THIRD EDITION

A Guide to Teaching
The Norton Field Guides to Writing

THIRD EDITION

A Guide to Teaching

The Norton
Field Guides
to Writing

Richard Bullock
WRIGHT STATE UNIVERSITY

Maureen Daly Goggin
ARIZONA STATE UNIVERSITY

W. W. NORTON & COMPANY

New York • London

Copyright © 2013, 2010, 2009, 2007, 2006 by W. W. Norton & Company, Inc.

Composition: Westchester Book Group
Manufacturing: Sheridan Books, Inc.
Production Manager: Andrew Ensor

ISBN 978-0-393-91953-0 (pbk.)

W. W. Norton & Company, Inc., 500 Fifth Avenue, New York, NY 10110
www.wwnorton.com

W. W. Norton & Company Ltd., Castle House, 75/76 Wells Street, London W1T 3QT

1 2 3 4 5 6 7 8 9 0

Contents

PART 3: Teaching the Readings

Preface

First-year writing is the best course
in the university to teach.
—*Toby Fulwiler*

Toby is right: First-year writing courses may be hard work, requiring of instructors more time and energy than some other courses, but they're immensely rewarding. We get to work with small classes, coming to know our students in ways lecturers in large halls seldom do. We get to help students learn their way around the new academic environment of college, sharing in their excitement and anxiety. And we get to help them explore ways of writing and reading that are often utterly new to them, from embedding significance in a narrative to dissecting a nonfiction text, from immersing themselves in research to considering how best to persuade an audience. When we teach first-year English or other writing courses, we combine complex, challenging content and strong interactions with individual writers as they go about creating unique texts. This is a set of resources for teachers using the third edition of *The Norton Field Guide to Writing*. No matter which of the *Field Guides* you use—with the handbook, with the reader, with both, or the rhetoric alone—this guide

to teaching includes resources you'll find useful.

Like the *Field Guide* itself, this guide doesn't try to tell you everything there is to know about teaching writing. Instead, it tries to tell you what you're most likely to need to know as you teach first-year writing courses. If you want to know more, you can find additional information at the end of each chapter in lists of useful readings. These lists are not intended to be comprehensive. Instead, they present one, two, or more essays or websites that offer useful information and helpful advice for teachers—and, usually, a good bibliography of additional sources on that topic. You're busy and may not want to wade through a lengthy bibliography; therefore, these readings are good starting places for learning more about basic issues in teaching writing.

This guide to teaching has three parts. Part 1 consists of twenty-one chapters with advice on teaching writing, from designing a writing course to meeting the needs of students and adapting to a new role as a teacher. Each chapter offers specific guidance on developing and teaching a first-year writing course and aims to be as practical as possible. Although knowing rhetorical and composition theory is important—you need to know why you teach as you do, and theory provides that understanding—this guide isn't the place to provide theory. Our assumption is that you need first of all to be ready to walk into your own writing course on the first day of class and both be prepared and seem prepared to your students: to have a plan for your course, a syllabus to share with students, activities to do in class, and the ability to respond to and grade students' writing. These chapters will help you do that.

Part 2 gives advice on teaching with the *Norton Field Guide*. The *Field Guide* is designed to be flexible: you can create any number of course plans and sequences of writing and reading assignments by combining its chapters in various ways. If you're new to teaching or comfortable with a traditional guide to writing, you might start by using Chapters 7–10: WRITING A LITER-ACY NARRATIVE, ANALYZING TEXTS, REPORT-ING INFORMATION, and ARGUING A POSITION. These four chapters present sequences of readings and assignments that lead students from understanding of the key features of the genre to the completion of a finished essay in that genre, and you can structure your class activities and assignments to follow the chapter's advice. Whichever path you choose—or if you decide to mix writing guides and assignments you yourself create—you should find useful advice in Chapter 22, "Developing Course Plans Using *The Norton Field Guide*." More course plans—for stretch, accelerated, and basic writing courses—may be found in Chapter 21, "Helping Struggling Writers

and Readers." The other chapters offer advice, tips, and ideas for using each of the chapters in the *Field Guide*.

Part 3 provides guidance for teaching the readings in Chapters 57–66 of *The Norton Field Guide to Writing with Readings* and *The Norton Field Guide to Writing with Readings and Handbook*: literacy narratives, textual and literary analyses, reports, arguments, evaluations, memoirs, profiles, proposals, reflections, and texts that mix genres. In particular, we offer a rationale for each of the discussion questions and writing prompts that accompany the readings, along with guidelines for working with each question. Additional questions for discussion are included for each reading. This section is guided by the assumption that since part of learning a new genre is learning to recognize that genre and its conventions, reading deeply and purposefully in a specific genre helps students develop that awareness. The readings can also serve both as models and as inspiration for relevant topics and treatments. The discussion questions are designed to help students learn how to read purposefully and to mine texts rhetorically—how, in other words, to *engage with the text*. Some questions focus students' attention on key features of the specific genre, others on specific rhetorical strategies, and still others on issues and claims raised in the reading. The rationale offered for each question indicates the intended goal and may inspire you to design specific individual, small-group, or whole-class activities and out-of-class assignments. You can find additional advice in Chapter 8 of this guide,

"Using Readings to Teach Writing." The writing prompts offer you an additional resource for helping students generate topics and approaches for writing in a particular genre.

We asked some of the best writing teachers we know—some of them former students, others colleagues and collaborators—to contribute chapters to the guide. We think you'll find that they succeeded admirably, presenting good advice on teaching narrative, teaching ways to use readings, being an effective teacher and graduate student, and dealing with special populations of students, including those whose first language isn't English and those with various disabilities. We want to thank these teachers publicly for making this guide for teaching better than it would otherwise be: Brady Allen, Mike Boblitt, Adrienne Cassell, Jimmy Chesire, Carol Cornett, Deborah Crusan, Melissa Faulkner, Scott Geisel, Paige Huskey, Carole Clark Papper, and Melissa Toomey.

There are others we need to thank, too. Jane Blakelock, assistant director of writing programs for computing in Wright State's English Department and also the department's and our college's webmaster, taught Rich most of what he knows about designing electronic texts and how best to teach them. Catherine Crowley sensitively edited several chapters, and other instructors, lecturers, and professors in Wright State's English Department contributed many ideas that found their way into the book: Debbie Bertsch (now at Columbus State Community College), Vicki Burke, Byron Crews, Sally DeThomas, Stephanie Dickey, Andrea Harris, Karen Hayes, Chuck Holmes, Jeannette Horwitz, Beth Klaisner, Peggy Lindsey, Nancy Mack, Cynthia Marshall, Sarah McGinley, Michelle Metzner, Kristie Rowe, Bobby Rubin, Cathy Sayer, David Seitz, Tracy Smith, and Rick Strader. Thank you all.

We owe a special debt to Paige Huskey, Mike Boblitt, and Carole Clark Papper, whose work in revising and editing this manual has greatly improved it.

Special thanks are also in order for the people who have supported us as we've worked on these field guides. Henry Limouze and Carol Loranger, the former and current chairs of Wright State's Department of English, have been unfailingly supportive. Neal A. Lester, associate vice president of humanities at Arizona State University, has also offered unwavering support. Marilyn Moller is the finest editor in the textbook business and has helped us in ways too numerous to mention. Rebecca Homiski, our project editor, was so helpful and kind, and senior developmental editor John Elliott offered useful advice. Thanks also to the other fine people at W. W. Norton who helped make this book happen; all deserve their share of the credit for this book. And finally we offer gratitude to our spouses. Rich thanks Barb Bullock, his wife and best teacher, who each day by precept and example teaches him to open up to life. Maureen thanks Peter Goggin, her husband, who nourishes her spiritually, physically, and intellectually.

part 1

Teaching Writing

Designing a Writing Course 1

Whenever we teach, designing the course we're about to teach presents challenges. If you're a new teaching assistant, you've been given a general outline of the writing course you're to teach, along with some intensive training. When you've never taught before, though, organizing the weeks that stretch ahead is daunting, even with the help you've been given. If you're a newly hired adjunct instructor, you may already have experience in the classroom, but you need to adapt what you've done before to the requirements of a new writing program. If you're a seasoned faculty member, you've taught many writing courses, but perhaps not recently, and not with this text or this course outline. No matter where you fit in these scenarios, you can use some help in designing your course. This chapter offers advice on planning a writing course that suits your preferences and your students' needs.

Thinking about Course Design

A writing course is akin to a set of boxes within boxes: the largest, outermost box is the complete course from start to finish. Within that box are instructional units that typically begin with the introduction of a writing assignment and end with its completion. Each unit is made up of sequences of assignments that move the class and the assigned writing along. And each class period includes various activities that move students through the sequence of assignments. Considering your course on each of these levels enables you to plan every period of every week of the term so that every class period's work builds on what went before and prepares for what comes next. Having a plan gives you something to diverge from and improve on without losing your way or being reduced to wondering, "What do I do on Monday?" Here's how to devise such a plan.

The course as a whole. Determine the writing program's goals for the course: What does the program or department or university want students to achieve by completing this course? Sometimes these goals are clearly spelled out, but you may need to ask the writing program administrators, the department chair, or faculty who regularly teach the course what the institution's expectations are. If the goals of the course are left to you, consult the WPA Outcomes Statement available online at wpacouncil.org/positions/outcomes.html. That statement defines outcomes that soundly designed first-year writing courses should include, according to the Council of Writing Program Administrators, a national organization of writing program directors and specialists in composition and rhetoric.

Use the goals for your course to guide your planning. For example, if a goal is to "develop flexible strategies for generating, revising, editing, and proofreading," then you need to include those activities in your course plan. If a goal is to "respond appropriately to different kinds of rhetorical situations," then your plan should include opportunities for students to write in various genres for various reasons. If a goal is to "control such surface features as syntax, grammar, punctuation, and spelling," then including instruction in those surface features should be part of your overall plan. Once you've established your goals for the course itself, you can meet those goals by dividing the course into units.

Units. Designing a writing course is akin to other complex tasks best broken down into smaller parts that can be dealt with more easily, rather than trying to think of the whole at once. A writing course usually consists of a number of units within which students create a certain sort of writing, such as a personal narrative, an argument, an analysis, or a researched report. As you teach each unit, you lead students through a sequence of assignments that help students through writing processes from finding a topic, thinking about and researching it, and drafting and revising to polishing a

final draft and assessing their work. The number of units you create depends on how many pieces of writing you want students to finish and how much time you want to spend on each of those pieces. For example, a typical first-term, first-year writing course might consist of three or four 3-week units, each of them focusing on a single genre.

An alternative model would take a rhetorical approach designed to help students develop an understanding of the major rhetorical considerations—genre, audience, purpose, stance, and style—as they develop their writing processes. This approach reinforces the idea that writing (especially beyond the classroom) has more to do with intentionally choosing from a variety of strategies (and sometimes combining them) to meet the needs of particular audiences and situations. During each unit, students would identify and address the needs and constraints of particular rhetorical situations. Here are two sample unit-based schedules:

14-Week Semester
Weeks 1–3: Literacy Narrative
Weeks 4–7: Text Analysis
Weeks 8–10: Evaluation
Weeks 11–13: Argument
Week 14: Portfolio preparation and assessment

10-Week Quarter
Weeks 1–2: Literacy Narrative
Weeks 3–6: Text Analysis
Weeks 7–9: Evaluation
Week 10: Portfolio preparation and assessment

The length of a unit is highly flexible, of course. Some instructors may teach five- or six-week units to allow students to delve deeply into a subject and write lengthy, extensively researched essays; others may design two-week-long units to give students a flavor for certain genres and to make time for others. The length of each unit is finally like the length of a good essay: as long as it has to be to get the job done.

Assignment sequences. Within a unit, the sequence of specific assignments creates the momentum that gets students writing and keeps them progressing from beginning to end. This sequencing involves several variables: how many days your class meets each week, which days you meet, how long your class sessions are, and what you can expect students to do in class and between classes. Let's deal with each one separately:

How many days each week does your course meet, and on which days? Your course schedule—Mondays, Wednesdays, and Fridays for fifty minutes each day; Tuesdays and Thursdays for seventy-five minutes; Monday nights for three hours—determines the rhythm of your assignments: what you ask students to do, how much you ask them to do, how much work you do in class, and how much work you ask students to do independently. For example, if your course meets on Tuesdays and Thursdays, you will probably ask students to do much more work outside class over the long period between Thursday and Tuesday than between Tuesday and Thursday; if your course meets Mondays, Wednesdays, and Fridays, you'll probably assign more balanced amounts of independent work. Here are a couple of examples, one from a Tuesday–Thursday course (below) and one from a Monday–Wednesday–Friday course (p. 6).

Sample Assignment Sequence: Tuesday–Thursday Schedule

Day	In-Class Activities	Assignment for the Next Class
Tue	Introduce literacy narrative assignment, begin generating activities.	Read essays in Ch. 7; write 1-page responses to each.
Thu	Share responses and discuss essays; go over Key Features; start developing possible topics through freewriting, looping; introduce the rhetorical situation.	Read "Choosing a Topic" in Ch. 7; choose a topic; answer questions in "Considering the Rhetorical Situation."
Tue	Topic conferences: Be prepared to describe your topic and the rhetorical situation as you see it.	Do Ch. 7 "Generating Ideas and Text" activities.
Thu	Workshop on choosing pertinent details; mini-lesson on organizing a narrative.	Read "Ways of Organizing a Literacy Narrative" in Ch. 7 and "Beginning and Ending" in Ch. 30. Write a complete draft, 3–5 pp. long.

Sample Assignment Sequence: Monday–Wednesday–Friday Schedule

Day	In-Class Activities	Assignment for the Next Class
Mon	Introduce assignment; begin generating activities.	Read Vallowe and Agosín essays in Ch. 7; write a 1-page response to each.
Wed	Share responses and discuss essays; go over Key Features.	Read Nichols and Gomez essays in Ch. 7; write a 1-page response to each.
Fri	Discuss Nichols and Gomez essays; start developing possible topics through freewriting, looping; introduce the rhetorical situation.	Read "Choosing a Topic" in Ch. 7; choose a topic; read and answer questions in "Considering the Rhetorical Situation."
Mon	Topic conferences: Be prepared to describe your topic and your rhetorical situation as you see it.	Read "Ways of Organizing a Literacy Narrative" in Ch. 7 and "Beginning and Ending" in Ch. 30. Write an outline and first paragraph.

In each, students are beginning to write a personal literacy narrative. The left-hand column shows the day of the week; the middle column describes the activities to be completed during class, and the right-hand column shows the students' assignments for the following class.

Charting your assignment sequences can help you see how each class relates to those preceding and following it and how each assignment helps students make progress, using what they learned in class to do something that prepares them for the activities of the next class.

How long are your class periods? Within the term, unit, and weekly schedule, you need to develop a rhythm for your class periods, too. A fifty-minute period has a very different feel to it than a seventy-five or ninety-minute period. Chapter 4, "Managing Class Activities," in this guide to teaching provides more detailed advice on structuring your class meetings, but in general, in an effective class period you will accomplish the following:

- Review what the class has done so far.
- Clarify the relationship of students' previous work and current tasks.
- Introduce activities or help students with upcoming tasks.
- Prepare students to do the next assignment.

Putting the parts together. Here is a set of guidelines for planning a course by considering the course as a whole, the units that make it up, the assignment sequences that students will follow, and the class activities that will help them progress.

1. Determine the goals of your course and what you must do to achieve them.
2. Decide on the number of units and what each will achieve.

Sample Unit Plan

Unit			
Class Day	Goal of Day's Work	Class Activities	Assignment

3. Estimate how many weeks—or how many class days—the class will need to achieve each unit's goal; make sure your units don't exceed the number of class periods in the term. Note that some tasks take more time and instruction than others.

4. Consider how much preparation students will need in order to write a draft. For example, students might draft a literacy narrative after a day or two of generating ideas and material, but they might need several weeks to write a report. Consider also what they will need to do—what assignments you will give them—before they write a draft, during drafting, and afterward. Consider too how many drafts you want them to write and what sort of response you can give them along the way. (See Chapter 9, "Responding to Student Writing.")

5. Plot out the unit on a calendar or chart, playing with the placement of the due dates for each student assignment. Think about how much time each assignment will take and how that fits into the time students have between class meetings.

6. Now start filling in the details. What, exactly, will you expect students to have done before each class meeting? What will you do during each class meeting? Chapter 4, "Managing Class Activities," offers detailed advice on using your time with your students effectively. What will the assignment for the next class meeting be? Chapter 3, "Designing Writing Assignments"; Chapter 7, "Using Writing Activities in Class"; and Chapter 8, "Using Readings to Teach Writing," can help you create appropriate tasks for students to complete on their own. For each unit, consider creating a plan in the form of a table that provides you and your students with that information.

Being Prepared and Flexible

Creating a plan for your course can relieve much of the stress of teaching, especially the first time you teach a course. Just don't let it become a straitjacket that confines, rather than enables. Students may need more or less time on a task than you've scheduled; you may find that providing students with the instruction they need takes more or less time than you had thought; and events beyond your control, such as the weather or electrical power interruptions, may force you to change your plans. Maintaining flexibility to meet students' needs and to anticipate the unforeseeable is just as important as knowing what you'll do each day. You can incorporate flexibility into your plan in several ways. You can build a couple of open class periods into your schedule at the end of a unit, so if you need more time you can use those periods without squeezing the next unit's schedule. Or you can create detailed unit plans one at a time, giving students the overall unit topic and main deadlines but waiting until you've gone through much of one unit before filling in the details of the next. As you gain confidence in your teaching abilities and get to know your students, you'll find balancing planning with flexibility will become easier.

Useful Readings

Deen, Rosemary. "Notes to Stella." *College English* 54.5 (1992): 573–85. Print.

Elbow, Peter. "Embracing Contraries in the Teaching Process." *College English* 45 (1983): 327–39. Print.

Murray, Donald M. *A Writer Teaches Writing*, Revised 2nd ed. Boston: Heinle, 2003 (especially Chs. 5 and 9). Print.

Creating a Syllabus **2**

In every class you took in college, the instructor gave you a syllabus that provided an outline of the course. As an instructor, you may be required to provide a copy of the syllabus for your own course to your department office to be kept on file. A course syllabus is more than simply information for students; it is both a promise to those students that the course will be conducted in a certain way and a record of how the course was conducted. The audience for your syllabus includes students, faculty, and administrators, so taking care to create a complete, clear syllabus is well worth your time. This chapter offers advice on how to construct a good syllabus for a writing course.

Contents of a Good Syllabus

A good syllabus anticipates and answers students' questions:

- How does this course fit into the curriculum? Why must I or should I take it?
- What is the content or subject matter of the course?
- What teaching style or methods of instruction will be used? Will the course be primarily a workshop course? Lectures? Discussion? Online? A combination?
- What are the prerequisites? What knowledge or ability does the instructor assume I already have?
- What are the requirements? How much work is there?
- How will my work be evaluated? Will there be a portfolio, tests, quizzes, written assignments, projects, presentations? How many?
- When are assignments due? How will I need to use my time to get the work done?
- What books and materials must I have? What must I purchase? What will be available through the library, online, in class, or as handouts?
- What are the rules for the course, for attendance, submitting work, and participating in class?
- How can I contact the instructor, and when can I do so?

Building a Course Syllabus

A typical syllabus for a writing course contains much of the following information but is unlikely to include all of it. Even if you don't want to put an item in your syllabus, you may find that thinking about your policy on that issue can help you anticipate students' questions or behavior.

Basic Course Information

- Course title, section number, call number, and number of credits
- Room and time(s) where the class meets
- Semester or quarter and year
- Prerequisites: other courses, placement scores, or test scores

Your Personal Information

- Your name and title
- Your office location, with directions if it's hard to find
- Your office hours, email address, office phone number, and website URL, if you have one
- Your home phone number and times when students may call, if you wish
- How you'd like students to address you (as Mr. or Ms. _____, as Professor or Dr. _____, or with your first name)

Textbooks and Other Materials

- Each textbook's title, edition, author, publisher, and date of publication; ISBN number; clear identification of required and recommended texts; URL of textbook website
- Additional materials to be assigned and where they may be found (in the library's reserve room or in your learning management system, for example)
- How to access and use the learning management system for the courses, if there is one
- Where students may get help with accessing electronic materials (online reserve materials or materials in your learning management system, for example)
- Other required materials or fees (such as lab, printing, or photocopying fees; flash drive; two-pocket folders)

Course Description

- Can repeat your school's catalogue description, or you may write one (or both)
- Typically includes the major themes, topics, knowledge, and skills to be addressed in the course

Course Objectives

- Cognitive: what students should understand
- Affective: what students should appreciate
- Behavioral: what students should be able to do

Course Requirements

- Summary of assignments and due dates

- Reading assignments
- Number and type of papers and other assignments such as oral presentations or group projects
- Attendance requirements
- Class participation requirements (in-class, electronic, or both)
- Your expectations of the amount of time and work students should anticipate

Course Calendar

- Reading assignments with due dates
- Deadlines for drafts and other projects
- Dates of tests, special events, final exam, and course evaluations
- Deadlines for dropping or withdrawing from the course

Grading Policies and Procedures

- The course grading system (A–F, plusses and minuses, points, percentages, etc.)
- Percentage or amount each course requirement counts toward final grade (make sure percentages add up to 100%)
- Rubrics for evaluating papers
- Use of quizzes, surprise or scheduled, and whether or not they can be made up
- Penalties for late work (for example, "All assignments must be submitted at the beginning of the class on their due date in order to receive credit")
- Extra-credit policy, if any

- Policy on incomplete grades (for example, "No Incomplete grades will be given except in extreme circumstances")
- Policy on incomplete portfolios (for example, "Incomplete portfolios will receive an F")
- Policy on making up work (for example, "No work may be made up unless you have talked with me. It is your responsibility to initiate this meeting. Penalties for turning in work late may still apply")

Academic Honesty Policy

- Your academic honesty policy must correspond with your department's or university's policy. Check with your chair to see if there's a prescribed version to include.

Other Useful Information

- Campus resources such as a writing center, study skills center, technology help desk, or counseling center
- Space for 2–3 classmates' names, telephone numbers, and email addresses

Some Tips to Help Students Do Well

- Most learning takes place out of class. The time students are expected to work outside class is usually two hours for every class hour.
- Read each reading assignment several times. Once is seldom enough.
- Come to class; sit in the front of the room.
- Ask questions and participate.

- Go to the writing center.
- Study with peers.

Course Rules

- Recording class discussions
- Eating food in classrooms
- Using electronic devices in class
- Other class decorum issues

As you can see, a course syllabus may be quite elaborate—or it may be fairly brief.

Look at syllabuses for other courses like the one you're teaching to see what instructors at your school customarily include in their syllabuses (or syllabi, or course plans—that's another term that varies from school to school).

A Useful Reading

Baecker, Diann L. "Uncovering the Rhetoric of the Syllabus." *College Teaching* 46.2 (1998): 58–63. Print.

A Sample Syllabus

Here is a sample syllabus for a fifteen-week writing course, annotated with commentary.

ENG 101: Processes of Writing[1]

Call no: XXXXX

Section XX, Fall 20XX, 0XX Millett Hall, 11–12:15 Tuesdays and Thursdays

Instructor: Richard Bullock

Office: 541 Millett

Phone & voice mail: 770-0000; **email:** rbinstructor33@wrightstate.edu

Office hours: Tuesdays and Thursdays, 2:00–4:00 and by appointment

This course aims to help you become a better reader and writer of academic and other nonfiction writing. You'll write several drafts of four essays: a narrative focused on your own literacy, two text analyses, and an evaluation of a film or television show. You'll also write several evaluations of your own work, all of which you will compile in a writing portfolio. Along the way, I hope you'll come to understand yourself as a writer and reader better than you do now and be able to assess your own writing's strengths and weaknesses.[2]

In some courses, you must read and learn a certain amount of material that is fairly well-defined. In a writing course, however, you can interpret writing activities as requiring a lot of time and effort, or a little. Consistently interpreting assignments as something to dash off quickly, rather than as something to think about, consider, and spend time on, is likely to affect your performance and final grade. Note, too, that in college, you're expected to spend about two hours studying and working independently for every hour you spend in class.

Note: Everything you turn in should be as error-free as you can make it. Get into the habit of editing and proofreading, because your instructors will expect clean, correct prose, in informal as well as formal writing—and in emails.[3]

ATTENDANCE AND PARTICIPATION: You'll be doing a lot of group work in this class, and failing to attend hurts both you and your group members. So don't miss, and don't schedule other activities during class time. As an incentive, remember that something will be due every class period—something either written for the class or written during the class; I won't accept it from anyone but you, and I won't accept it after I've collected it in class.[4]

---

[1]Provide basic information at the top.

[2]Give a general description of the goals and desired outcomes of the course.

[3]This note is intended to counteract the effects of students' texting and email habits while continuing to establish expectations.

[4]Some instructors prefer a simple policy, e.g., 3 absences and the student's grade drops a letter, and drops another letter for each additional absence. If you prefer such a policy, combine it with an attendance sheet students sign on arriving each day, to eliminate arguments over whether or not a student was present; if the student doesn't sign the sheet, the student is counted absent.

Much of the work of the class comes during class time, so you must be present, doing the work along the way; note that daily work comprises 15% of your final grade. *I won't accept at quarter's end a portfolio of work I haven't seen beforehand in draft form.* If I haven't seen it while you've worked on it, how can I know that you wrote it?[5]

I also reserve the right to let your preparedness and participation affect your grade. In other words, if you don't come prepared, or if you choose not to participate in class activities, your grade may[6] suffer.

EMERGENCIES: Sometimes—very seldom, but sometimes—things come up that may force you to miss class or be unable to submit an assignment. If they do, CALL or EMAIL ME ahead of time. I'm more inclined to be flexible if you talk with me than if you stop coming to class or simply disappear.[7]

TEXTS AND MATERIALS: Richard Bullock and Francine Weinberg, *The Norton Field Guide to Writing with Handbook,* 3rd ed.
   At least $5 worth of copy card credit—you'll be making copies
   Your campus username, password, and email address

WEEKLY LETTERS: Each Tuesday, plan on writing a letter from you to me. Make it at least a page (250+ words) long. Address it "Dear Rich." Each Thursday, I'll write a "Dear Class" letter via email.[8]

GRADES:
- **15% Daily work, including weekly letters.** 5 points per class, 150 in the term; lose more than 20 points or 4 days' worth and you lose all. Showing up matters.
- **20% Midterm portfolio.** Must include literacy narrative and self-evaluation, your weekly letters, and your daily work.
- **65% Course portfolio.** Must include two of these three: literacy narrative, one of the two text analyses, and evaluation; self-assessment of portfolio contents; and all drafts of all 3 essays listed above.[9]

INTERIM EVALUATION: Anytime you want to know what your grade would be before the course portfolio is due, make an appointment with me and I'll gladly go over your work with you, to let you know your grade if I had to give you one at that time.[10]

---

[5]This rule, along with deadlines for committing to topics of essays, can greatly reduce students' opportunities to submit plagiarized work and establishes your expectation that they must write multiple drafts and participate in the course activities.

[6]Soft language here gives you flexibility to take individual students' situations into account.

[7]Advice on how to behave responsibly in a new environment. Some students believe that if they're absent when something is due, instructors have to let them turn it in late.

[8]Toby Fulwriler's assignment idea helps you know your students and gives them a way to ask questions they may not feel comfortable asking in class.

[9]Make sure your points or percentages add up to 100%!

[10]Knowing that students can take this option relieves many of their fears, even though very, very few students will do it!

COURSE PORTFOLIOS: Rather than being graded on every piece of writing you do, you're better off if you're evaluated on a body of work you've compiled over an extended period. Here's why:

- You've got more chances of doing a good job. If you buy 10 raffle tickets instead of one, your chances of winning improve.
- You'll present a more realistic view of your writing abilities and achievements than you can with any single piece of writing. An album of photos better shows what you look like than your driver's license photo does.
- You'll have the opportunity to rewrite, revise, edit, and polish, to visit the Writing Center—to show me your best work—right up until finals week, so you can do a better job than you might otherwise do.

For all those reasons, the midterm and course portfolios represent your evidence to me that you deserve a certain grade.[11]

Note: Your course portfolio grades are based on your achievements—on the quality of the writing—not on effort (how hard you worked) or intention (what you meant to do). *An incomplete or missing midterm or course portfolio will earn a final course grade of F.*[12]

FORMAT: The portfolios should consist of printed final drafts submitted in a two-pocket folder. Final drafts should be formatted in MLA style, as modeled in Chapter 50 of the *Field Guide* (pp. 522–32). Assignments marked "informal" may be handwritten, but must be legible and not written on paper ripped out of a spiral-bound notebook. Submit weekly letters, essay drafts, and other work during the course in the appropriate dropbox in Desire2Learn.[13]

Keep everything you write for this course in some organized fashion: an accordion folder, a three-ring notebook, a stiff plastic or cardboard envelope, or a separate folder in your computer files. (See Chapter 55, "Writing Online," for help.) Save your work in at least 2 places!!! Keep everything in order—you'll need it to compile your portfolio and write your self-assessment essays.[14]

UNIVERSITY WRITING CENTER:[15] The University Writing Center, in 104 Wilson Hall, can help you improve your writing through one-on-one conferences. Please go early, go often—it's

---

[11]Many students are used to receiving grades on every piece of writing they submit. Explaining the rationale for portfolios can start the process of relieving their worries; their experience in the class will help them see the advantages of earning a grade on a portfolio of work they've revised extensively.

[12]Lack of evidence for a grade makes grading impossible. This policy shows that you're serious about them doing the work—all of the work. You also establish your expectations—that they submit the best work of which they're capable—and forestall arguments of this sort: "I came to class every day and worked really hard, so I deserve a better grade."

[13]Explain how students should submit assignments: on paper, as email attachments, or in an assignment posted on your learning management system.

[14]Again, advice to help students be successful in a course in which they'll generate a lot of material.

[15]It's always good to tout support services available to students.

free and will be useful to you. (I may require some of you to go there, if your writing shows that you need additional help.)

DISCLAIMER: This syllabus may well change to reflect my sense of your needs. I won't make changes that are potentially harmful to you, however, without negotiating.[16]

CONTACTS: Write down the names, phone numbers, and email addresses of three class-mates. Call or write them if you need help with something to do with this class and you can't contact me.[17]

_____

_____

_____

Advice from students who've taken ENG 101 in the past:[18]

"If you are taking English 101, then you are probably a new student. College isn't what you thought it would be, is it? . . . if you don't like taking advice, get over it. Next off, go to class and finish all of your assignments. (You will find that this tip is useful in any class.) Grades can easily fall without you even noticing."

"My first word of advice is—make sure you have your papers in the dropbox or on a flash drive before you leave the house! When you have a draft or a revision due, always do it—write something. Even if you're having trouble, and it's not your best work, it will most likely help you work towards your final draft."

"Do not take the little assignments lightly. Those little assignments, in the long run, make or break your papers. He gives you things like that to better prepare yourself for the big assignments, and trust me when I say, you need those little ones."

"I can tell you now that I am not, nor ever will be an English major. So here are a couple of suggestions to help you get through this class smoothly. First of all, procrastination has got to go. Until this year I was the crowned queen of procrastination. I'll let you know now that it is considerably <u>less stressful</u> to do things in bits and pieces and not to wait until the last minute to start things. It will also improve your grades greatly."

"You can never have too many drafts! We all hate revising and changing our papers, I understand. However, sitting down at midnight to start your paper that is due at 11 a.m. is not going to cut it in college! Trust me."

---

[16]The class you teach depends in part on your students' abilities and needs as well as your developing sense of how to teach them. Language like this lets you adjust your course to meet the students' needs.

[17]If your school doesn't place students in learning communities—and even if it does—helping your students create support networks with their peers can help them succeed.

[18]As in many things, students often take the advice of other students more seriously than they take ours. Asking them at the end of the course to give advice to future students can give you a wealth of good ideas to share—and give you insights into your course as students see it.

"English is not like most of your other classes. There are few people per class, so the prof knows if you're there and attentive or not."

"My advice to you is to take risks and enjoy what you are writing."

"You don't have to write a perfect paper the first time. Take your time; you will have many chances to revise papers. I'm sure this will annoy you, because I know it did me, but it really does benefit you a lot."

3   Designing Writing Assignments

When you hear faculty complain that the writing their students submit to them is horrible, the fault often lies not so much with the ability of the students but with the quality of the assignment. Vague, incomplete, poorly constructed assignments elicit—guess what?—vague, incomplete, poorly constructed student writing. On the other hand, carefully constructed assignments can aid students as they write, guiding them to well-written texts. That's why it's important to craft your writing assignments carefully: You get what you ask for.

Developing Assignment Sequences

When you plan assignments, think in terms of sequences that move students through a series of activities toward the goal of a finished piece of writing. Reading, working in groups, generating ideas and text, drafting, getting response, revising, editing and proofreading, and evaluating—each of these activities helps students write better texts. You may well think initially of a course as made up of a few assignments—a literacy narrative, a text analysis, a report, and an argument—but each of these products results from a carefully plotted sequence of in-class and out-of-class assignments, each of which contributes to the quality of that final product.

Using *The Norton Field Guide to Writing*

The *Field Guide* is designed to help you develop clear and effective assignments. You may use one of the longer genre chapters (Chapter 7, WRITING A LITERACY NARRATIVE; Chapter 8, ANALYZING TEXTS; Chapter 9, REPORTING INFORMATION; and Chapter 10, ARGUING A POSITION), each of which presents a sequence that leads students from initial exploration of a genre through editing and proofreading and self-assessment of their work. If you're new to teaching, you may find those chapters to be useful models of successful assignment sequences. If you'd like to design your own sequences, the activities in those chapters can provide a framework for creating assignments using various parts of the *Field Guide*. At its most basic, creating a sequence of assignments involves these steps:

1. Introduce the genre (Chapters 7–21), using readings.
2. Define Key Features of the genre (as defined in the Genre chapters).
3. Provide help in choosing a topic (presented in each Genre chapter and in Chapter 24, GENERATING IDEAS AND TEXT).
4. Have students consider the Rhetorical Situation (Chapters 1–6, with advice in each Genre chapter as well).
5. Ask students to generate ideas and text (with activities in each Genre chapter or in Chapter 24) and do appropriate research (Chapters 43–51).
6. Have students organize their material, plan their text, and use appropriate writing strategies (from Chapters 30–42) as they draft (Chapter 25).
7. Ask students to assess their drafts (Chapter 26), get a response and revise (Chapter 27), and edit and proofread (Chapter 28).
8. Have students assess their written product, either by itself or as part of a portfolio of their work (as described in Chapter 29).

Of course, each of these steps may be expanded or contracted to suit the assignment and the needs of your students. For example, you may give students only a few days to generate ideas and text and organize a memoir, on the assumption that they are familiar with narratives and have the necessary information in their memories. By contrast, students writing a researched essay arguing a position may need several weeks to generate ideas and find sources before they attempt a draft. For more assignment sequence possibilities, see Chapter 22, "Developing Course Plans Using *The Norton Field Guide*."

Making Your Expectations Clear

A good writing assignment gives students all the information they need to complete it. As Erika Lindemann notes, providing clear information about the rhetorical situation of the text you expect them to produce will help students understand both what you want and what they should do. The elements of the rhetorical situation that you should address include the following (adapted from Lindemann 212):

- Students' interest in the topic and what they understand about it
- Purpose of the text—what it should try to accomplish
- Intended audience for the text
- Genre in which students should write, including its key features
- Stance students should adopt
- Criteria such as format and deadlines

All of the Genre chapters in the *Field Guide* provide questions for each element in the rhetorical situation as well as a list of each genre's Key Features. You can ask students to explore what they know about their topic using several of the activities in Chapter 24 of the *Field Guide*, GENERATING IDEAS AND TEXT.

Here's an example of a good writing assignment:

> **Arguing a Position.** Take a stand on an issue that affects your life as a student, a worker, or a citizen. Your argument should include: a *thesis* declaring your explicit position, a response to what others have said, appropriate background information, a clear indication of why the topic matters, good *reasons* and *evidence* supporting your position, attention to more than one point of view, an authoritative tone, and an *appeal to readers' values.* Your purpose is to convince your readers that your position is reasonable—though you may attempt to persuade them to consider a certain position or to do something. You are writing to an informed, intelligent audience, perhaps readers of the *New York Times* or the *Atlantic,* so your stance should be thoughtful, balanced, and reasonable. Your essay should be 4–6 pages long. You must submit a topic proposal on February 1, have a draft for peer review on February 10, and submit a complete draft on February 15. You may revise until the course portfolio is due during finals week.

This assignment provides students with considerable freedom to choose a topic of interest to them while giving them a clear indication of the rhetorical situation in which they must write, including important due dates and procedural information.

Assigning Topics or Giving Choices

Whether you assign specific topics or let students choose their own depends on numerous factors. If you want students to work together as a class on a project, you may assign a topic or a cluster of related topics on which individual students or groups of students might work. When asking students to evaluate a film, for example, you might provide a list of suitable movies and ask groups of students to choose one. If you're using the assignment to teach specific skills, you might assign everyone the same task so they can discuss its intricacies and compare their attempts, a useful tactic for teaching summarizing and paraphrasing, for example. Some instructors ask students to work from a limited set of source materials to write a researched essay on a controversial topic chosen by the instructor in order to teach them how to use sources appropriately. When you assign a topic, you gain control over significant aspects of your course. However, you run the risk that your students may not find the topic as engaging or as interesting as you do. Even if your writing program offers courses identified by their theme, students more often sign up for courses by time of day and availability than by course topic. Also you lose variety in your student drafts, something to consider when it comes time to read and respond to twenty or twenty-five drafts—or more.

If you allow students to choose their own topics, you must help each of those two dozen students solve unique writing problems; however, you gain the opportunity to read and discuss many subjects you might never have otherwise encountered. More important, you offer students the opportunity to explore topics in which they have an interest, resulting in more engagement in the work of your class and better writing. In general, don't leave assignments completely open. Stipulate a genre within which students must write, help students narrow or broaden topics to fit the constraints of their abilities and the course, and veto topics that are unmanageable or difficult to write well on. Consider an assignment to be like a game: Establish the rules and set the boundaries of the playing field, and then let your students be as creative as they can within those rules and boundaries.

Helping Students Interpret Your Assignments

No matter how elaborately instructors define assignments, students need to interpret them in order to begin. Part of that interpretation involves making a judgment about the ease or difficulty of accomplishing the tasks. One student may understand an assignment as requiring several hours of library research, the creation of a detailed outline, and a schedule that will permit the writing of several drafts. Another student in the same class, interpreting the same assignment, will assume that it can be knocked off with an hour's research on the web and a single, quickly written draft. One, if not both, of these students may be misinterpreting your expectations, so it's important to clarify them. Breaking a large assignment into a sequence of activities, each with a due date and a product to be submitted, is helpful; so is a suggested timetable. Consider, too, showing good examples of the amount and quality of work you expect. You don't want your conscientious students spending hours on an assignment you consider a brief learning tool, and you want to prod your less conscientious students to adopt suitable work habits.

Doing the Assignment Yourself

Whenever possible, do assignments yourself before you give them to your students. You will accomplish two important things: (1) you can find out whether the assignment works—if it's doable or leads to unanticipated difficulties—before students are led into a swamp; and (2) you develop an example that you can show them and discuss, not necessarily as an expert, but as a fellow writer who sometimes struggles with an assignment. Students rarely see the writing of their teachers and even more rarely see that writing with its dead ends, revisions, and rough edges, and they find the process fascinating. Show students your own writing, and you'll not only show them how they might approach assignments, you'll gain credibility in their eyes as someone who does what you ask your students to do.

Useful Readings

Lindemann, Erika. *A Rhetoric for Writing Teachers,* 3rd ed. New York: Oxford UP, 1995. Print.

Rankin, Elizabeth. "From Simple to Complex: Ideas of Order in Assignment Sequences." *Journal of Advanced Composition* 10.1 (1990): 126–35. Print.

Sommers, Nancy. "Revision Strategies of Student Writers and Experienced Adult Writers." *College Composition and Communication* 31.4 (1980): 378–88. Print.

Managing Class Activities   **4**

You may remember most vividly your upper-division courses, which were probably a mix of lecture and discussion. As a new teacher of writing, however, you're faced with a different situation, a course in which the subject is writing, and the goal is primarily the improvement of students' writing. How can you fill 150–200 minutes of class time a week on writing? This chapter offers some advice on structuring your class time in ways that will engage students and help them improve their writing.

Structuring Classes

The primary model of college teaching is the lecture that fills the entire class period, no matter how long. Various observers have noted, though, that students' attention begins wandering after about twenty minutes, suggesting that varying class activities will maintain students' interest and improve their learning better than doing any one activity for the whole class period. Your class will likely run more smoothly and be more interesting to you and your students if you follow a predictable overall pattern during class but vary the activities within the pattern. One pattern that works well includes these tasks:

- Review what the class has done so far.
- Clarify the relationship of students' previous work and current tasks.
- Introduce activities or offer information to help students with current and upcoming tasks.
- Prepare students to do the next assignment in the unit.

Each of these tasks may require one or more activities and take up more or less time, depending on your purposes and your students' needs. For advice on coordinating your class activities with your assignment sequences and overall course goals, see Chapter 1, "Designing a Writing Course."

Planning Class Activities

Here are some activities that successful writing teachers use to achieve their purposes in class.

Workshops and conferences. Writing workshops and student conferences are the primary activities in most writing courses, often being the predominant use of class time. See Chapter 5, "Conducting Class Workshops," for detailed advice on setting up and running workshops in class. As preparation for workshops, you can ask students to read about COLLABORATING in Chapter 23 of the *Field Guide*, and to do several of the activities together in workshops. Many activities in the Genre chapters lend themselves to collaboration. For example, several of the activities in Chapter 8, ANALYZING TEXTS, are best done in class by groups of students working together.

Although students working together can accomplish much, sometimes you need to discuss each student's writing individually. Chapter 6 in this guide to teaching offers detailed advice on scheduling and holding conferences.

Mini-lessons, presentations, and lectures. Mini-lessons are brief, 5–10-minute lessons on a specific topic. They may include information students need to know, such as the importance of the rhetorical situation; procedures for class activities, such as how to respond to others' drafts or how to collaborate successfully; lessons in specific writing strategies or processes, such as options for generating ideas and text, editing, or narrating; lessons on topics that may give students trouble, such as citing websites; or lessons on specific aspects of writing, such as using semicolons. Mini-lessons are successful because they are clearly focused and brief. Many instructors start class periods with mini-lessons that focus students' attention on the day's work or answer a question that came up in a previous

class. You might end some days with a mini-lesson that explains an aspect of the students' assignment or intersperse mini-lessons throughout a class period as you move from activity to activity.

Presentations using *PowerPoint*, *Prezi*, audio, or video often accompany mini-lessons or may comprise longer segments of a class period. For example, you may show a brief video clip to introduce a writing or research assignment. As always, though, such a presentation should have a clear pedagogical purpose. Although students like to be entertained, they understand that what goes on in class should relate to their purpose for being there. So make the connection between a presentation and their writing explicit, both orally and through follow-up activities that ask students to analyze or use the presentation in some way. For advice on creating effective media presentations, see Chapter 56, GIVING PRESENTATIONS, in the *Field Guide*.

Lectures may be useful for transmitting content, but they are usually inappropriate for writing classes. You may find an occasional lecture useful, but if you do, treat it as a carefully crafted, focused explanation of a specific topic appropriate to the assignment students are engaged in developing. To aid students' understanding, accompany your lecture with visual presentations of the material.

Discussions. Discussions can be useful for helping students develop and articulate their thinking on issues related to their writing and reading. After asking students to read several literacy narratives, for example, you might ask them to discuss the way each writer expresses the significance of the events portrayed in the narratives and which ways are most effective. Or you might ask students to describe a situation in their lives where they evaluated a movie or a song and then compare that evaluation to a formal, written evaluation of a movie or a song. Having a good discussion involves getting students to participate, moving the discussion forward toward your goals, and dealing with emotional or interpersonal issues as they arise. Here are some tips for conducting whole-class discussions.

Getting students to participate. Students are often hesitant to participate in discussions. They may be unsure of the reaction their comments will elicit from you or from their classmates. They may feel unprepared. They may not know where to begin. When you start a discussion, consider these tactics to help students become comfortable and more likely to respond:

- *Consider the seating arrangement.* It may sound touchy-feely, but people's physical relationships to one another influence the quality of their interactions. Having students face one another, in a circle or some other arrangement, creates a better dynamic for discussion than sitting in rows. It's also harder for students to hide.

- *Begin with writing.* Ask students to write for five minutes on the topic you wish them to discuss. Then ask some or all students to share what they've written. This simple technique gives students a chance to think about the topic and rehearse what to say; it relieves pressure and permits thought.

- *Start with a common experience.* If students can relate the topic to something in their own lives, they're likely to have something to say; for example, a life event that everyone has likely gone through or knows about such as the loss of a pet or a family member. A shared event or presentation might take place in class: a brief video, a common reading, even a staged skit.

- *Pose a problem.* You might present a scenario or point out a contradiction between two ideas or positions and ask students to explore ways of dealing with it. Your challenge here is to keep the possible options for dealing with the situation open as long as possible so students don't latch on to the first solution and settle for it, effectively ending the discussion.

- *Start with a group activity.* Some students, indeed some classes, find discussing topics in small groups easier than talking as a class. If so, begin discussions by asking students to write briefly; to share their writing with three to five classmates in a group; and then to solve a problem, reach a consensus, or otherwise carry the discussion forward. Have the groups report to the class, using their reports to start the whole-class discussion. This activity can be done quickly: for example, in workshops on writing across the curriculum, Toby Fulwiler asks participants to write for five minutes, share in groups for five minutes, and then report. The discipline of a brief time limit keeps everyone on task.

- *Conduct discussions online.* Holding a classroom discussion through computers may seem odd, especially as you hear students engaged in discussion only by the clicking of fingers on the keyboard. However, some students who would never contribute to a spoken discussion will reveal strong voices in online discussions. And some classes that simply won't talk to one another will write to one another.

Moving the discussion forward. Once you have a discussion going, here are some tips for keeping it going:

- *Plan for possibilities, but don't assume you can predict the shape of the discussion.* To prepare, know the subject as well as you can and identify your goal in having the discussion. Then, as students talk, you can interject responses and questions to nudge the discussion in the direction you want it to head. Avoid creating a script or flowchart for the discussion, however; your plan is likely to be useless within five minutes.
- *Use silence as a tool.* Too often, when teachers ask a question, they don't wait long enough: The silence makes them uneasy, and they either call on someone or answer the question themselves. Don't. The silence following a question

may make you uneasy, but it makes students uneasy, too, and sooner or later one of them will say something to break the tension. Allowing a period of silence following a question also shows respect for students' need to think before speaking.

- *Use writing and groups to refocus students' attention or jumpstart a dying discussion.* If a discussion heads in a direction you don't want—it peters out, dissolves into irrelevancies, or becomes argumentative, emotional, or personal—reset it by having students do a brief writing, share it in groups, and then come together again as a class. Small index cards are useful tools for this sort of writing, as their size makes them less intimidating; you can ask students to write on two topics, one on each side; and you can collect and read them aloud yourself or have students read their own.
- *Make sure everyone participates or has the opportunity.* You may have a couple of students who monopolize the discussion. If that happens, you may need to deal with the problem. For example, you might take the monopolizers aside, thank them for their strong contributions, and ask if they would allow others to participate more, to help their classmates gain the skills they already have. Chronic nonparticipants should be drawn out, again privately. Tell them you value their opinions and contributions and want them to share with the class. Asking students to

write, and then asking all students to read what they've written, allows everyone to participate, too. Also consider offering students a couple of "free pass" opportunities; if called on, they can cash in one of their free passes if they aren't ready to respond.

Dealing with emotional or interpersonal issues. Sometimes students become agitated, angry, or upset during a discussion. This display of emotion can be a positive sign that students are engaged in the topic, but it can also make you (and them) feel uncomfortable or threatened. If you feel that you are losing control of a discussion or that students are becoming too argumentative, you can ask the class to stop and write briefly on the contended topic, giving everyone a chance to gather their thoughts. Then ask the class to articulate the arguments on both sides, perhaps listing them on the board and asking the class to look for areas of common ground. Refer to authoritative sources to resolve disputes that have a basis in fact or turn the dispute into a writing assignment, which can lead to a follow-up discussion during the next class period or be posted on an online discussion board. In a particularly contentious situation, you may need to spell out rules—perhaps creating them with the class—for acceptable behavior during discussions, for example, "No personal attacks," or "Before you attack someone's position, you must restate it in your own words." Your goal should be to create a class atmosphere in which students feel safe in expressing their opinions.

Using Class Time Effectively

Taking attendance. Most instructors maintain an attendance policy, stated in their syllabus. You may take attendance orally, checking off each student as you read his or her name. This method is useful at the beginning of the term, when you're trying to learn everyone's name, but it can be time-consuming unless you combine it with another activity, such as a workshop "status-of-the-class" check (see Chapter 5, "Conducting Class Workshops") or a brief written response to a reading. You might also take attendance silently, noting who's present during workshop or group activities. Some instructors ask students to sign an attendance sheet at the start of every class, making the point that if their name isn't on the attendance sheet, they'll be considered absent. This method puts the responsibility for taking attendance on the students, rather than on the instructor, and produces a paper trail of student attendance—or lack of it. A variation relies on simply collecting something from each student every day—a draft, a piece of in-class writing, a report of group work that all group members sign—and using it as evidence of attendance. The virtue of the daily assignment is the emphasis not merely on attending, but on doing the work of the class.

Stating class goals and objectives, on the board or on a *PowerPoint* slide, establishes expectations for both you and your students; sets a consistent tone for the class; and ensures that everyone is on the same page. Spend a few moments reviewing them orally to get the class rolling.

Structuring class time. Most of the time, instructors feel that class periods aren't long enough, no matter the number of minutes in each one. Here are some suggestions for using your class time wisely:

- Take attendance as part of another activity, as described above.

- Begin each class promptly on time with a brief writing activity. If you do this every day, students will get to class and out of their coats in time to do the activity, rather than straggling in and getting themselves arranged while you try to start class.

- Maintain a schedule for each class that includes an estimate of the time each activity will begin and end. Even if you can't keep to this plan—students are engaged in a good discussion or workshop, they have more questions than you anticipated, a piece of technology you're using stops working—you can adjust the schedule by shortening an activity, moving it to the next class period, eliminating it, or turning it into an out-of-class activity.

- Have some activities on hand that you can insert if, for some reason, you have time on your hands that you didn't anticipate. A couple of mini-lessons, an engaging group exercise, even an essay or a couple of children's picture books relating to the assignment that you might read to them can help you fill extra time with a worthwhile activity. Although dismissing class early will seem like a treat, most students, especially those who are working to pay their own way, will object if classes are abbreviated with any regularity. Experienced instructors are good sources of backup plans and activities, and they are usually happy to share, so don't hesitate to ask.

- Hand back papers while students are working in groups. As you circulate, returning their materials, you can monitor the groups' work.

- End each class with a writing activity. If you do this every day, students will be less likely to start packing in anticipation of the end of the class period.

Motivating Students

Some students want to do well and consistently come to class prepared, having read and written what you've assigned. Other students are less inclined to work without prodding, motivated more by their sense of how their peers will see them than by their desire to please you or to earn a good grade. You can help those students by creating class activities that ask them to perform for other students. A traditional approach is to ask questions and call on students at random for the answers, but that method is hard on shy students and isn't often appropriate to a writing class. A better way is to build in occasions for students to present their work to the rest of class. Ask students to read parts of their drafts aloud within small groups and to the class. Require that groups report their work to the class, alternating the role of speaker. Have students read in-class writing to start, refocus, or conclude a discussion. Alternate various methods of asking for student performance: go around the room, asking each student to read or respond; ask for volunteers; call on a few individuals at random; require postings on an online discussion board. The key is to use class activities that demand everyone's participation and don't allow students to become unengaged, invisible, or mute.

Observing Other Classes

While reading about and discussing how to design class meetings is useful, the best way to come to an understanding of how classes work is to experience them. Ideally, you should sit in on several veteran instructors' classes in order to watch them as they teach. Observe how they structure their time, establish rhythms, move the class from place to place, and deal with surprises or unanticipated issues. Some tips on visiting include the following:

- *Ask permission first.* Some instructors are hesitant to let other instructors observe their classes, or they may want you to visit when certain activities are planned.

- *Arrive on time, even a bit early.* You want to disrupt the class as little as possible, and already being seated when students arrive is one way to do that.

- *Ask the instructor where you should sit.* Remember that you're a guest, and, more than that, your mere presence changes the dynamics of the entire class, at least at first. Once the students get used to you, they'll ignore you, but during the first ten minutes or so, they'll be aware that you're there.

- *Take your cues from the instructor.* Some instructors will introduce you to the class and explain why you're there; others won't. Some instructors will want you to participate as much as you'd like, sitting in on groups, speaking up during discussions and contributing during lessons; others will want you to sit quietly and apart from the class to minimize the effects of your presence.

- *Take notes—lots of notes.* Take notes on whatever you see and hear—eavesdrop on students' conversations to one another or in groups, look over students' shoulders (if you can) to see what they're writing, describe what the instructor is doing when he or she's moving around the room or sitting at the desk in front. If you vow to yourself that you'll take notes more or less continuously, you'll force yourself to pay attention to the class so you'll have material to write about later. Jot down the time in the left-hand margin every few minutes, so you'll know what happened at what time. Divide your notes into three columns: one for the time, one for the notes you take as you observe, and one for additional observations, comments, and responses that you add later.

- *Focus on students as well as the instructor.* In a workshop class there's a lot of activity going on, whether or not the instructor is talking: students are working in groups or individually, the instructor is conferring with individuals, modeling desired behavior, or preparing for the next set of class activities. Remember that a classroom is a rich milieu filled with twenty or twenty-five people engaged in a common enterprise: things are happening, even when the room is silent and everyone is working quietly at their desks or computers.

- *Expand on your notes as soon as you can* after the class meeting ends. Add additional details and your reactions while you still remember them.

- *Offer to share your observations* with the instructors whose classes you observe. Most will welcome the opportunity to see their classes through the eyes of another instructor.

Useful Readings

Elbow, Peter. "Collaborative Peer Evaluation by Faculty." *Embracing Contraries: Explorations in Learning and Teaching.* New York: Oxford UP, 1986. 179–205. Print.

Frank, Carolyn. "Classroom Observations." *Ethnographic Eyes: A Teacher's Guide to Classroom Observation.* Portsmouth, NH: Heinemann, 1999. 82–93. Print.

A Sample Observation

Chris Massey, a first-year graduate teaching assistant at Wright State University, wrote this report of his observation of a class taught by Catherine Crowley, an instructor in the English department. He notes the time periodically to help him remember the pacing of the class, and he intersperses his reflections (in italics) with his report of his observations.

I sat in on two classes taught by Catherine Crowley, an instructor at Wright State University. The two classes met on Wednesday and the following Monday during the 6th and 7th weeks of the 10-week fall quarter, as students finished writing an analysis of a text and began working on a profile. Each class period lasted 65 minutes and took place in a classroom equipped with networked computers for each student. Students have access to Microsoft Office applications as well as the internet and courseware that includes Desire2Learn.

Wednesday, October 13

1:30 p.m. Professor Crowley returns papers and passes around the attendance sheet. While the students review their graded papers, Professor Crowley reviews the lesson from Monday and connects Monday's activities to the students' objectives for today. Here, she accomplishes two tasks at once—she gets "housekeeping issues" out of the way while, at the same time, bridging the gap between Monday's lesson and today's lesson. *I like the way she accomplishes this task: effortlessly. The students are not even aware of the teaching taking place.* Upon successfully transitioning from Monday's assignments to those scheduled for today, Professor Crowley asks the students if they are ready to submit their rhetorical analyses as final drafts. As you might expect, the entire class responds with a resounding "no." She then agrees with the students and tells them that they can have the weekend to polish their papers. *I hope I have this same connection with my students. I also need to realize that the goal is to get a set of well-written papers. Who cares about the deadline? I hope I have enough foresight to make changes to due dates when necessary.* She then gives the class the plan for the day: She will visit each student and discuss topics for the upcoming paper, the profile. While she is visiting with each student individually, the rest of the class is to begin researching the topics for the profile paper using the internet. While talking, she begins passing out the assignment; she has posted it to D2L and has printed them each a copy. *I wonder if I should use hard copies for my students. I always put the assignments on D2L, but I never give them a handout. I do this to keep from wasting so much paper, but I wonder if it helps to reinforce the assignment if the students have a paper copy to refer to later on.* Moving from the next scheduled assignment, she asks her students to recall specifically what they observed on Monday: "Stephen, what did we do Monday?" Stephen answers that they went outside and observed activities in the quad. At this point, she links their individual responses ("rustling leaves" and "the hot chick with the pink book bag") to the assignment: observing behaviors and places. *Here, the questions serve to reinforce the assignment from Monday and allow the students to link both assignments. It serves as a review of sorts. . . . I need to remember to do this. I tend to move too quickly. Take the time and review prior assignments.*

1:36 p.m. At this point, Professor Crowley mentions that students who use Apple computers need to review their font choices before submitting assignments to websites. She gives this information because the sheet she passes out is from her computer, a Mac. *This information is not related to the assignment, but it serves to link Professor Crowley to her students; they see her as one of them. She becomes human. I thought this was nice of her—students appreciate any information their instructor gives them that helps them out in the real world.* Next, she tells the students that, "We need to make a plan, man." Here, she relates the observation in the quad to the assignment: to come up with topics for the profile paper. She calls on individual students to relate their observations to their topics—Ryan wants to observe the Dayton Mall, and she warns that malls can be generic; Pam wants to observe a football game from her old high school, and Jessica wants to observe a homecoming. Professor Crowley gives constructive criticism here—some topics are good, others too general. *Going around the room serves to make the assignment real—the students get to hear each other's ideas, and it cements the profile topics in their minds. I sometimes back away from having my students share their ideas publicly, but I see now it can work to the students' advantage.*

1:43 p.m. At this point, Professor Crowley gives the students pointers for getting started on their plans. She tells them to take notes on a piece of paper, type it, etc. She then writes on the board: "What is your topic? How will you take your observation notes (laptop, pictures, video, etc.)? Remember to include the date, time, and specific place. Who do you plan to interview (may not know yet)? How will you make your interview (live, contact)? Write down possible questions. Create a survey?" *This allowed her students to have a starting point (they took notes and made their own lists) to think about what they wanted to do.* She then asks her class, "How will you find published sources about your topics?" She responds to their answers and advises them to look on the internet for possible sources. She also reminds them to identify and document their sources.

1:51 p.m. Here, a student—Katie—asks a question: "When researching soccer, do I research soccer in general or soccer about my high school?" Professor Crowley responds and compliments her student on a good question. She tells her entire class the question and responds that they should research specific topics, not general ones. She even responds to one student by telling him to ask his grandparents about his topic. *She has a good connection with her students . . . they respect her and value her opinion.* Professor Crowley then logs on to the main computer console and pulls a website up:

St. Anne's Hill, a website for the community where she lives. She informs her students that many websites are themselves profiles. She shows them the community homepage and the information located on the website, such as the demographics. She reminds her students that you can put opinions in a profile and she clues in the class that their main job now is to get information—concentrate on detail, detail, detail. *I like the way Professor Crowley demonstrates how to utilize a website—I would have never thought of this. Good idea. Sometimes the simple ideas are the best.*

1:55 p.m. She reminds them that their text analyses are due Monday. She tells them they have plenty to do this weekend. She tells them to use their fellow students as sounding boards: use each other to come up with ideas and comment on each other's.

1:56 p.m. Professor Crowley begins individual conferences with students; other students are working on gathering information—she encourages them to talk to each other, to utilize the class time. *I really like the idea that she encourages her students to talk to each other. It seems so simple, yet I have never used this. Good mix between individual time and group time. This approach allows Professor Crowley to spend time with each student while, at the same time, allowing students to work on their papers.* Some students are typing answers to questions. Others are searching the internet and discussing ideas with their peers. One student asks, "Is first person OK?" She repeats the question to the class and answers yes to the class. She reminds the sports people that they don't want just a play-by-play account; they need to interview players, cheerleaders, whatever will make the account realistic. She reminds them to zero in on the hometown event. *Professor Crowley maintains excellent control of the room even when talking to students individually. I noticed several students who wandered from the assignment, but they only did so momentarily.*

2:16 p.m. Professor Crowley continues to consult with individual students. She asks the class: "Is everybody working on something here?" *Again, nice control of the room—this one statement reels in those students who are not working on the assignment.* She responds to one student's question about chat rooms, that you can use quotes from these sources. She also responds to a student who asks her about D2L and tells her to ask at the helpdesk. She reminds her students that they are going into this assignment as reporters and need to be as objective as possible.

2:27 p.m. Professor Crowley reminds the students that there is no class on Friday and tells them that she wants their topic choices. Dismisses class.

5 Conducting Class Workshops

Workshops play an important role in most writing courses. In fact, workshops are often the predominant use of class time. Most simply, a workshop includes any activity in which students write or respond to others' writing, providing them the opportunity to give and receive focused response to their writing in order to revise it. When students confer with their instructor, they also receive focused response leading to revision.

Getting Started

You may offer workshop time as a regular feature of your course, so that during a workshop your students are engaged in various activities at once: generating ideas and text, drafting, conferring, evaluating, revising, editing, or proofreading. You may want to structure workshop times to focus on a single set of activities, such as editing final drafts before submitting them or on collaborative activities such as analyzing a text in groups. However you use workshops in your course, here are some guidelines to help them run smoothly.

Define workshop tasks clearly. Students should know what you expect them to do during workshop time and what to produce by the end. You may begin the workshop with a brief lesson outlining the tasks and the reasons for doing them as well as provide structure for the activities, as appropriate. If students are writing during class, clearly define what writing activities are acceptable and how they should carry them out. If you expect a certain product (a draft, a worksheet, a report to the class by a group), provide clear instructions.

Establish rules of behavior. At a minimum, you should expect students to come to workshops ready to do the assigned tasks. If you want students to follow specific rules (when responding to one another's drafts in groups, for example, or when editing one another's essays), state them clearly and enforce them.

Hold students accountable for their workshop time. If students are working independently, you might take a few minutes to conduct a quick "status-of-the-class" check by asking each student to declare orally what they will be working on during

Sample Workshop Intentions Form

Class:		Section _____ Week _____	
Student's Name	Focus		
Connor, Siobhan	Mon: Work on draft		
Henton, Joe	Mon: Peer conference		
Jones, Rik'kia		Wed: Revise draft	Fri: Editing conference, work on draft

the workshop. As they do, jot down their intended focus. Then you can use the notes to determine who might need help, who should work with another student—in other words, individualize your workshop instruction. Many instructors create simple forms that allow them to record students' workshop intentions quickly. (An example appears above.)

You can require each group to present a report to the class on their achievements, or ask each group to produce something in writing—a worksheet or an informal report—that each group member signs.

Allow for some chit-chat. Students forming groups often need to establish a social connection before they can get down to work. To do that, they may talk informally together for a few minutes first. Also, if the group discussion becomes more serious than group members can handle, they may cool off by diverting the discussion away from the topic at hand. If they don't return to the main topic, you may need to nudge them or give them a follow-up task.

Circulate and monitor. Workshops work best when students are given tasks that they complete independently, using you as a resource when necessary. Give them space to do that by staying at your desk for a few minutes after getting them started. Then circulate around the room, pausing to answer questions or listen to groups as they work. Students will ask questions if you're in their vicinity, and you can glance over shoulders and initiate impromptu conferences as students work. Your presence may also keep students or groups on task, at least while you're in the area. If your classroom layout permits it, sit at a student desk in the middle of the room. You'll be able to hear all the groups as they work without seeming overly intrusive.

Model writers' behavior. Just as students benefit from seeing your writing, they benefit from seeing you write and share your writing. You might spend classroom workshop time working on a draft of something you're writing—a piece you're asking students to write, a professional essay, a personal piece—and at some point share it with them, perhaps showing your revisions and describing your own process. Ask students to respond to your draft, using the same techniques you want them to use when responding to one another's writing. Your students can be perceptive readers, especially in helping you explain concepts clearly.

Conduct conferences or small-group mini-lessons. You may schedule individual conferences during workshop time, speaking softly to students at your desk while the rest of the class works independently. If several students are having a similar writing problem, you might use workshop time to work with that group while the students who don't share their problem work on their own.

Selecting a Workshop Format

Here are some common formats for writing workshops.

Independent workshops. In these workshops, students work on their own writing assignments, so in a class of twenty-five students, ten may be writing drafts, eight may be revising, five may be doing research on computers, and two may be editing a final draft. Have students declare their intentions through a status-of-the-class check; circulate and be flexible, nudging students when they finish one task to begin another. For example, a student who finishes a draft may need to get you or a peer to respond to it and then begin revising. A few minutes before the end of a workshop class period, it's useful to stop students and ask them, either orally or informally in writing, to review what they did and what they plan to do next.

Whole-class response workshops. In these workshops, the entire class discusses one or two students' drafts. Establish rules: The writer provides a draft a couple of days ahead of time, either bringing copies for everyone or posting it online, where the other students must read the draft before coming to class. In class, the writer reads the draft aloud while the class follows along and the writer provides background by describing the rhetorical situation and the stage of writing (rough draft, revision, or final draft). Classmates respond to the draft, offering suggestions and guidance, orally or in writing or both. Students should be reminded of their need to balance honesty and tactfulness.

Group response workshops. Students work in groups of three or four in these workshops, responding to one another's drafts. In one method, students take turns. The writer reads his or her draft aloud, while the other group members listen, taking no notes. When the writer finishes, the others write a brief response. The writer reads the draft again, and this time the others take notes on what they liked, what they didn't like, and what they had questions about. When the writer finishes, each group member describes his or her response while the writer takes notes. The writer does not engage in conversation or debate with the others, since they are simply reporting their reactions to the draft, which are not arguable. The writer then decides how to revise based on the various responses. Here are some variations:

- Students trade drafts and read them silently before responding as described above. If left to themselves, some groups will decide to follow this procedure to avoid reading aloud. Encouraging reading aloud helps students hear both their own voice and potential trouble spots in their writing, but if you encounter a group of students who are very reluctant to read aloud, consider offering this silent option.

- Students read their drafts aloud to a group, which listens but does not respond, except with applause (which may consist of finger-snapping, to keep the noise level down). Especially early in a term, students may need to get used to the idea of sharing before they can work up the courage to give or get response.

- Students respond to one another's drafts based on specific criteria, such as the Key Features of genres defined in the *Field Guide*. In this sort of workshop, have individual students or groups fill out a worksheet that outlines the criteria to ensure that students address everything you want them to.

Focused-activity workshops. The instructor defines a particular task for individual students or groups of students to complete. These tasks might include asking students to work individually on any of the processes of writing as part of their work on their own drafts; to analyze their own drafts or the drafts of classmates, answering specific questions about the writing; to collaborate to complete a writing task; or to choose one group member's essay for oral publication to the entire class.

Online groups. In online courses, groups may still work together in discussion forums within learning management systems or through email. They can respond to one another's drafts using such tools as *Word*'s Comment and Track Changes features and by highlighting parts of one another's essays.

Useful Readings

Murray, Donald M. *A Writer Teaches Writing.* Rev. 2nd ed. Boston: Heinle, 2003. Print.
Garrison, Roger H. "One-to-One: Tutorial Instruction in Freshman Composition." *New Directions in Community Colleges* 5 (1974): 55–84. Print.

6 Working One-on-One with Students

Individual conferences with students to discuss their writing are time-consuming but can be very effective. If your school has a writing center, you can also refer students to work with the tutors there, but in fifteen or twenty minutes, you yourself can establish a personal relationship with a student and offer focused, detailed advice to help the student write and revise. While you may have specific goals for some conferences (for example, you may hold conferences solely to help students settle on a topic for an essay), you can use conferences for a number of purposes:

- Provide one-on-one help.
- Listen and respond respectfully to students' writing, working with the text they have—or discussing the text they don't have.
- Offer whatever help students need, such as generating ideas and text, organizing a draft, working on various writing strategies, or exploring research options.
- Help students understand their own writing processes and identify areas for further work.
- Answer students' questions.

Whatever you do, avoid taking over the draft or telling the student what to write. Most of the time, instructors and tutors make no marks on students' drafts, leaving that job to the students themselves. The best conferences consist of conversations between two writers who are trying to improve one writer's work. You should remind students that it's up to them to interpret and enact, modify, or reject the advice they've been given. Here are some common questions instructors ask about conferences.

How often should you schedule conferences? The simple answer is, as often as possible; working one-on-one with students allows you to tailor your instruction to each student's needs, making conference teaching "the most effective—and the most practical—method of teaching composition," as Donald M. Murray says in "Conference Teaching: The Individual Response." In that essay, Murray outlines approaches for turning an entire course into a series of conferences. Before you structure your course that way, however, you need to know your school's policy on canceling class periods for conferences, and you need to gain experience in conference teaching. Although it's rewarding, it's also challenging, because you need to think on your feet, which can leave you mentally exhausted at the end of a day of conferences. Typically, instructors schedule one mandatory conference for each major assignment, usually two or three per term.

How long should a conference take? Conferences can vary from five minutes for a very focused conference on a limited topic to a half-hour or more. If you're teaching writing for the first time, schedule twenty-minute conferences the first time, and see how they feel. Then adjust the length for subsequent conferences.

How should you schedule conferences? If you're holding twenty-minute conferences for twenty-five students, your conferencing time totals eight hours and twenty minutes. You should schedule four conferences in a row, followed by a twenty-minute break, to allow for conferences that run long (some will) and to give you time to use the bathroom, eat, and recharge. So you'll need a day and a half or so, with most conferences taking place on a day you cancel class. Setting a timer can help you keep to your schedule—both you and your student will wrap up your conversation once the bell rings.

What if students can't meet during the times you've scheduled? If attending a conference is a course requirement, you have the obligation to make the requirement possible to complete. You may have to negotiate with some students for a special time or, if a meeting isn't possible, a telephone or online conversation.

How can you hold conferences without spending so much time on them? You can schedule briefer conferences of ten to fifteen minutes each. When you're crunched for time, you will need to be more focused, but most instructors find that it's possible to get all the work done. Another option is to hold small-group conferences, scheduling three or four students for one thirty-minute conference—in essence, establishing a workshop of which you're a member. If your class periods are lengthy, you can set aside the last fifteen to twenty minutes for conferences, meeting with three or four students each day.

At what point in a sequence of assignments should you schedule conferences? The glib answer is, anytime you want. Students will benefit, no matter when they have a conference with you.

What should students bring with them to a conference? Depending on the nature of the conference, in general it's useful to ask students to bring something in writing: a thesis statement, a rough draft, an introductory paragraph, a set of questions. That writing gives both of you something concrete to work with. Since few students will have had conferences before, it's a good idea to let them know what to expect, as teaching assistant Ozlem Wierzbicki did: "I gave them a mini-lesson on one-on-one conferences, which made a big difference in terms of their expectations for the conference. This mini-lesson was basically an outline explaining to them how the conferences would be conducted."

Should you read students' drafts ahead of time? Inexperienced instructors who haven't read many student essays may feel more confident in their ability to give good advice if they collect drafts and read them ahead of time. Most instructors, though, find that they can answer students' questions or deal with the conference's main issue after quickly skimming the essay at the start of the conference—or after having students point out the parts of the essay that concern them. Also, the time spent reading first and then conferring can double the time you spend with each student.

What if students come unprepared? Some instructors turn away students who come to a conference without a thesis statement or a draft. I believe, however, that if students come unprepared, they're genuinely stuck: they can't think of anything to write, they're blocked, or they have personal problems that prevent them from doing the work. So I work with what they have, helping them get caught up so they can progress toward success in the course.

How do you start a conference? What do you say? Invite students to sit and make them comfortable with a few words of welcome. As Murray points out, you may not need to say anything, or you may begin the conference with a question like "Well? What questions do you have?" For

students who don't know what to say, ask some general questions like these:

- What's the strongest part of your draft? What makes it good?
- What's your purpose for writing?
- Who's your audience?
- What gave you the most trouble as you wrote?
- Where do you think you need more information?

If students come without a draft, these questions won't work, of course. Then you need to shift gears with questions to generate ideas for topics:

- What interests you?
- What do you do for fun or relaxation?
- What makes you mad?
- What puzzled you in the reading we did? What made you uncomfortable?
- If you *could* write about _____, what would you write? (This "fill-in-the-blank" approach is surprisingly effective, and is useful in many situations.)

How can you use The Norton Field Guide ***effectively as you confer with students?*** Because the book is organized for easy reference, you can quickly find the advice you need at the time you need it. When you hold a conference, you might keep the book open to the glossary/index. As you work with students, you—or, better, your students—can go quickly to the advice they need. In the process, you'll be teaching them how to use the textbook as a reference tool.

What should students do while you're reading their drafts? You might give students something interesting to read while they wait. You can also ask them to bring two copies of the draft and read it while you do, so it's fresh in their minds when you start discussing it. Here's what teaching assistant Holly Gilbert discovered:

> I had the students bring two copies of their draft to conferences with them. I found it to be extremely helpful because we both were not trying to flip through the same document at the same time. While I read through each draft, I had the students find specific points in their drafts that they wanted to talk about and star them; some even jotted down little notes in the margins to explain to me what they think works and what doesn't and why they think it does or does not. I really found this to be helpful. It helped those students who even after writing a self-assessment had no idea what to discuss in the conference. The students who took the time to reread their drafts and star specific parts really got into discussing how they wanted to make their draft better and where they wanted to go from this point. Instead of staring at me and fearing what I was going to say about their drafts, they had something to do that kept them engaged and refreshed their memory about certain aspects of their drafts that they may want to discuss in conferencing. Our conferences started to have the tone of a conversation (as Murray would say).

How should the conference end? Each student should leave the conference with a clear sense of what to do next. It's a good idea to ask students to state their plans in writing before leaving the conference, as the act of composing it together forces both of you to be specific and clear. You might ask if they have questions about any other aspects of the class or about their progress in the course.

How should you handle students who don't show up? I usually count a conference as the equivalent of two absences because I value my time. Since I've canceled a class period, replacing 50 to 100 minutes of group instruction with 15 minutes of individual attention, I want students to take the conference seriously. As teaching assistant Chuck Holmes notes, there's also a personal dimension when students don't come to conferences:

> The most powerful response I had to any of my first conferences was the way it felt when students didn't show up. I was pretty indignant about that. The vast majority of the students did attend the conferences and I think we all got something worthwhile out of it, so I have made myself a promise that I won't say anything in the next class about how it made me feel, being stood up that way. As a matter of fact, now that I think about it, being stood up is exactly what it felt like.

How can you use your campus writing center to best advantage? First, make sure your students know the writing center exists and encourage them to seek help there with their writing, whether they're seeking a topic or polishing a final draft.

Include writing center information on your syllabus and on each assignment handout. You might contact the center's director to ask for brochures or other material describing the center's services to give your students. Some writing centers will send tutors to classes to describe its services to students. You could give students a bit of credit toward their grade for attending a tutoring session. Send a copy of your course syllabus and assignment descriptions to the writing center, and make sure they have copies of the *Field Guide* available for tutors. The more tutors know about your course and expectations, the more they can help your students. You may be able to require some students to get help at the writing center, but check with the center's director first since some centers have limited scheduling ability. Also check to see if your campus center has an explanation of what to expect on its homepage.

Useful Readings

Boynton, Linda. "See Me: Conference Strategies for Developmental Writers." *Teaching English in the Two-Year College.* 30.4 (2003): 391–402. Print.

Murray, Donald M. "Conference Teaching: The Individual Response." *A Writer Teaches Writing,* 2nd ed. Boston: Houghton, 1985. 147–75. Print.

Using Writing Activities in Class **7**

Writing is a form of learning. As we write, we generate thoughts we wouldn't have had if we hadn't put pen to paper or fingers to keyboard. In our own writing as well as our students', we can see that thinking improves as drafts evolve. More than once, a student of mine has exclaimed, "I didn't know this essay would head in this direction!" Because writing helps us generate ideas and clarify our thinking, the act of writing is a useful tool for teaching. This chapter explores some ways you can use writing to both enhance your teaching and improve students' learning.

Freewrites

Freewriting is a tool used by many to generate ideas and text. By writing without stopping for a specified amount of time, writers frequently discover that they articulate complex ideas and sentences of unanticipated power that can then be more fully developed. Having students freewrite on index cards often reduces their anxiety, because, after all, anyone can fill up a small card. Here are three times when you can use brief, informal freewrites as pedagogical tools:

At the beginning of class. Ask students to write questions they have about the assignment that's due or reactions to a reading. You can use their answers to start a discussion or to begin the class with a brief question-and-answer session, or you can collect the cards and skim them later to find out how well students understood the assignment—or if they did it. If students write on index cards, you can give them two assignments, one on each side. For example, "What's one question you have about this assignment?" and "What's one thing you liked about the reading for today?" Alternately, set aside the first ten minutes of every class for writing. Expect students to spend ten minutes writing whatever they want, an activity that settles them down and warms them up for the day's activities. Starting the class with a writing activity is a good way to let students know that they need to arrive on time and be prepared and gives you a way to take attendance: if students turn in the writing, they're present and on time.

At the end of class. Ask students to sum up the day's activities or what they learned during class. Ask them to relate the day's discussion to their reading, to ask questions about the assignment, or to predict what they'll do with their drafts after working on them in class. These end-of-class freewrites help students synthesize course material and think about how to apply it to their own writing. They also forestall students' tendency to start packing up several minutes before the end of class and let them know that you've planned their class time carefully.

During class. Brief writing activities can be valuable during class, too. When you finish one class activity, have students reflect on it before moving on to the next. If a discussion bogs down or becomes heated, ask students to stop and write briefly on the topic to get everyone on track (and give you a few minutes to regroup!). These brief freewrites may take as little as two minutes—just enough to give students a chance to think on paper.

Here's how teaching assistant Andrea Nay uses brief writing assignments on index cards:

> Every single class period, students must write on a topic I assign for the first 3–4 minutes of class. Some assignments are designed to be funny and simply serve as a means to capture attendance. Others are in keeping with the day's lessons. In advance preparation for Wednesday's mini-lesson on sentence breaks, for example, I had the students take the first few minutes of class Monday to write the longest grammatically correct sentence they could concoct on the front or back of an index card. The "winner" got a prize on Wednesday, and I used that sentence as a good

example to illustrate the proper use of coordinating conjunctions.

For more on freewriting and other generative writing activities, see Chapter 24 in the *Field Guide*, GENERATING IDEAS AND TEXT.

Letters

Everyone knows how to write a letter. The form is simple, the stance and tone natural. As such, letters are a great way to communicate with your students. Sue Dinitz and Toby Fulwiler suggest that you require each student to write you a letter of at least 250 words—one page—each week. You might specify a topic, but I've found that simply requiring the letter and leaving the contents up to the students produce wonderful results. You might ask students to send you an email letter or give you a hard copy, or let them choose the medium they feel most comfortable with. Then read the letters quickly, highlighting or copying interesting passages or good questions. Respond with a "Dear Class" letter in which you use the passages you've chosen as the basis for your own remarks, sharing interesting thoughts they've expressed, answering questions, and exploring ideas with them. Give students credit for their letters.

You'll find that these letters have several good effects. Students will be doing more writing, always a good thing. They'll be writing to a real audience—you—on topics of importance to them. As a result, you'll learn much more about their interests, backgrounds, emotional states, and circumstances than you would otherwise. You'll be able to tailor your instruction to meet their needs and answer their questions promptly. And through your exchanges of letters, you'll get to know one another far better than students and instructors normally do. In colleges and universities, where young people may be living away from home for the first time, this personal connection between students and faculty can be crucially important to the students' success, not only in your class but also in making it through their first year. Besides, learning about your students' lives and thoughts is at turns touching, interesting, sad, and funny—but thoroughly rewarding.

Consider, too, asking students to write letters to one another, perhaps providing a copy for you. After several rounds of letters to and from you and each other, discuss the effects of varying audiences on the letters' form, content, and stance.

Online Discussion Lists

You can use online discussion lists to engage students in conversations about any topics you might otherwise use class time to discuss or to extend discussion that begins in class. You can post a specific topic or question for students to discuss, or you could also ask students or groups of students to create discussion topics. It's best to require students to post responses; otherwise, participation will likely be spotty. Most colleges and universities offer you the ability to set up a group consisting of members of your course through a website portal, email, or online courseware. For more advice on online discussions, see Chapters 13 and 14 in this guide to teaching.

Journals/Blogs

Journals—also known as daybooks, logs, or personal notebooks—and their online manifestation, blogs, have been popular with high school and college English teachers for many years because they give students practice in writing and thinking on paper or online without the pressure of crafting polished prose. Some instructors focus their journal assignments on practice, simply requiring a certain amount of writing, such as a page or post each day or five pages/posts each week. More often, though, students are given more direction, so that their journal writing contributes to the overall goals of the course. The sorts of assignments you might ask students to complete in a journal include the following, adapted from a list of characteristics described by Toby Fulwiler in *The Journal Book* (2–3):

- *Questioning.* Students can explore questions about their assignments, their research material, or class activities. They can also work out conflicts between what they've previously thought or learned and new information.

- *Responding.* Students can play with ideas or react to aspects of the course, giving them a chance to work out their thinking and giving you a window into their difficulties.

- **Consolidating and connecting.** Students can explore the ways that the various course activities and assignments interrelate, or how your course relates to their writing in other courses.

- **Analyzing.** Students might reflect on their own processes of writing, explaining how their activities helped (or didn't help) them write an assignment. Periodically, they might also analyze the course itself: what's been helpful so far, how the course differs from or matches their expectations, and what might be done differently to help them learn better.

- **Playing.** Students might use journal entries to play around in a safe environment: to write parodies or poems, draw cartoons, or explore hypothetical situations that they or you create.

- **Conversing.** Dialectical journals (also discussed in Chapter 8, "Using Readings to Teach Writing") give students an opportunity to reflect on their own earlier journal entries. The technique is simple: students write journal entries on one side of a notebook page, leaving the other side blank, or they fold a page in two and write only to the left of the fold. Later, they read their entries and, on the other page or right-hand side of the page, they comment on those earlier entries. If students keep class notes, you might ask that they follow the same procedure.

Tips for assigning and evaluating journals. If you ask students to use a three-ring binder for their journals, they can use the same binder for all course materials and you can collect only the entries you want, rather than having to lug two dozen spiral notebooks around. Make sure students date each entry and begin each entry on a new page. Alternately, set up a system that allows students to post their entries online. Designate a minimum word length for entries; often, writers' best insights appear near the end of an entry. To manage your workload, consider collecting the journals from half the class each week, so you'll see each student's journal every two weeks.

When you evaluate journals, remember that they are places for students to play, experiment, and explore. You should respond to their content as a reader. To evaluate the journals, you might give credit based on quantity; for example, journals with lots of writing earn high grades, journals that meet the minimum requirements get a C. Or combine quantity with quality: doing the minimum earns a C, and higher grades depend on such qualities as elaboration, thoughtfulness, and playfulness.

Blogs. Blogs may be used as online journals. Blogs, which at their simplest are personal websites built upon a template, are easy to create and allow writers to include photos, documents, links to other websites, and even video as they explore ideas. One significant difference between a traditional journal and a blog, of course, is audience; instead of an audience of the writer and the instructor, the blogger's writing is posted on the web, where it can be accessed by classmates and people all over the world. As a result, students may avoid certain topics that they might write about in a more private journal.

Useful Readings

Bean, John. "Informal, Exploratory Writing Activities." *Engaging Ideas: The Professor's Guide to Integrating Writing, Critical Thinking, and Active Learning in the Classroom.* San Francisco: Jossey-Bass, 1996. 97–118. Print.

Dinitz, Sue, and Toby Fulwiler, eds. *The Letter Book: Ideas for Teaching College English.* Portsmouth, NH: Boynton/Cook, 2000. Print.

Emig, Janet. "Writing as a Mode of Learning." *College Composition and Communication* 28 (May 1977): 122–28. Print.

Fulwiler, Toby, ed. *The Journal Book.* Portsmouth, NH: Boynton/Cook, 1987. Print.

8 Using Readings to Teach Writing

Maureen Daly Goggin

Like writing, reading is not a natural act; it's a learned activity. Because there are many genres in writing, readers attend to these genres in different ways. Reading, then, is not a single act but multiple practices that vary with the purpose, context, and kind of text. As the first readers of their own work, writers need to anticipate other readers' needs, concerns, and levels of knowledge about a topic. Writers must predict readers' expectations for the genre and relationship to the writer. In other words, writers need to learn to read as well as write rhetorically: They need a strategy for reading a text for its purpose, audience context, expected conventions, and style. Using the *Field Guide*'s sample readings in the genres you're teaching offers you an important opportunity to show students how to read a variety of genres rhetorically. This chapter offers strategies for assigning readings and using them in the classroom.

Writing teachers assign readings for many reasons. As Wayne Booth so powerfully observes, embedded in readings of all kinds are worldviews and values: "To teach reading (or viewing or listening) that is both engaged and actively critical is central because it is in stories, in narratives large and small rather than in coded commandments, that students absorb lessons on how to confront ethical complexity.... It is in stories that we learn to think about the 'virtual' cases that echo the cases we will meet when we return to the more disorderly, 'actual' world" (48).

To become critical citizens and consumers, students need to learn how to make sense of ethical complexities and to understand multiple perspectives. Readings you assign can support this critical thinking at the same time they demonstrate the key features of a genre, explore a topic or an issue, and initiate research in an area of interest for the class. Most important, readings teach students how to read other writers rhetorically so they can read their own writing rhetorically.

Regardless of your purposes for incorporating readings into your writing class, make your reasons clear so students will understand how the readings relate to their own writing. The suggestions here are by no means exhaustive but are meant as examples that may spark additional ideas.

Preparing Students to Read

Let students know why you have assigned the readings, either by including your purposes in the assignment or by giving a brief lecture or mini-lesson before they begin the reading. You might save the last five minutes of class to prepare students for the following class's reading assignment by giving them a focus or a series of study questions. You can also prepare them for any unfamiliar vocabulary by playing a version of Balderdash: you say and spell one or more of the words you suspect will be unfamiliar, then have students write impromptu definitions. They pass the definitions to you or a chosen speaker in the class to read aloud. Students then vote on the most likely definition. The writer of the definition chosen gets a point, and all those who defined it correctly get a point. Points can be accumulated throughout the semester in this manner. Here are some other ways to use readings effectively.

Models. Readings can serve as good examples of the genres being studied but *only* if students are taught *how* to look at them as models. In ancient Greece, Isocrates offered a caution against placing models in front of students and expecting them to know how to compose a similar piece, offering the analogy that it's like placing a row of shoes in front of novice cobblers and expecting them to understand how to make a shoe. How would the would-be cobblers know what raw materials were needed and where to get them? How to prepare those materials even if they could locate them? How to fashion the shoe? In writing as well, students need to be taught how to look at models.

It's worth spending class time early in the term going over at least one essay in depth to demonstrate how to read it for its rhetorical features. Students can then continue this process on their own, guided by questions or perhaps by keeping a reading journal. You might ask students to write out their understanding of the essay's rhetorical situation:

Purpose: What is the writer's purpose? To entertain? To inform? To persuade readers to think something or take some action?

Audience: Who is the intended audience? Are you a member of that group? If not, did you need to look up unfamiliar terms or concepts or run into assumptions you don't necessarily share?

Genre: What is the genre? Is it a report? an argument? an analysis? Something else? What are the key features of this genre, and where are they found in this essay?

Stance: Who is the writer, and what is his or her stance? Critical? Curious? Opinionated? Objective? Passionate? Indifferent? Something else?

Medium/Design: What is the medium, and how does it affect the way you read? If it's a print text, do you know anything about the publisher? If it's on the web, who sponsors the site, and when was it last updated? Are there any design elements—such as headings, summaries, color, or boxes—that highlight key parts of the text?

Collecting their responses and reviewing them in class will help students take the readings and their responses to them seriously and will also help to show how reading is an integral part of writing. More advice on responding to reading may be found in the *Field Guide* Chapter 41, READING STRATEGIES.

Reader's logs. You can ask students to keep a reader's log or journal where they record their impressions of assigned readings, focusing on their reactions to the lines of argument or the writer's position or the rhetorical stance of the readings. You can provide specific questions tied to each reading or provide a template of questions that students apply to all readings. If you ask students to bring their logs to class, their entries can be a starting point for discussing the readings. You can also ask students to reflect on their entries either during class or outside of class following discussions in class. At the end of the term, you might ask students to review all of their entries and write a reflection on that review.

Summarizing and outlining. You can ask students to summarize or create outlines of readings. These activities force students to read carefully and attend to the structure as well as the content of the text. They also allow you to see how well the students understand the reading, and offer a starting

point for discussions of the reading. You can find advice on summarizing in Chapter 47, QUOTING, PARAPHRASING, AND SUMMARIZING, and advice on outlining in Chapter 41, READING STRATEGIES, both in the *Field Guide*.

Double-entry notebooks. Ann Berthoff developed the concept of a double-entry reading notebook. As she explains,

> What makes this notebook different from most, perhaps, is the notion of the double entry: on the right side reading notes, direct quotations, observational notes, fragments, lists, images—verbal and visual—are recorded; on the other (facing side), notes about those notes, summaries, formulations, aphorisms, editorial suggestions, revisions, comment on comment are written. (48)

With a double-entry notebook, the opposing pages are seen in dialogue with one another. According to Berthoff, this kind of reading notebook helps students develop critical reading and writing skills because they are conducting a "continuing audit of meaning" (I. A. Richards, qtd. in Berthoff 42). Questions and observations that appear in these notebooks can launch vibrant classroom discussions.

Discussions. Discussions of readings can take place either face-to-face in class or in a synchronous or asynchronous online forum. The goal of these discussions should be to help writers advance their own writing. Unlike literature classes where the readings serve as the focus for literary analysis, in writing classes discussions of the readings ought to be tied directly to the aspects of writing with which your students are grappling. If, for example, you're teaching a unit on how to write a profile, you might have students analyze readings in this genre for rhetorical moves that would be useful for their own writing. Students might read the model in Chapter 16 of the *Field Guide* or a profile they find in a magazine or newspaper. Does the writer begin with an anecdote? What kind of information does the writer provide about the subject (person, place, or thing) profiled? How did the author get the information she or he uses in the profile? How does the author end the profile? Also, to help students prepare for discussions, you might ask them to freewrite any questions, concerns, or observations they have about the assigned reading. This task jogs their memory and provides a framework for discussion.

Small-group discussions and activities. Small-group activities help students practice collaborative work and are central to active learning. Variations on games students know can produce lively discussions. For instance, students can play a form of Jeopardy where they form groups and devise answers to questions relevant to the readings. They then challenge other groups by stating their answers and asking the other groups to form an appropriate question. Another strategy is to have student groups identify the rhetorical or content points they feel everyone should attend to. The small groups then share their recommendations with the whole class. Finally, students can be asked to select readings for the class and then lead the discussions either by themselves or in groups.

Quizzes and essay exams. Although some teachers assign quizzes as a way to make sure that students are doing the readings, an alternative and perhaps better approach is to use quizzes to help students learn how to write quiz and exam answers. Let students know that they will be taking periodic quizzes on the readings as a way to help them become strong quiz takers throughout their educations.

You may also want to help your students learn how to write essay responses to exam questions under pressure. A twist is to have students design a final exam on the readings and to write a rationale for their exam. Students find that they have to understand a whole lot in order to write good essay exam questions.

There are lots of valid reasons for incorporating reading into the writing classroom, and there are many creative ways for doing so. Still, a note of caution is in order: because they often have a strong background as readers, some new writing teachers are tempted to spend too much time on the readings instead of the writing that should be the primary focus of the course. Keep your goal in mind: use readings to help your students improve their writing.

Useful Readings

Berthoff, Ann E. "A Curious Triangle and the Double-Entry Notebook: or, How

Theory Can Help Us Teach Reading and Writing." *The Making of Meaning: Metaphors, Models, and Maxims for Writing Teachers.* Upper Montclair, NJ: Boynton/Cook, 1981. Print.

Berthoff, Ann E. "Is Reading Still Possible?" *Composition in Four Keys.* Eds. Mark Wiley, Barbara Gleason, and Louise Wetherbee Phelps. Mountain View, CA: Mayfield, 1995. 45–49. Print.

Booth, Wayne C. "The Ethics of Teaching Literature." *College English* 61.1 (1998): 41–55. Print.

Foster, David. "Reading(s) in the Writing Classroom." *College Composition and Communication* 48.4 (1997): 518–39. Print.

Roth, Audrey. "Students Collaboratively Choose Reader Selections." *Teaching English in the Two-Year College* 20 (1993): 298. Print.

Responding to Student Writing 9

You want to give your students as much help as you can because you want them to succeed in your class—but you also need to get your own work done and, you hope, cook an occasional meal and get some sleep. Ways to respond helpfully to students' work and still manage your own time are the subject of this chapter.

Responding and Grading

First, remember that responding and grading are two different activities. When you respond to students' writing, your goal is to help them improve their writing of the draft at hand and in future writing. For that reason, you should respond in greatest detail to drafts that will be revised. Grading, on the other hand, ranks the writing's overall quality in relation to standards you or your writing program has set. You'll find advice on grading in Chapter 12 in this guide to teaching, "Grading Student Writing." Once a grade has been assigned to a piece of writing, students are likely to see the writing as finished. At that point, detailed responses are more often an attempt to justify the grade and function primarily as an autopsy. Here is advice on

responding usefully and efficiently to students' writing.

Developing Criteria for Response

Since most students have been taking English in school for many years, they may have some definite ideas about what makes good writing. However, their ideas may not match one another's ideas or your criteria. So a good first step in preparing to respond to students' writing—and a good way to help them understand what you want—is to describe, as clearly as possible, the criteria you'll use when you respond to their writing. Here are a couple of ways to do that.

Use rubrics and checklists. Checklists and rubrics or scoring guides are excellent tools for responding to students' work in progress. They spell out as clearly as possible your expectations and provide detailed response to as few or as many characteristics as you want students to be responsible for. Students can use them to evaluate their own and one another's work. And they control your response by reminding you what to look for as you read students' work. On page 54 is a sample

53

Arguing a Position: Response Criteria

Author: _____   Assessor: _____

	Very well	Well	Some-what	Poorly or not at all
The Assignment				
The essay presents an argument.				
Required drafts and other related assignments are present.				
The Rhetorical Situation				
The essay accomplishes its PURPOSE.				
The essay meets the needs of its AUDIENCE.				
The essay fulfills the demands of its GENRE.				
The essay's stance is reasonable and fair with an appropriate tone.				
The essay's design is appropriate and effective (readable, clear).				
The Argument				
The position is stated clearly in a THESIS statement.				
The position is appropriately qualified.				
Reasons are clearly stated.				
Reasons are adequately supported.				
Supporting evidence is accurate, current, appropriate, and sufficient.				
Counterarguments are addressed, acknowledged, refuted.				
The draft is clearly organized.				
The argument is presented logically throughout.				
Writer works to build common ground with the audience.				
Transitions help the reader move from idea to idea.				
Use of Source Material				
The essay includes adequate and appropriate source material.				
Sources are introduced and identified.				
In-text citations are present and correctly formatted.				
Summaries and paraphrases are accurate and avoid plagiarism.				
The Works Cited section is correctly formatted (MLA).				
In General				
Sentences are consistently correctly phrased and punctuated.				
The language is precise, and the wording exact and accurate.				
Mechanics, usage, grammar, and spelling are correct.				

checklist for an essay that argues a position. To respond, you would simply place a check mark along the continuum from "very well" to "poorly or not at all."

You could substitute "well," "acceptable," "poorly," "not at all," "early," "middle," or "late"—whatever method of response you choose. Having an even number of response levels prevents grouping checks or credits in the middle. Why not use numbers or letters? For one thing, students will expect you to tally them up to create a precise grade for the whole rubric, increasing your workload. For another, the criteria on the rubric are not equal in value and, in fact, may change in value from draft to draft. For example, you may not want to weight "mechanics, usage, grammar, and spelling" as much as "adequate and appropriate source material," but if the mechanics are flawed enough that the writer's credibility comes into question, those problems will likely outweigh other criteria. And absence of a grade reinforces the idea that this checklist is a response to a work in progress.

Develop evaluation criteria collaboratively.
Students understand and accept evaluation criteria more readily when they participate in developing them. You'll find, too, that students know and can articulate standards very well; they know what makes for good writing, even if they have trouble achieving it. (Here's a useful analogy: you may know what qualities characterize a good tennis backhand, guitar lick, or pastel drawing technique but still be unable to do it.) Here's a way to work with your class over one or two class periods to develop a checklist of evaluation criteria collaboratively:

1. Ask students to jot down a list of the criteria on which the type of writing they're currently working on should be judged.
2. Place them in groups of three to six students. Each group's task is to share their individual lists and come up with a single list on which they can agree.
3. Ask one member of each group to write the group's list on the board, which you have divided into sections for each group's list plus one in the middle that you've reserved.
4. Once all groups' lists are on the board, ask the class to find common criteria. If, for instance, every group's list contains "focused topic," write that term on a class list in the middle section. As students find common criteria, they'll note that groups use various terms to describe some criteria. Discuss possible differences in the terms and help the class decide on a single term that everyone agrees will be used to mean one criterion. This discussion will help students understand the criteria and develop a common language for discussing their work.
5. After the groups' lists are merged into a single class list, you may find that criteria important to you are missing. Now is the time to add them, explaining what they mean and why they're important.

This procedure results in a class-specific set of criteria on which you can base checklists and rubrics that you and the students will follow in responding to and evaluating their work. You may want to extend the exercise by comparing the class criteria with generally accepted criteria from your school's writing program documents, your textbooks, and other sources. For example, share with students three or four checklists or rubrics that define criteria for the kind of writing you're working on. (The WPA Outcomes Statement, reprinted in Chapter 23 of this guide to teaching, is a good starting point.) As out-of-class work or in groups, have students compare their class criteria with these other criteria and then discuss the comparisons: What does the class list contain that these others don't? What do they include that ours doesn't? Should we consider adding these other criteria or changing our criteria to match theirs more closely?

Responding to Drafts

Don't. Many writing teachers think that if students write something, they need to respond in detail. That's not true. If a student writes in a journal or does in-class writing as part of class work, a check or date stamp to acknowledge that it's done may be all that's needed. Much other informal writing may only require a brief comment on some part of the content—"Really? That's interesting," "I didn't know that," or "Is this always the case?"—to show that you've read it.

Ask students to respond first. Ask them to keep track of their writing process as they compose from the earliest invention strategies through the final draft. If you ask students to turn in a self-assessment of their writing, you can then respond to their assessment, which is often exactly right or even excessively harsh. Engaging in a written dialogue with students over the merits of their drafts in which you can affirm their evaluation rather than having to point out problems yourself can be very positive—and even better is pointing out strengths they may have overlooked.

Respond as a reader. Respond to students' writing as an interested reader, and you'll provide them with a lot of useful information on which to base revisions. Respond to content with reactions ("Really?" "Wow!"), personal responses ("That happened to me once, too," or "I'd like to know more about this."), questions ("How do you know this?" or "Do others have the same opinion?"), and suggestions ("What if you . . . ?" "Consider moving this to . . . ?").

Highlight strengths as well as weaknesses. Research suggests that we learn best when criticism is balanced with praise—when our strengths as well as our errors are pointed out. Frequently, however, praise for what students do well in writing has been far outweighed by "correction" of their errors. Look for ways to respond positively and show that you're taking their writing seriously, itself a positive gesture. Note interesting ideas, well-organized paragraphs, graceful turns of phrase, and striking words and images; sprinkle the margins with smiley faces and stars when something strikes you positively.

Look for patterns. Many students' errors result not from ignorance but from their attempt to create order by inventing rules that are consistent but wrong. If a student consistently links two closely related sentences with a comma, for example, that student needs lessons in editing for comma splices in the context of showing how one sentence follows logically from the previous one. Unlike random errors, which suggest a lack of editing skills, patterns of error can be identified, after which you can help students learn the correct rules. You can show students such patterns in several ways. Once you identify two or three patterns, you can mark only those patterns by underlining the problem, circling it, or putting a notation in the margin next to the line on which the error appears. You might draw lines connecting each instance of a pattern to show that the same problem occurs several times. If you're commenting with a word processing feature, you might highlight each instance of a pattern in a certain color: yellow for comma splices, green for a certain type of misspelling, and so on. Or you can mark one example and ask the student to locate others as a way to recognize and eventually edit that error.

Limit your responses. If you're having a tennis lesson and the coach criticizes your stance, your grip, your swing, your serve, your racquet, and your clothing all at once, you're more likely to walk off the court in frustration than to improve your game. The same is true with writing, so concentrate on a small number of issues on any given draft and ignore the rest—for now. If you're reading an early draft, pointing out errors in sentences that may well be changed or deleted as students revise is wasted energy. As a rule of thumb, comment on issues in students' drafts according to a hierarchy, dealing with the biggest issues first.

- *Focus.* Does the student have a workable topic? Is it appropriately narrowed or focused?

- *Development.* Does the draft say enough? Does it cover the topic in appropriate depth?

- *Organization.* Does the draft have a clear beginning, middle, and end? Are the paragraphs in the best order? Are the paragraphs themselves organized appropriately?

- *Coherence.* Can the reader follow the logic throughout the draft? Does the writer include transitions and other signposts to help the reader?

- *Sentences.* Does each sentence contribute to the whole? Is each sentence correct? Is there appropriate variety in sentence construction?

- *Phrasing and tone.* Are phrases idiomatic? Is the tone consistent? Appropriate?

- *Editing, proofreading, and design.* Is the draft correct? Is the design appropriate for the genre and the audience's expectations?

As you read the draft, try to identify strengths, the areas most in need of improvement, and strategies to suggest to the student for revising.

Recognize the stages in the writing process. One way to encourage students to see their assignments in terms of work accomplished and work yet to be done is to respond at stages in the process. Edwina L. Helton and Jeff Sommers have described a useful method: E-M-L, or early, middle, and late. A draft marked early is early in the process: it may lack a clear thesis; it may be unfocused and underdeveloped. A middle draft likely has a clear direction but needs significant work on development and clarification. A late draft may be almost finished, needing only editing and proofreading.

Use minimal marking. Students, like the rest of us, often know more than their writing shows; they make mistakes that they know are mistakes but simply don't see as they put together a draft. To place the responsibility for finding and fixing errors on the students, consider this method, first described by Richard Haswell: note errors in grammar, spelling, mechanics, and usage by a check mark in the margin next to the line on which the error appears. Students then must identify and fix the errors. Problems that remain after they've gone through the draft are probably problems they need assistance with in conference, through lessons in class, or in a visit to the writing center. The checkmarks in the margin of the second draft of the student essay in this chapter (pp. 61–64) show minimal marking at work: in the third line, the student omits the final -s from the verb *consists*, so a checkmark is placed in the margin next to that line to alert the student to the presence of an error.

Respond to errors in context. Many of us are good at seeing errors; in fact, marking formal errors is the easiest part of responding to writing. Although there's no question that errors in a piece of writing can seriously undermine its effectiveness and its writer's credibility, a resolute focus on error leads student writers to the conclusion that what they have to say doesn't matter as long as they write error-free prose. Let students know that errors are like bee stings: a few are an annoyance, but too many can be fatal. It's not useful to create a rigid policy on errors, such as "Three errors and your paper automatically fails." Your role is to teach, not punish, and if student work has errors, it's likely that the student didn't know they were there; otherwise, he or she would have corrected them. You can teach students how to edit and proofread, what to look for, and where to get additional help, whether from computer spelling and grammar checkers, handbooks, classmates, or the school's writing center.

To respond to error productively, remember that correctness is one of a constellation of goals. Here are some questions to help you think about errors:

- Which errors are most serious? Problems involving sentence structure and boundaries, such as sentence fragments, comma splices, and run-on sentences, are usually seen as more serious than misspellings or nonstandard verb forms.

- Do the errors interfere with the reader's ability to understand the text? If so, the writer needs to know.

- Do the errors affect the writer's credibility? Rightly or wrongly, readers often judge the writer's intelligence by the correctness of his or her prose.

- Do the errors form patterns? A pattern of errors can be corrected through instruction; random errors are most likely the result of poor proofreading.

Making Specific Comments

When you respond to students' drafts, you should consider these questions: What response will help the writer at this stage of the writing? What does the writer need to know—and what does the writer not need to know—right now? How should this response be given? Your response will vary, depending on your knowledge of the student and the student's needs, the timing of the draft (rough, revised, or final), and the text of the draft. For example, consider the following responses to two drafts of a student's argument essay on the dangers of the Atkins and other low-carbohydrate diets. Here's the student's first draft; the comments were made using *Microsoft Word*'s Comment function.

Atkins Diet, Good or Bad?

first draft

[With the general population in the United States being obese and constantly more and more people becoming obese,] many consider the Atkins diet. This diet is simply [low to no carbohydrates and a great intake of protein.] This diet has been around for many years, but is currently getting more publicity and many people are starting to consider it. [The main focus now is, is the diet really healthy for ones body?]

[The Atkins diet is broken up into stages.] The first stage is where the weigh becomes off the fastest because it is predominately water fat, but [after this stage] is when the weight loss slows. Constantly eating protein everyday is not merely the healthiest way to remove those unwanted pounds. There are many health risk involved with this diet.

Studies reported that weight loss was associated with the length of time being on the diet and not the reduced intake of carbohydrates (PCRM pg7). Low carbohydrate diets induce a chemical known as ketosis which is an abnormal state that occurs in starvation. [In

Comment: It's good to explain the context for your topic, as you do here. In fact, I'd like to know more about why Americans are diet-crazy!

Comment: Good, brief summary of the diet.

Comment: Is this your thesis? Can you restate this as a statement? "The Atkins diet is _____." (See FG on Thesis Statements)

Comment: I like the idea of discussing the stages—it's a good way to show the effects of the diet.

Comment: I'd like to know more about these stages. Are there more than 2?

the long run| this chemical can effect ones body physically, having

> **Comment:** Wow! This sounds serious! I like this specific information.

calcium loss, a high risk of osteoporosis, and a high risk of forming kidney stones. Your body can also be in high risk of problems dealing with bones, the cardiac system, and the liver. Food containing a high count for protein usually lack important healthy ingredients such as fibers which results in problems with the body.

Many people don't look at the risk factors for this diet, but their focus is primarily on, Am I going to lose weight, how fast, and is it easy? The Atkins diet fits these three questions and that's why many people decide to go on it. This diet is said to burn your fat for energy. This attracts the so called "busy" people fast. Those always on the go can lose pounds fast because they need the energy and their fat is their supplier. [Research found this diet to be top notch over almost any other diet.] Low fat diets, Weight watchers, and many others

> **Comment:** This seems to contradict the first part of your paper. How can it be harmful and yet the best?

were compared to the Atkins diet and more results were viewed in favor of Atkin. More pounds were shed and blood pressure, glucose, and other body problems in question were all in normal range.

I guess depending on the person Atkins might be for you, but for those concerned with their body in the future may take more consideration into what diets they partake in.

> **Comment:** You'll need more sources than this one, and your sources will need to be documented accurately. See Chs. 44 (Finding Sources), 45 (Evaluating Sources), and 50 (MLA Style) in FG for help.

Work [Cited]

PCRM: http://www.pcrm.org/health/reports/pdfs/
    HighProteinReport.pdf

This draft has several problems, ranging from its lack of a clear thesis to problems with sentence structure and wording. Since it's a rough draft, however, your goal in responding should be to give advice to help the student revise it. You may have a checklist or rubric for the assignment that moves from more global issues (focus, development, and organization) to more local (coherence, sentence structure, mechanics, and editing and proofreading). Generally, when you respond to early drafts, emphasize global issues first. Marking errors in sentence construction, wording, mechanics, and spelling is inappropriate because at this point your response will advise the student to rewrite much or all of the essay, eliminating the material you've marked. Here's how this student's instructor responded in a summary comment:

> I think this topic is really interesting; I tried the Atkins diet once and couldn't stand how I felt after just one day! Your information is troubling; it sounds as if you don't think Atkins is a good diet. Try to make your position clearer in a thesis statement. Then organize your ideas so you can discuss one at a time, completely. You need more information in the essay: What is the Atkins diet and how does it work? What are the bene-

fits in the short term? What are the worst effects in the long term? Look in more sources for answers to these questions.

The student then revised the draft twice, eventually submitting the following final version in her midterm portfolio for a grade. In this situation, your response can be more comprehensive, covering all the requirements for the essay; however, if you allow students to revise throughout the term, you can still urge improvement, as this instructor does, both in the comments and through minimal marking of errors.

Atkins Diet, Good or Bad?

With the general population in the United States being obese and constantly more and more people becoming obese, many consider the Atkins diet. This diet consist of little to no carbohydrates and a high ✓ intake of protein. This diet has been around for many years, but is currently getting more publicity and many people are starting to consider it. The main focus now is, whether or not the diet is really ✓ healthy for ones body? In my opinion [this diet is too risky and ✓ unhealthy to partake in just to lose a few pounds.]

> **Comment:** Much better statement of your thesis!

The Atkins diet has [four stages:] the induction phase, ongoing weight loss, pre-maintenance, and lifetime maintenance. The induction stage last for approximately two weeks. This switches your ✓ body into ketosis [where] your metabolism begins to burn fat for energy. In this stage you are consuming protein and vegetables. [Ongoing weight loss] is where more vegetables, nuts and berries are included in your diet. This is where you are changing the ratio of carbohydrates to protein and fats ("The Science Behind Atkins"). Stepping into the pre-maintenance stage is the crucial change. This is

> **Comment:** You explain the four stages much more clearly in this draft. Good work!

> **Comment:** All 4 stages start with "this is where." Vary sentence structure.

> **Comment:** Another stage?

where you begin to change your eating habits to something you will stick to for the rest of your life. During this stage your weight loss will slow. The last stage is where you are controlling your intake of carbohydrates and focusing on the future. This stage refers to your permanent eating habits. [The Atkins diet is broken up into stages.] The first stage is where the weight comes off the fastest because it is predominately water fat, but after this stage is when the weight loss ✓ slows. What makes the fat come off so fast the first stage of this diet ✓ is because eating fewer grams of carbohydrate results in fewer spikes in blood sugar, resulting in less insulin output. Insulin makes the body retain sodium, which makes your body retain water. When you are not producing as much insulin, the cycle slows and the effect is like taking a diuretic which is a drug that increases the output of urine. ✓ After a few days, that's when you will also begin to lose body fat. [Young men and people who have a lot of weight to lose are more likely to lose weight more rapidly at the start of the Atkins program] ("FAQ").

> **Comment:** You already outlined the 4 stages; why not combine that discussion with this one—don't repeat yourself.

> **Comment:** Why?

Supposedly many health benefits are to come out of this diet. [It is suppose to lead you into a way where you can control your ✓ eating habits and stay slim for the rest of your life, maximize your carbohydrate intake and staying within three to five pounds of ✓ your ideal weight, prevent you from getting caught up in those foods that cause severe weight gain, help you to make healthy food choices, reduce risk factors for various disorders including diabetes, and give you a sense of accomplishment.] However, these health benefits are not clearly what you are going to get out of this diet in the long run. Constantly consuming protein for several weeks is not nearly the healthiest way to remove those unwanted pounds. There are many health risk involved with this diet. Studies reported that ✓ weight loss was associated with the length of time on the diet and not the reduced intake of carbohydrates ("Health Advisory"). Low carbohydrate diets induce a process known as [ketosis] which is an abnormal state that occurs in starvation. The increase of this and

> **Comment:** A long sentence—break into at least 2: one on weight benefits, one on health benefits.

> **Comment:** You discuss ketosis more below. Keep discussion together.

uric acid can lead to severe headaches. It also has said that people on this diet have bad breath odors, maybe causing halitosis. Many experience [weakness, drowsy and having a lack of energy.] Others have also experienced the case of hair loss. Food containing a high count for protein usually lack important healthy ingredients such as ✓ fibers which results in constipation and chronic bowel disease.   ✓

> **Comment:** These 3 terms should be parallel in form.

This diet doesn't even fit the guidelines for the American Heart Association. These guidelines include: eating fruits, grains, drinking milk, limiting food high in saturated fats, eating less than 6 grams of salt, exercise, and drinking no more than one alcoholic drink a day for a woman and two for a man ("Diet and Lifestyle"). In the long run *this ketosis* can effect ones body physically leading to having ✓ calcium loss, a high risk of osteoporosis, and a high risk of forming ✓ kidney stones. Your body can also be in high risk of problems dealing with bones and the liver. The cardiac system can be effected also because of the high counts of animal fat consumed on this diet. Animal fat leads to cardiac disease and/or high cholesterol. Many case studies show many people to have dealt with high cholesterol ✓ even though this diet is said not to have any effects of an increase of cholesterol. Many people don't look at the risk factors for this diet, but their focus is primarily on, Am I going to lose weight, how fast, and is it easy? The Atkins diet fits these three questions and that's why many people decide to go on it. This diet is said to burn your fat for energy. This attracts the so called 'busy' people fast, those always on the go can lose pounds quicker because they need the energy and their fat is their supplier. Research found this diet to be one of the top sellers right now. Low fat diets, [Weight Watchers, and many others were compared to the Atkins diet and more results were viewed in favor of the Atkins diet. More pounds were shed and blood pressure, glucose, and other body problems in question were all in normal range.] Unfortunately it is still putting your body in a higher risk of health problems in the future ("The Science Behind Atkins").

> **Comment:** Who did this comparison? Can we trust them? Seems to contradict the rest of your argument. Maybe it belongs with the earlier section on "Many health benefits."

Many studies done came to the conclusion that the Atkins diet is good for a short period of time, but not a lifelong thing. I feel short or long, you will still be in a higher risk for health problems either ✓ now or in your future. Some how this diet will effect your body, by ✓ not just having you lose weight. It has proven to help lose more ✓ weight in a six month period, but after about one year ⅓ of the weight is regained (diets nutrition). Though this diet may work in ones favor for a few months it still has its share of serious disadvan- ✓ tages. I guess depending on the person Atkins might be for you, but ✓ [for those concerned with their body in the future may take more consideration into what diets they partake in.] I see it as the only healthy way to lose weight is to change ones eating habits and ✓ exercise. Not only are you losing weight, but it's healthy for the body and you don't have to worry about what future side effects may occur due to your early years of dieting.

> **Comment:** You lose control of your sentence structure here—rework.

Works Cited

"Diet and Lifestyle Recommendations." *American Heart Association.*
    American Heart Association, 29 June 2012. Web. 23 Sept. 2012.

"FAQ." *Atkins.* Atkins International, n.d. Web. 27 Sept. 2012.

"Health Advisory." *Atkins Diet Alert.* Ed. Neal D. Barnard, M.D.
    Physicians Committee for Responsible Medicine, n.d. Web.
    27 Sept. 2012.

"The Science Behind Atkins." *Atkins.* Atkins International, n.d. Web.
    27 Sept. 2012.

This draft shows many improvements over the first draft, but it still has problems with organization, wording, editing and proofreading, and sources. The instructor said as much in the summary comment:

> You've improved this essay considerably. You take a clear position on the Atkins diet

and provide a lot more information on it— just what it needed! I like the way you describe the four stages of the diet and how you rebut the Atkins claims. It still needs work on organization, however: you discuss 3 different topics in two different places in the essay, so the essay seems to repeat itself. For example, discuss the benefits of Atkins all at once, and discuss the aspects of each stage as you introduce it. Your reliance on only three sources, all from the web, is worrisome, too—getting additional support in some academic sources and getting help from a reference librarian would strengthen your argument. Also, look through each sentence to make sure it works grammatically, and proofread carefully—spell checkers won't pick up on "effect" when you mean "affect," for example.

Marking Student Writing

Respond in pencil. If you're responding to printed drafts, pencil is less intimidating to students than ink, red or otherwise. Also, I've learned that occasionally I make a comment that I want to reconsider, and comments in pencil can be erased without making a mess of the student's draft. Of course, if you're responding using computer or online programs, you can change or delete comments easily.

Comment electronically. Another way to write comments that you can revise or reconsider is to comment electronically on drafts students submit electronically. Some learning management systems offer the ability to insert comments wherever you want, simply by mouse-clicking on a word in the document. *Microsoft Word*'s Reviewing toolbar offers a Comment feature that works the same way—and some versions even allow you to record a voice comment. These tools offer the advantage of legibility, since you don't have to worry whether students can read your handwriting.

Respond on a separate sheet. Marginal comments offer the benefit of being visually tied to the text to which they are responding, and patterns can be marked easily. If you need to say more than a few words or a phrase, however, the margins can become crowded and your comments hard to read. For that reason, consider making up response sheets that you can attach to each draft. On the sheet, you can print any rubric or checklist you're using, or you can simply provide space for comments. When you want to comment on a student's work, simply place a number near the passage on which you want to comment. Number and write your response on the attached sheet. As an alternative, compose a response as a letter to the student; if you use your word processor, you can save a copy of your feedback.

Use correction symbols or abbreviations sparingly. Handbooks traditionally provide a list of correction or revision symbols that instructors may use to save time. Unfortunately, students seldom know what those symbols mean, and too often they are too vague to be helpful. (AWK, for example, usually means, "There's something wrong with this sentence, but I can't tell you what it is." X, for "obvious error," suggests that the error is obvious to you, but if it had been obvious to the student, he or she probably wouldn't have made it.) If you use such symbols, use only a limited number and explain to students what they mean. I've found that the slight increase in time spent identifying the problem in plain English benefits student understanding.

Useful Readings

Blumner, Jakob S., and Francis Fritz. "Students Using Evaluation in Their Writing Process." *Alternatives to Grading Student Writing.* Ed. Stephen Tchudi. Urbana, IL: NCTE, 1997. 233–42. Print.

Elbow, Peter. "Ranking, Evaluating, and Liking: Sorting Out Three Forms of Judging." *College English* 55.2 (1993): 187–206. Print.

Haswell, Richard H. "Minimal Marking." *College English* 45.6 (1983): 600–604. Print.

Helton, Edwina L., and Jeff Sommers. "Repositioning Revision: A Rhetorical Approach to Grading." *Teaching English in the Two-Year College* 28.2 (2000): 157–64. Print.

Sommers, Nancy. *Beyond the Red Ink.* New York: Bedford/St. Martin's, 2012. DVD.

Teaching with **10** Writing Portfolios

Take a good look at the snapshot on your driver's license. How well does it capture your looks? When you read a draft of a student's writing, you see a snapshot of their writing at a particular time, in response to a particular prompt or assignment. And, like any snapshot, it's not clear how well that draft represents the student's overall writing ability. For that reason, many writing teachers ask students to create and submit portfolios of their work during a course. Portfolios allow instructors to examine several samples of students' writing for patterns, trends, strengths, and weaknesses—and, depending on what the portfolio includes, to see the students' processes as they researched, drafted, and revised the texts in the portfolio. Portfolios also provide students the opportunity to create written reflections on and evaluations of their own work to help them see what they've accomplished and what they need to work on in the future. This chapter offers advice on creating a writing course that will foster the creation of writing portfolios along with tips on managing student portfolios.

Self-Assessing Writing Portfolios

Many writing teachers who require portfolios see the students' written assessment of the contents as the most important element because it moves students toward independence through the ability to assess their work themselves, instead of relying on teachers. This reflective self-assessment may be written in the form of an informal letter or a formal essay asking students to use the materials in the portfolio as the evidence on which they base thoughtful examination of their writing and their work in the class. Chapter 29 of the *Field Guide* offers guidelines on assembling a writing portfolio, including what to include, how to reflect on one's writing, and how to organize both print and electronic portfolios. Bonnie Sunstein's essay, "Be Reflective, Be Reflexive, and Beware: Innocent Forgery for Inauthentic Assessment," offers additional guidelines and questions for students as they self-assess.

If you ask students to include all drafts and revisions as well as in-class work and research materials, you can evaluate how diligently they worked; usually that diligence will result in good final products. Some students will use their self-assessments to argue that their grade should be based on their effort, rather than on the writing they produce. Also, some students will use the self-assessment to try to flatter you. Emphasize the goal of focusing their attention on their writing and observable class performance, not on evaluating the course or instructor. Let students know that flattery will not persuade.

Assigning Writing Portfolios

What should go into a portfolio of writing? In its barest form, a portfolio is simply a paper or online folder in which students keep their writing. If you assign, collect, and grade individual assignments and then ask students to submit them again in such a portfolio, they can write an assessment of the contents before submitting it at term's end. More often, however, instructors ask for a portfolio of students' work once or twice during a term and evaluate the contents as a whole, looking for patterns and trends that persist over several pieces of writing. However you design your portfolio requirements, explain them to students clearly, preferably on the first day of class, because they'll need to know what writings to keep in order to have a complete portfolio. Here are some suggestions for what portfolios might include.

Polished, final drafts of assigned essays. You may ask for every assigned essay or offer students a choice among their assignments, since every writer drafts some texts that don't work out. Or, you might require some and make others optional. For example, if students work on a literacy narrative, a text analysis, and an evaluation, they must include in their portfolio the analysis plus either the narrative or the evaluation. To prevent students from assuming they don't need to write the essays they will exclude from their portfolios, you might insist that at least one complete draft of those omitted essays be included. Their self-assessment can then address the reasons why they were abandoned.

All drafts of assigned essays. Drafts are useful for seeing the progress students make from first to finished draft and for jogging your memory if you've seen an earlier draft. Ask that students label and date each draft and, in print portfolios, place them in order from finished on top to first on the bottom.

Cited source material. It's easy to check the accuracy of summaries, paraphrases, quotations, and citations if photocopies of the sources are in the portfolio. Again, ask students to label each source; consider asking students to highlight or underline the passages in each source that they used in their own essays. Even if you require electronic portfolios, having labeled and annotated copies of sources used will save you time as you evaluate students' research and use of source material.

Student assessment of the contents. Some instructors ask for an informal letter that discusses the strengths of the contents and the writer's plans for improvement in the future. Others assign a lengthy self-assessment essay that includes quotations from and references to the essays the student is assessing, treating this essay as an additional sample of the student's writing or the equivalent of a final exam.

Other materials. Other course-related writing, such as collaborative work or in-class writing and tests, may be included. Also, some instructors allow students to include other writing—essays from other courses, fiction or poetry, work-related writing—that shows aspects of their writing ability that the course writing does not.

The portfolio itself can be a simple two-pocket folder. Ask students to place pieces to be graded in one pocket and drafts and other materials in the other, to simplify your reading. Insist that they write their names on the outside of the folder, again to make recordkeeping easier. If, of course, you allow or require students to create online portfolios, their work must be organized through links or other means, depending on the software and online resources available to them. What's important is that their work be organized so that you don't have to wade through it to find what you need to respond appropriately. Also, organizing their selections helps students review their own evolution as writers.

Organizing Electronic Portfolios

If you ask students to submit their work in electronic portfolios, you need to create ways for students to organize their essays and files. Learning management systems such as *Desire2Learn* allow you to create specific assignments to which students post their drafts, so you may set up portfolio assignments like "Position essay portfolio draft," "Evaluation portfolio draft," and "Self-assessment." If you're relying on email, you might require students to attach their final drafts to a single message. If students create online portfolios on websites or blogs, you need only visit each site to read their work—though you may need to respond to their writing in an email, since commenting within the body of the text may not be possible online.

Reading Portfolios

The guidelines presented in Chapter 9 of this guide, "Responding to Student Writing," apply to portfolios of writing, too. A significant difference is that instead of or in addition to evaluating individual pieces of writing, you may evaluate students' overall performance for your course as well as their self-assessment. Here, for example, is a list of the qualities writing program faculty at Wright State University look for in portfolios in a course focused on argumentative writing.

Content

- Defines the issue and its context
- Enters a debate (engages the issue, not just a literature review or detached analysis of the argument: "One might argue . . .")
- Shows awareness of the audience and needs of that audience
- Is focused (appropriately chosen and limited topic)
- Is developed (uses sources but doesn't create a collage of quotations or paraphrases; creates and sustains a line of reasoning; covers topic appropriately; explains thoroughly and clearly)
- Is convincing or reasonable
- Presents differing arguments
- Bonus: displays passion in arguing

Evidence

- Evidence is present
- Evidence relates to point
- Evidence is properly cited and documented
- Evidence shows synthesis of ideas with multiple citations

Form

- Coherence and cohesion (at the essay and sentence level: transitions, signal phrases, repeated words, and integrated quotations)
- Thesis statement or equivalent
- Satisfying conclusion
- Control over sentence construction
- Subject and verb agreement
- Mechanics, usage, grammar, and spelling (don't distract or cause credibility problems)

Assessment

- Critical assessment of own work, supported by evidence from portfolio

You might combine criteria common to each individual essay's rubric to develop a single rubric for the portfolio as a whole, separating out only those criteria that apply only to a single assignment. You might also combine the rubrics for each individual

Self-Assessment Rubric

Selection	3	2	1	0
Analyzes work habits from invention to polished work				
Analyzes strengths and weaknesses of each item in portfolio				
Analyzes strengths and weaknesses of overall writing ability				
Discusses how writing has changed over time				
Analyzes performance in this class				
Offers evidence from portfolio papers to support assertions				
Avoids argument from effort or undue flattery as persuasive techniques				

essay with a rubric for the self-assessment or reflection, such as the one at the bottom of p. 70.

Delaying Grades

If you design your course to include portfolios, you may assign grades much less often than if you grade each assigned essay separately. As a result, some students will express anxiety over not receiving frequent grades, as they did in high school or other classes. To allay their fears, make this offer: "Anytime you want to know your grade as it stands at this point in the course, schedule a conference with me. Bring your portfolio with the work you've done so far, and I'll go over it with you and tell you what your grade would be if I had to give you one at that time." Interestingly, almost no students will take you up on your offer. Although they are disoriented at first by the lack of grades, students quickly realize that they are now free to concentrate on their writing, which they can work to improve over a much longer time span than they're used to. Portfolios encourage multiple revisions precisely because students have not received grades, which they consider the mark of a finished assignment.

At the same time, students do need some indication of their standing in your course before the very end, and some may need a grade in order to understand your grading standards. To give students an indication of how you'll be grading their work, consider putting a grade on a draft early in the course. Give it a low value, and grade it using the rubric you'll use when assessing their work at the end of the term—the grades will likely be far lower than your students expect, and you can then explain the advantages of multiple revisions and delayed grading.

Later in the term, you can give students a progress report by asking them to submit a midterm portfolio that contains the work done through the first half of the term, along with their self-assessment of that work. They'll get practice in compiling, organizing, and assessing a body of their work as well as an indication of their grades so far. To maintain an incentive for continued revision, you might consider weighting the portfolio grades unevenly. For example, make the midterm portfolio worth 20 percent of the final grade, while the final course portfolio (which might contain some or all of the contents of the midterm portfolio in addition to the work done in the second half of the course) is worth 50 percent. You might offer students an additional incentive to continue working hard (or start working harder!) by offering them a choice: if they wish, they may drop their midterm portfolio grade and add its weight to the final portfolio. In the example above, the final portfolio would then be worth 70% of their final grade.

Useful Readings

"CCCC Position Statement: Principles and Practices in Electronic Portfolios." *CCCC (Conference on College Composition and*

Communication). National Council of Teachers of English, Nov. 2007. Web. 4 Jan. 2013.

Conway, Glenda. "Portfolio Cover Letters, Students' Self-Presentation, and Teachers' Ethics." *New Directions in Portfolio Assessment: Reflective Practice, Critical Theory, and Large-Scale Scoring.* Ed. Laurel Black, Donald A. Daiker, Jeffrey Sommers, and Gail Stygall. Portsmouth, NH: Boynton/Cook, 1994. 83–92. Print.

Electronic Portfolios. Washington, DC: American Association for Higher Education and Accreditation. 2005.

Peet, Melissa. "The Integrative Knowledge Portfolio Process: A Program Guide for Educating Reflective Practitioners and Lifelong Learners." *MedEdPORTAL.* Association of American Medical Colleges, 22 Apr. 2010. Web. 4 Jan. 2013.

Sommers, Jeffrey. "Bringing Practice in Line with Theory: Using Portfolio Grading in the Composition Classroom." *Portfolios: Process and Product.* Ed. Pat Belanoff and Marcia Dickson. Portsmouth, NH: Boynton/Cook, 1991. 153–64. Print.

Sunstein, Bonnie S. "Be Reflective, Be Reflexive, and Beware: Innocent Forgery for Inauthentic Assessment." *The Portfolio Standard: How Students Can Show Us What They Know and Are Able to Do.* Ed. Bonnie S. Sunstein and Jonathan Lovell. Portsmouth, NH: Heinemann, 2000. 3–14. Print.

Yancey, Kathleen Blake, ed. "Special Issue: Electronic Portfolios." *Computers and Composition* 13.2 (1996). Print.

Managing the Paper Load **11**

Consider the situation described by Chris Massey, a TA: "My students are constantly writing, and that means I am constantly reading what they are writing. Even though I am not marking every piece of writing they submit to me, I am reading each piece and responding to their writing in some fashion. My students are writing and writing well; the only downside is that I am spending a great deal of my time reading." The problem Chris describes, responding adequately to students' writing while not overburdening the instructor, is common among writing teachers. Fortunately, there are ways to teach writing that can make responding and grading manageable, including the techniques described in Chapter 9 in this guide to teaching on responding to students' writing. Here are some more suggestions.

Don't read everything. Just because you assign it doesn't require you to read it, let alone respond to it. Some things you read carefully (drafts); some things you skim and, maybe, respond with underlinings, stars, exclamation points, and question marks (letters, some in-class writing); and some things you simply put a check on or stamp, record if they did it, and move on (much daily work). The more writing you assign, the more you need to beware of overextending yourself.

Read all the drafts first. We evaluate things by comparing them with others, and student drafts are no different. To get an overall sense of how your students did on an assignment, read quickly through all the drafts you collect, perhaps sorting them as you read into three groups: strong, middling, and weak. This process helps you see the criteria by which you'll read each draft in concrete terms and gives you choices of what to read: Some instructors like to read some strong drafts first to establish what's possible, while others like to save some of the best for last.

Set a schedule. As a new instructor, you're likely to spend thirty minutes reading and responding to each draft of an essay; in a class of twenty-five students, that totals twelve-and-a-half hours. Establish a schedule for responding and keep to it. If you collect drafts late in the week and keep them over the weekend, spread out your responding sessions over three or four days. Include time for breaks to rejuvenate yourself, because reading and

73

responding is taxing work. Use a timer set at thirty-minute intervals to keep yourself disciplined. If you're teaching more than one course at a time, consider establishing a regular, daily schedule: every afternoon from 3 to 5, you read student writing.

Use rubrics. If you clearly articulate the requirements of an assignment, you can create a chart-style rubric that lists them in the form of a table. The rubric helps you maintain discipline over your read-ing, forcing you to pay attention to the features of each student's writing in similar ways. It also provides a clear, descriptive response for students to use as they revise or contemplate their grades. Make copies and do most of your responding on the rubric sheet, placing a check mark at the appropriate place on the right-hand side. Other comments may be written below the table. An example using statements of desired criteria is printed in Chapter 9 of this guide to teaching. Below is another example that phrases criteria

Argument Draft Assessment

Author: _____   Assessor: _____

Circle one: First draft   Rewritten draft   Further revision

Answer each question on a scale of 1–5 (5 = very well, yes indeed; 1 = no, not at all). Comment below the question.

Assessment questions	1	2	3	4	5
Is the thesis clear and appropriately qualified?					
Are the reasons plausible? Do they make sense?					
Does the writer provide enough appropriate support for the reasons?					
Can you follow the steps in the argument's reasoning? (*If not, identify where you lose track.*)					
How well does the argument deal with potential objections or counterarguments?					
Is source material documented carefully, with in-text citations and works cited?					
Does the writer use signal phrases to introduce information from sources?					

as questions. If you provide space between each question for comments, you can provide a summary response as well as commentary.

Have students evaluate their drafts. Before students give you their drafts, have them write a self-assessment, pointing out strong elements, parts that need to be improved, and questions they have. You might also have them fill out the same rubric you'll use when you respond. When you respond to their drafts, you can then respond to their assessments, continuing a conversation they've already begun. You'll be surprised at how much easier it is to write comments.

Avoid overresponding. If you identify a few strengths, problems, and patterns and use minimal marking, you'll avoid the trap of making too many marginal and in-text comments that take time and energy (and overwhelm many students). Also, avoid a too-long end comment; some instructors' comments end up longer than the student's draft. Work toward a single paragraph that offers a couple of positive comments, a couple of suggestions or goals for the next draft, and a helpful strategy or two—and then stop.

Don't worry about originality. Several students' drafts will have similar problems, so responding with the same comment can save you time—and they're unlikely to compare their comments' prose style. If you respond using a computer, you can even program certain comments to print with a single keystroke.

Stagger due dates. If you're teaching more than one section of a course or more than one course at a time, create course plans with due dates that don't coincide. Making one syllabus for multiple sections may save time up front, but you might have fifty drafts or portfolios to respond to during one weekend, a task that will not be to your or your students' best advantage.

Keep good records. Be sure to keep records of your students' work as you read so you don't have to go through the stack one more time to record grades or other marks. Many instructors use a "received—date" stamp to show that assignments, especially those that don't require much attention, have been received. Some learning management systems automatically date-stamp assignments as students post them. If the papers are stamped, they earn full credit when presented in the student's portfolio. If papers are presented but not stamped, they get half credit (for doing the work but turning it in after the due date). And, if the papers are not present at all, they get zero credit.

Useful Readings

Ketter, Jean S. "Using Rubrics and Holistic Scoring of Writing." *Alternatives to Grading Student Writing.* Ed. Stephen Tchudi. Urbana, IL: NCTE, 1997. 291–95. Print.

White, Edward. "Using Scoring Guides to Assess Writing." *A Sourcebook for Responding to Student Writing.* Ed. Richard Straub. Cresskill, NJ: Hampton, 1999. 203–12. Print.

12 Grading Student Writing

If you've developed good assignments and responded to drafts of students' writing, grading will be less onerous. If you clarify expectations up front, students will know what you want and will usually have a fairly good idea of how well they performed. Still, grading is often difficult work for experienced and inexperienced instructors alike, so the following advice can help you as you face a stack of essays or portfolios to grade.

Developing a Method

Preview your students' work. Avoid the temptation to jump in and start reading with an eye to a grade. First, reread your assignment to remind yourself what you asked for, and then read quickly through the whole stack (if you're new to teaching) or a random sample (if you've given the same assignments before) to give yourself a sense of how students did. You may find it helpful to create three stacks as you skim: good, middling, and poor. Simply dividing students' work into those three piles helps you internalize your criteria and how those criteria translate into various letter or number grades.

Use rubrics. Rubrics help you maintain your focus on the criteria for evaluating students' work. Even if the rubrics are fairly general, they also provide a vocabulary to help students understand why they earned the grades they did. See Chapter 9, "Responding to Student Writing," and Chapter 11, "Managing the Paper Load," for sample rubrics and advice on creating your own.

Write a final comment. Whether or not you use a rubric, it's helpful for students when you sum up the strengths and problems in an essay or portfolio as a guide for their future writing and as an explanation for the grade. A good final comment offers an overall assessment of the work, discusses how well it meets the demands of the assignment, and briefly outlines the work's strengths and weaknesses. The final comment should be an occasion for you as a serious reader to discuss the writer's work honestly and respectfully. At the same time, it shouldn't be overly long or detailed—about 100 words is usually sufficient.

Use the full range of grades. After working with a group of students for ten or fifteen weeks and getting to know them and their work, we all have difficulty assessing that work fairly. Most often, we give higher grades than an objective grader who doesn't know the students. You should resist the temptation to give most students grades of B and a few grades of A or C, reserving the D or F for students who didn't do the work or disappeared but didn't drop the course. Why? Because your credibility and your writing program's credibility in the university will suffer if students leave your course having earned a high grade and then do poorly in a subsequent writing course. Conversely, if your writing program includes a sequence of courses, you could end up with students whose grades in the first course mask their lack of preparedness to do the work of the second—and that's no favor to the students. The hardest part of grading is giving students (especially students who have worked hard) the low grades that they have earned and that reflect your and your school's expectations. It's advisable to discuss grading criteria with other writing instructors, to get help in understanding and applying the writing program's and university's criteria to your own students' work.

At the same time, don't expect the grades in your classes to form a bell curve. Writing classes are relatively small, so the group of students you have in any one class may consist of many strong writers, many weak ones, or a mix, depending on how courses are scheduled, whether or not students register by major, or even time of day. You may well have a class in which more than half the students earn Bs and As—and in your next course, the reverse may be true. Remember, though, that few instructors consistently attract only the best writers, so monitor your grades over several courses to see how they average out.

Ask for second opinions. All writing teachers encounter student work that they have trouble grading. No matter what the reason, ask another instructor what grade they would give to a troublesome portfolio or essay. Your conversation about the merits of the work and the reasons for your grades will not only help you grade that student's work fairly; it will help you understand your own grading better. If you share grading with several other instructors, you'll also develop a clearer sense of the standards held for student work at your institution and have to worry less about whether you're grading too high or too low.

Don't grade every revision. Once expectations have been established, offer the option to revise for a higher grade, but don't fall into the trap of regrading every draft a student submits. Some students will change exactly what you point out, with the expectation that if they follow your instructions, they will earn a higher grade. A few will resubmit several times, assuming that enough incremental changes will turn a C paper into an A paper. As the grader, you, too, will feel pressure to add points or raise a grade on a draft that a student submits repeatedly. Better to offer a deadline for resubmitting work for reconsideration of the grade along with an offer to help students improve their drafts at any time before that deadline—but refusing to put grades on each successive draft.

Don't assume that grades motivate. As you teach, you'll find that some students are motivated only by a grade and will ask, "What do I have to do to get an A in this course?" Many of us who pursue advanced degrees and teach in college were motivated as undergraduates by the desire to excel, not just by earning high grades but also by working hard to learn. As statistics show, though, we are a distinct minority of the population. As you teach, you'll encounter students who are happy to earn Cs, even if they could do better, and occasionally you'll run across students who are trying, for one reason or another, to flunk out. These various students create a rich mix that you may find alternately frustrating and delightful, and you'll need to find various ways of reaching them; grades alone won't do it.

Keeping Records

It's important to keep students' grades organized so that you can calculate their final grades without difficulty. One way to lose credibility as a teacher is to lose students' work or fail to record their grades accurately, and for good reason: students' grades are their record of having done the work of a course. Here are some ways to keep track of students' work and grades.

Note cards. Many instructors ask students to list information on index cards on the first day of class. Those same cards can then be used to jot notes about the students' work: goals framed in conferences, ongoing progress in drafts, and various other assessments that might not lend themselves to a letter grade or number of points.

Three-ring binders. If you ask students to sign an attendance sheet, using three-hole-punched paper that you can slip into a three-ring binder simplifies maintaining attendance records. In fact, you can organize your entire course—syllabus, assignment sheets, daily class plans, handouts, and student records—in a single binder that you can bring to class and keep with you as a ready reference for whatever questions students might have about the course.

Gradebooks, online gradebooks, and spreadsheet programs. To keep track of students' grades and attendance, you should have a means of identifying each assignment and noting students' performance—a system that won't take too much time. The traditional gradebook offers a grid, but its spaces tend to be very small and uniform, forcing you to abbreviate assignment titles and, at the same time, providing far more spaces for grades than you're likely to need. Online gradebooks provided with some learning management systems can be flexible and useful, even tallying up grades automatically. A third alternative that can meet your specific needs is a spreadsheet program like *Excel*. Not only can you create a customized grade sheet that you can program to figure grades automatically, you can create a color-coding scheme for such things as attendance and daily work assignments: if a student was present, you simply color the appropriate square, so that absences are visually obvious. You can also color graded assignments, making them easy to find. Here's a simple example, showing one month's class attendance.

	A	B	C	D	E	F	G	H	I	J	K
1	**ENG 101-18, Winter 20XX**								present		absent
2	Attendance	2/7	2/14	2/19	2/21	2/26	2/28	3/4	3/6	3/11	3/13
3	D—, Dominic										
4	D—, Mary										
5	G—, Michael										
6	H—, Veronica										
7	H—, Charrelle										
8	H—, Alison										
9	J—, Matt										
10	J—, Cara										
11	K—, Chelsea										
12	K—, Kelly										
13	P—, Lauren										
14	R—, Julia										
15	R—, Alexandra										
16	S—, Anthony										
17	S—, Allison										
18	S—, Chelsey										
19	S—, Latesa										
20	S—, Kyle										
21	S—, Amanda										
22	T—, Erin										
23	U—, Brittany										
24	W—, Antonio										
25	Y—, Steven										

Returning Students' Work

The final step in responding to and grading students' work is returning it to them. Here are a few hints on doing that effectively.

During the term. Strive to return students' work as quickly as you can; within a week or ten days is reasonable. If you bring a stack of essays or portfolios to class, resist the pressure to hand them back at the beginning; wait until the end, when you can briefly discuss the class's overall performance after completing the day's agenda. When you return the work, let students know that you'll be available for conferences, but not right after class. Give them time to review the paper and your comments before you meet. Also, asking students who wish to dispute their grades to write out a response rather than present an oral argument will help defuse emotions that might get in the way of a fruitful discussion.

At the end of the course. Most writing instructors schedule the due date of final portfolios or essays during final exam week. As a result, students often cannot pick them up until the following term or until the next fall term. If your school has no policy on keeping or returning student work, the easiest way to deal with these portfolios or essays is to tell your students that they may pick up their work in your office during your office hours in the first five weeks of the following term. Place them in a box in your office and give them to students as they show up. Students who want their work before the next term may provide a self-addressed envelope with sufficient postage, so you can mail it to them. If students do not plan to pick up their work, having saved it on their computers, ask them to write "Discard" on it so you don't need to keep it. Don't place student work outside your office door or in an unguarded room—doing so invites theft and plagiarized essays.

Useful Readings

Adkison, Stephen, and Stephen Tchudi. "Grading on Merit and Achievement: Where Quality Meets Quantity." *Alternatives to Grading Student Writing.* Ed. Stephen Tchudi. Urbana, IL: NCTE, 1997. 192–209. Print.

Carbone, Nick, and Margaret Daisley. "Grading as a Rhetorical Construct." *The Theory and Practice of Grading Writing: Problems and Possibilities.* Ed. Frances Zak and Christopher C. Wheeler. Albany: SUNY, 1998. 77–94. Print.

Haswell, Richard H. "Minimal Marking." *College English* 45.6 (1983): 600–604. Print.

Teaching in a 13 Technology-Enriched Classroom

Today, classrooms come in all manner of configurations, but one constant is that the students are conversant with and expect to see technology. They'll also likely be carrying smartphones and perhaps laptops or tablets. This chapter will offer advice on teaching writing in a classroom equipped with computers for you and your students. In addition, check out the activities and advice in Chapter 14 of this guide to teaching, "Teaching Writing Online."

Getting Started

The availability of technology always implies an imperative that we use it. When you teach in a technology-rich classroom, you may feel pressure to use whatever is in the room, every day. Resist that pressure. Instead, use the equipment and software as you feel comfortable and as they support writing instruction. Especially if you're teaching for the first time, you have a lot to get used to; there's no need to increase your anxiety by struggling to master the principles and practices of effective teaching as well as hardware, software, and a learning management system (LMS).

You can always increase your use of technology as the term progresses, or use a few, simple tools one term and add a few more tools to your repertoire each term. It's more important that you use a technological tool effectively than use every tool that's available.

Using the Available Tools

The configuration of electronically enhanced classrooms varies from school to school. The following tools are available for your use, but before term begins, go to the classroom where you'll be teaching and find out exactly what's available and how each piece of equipment works as well as how to get technical support.

Networked computers for each student. When your students arrive in class, they sit in front of a computer at a workstation or get out their laptops. Typically, they'll need to log into your university's computer network just as you do, with a username and password. While most students master this procedure easily, there are always a few students—usually ones new to the university—whose password doesn't

81

work or who don't remember it. Find out how to assist these students, usually through your school's Help Desk, so they can gain access as quickly as possible. Beware the temptation to become so embroiled in helping one student that you lose significant class time; you can always suggest that students look on their neighbor's screen or do the day's work with paper and pencil during class, and find the answers to their computer problems after class.

Once students are logged in, you can immediately give them tasks on the computer such as creating a writing sample, sending you an email (to which they can attach a writing sample, if you ask for one), finding your course syllabus if you posted it online, or registering for the LMS you'll be using. Provide complete, step-by-step instructions on the board, projected onscreen, or on a handout and be prepared to circulate, offering help and making sure students' screens show the desired destination.

When you want to engage in a face-to-face discussion, lecture, or some other activity, some students will keep working at the computer. Computers are compelling, after all, and one way classes using computers differ from other classes is that the presence of the computers forces instructors to find ways to divert students' attention away from the machines and toward the instructor or one another. Have students move their chairs toward the front of the room, if possible, or ask students to turn off their monitors or place a sheet of paper over the keyboard.

Another difference that you may need to take into account is the noise of the computers. Most computers contain one or two small fans to dissipate heat, and the low hum generated by twenty-five computers running at once can add up to a level of noise that makes hearing speech across the room difficult. If you can't hear students, they probably can't hear you, either, so you all may need to project your voices more than usual. Students may need to stand up when they speak so they'll be seen and heard.

A printer is usually available, either in the classroom or in a central location nearby. If students have to pay for printed copies, they may prefer to use their own printers, so it's a good idea to reserve in-class printing for special occasions or leave it up to students whether or not to print in the classroom.

Instructor's station. Familiarize yourself with the instructor's station: how to log on to the computer, how to raise and lower the projection screen, how to turn on the projector and show or hide the image being projected, how the other available features work. Your school's computer services office may offer sessions to teach faculty how to use this equipment; if so, you'll find it time well spent. If not, you may be able to enlist the aid of a Help Desk employee or an experienced teaching assistant or faculty member.

Your room will probably also be equipped with a whiteboard, rather than a chalkboard (to eliminate chalk dust, which can harm computers), so find out what kind of markers you should use—usually water-based and erasable—and take several with you. These markers dry out quickly, so having your own supply is a good idea, and if you want several students to write on the board at once, you'll know you have enough for everyone. If the room has electronic whiteboards, you'll need special markers and training to use them. Your room may not contain such items as an overhead projector or document camera, television monitor, or DVD player (unless it is built into the computer in the instructor's station). Find out how to request such equipment well before you need to use it.

Access to the internet. If your students have internet access on their classroom computers, the world is literally at their fingertips. You might have them search for examples to support class discussion topics, for example, or compare various news sources to get a sense of how authors appeal to specific audiences. Using sites like *Inklwriter*, students can compose progressive, interactive short stories or reports. *Google Docs* enables both group work and instructor assessment by making it easy to compose, share, and revise collaboratively. The internet has fundamentally changed the way we access information—and the way we create and share knowledge. Use the tools students are most comfortable with, including social media sites like *Twitter* and *Tumblr,* to expand their understanding of the rhetorical power inherent in communication that reaches beyond their immediate environs.

Library resources. So much academic material is available online through academic libraries—through the catalogue, hundreds of databases and online scholarly journals, and even librarians available to answer research questions—that students can do substantial library research in class while you circulate, offering help and instruction in the research avenues available through the library. At some schools, research librarians will visit your classes to introduce the library's resources and help your students start searching for information on their topics—a service worth taking advantage of.

Learning management systems. Learning management systems, sometimes called *courseware,* are sophisticated web-accessed software systems used at many universities. These programs allow you to post course materials, including readings, lessons, your syllabus, and photographs; to create links to various websites, such as your school's library and writing center and other sites you want students to have easy access to; and to create discussion boards where students can post responses to questions you pose or topics you specify and then follow threads of postings, responding to one another. They also include course management features, such as the ability to email all students at once as well as individuals or groups; to sort students into collaborative groups, either randomly or by your choice; to create assignment dropboxes and folders into which students post assignments; and to track students' attendance and grades.

Many programs are available through a university-purchased license, so your choice may be limited to the program supported by your school. As with other aspects of a computer classroom, you may find the easiest introduction to be a workshop presented by your school's computer services department.

Making Choices about Technology

You can use courseware to effectively reduce or eliminate paper in your classroom, as you make assignments, collect drafts and comment on them, and even have students compile portfolios of their work, all online—but you don't have to. You can select the features of the courseware that you feel comfortable using and ignore the rest. If you like the idea that students have access to the course syllabus and all the assignments whenever they have access to a computer, post those materials online. If you prefer to read students' drafts on paper, ask students to present you with printed copies. If you'd like students to send you drafts as email attachments instead of posting assign-ments on the LMS, that's okay, too. It's better to teach effectively using technology to enhance your teaching and students' learning than to struggle with technology with which you aren't familiar or that you aren't convinced improves students' writing or learning. See Chapter 14 in this guide, "Teaching Writing Online," for activities adaptable to the computer classroom.

Useful Readings

Computers and Composition: An International Journal. Bowling Green State University/ Elsevier, 2008. Web. 8 Jan. 2013.

McGee, Tim, and Patricia Ericsson. "The Politics of the Program: MS Word as the Invisible Grammarian." *Computers and Composition* 19.4 (2002): 453–70. Print.

Selfe, Cynthia L. "Technology and Literacy: A Story about the Perils of Not Paying Attention." *College Composition and Communication* 50.3 (1999): 411–36. Print.

Yancey, Kathleen Blake. "Made Not Only in Words: Composition in a New Key." *College Composition and Communication* 56.2 (2004): 297–328. Print.

Teaching Writing Online **14**

Adrienne Cassel

The Sloan Consortium's overview of *Going the Distance,* a 2011 survey of online learning, reveals that the "number of students taking at least one online course has now surpassed 6 million. Now nearly one-third of all students in higher education are taking at least one online course." With enrollments increasing this quickly, there is a need for more faculty who can effectively and efficiently teach online classes. Thus, whether you are a TA teaching for the first time, an adjunct faculty member, or a full-time faculty member who has considerable teaching experience, you are likely to be given the opportunity to teach in a virtual learning environment. This chapter aims to help you successfully meet that challenge.

Online teachers, like online students, can connect anytime day or night on any computer that has an internet connection. You can avoid the hassles of driving to campus, finding a parking place, and designing and maintaining a schedule that requires your physical presence at a certain time or place. However, you also share in the frustrations of the online learning environment. Computers crash, programs fail, support isn't always available, and it's often difficult to create and maintain a community that supports and fosters successful learning. Further, all of the challenges of teaching in a face-to-face classroom are present in the online classroom as well. You still have to motivate students who don't know why they need to learn to write, communicate standards and concepts to students who are new to the academic community and unfamiliar with its methods and requirements, and figure out ways to help each student improve his or her ability to successfully conduct research and write essays in an academic environment. So, how do you do that?

Preparing to Teach Online

Fortunately, most colleges have a department devoted to distance learning. The first step after you've been assigned a course is to contact the department and inquire about the format and expectations. For courses already set up in a virtual environment, the instructor's role is to simply maintain the course, answer email about it, and grade the assignments. In many cases, instructional designers have worked collaboratively with content experts (faculty members) to design a course that is user-friendly and provides pedagogically sound methods for teaching online, and so the most important role of the instructor is to provide timely and accurate feedback.

Before the term begins, be sure to look over all the lessons required of students and to contact your liaison with questions or concerns about the course. Although you can teach online without a learning management system (courseware), many teachers and students prefer access to reliable, user-friendly courseware and both training and technical support from the university. If you are being asked to teach online by administrators, the courseware and technical support most likely are already in place. Your job is to find out what is available to you and to ascertain the technical capabilities of your students.

In order to develop the best course design, you need to gather some information about the students and the institution where you are teaching. Find out the following:

- Does your institution already provide courses online? If so, which courses?
- Who teaches them?
- Which learning management system do they use? (*Blackboard* is the most common, although some universities create their own or use freeware like *Moodle* or *Sakai*.) Once you know what's available, work with an IT person or a more experienced colleague to learn

how to maximize the capability of your system.

- How are the courses put together? Who sets up a course? Does a course need to be approved before it is offered? If so, by whom? Who populates the courses with students?
- How long does developing an online course usually take from start to finish?
- Who coordinates the development, delivery, and support?

Once you find out the answers to these questions, visit with some of the faculty already teaching online. Firsthand information from them will be some of the most valuable information you can collect. Contact any support organizations available to you. Many colleges provide workshops and help you set up your course and keep it running smoothly. If your university does not offer faculty support in this area, contact the company that provides the learning management system. They can often answer questions and provide materials to make your transition to online teaching easier and more effective. Give yourself ample time for testing the materials before you begin the term.

After you look into instructor support services, check into the support provided for students. Does your school have a help desk for students? What information is available concerning the technical literacy of students at your school or the students who will be targeted to take your class? Is there an orientation for students who are taking online courses? Do they have computers at home? Or will they be visiting a library or campus to complete their work? All of these factors will affect how you set up and manage the course.

Developing an Online Course

Planning the course. If a predesigned common course (often called the master course) is not available for your particular course, then you will need to consider the best steps for designing your own. As with preparing to teach in a face-to-face classroom, begin by determining your goals and objectives. (See Chapter 1 in this guide to teaching, "Designing a Writing Course.") Then determine the assignments and assessment tools for helping students meet those objectives.

There are many resources available online for helping you design online activities. One particularly helpful website is *MERLOT (Multimedia Education Resource for Learning and Online Teaching),* a free open-resource center that is designed primarily for faculty and students in higher education and offers links to online learning materials that have been peer reviewed and are accessible via smart phones and tablets, both iOS and Android. Instructors who have submitted their activities and learning aids to the site have agreed that anyone who would like to use them is welcome to do so without obtaining permission.

Determining assignments and assessments offers the greatest challenge to teaching online. You won't be able to simply transfer your syllabus, assignments, instructions, and lectures word for word to an online format. Instead, you'll need to identify new approaches and new techniques that take into account the limitations and opportunities of learning online. You might begin with a list of four or five techniques, strategies, or specific abilities that you would like your students to achieve by the end of the term. Here is a sample list of outcomes for a course on research and academic writing:

- Students will be able to formulate research questions that really matter to them.

- Students will know where to go to get credible research materials for an academic paper.

- Students will know how to evaluate research resources to determine their reliability, authority, currency, and relevancy.

- Students will be able to summarize, synthesize, and demonstrate an understanding of the information they have read from scholarly, credible sources.

- Students will be able to write and document research essays that demonstrate higher-level thinking skills and knowledge of one of the documentation methods used in academia (such as MLA or APA).

Generally, it's a good idea to work through the objectives individually, brainstorming about the learning activities, assignments, and assessments that will help students reach each goal, but often as you begin to work through the objectives in this way, you'll discover that many assignments and learning activities can fulfill multiple objectives. For instance, for the class outcomes mentioned above, an inquiry-based learning project utilizing topics selected by each individual student seemed the best approach for accomplishing the goals. Allowing students to choose their own topics engaged students in the process, and step-by-step instructions on how to complete the project gave students confidence in the online environment as they worked toward meeting the objectives for the course.

Presenting Materials and Activities Online

Most activities and assignments for teaching online will fall into one of the following general categories:

Instructor presentations. Online instructors have many of the same options as instructors teaching in traditional classrooms when it comes to presentation methods. Faculty can give online lectures, present online simulations, and conduct online demonstrations with *PowerPoint*, *Prezi*, and other multimedia software. *Power-Point* is the most commonly used presentation method; however *Prezi* is becoming more and more popular. For both of these presentation methods, slides are easy to create and post. Moreover, the slides can

be accompanied by audio files that contain instructor explanations of course materials. Most universities have multimedia labs that can help with the development of virtual presentations, but keep in mind two guiding principles. First, online learners do best with small chunks of information rather than huge blocks of text. Slides should provide a simple outline of the information students are to learn. For more detailed information, it is best to direct students to texts they can read offline. Second, because presentation software can take a long time to load, provide links to websites that offer the same information with faster load times or design a one-page summary sheet for students to review. If you are working in *Microsoft Word*, you can save the file as HTML and upload it into the courseware. It will open within the course frames, making it easy for students to read, and will load more quickly than a *PowerPoint* show. Another option is web pages on a web server or uploaded into courseware. Web development software is increasingly user-friendly, and web pages don't depend on specific software for display. The site for developing *Prezi* automatically saves your presentation in a format that can be accessed online. And don't be afraid to make short videos that can also be uploaded to the class site or even to *YouTube* or *Vimeo*.

Simulations and demonstrations. Simulations and demonstrations can best be provided on websites. If you give students a link to information instead of actual files, loading times will be exponentially quicker and frustration levels much lower. One of the best resources for online simulations and demonstrations can be found at *MERLOT*.

Discussions. Discussions are one of the best ways for students to demonstrate understanding of course material, and discussion tools are included with all of the learning management software packages. Research has shown that counting discussion postings as part of the grade for an online course is an excellent way to encourage student engagement in your class (Hannafin, Land, and Oliver). Interactive discussions demonstrate students' understanding of particular readings, allow them to summarize and synthesize information from various sources, and, if students post drafts in the discussion area, provide opportunities for peer review. Two basic types of discussion formats are available in most course management software packages: the chat room, which is synchronous—meaning students meet at a designated time—or the discussion board, which is asynchronous—meaning students can log on and post anytime that is convenient for them. In online learning environments, asynchronous discussions are often more successful than synchronous ones because students taking a class online often have schedules that prevent time-constrained meetings. That said, synchronous discussions (chat rooms) can be valuable for office hours. You can designate times that students can find you in a chat room; students can log on and ask questions that require some back and forth discussion. Chat rooms can also be valuable for student group projects, as they are most effective when used by four or five people at a time rather than large classes.

Group work. All types of group activities, from peer review to cooperative learning projects, are possible in the online environment. However, for group projects to be successful, pacing and organization are crucial. Consider the following as you design the group work for your course:

- Incorporate nongraded activities that allow students to get to know each other and develop working relationships before you require them to submit work that will be graded. Include activities that will allow them to become familiar with the technical skills needed to share and post information.

- Consider how, when, and where students will meet and how you will evaluate individual contributions alongside group contributions. Make all of this information available to students from the beginning of the project.

- Provide group members with as many ways of communicating as possible. Set them up with a chat room, a discussion area, a place to share files, email contact information, and if possible phone numbers. If *all* students are on campus, you may encourage face-to-face meetings; if not, do not do so because students who are off campus will feel slighted.

- Determine ahead of time how groups will be formed. It is not a good idea to allow groups to evolve organically, nor is it a good idea to determine groups arbitrarily. Groups formed around common interests are the most successful online—as they are offline.

- Clear and well-articulated guidelines for group work are imperative if the group assignments are to be successful. Also, clear assessment criteria must be given before the work is under way. Providing rubrics for online group work and discussion postings is an excellent way to help students successfully meet learning objectives.

Research. Much of learning to write in college involves learning how to effectively and efficiently conduct research. Fortunately, much of the research needed for first-year composition courses (in fact, for most university courses) can be effectively completed online. University libraries are on the forefront of developing online research tools and access to those tools. Many libraries provide online tutorials on how to find and evaluate sources that can be used for research projects, and often the tutorials are geared toward online students.

Assessing Online Classes

Every well-designed course—whether online or face-to-face—includes well-designed assessment measures. In fact, since the feeling of isolation is one of the biggest challenges for online learners, students have cited immediate and ongoing feedback as one of the most essential characteristics of a successful online course. Chapter 9 in this guide to teaching offers several options for responding to students' writing, many of which can be adapted for online courses, as can the advice in Chapter 12 on grading.

Ensuring Academic Honesty

Although concerns have been raised about the reliability of online assessment, in first-year writing courses many of those concerns can be assuaged with assignments that require students to submit multiple drafts that you review or by group projects. For more information on teaching to avoid plagiarism, see Chapter 32 in this guide, "Teaching Research and Documentation."

Designing a Syllabus

The next step after determining the design and structure of the online course is to create a syllabus. Generally speaking, the syllabus for an online course includes the same elements as the syllabus for a face-to-face course: course information, course requirements, grading, and scheduling as well as information on how to contact the instructor for individual concerns or problems. However, in an online course, the syllabus needs to include more information than in a face-to-face course. Make sure that the syllabus is visible on the entry level of the course so that students can easily find the information they need to get started.

In face-to-face courses, students obtain additional information about course policies by asking questions as they come up, but in an online course, you must anticipate some questions. Moreover, assumptions that students and faculty make about some course policies might not fit in online courses. Many students take online courses because they expect that they will be easier or take less time. Others expect a self-study approach where they move at their own pace. Some may even expect the instructor to be available twenty-four hours a day, seven days a week. Be sure your syllabus specifies the exact nature of the course: the hours a week devoted to class (typically nine for a three-credit hour class), type and frequency of student participation, and availability and response time for instructor (online equivalent of office hours). Class participation is another aspect of the online course that will require additional information for students. You may require that students log on a certain number of times each week or that they make a specific number and type of postings each week. Just make sure they know what you will be looking for to determine adequate participation.

Provide students with adequate and detailed information about policies and procedures for using the online tools. Step-by-step written instructions for turning in assignments, completing tests and quizzes, participating in discussions, and contacting you or other individuals who can provide technical support when needed are crucial to a successful online learning environment. Slide shows, screen shots, and short movies can illustrate some of the processes and can be linked to or referenced in your syllabus.

Useful Readings

Allen, I. Elaine, and Jeff Seaman. *Going the Distance: Online Education in the United States, 2011.* Babson Park, MA: Babson Survey Research Group, 2011. *Sloan-C.* Web. 2 Jan. 2013.

Bauer, John F., and Rebecca S. Anderson. "Evaluating Students' Written Performance in the On-Line Class." *Principles of Effective Learning in the On-Line Class: New Directions in Teaching and Learning*, No. 84. Ed. Renee E. Weiss, Dave S. Knowlton, and Bruce W. Speck. San Francisco: Jossey-Bass, 2000. Print.

Bean, John C., and Dean Peterson. "Grading Classroom Participation." *Changing the Way We Grade Student Performance: Classroom Assessment and the New Learning Paradigm: New Directions in Teaching and Learning*, No. 74. Ed. Rebecca S. Anderson and Bruce W. Speck. San Francisco: Jossey-Bass, 1998. Print.

Hanna, Donald E., Michelle Glowacki-Dudka, and Simone Conceicao-Runlee. *147 Practical Tips for Teaching Online Groups: Essentials of Web-Based Education.* Madison, WI: Atwood, 2000. Print.

Hannafin, Michael J., Susan M. Land, and Kevin Oliver. "Open Learning Environments: Foundations, Methods and Models." *Instructional-design Theories and Models.* Vol. 2. Ed. Charles M. Reigeluth. Mahwah, NJ: Erlbaum, 1999. 115–40. Print.

Hewett, Beth L., and Christa Ehmann. *Preparing Education for Online Writing Instruction: Principles and Processes.* Urbana, IL: NCTE, 2004. Print. (Includes an excellent bibliography.)

Kairos: A Journal of Rhetoric, Technology, and Pedagogy. Kairos, 2009. Web. 13 Oct. 2009.

MERLOT (Multimedia Educational Resource for Teaching and Online Learning). California State University. 2013. Web. 2 Jan. 2013.

Palloff, Rena M., and Keith Pratt. *Lessons from the Cyberspace Classroom: The Realities of Online Teaching.* San Francisco: Jossey-Bass, 2001. Print.

———. *The Virtual Student: A Profile and Guide to Working with Online Learners.* San Francisco: Jossey-Bass, 2003. Print.

Peterson, Patricia Webb. "The Debate about Online Learning: Key Issues for Writing Teachers." *Computers and Composition* 18.4 (2001): 359–70. Print.

Reeves, Thomas C., and Patricia M. Reeves. "Effective Dimensions of Interactive Learning on the World Wide Web." *Web-Based Instruction.* Ed. Badrul H. Khan. Englewood Cliffs, NJ: Educational Technology Publications, 1999. 59–65. Print.

Sloan Consortium. "Going the Distance: Online Education in the United States, 2011." *Sloan-C.* Web. 2 Jan. 2013.

Creating and Sustaining **15** a Teaching Persona

Scott Geisel

If you've never taught before, or if you find yourself in new teaching situations, you're probably going to have a period of adjustment. Getting used to your new territory won't happen overnight. No one is going to hand you a script with every line of dialogue you'll deliver, provide you with a wardrobe and makeup, explain your character's motivation, or coach you when to emote and when to be stoic. Getting comfortable with yourself as a teacher is a much more fluid process than that.

You might think of your new teaching context less like a play and more like the first time you went to a movie with a date and held his or her hand in the dark. You want to hold hands, and it feels nice, but there are worries: Do I hold the hand the whole time? What if my palm starts to sweat, or I have an itch? What if my date starts to sweat? What if my arm goes numb and I feel like I'm going to pass out?

Don't worry—you'll deal with the things that come up as you're getting used to teaching, just like everyone adjusts to new circumstances.

Teaching as a Writer

You're in a writing classroom because you're a writer. You know how to write, and you've done it successfully. Your experience as a writer should inspire both you and your students. As someone who's been where they are, you can serve as an example. Writing along with students can be a powerful teaching tool and can help remind you why you're there and what you have to offer your students: a passion for writing and an ability to show how to work through the challenges and difficulties they'll encounter in your class and as college writers. The ability to write is your strength and can help you find your comfort zone. Don't be afraid to use it.

Teaching as an Expert

Start by reminding yourself who you are not: you are not another student in the class. Your students shouldn't expect you to act like one of them, and you shouldn't suggest that's what you're trying to do. Think about it this way: you've got a lot of

93

jobs that your students don't. Among other things, you have to prepare materials that are current, useful, engaging, and productive for each class day; manage the pacing of daily activities and the course overall; keep students on task and move students productively both in and out of class; and pay attention and be prepared to adjust when students' needs don't fit as well as you'd like with what you've planned. Your students will look to you to model activities, answer questions, explain concepts, and keep control of the classroom.

At various times, you'll feel that you're acting as a writer, scholar, mentor, coach, friend, authority figure, organizer, manager, mediator, grader, and more. You can be the voice of good news and positive feedback to students, as well as the reality check they don't want to hear. And your responsibility as grader can often feel like it's in conflict with your other roles. Your teaching persona may be all encouragement while the course is getting underway, but if you're unprepared or haven't prepared your students, there can often be a change in the feel of the classroom when you hand back that first set of graded papers.

Tell your students your expectations up front. Let them know that you'll grade their work fairly and accurately when the time comes, but that grades aren't personal. You can help to clarify this new role by developing a set of grading criteria, soliciting additional input and revision of those items from students, and applying the criteria to a sample piece of writing to demonstrate how your grading process will work. You'll be giving your students the opportunity to begin to interpret the comments you'll put on their papers. Make sure to include characteristics of good writing in general as well as qualities specific to a particular assignment. Prioritize so students will know the greatest impediments to achieving the goals of an assignment and don't spend the majority of their time worrying about less important features like headings and margins. When students are aware of your expectations and know how you're going to grade their papers, you'll feel more confident in that role. Once you've squarely faced the reality of the balancing act that teaching can sometimes be, you'll be on your way to feeling comfortable and to making your students feel comfortable with your teaching style, too.

Balancing Your Roles

At the same time you're juggling your various roles in your classroom, you'll have a whole other life outside of the classroom and your responsibilities as a teacher. Your students will, too. Their lives are their own, and yours is your own, but there are bound to be points of intersection and common experience that come up in the activities and discussions and writing that you share. How you handle those intersections will depend mostly on you, but keep in mind that you'll want to maintain the ability to keep control of the course while still trying to show you're a real person. A key here is relevance. The class you're teaching is about your students much more than it is about you. Act honestly in the relationship you want to have and can afford to have with your students, but don't lose track of your responsibilities. You don't need to withhold personal information or remain distant and untouchable, but you also shouldn't deliberately work in or reveal details about your personal life without some reason for doing so.

At the same time, don't be afraid to think like a student—like your students. What questions might you have or would you want to know if you had to complete the assignment you've just given? What is its value and goals, and what would be your motivation to work hard and try to do well? What's likely to be difficult, and where would you start? What processes might you use to get everything done? Then remember that your students will have a range of experience, skills, and confidence about college writing. They won't all respond the same to everything you ask them to do, and some are likely to find more value in a particular activity than others.

Dressing Like a Teacher

Dress codes in an academic environment are often arbitrary, self-imposed, or even nonexistent. Look around you—what are other people wearing, and why do you think they dress that way? And do they look comfortable? If the people you're noticing have been teaching long enough, their appearance and demeanor probably reflect themselves as teachers, and that's what you'll be projecting, too, once you find your comfort level. It can be tempting to wear a new power suit, a jacket and tie, or even jeans and an old button-down to project an image, and sometimes when

you're starting out, dressing nicely may help you establish authority in the classroom (or at least feel like you are).

Consider, too, a balance between fashion and appropriateness. Short skirts or oversized baggy shorts may distract students from reading and writing tasks in class. Many teachers are comfortable in a similar wardrobe day after day; others dress in a variety of ways to suit their mood, what's happening at any given time in the course, and even the weather. It's useful to look around at what other English teachers and people in different departments are wearing, too. Your colleagues may not feel compelled to wear a tie every day, but faculty in the business college may put on a jacket to teach. You might want a rack of ties or skirts you can choose from on days you teach and a drawer of jeans for when you'll be on campus but not in the classroom. And then you'll probably want to start mixing it up. The point is that you should feel relaxed in the way you present yourself to your students, and comfortable that they accept you in a way that you're happy with.

Having Fun

Teaching can be serious business, but if you're not enjoying yourself, too, then why are you here? And if you're not enjoying yourself, how must your students feel? Doing some things for fun (especially if they have some inherent value or relate to what's happening in your course) can set everyone more at ease and help create a comfortable, positive learning environment.

I like to throw things like little chocolate bars or a soft, rubbery ball that we can toss up over the lights and off the walls to each other during a discussion without hurting anyone or anything. Getting students to smile once in a while eases the tension in the classroom and helps them relax and open up. I've seen students perform skits in class with more energy and fun than I could have imagined. Ask students to perform a draft of a paper or to draw their thesis as a cartoon. Assign groups to attend and review a film or play or restaurant. And serving popcorn while you show a movie in class can make the whole experience more worthwhile.

But don't force fun. Starting class every day with a joke that you think is funny will probably be about as enjoyable for students as you can imagine it would be for you if one of your teachers did that. You don't have to be funny; you just want to get to the point where you feel relaxed. Being prepared and knowing what you want to accomplish and what you want your students to accomplish on any given day will help you find opportunities to relax. Even a smile or a willingness to indulge a minor diversion into an amusing side trip during class can go a long way to making it a more enjoyable experience for everyone.

Gaining Confidence

When you first start teaching, some plans will work better than others, and some activities you may do once and vow never to repeat. If you have a backup plan, or several, you may feel more confident for those days when technology fails you or students just don't respond as you'd hoped. If you'd like to do more than there is time for in the term, have some of those other activities ready as alternatives: a field trip to practice observation and the power of details, an activity with magnetic poetry to explore new boundaries with language, a writing day when students simply work on their assignments with you there to answer questions and offer input, an editing sample for students to work on and present in class, a provocative reading, or a workshop day when students can work on their own, in groups, or with you. Knowing you've got options can help you to feel confident and to take charge of your classroom in the ways you want to.

Outside pressures can also influence your attitude in the classroom: a restless night of sleep, the stress of other responsibilities, your love life (or lack thereof), or a dead car battery on a cold January morning. You'll know you're getting somewhere when you appreciate the good days and don't dwell on the bad—just keep moving forward. And remember that gaining confidence is a key to becoming comfortable with yourself as a teacher. You're here because you've got something valuable to offer your students.

A Useful Reading

Greinke, Russell. "What I Learned about Teaching from Observing Stand-Up Comedians." *The Teaching Professor* 18.5 (2004): 1. Print.

Balancing Graduate Studies 16 with Writing Instruction

Melissa Faulkner and Melissa Toomey

Most of us speak and behave differently in a gym than a church or a neighborhood pub. We've had ample time, an entire lifetime, to learn the social norms of familiar places, and we recognize that there's an already established social hierarchy where we know our role. In a church, for example, we know that the priest or pastor stands at the front, behind the pulpit, and we sit in a pew facing the front. It would be highly unusual for a member of the congregation to walk straight to the front and take over the pulpit. Yet, as new graduate teaching assistants, that's what we feel we're doing.

Most of us have about seventeen years of experience learning how to be a student, from kindergarten through undergraduate school. On the first day of kindergarten we didn't know to raise our hands before we spoke. Through observation, practice, and reminders from the teacher, we learned to do so. High school teachers prepared us for college by saying, "When you get to college . . ." and the expectations gradually became clear.

The transition to graduate school, however, is usually abrupt, and the transition from student to teacher feels even more sudden. Most graduate programs provide some type of teacher preparation in the form of a crash course, but rarely do graduate teaching assistants feel prepared to deal with their dual roles as both teacher and student. As graduate teaching assistants ourselves, first in an M.A. program and now as Ph.D. students at another institution, we offer advice on how to wear both hats, that of student and teacher, simultaneously. We hope to ease your mind, to assure you that nearly all graduate teaching assistants feel the same apprehension and fear you are feeling, and to encourage you. You have the experience and the knowledge—all you need now is the confidence.

Teaching First-Year Composition

Before you ever step into the classroom, you can prepare yourself for teaching writing. Meet people. Introduce yourself to the other teachers in your program, the professors in your department, and—perhaps one of the most important groups of people to know—the office staff, who usually will help you make copies and assist you with scheduling questions, technological issues, and other logistical concerns.

97

As you prepare to enter your classroom, think about how you want to physically represent yourself to students. Dress nicely. Business casual is often appropriate. Dressing in slacks or a skirt and a nice top or a jacket and khakis can set you apart from your students and create a professional tone from the start, as well as make you feel more confident when you walk in on the first day. Consider how you and the students will address each other. Also, take a bottle of water or a can of soda with you, both to quench your thirst and to have something to hold in your hand. See Chapter 15 in this guide, "Creating and Sustaining a Teaching Persona," for more ideas.

Once your class gets going, don't feel that you can't vary your routines. In fact, you should try different pedagogical approaches in order to keep the students and yourself interested and refreshed. Don't hesitate to ask students for their views on new activities. In doing a midterm assessment one semester, Melissa Toomey discovered that students wanted more collaborative work where they talked in groups, went back to their seats and free-wrote about the peer workshop, and then discussed the results as a class. In trying their proposed technique, Melissa found that students were energized by the new use of class time. Reflecting on this activity, students commented that they like for teachers to "move things around so we don't get bored," and several others stated they were "surprised and happy [the teacher] even took their ideas into consideration." Giving students a voice in designing your course can keep them personally invested in what they do.

Cultivating Good Habits as Teacher and Student

Developing sensible practices as both a writing teacher and a graduate student is vital to your success in both roles. In order to manage your busy schedule, it's useful to create systematic records of what you are teaching and reading. Here are some tips for keeping records.

Be organized. Try constructing a basic or detailed lesson plan for each class that you can place into a binder or folder. Include key points you want to address in class, and write down any information you will want students to note. As soon as possible after you teach, reflect in writing on what you taught and on your students' reactions: How successful were the class activities? Why did they succeed—or why not? How should you change them next time? Completing such a metacognitive activity helps you organize and track your personal experiences as a new teacher, gives you a chance to think about your students' reactions and needs, and helps you improve your teaching in later courses.

Keep your work for each class you're teaching and taking in a separate folder or binder so you can locate information both during the term and later, when you want to use a handout from your fall section of English 101 or cite from an article that you can find easily in your folder marked "En-glish 700: Research Methods—Spring 20XX."

Manage your time wisely. Staying ahead of your students in the coursework is crucial. When you've gained some experience teaching, you'll be able to plan several class periods ahead of time, but the first time through, you're likely to be figuring out what to do as you teach. If possible, keep at least two classes ahead in your lesson plans to reduce your stress level and allow you to alert students about challenges they may face as they do what you assign.

If you walk into class without students' homework or class assignments ready, you quickly can lose credibility, so make copies of handouts or put information on reserve several days before you'll use or assign them. Unanticipated problems—broken copiers or scanners, delays in the library—often arise, and you want to avoid scrambling for an alternative to your planned lessons. You can then review the readings, copied handouts, and lesson plans just before your class.

It's equally important to manage your time wisely as a graduate student. Schedule time to write. We write in our planners (another good way to stay organized) that from nine to five on Mondays we will do nothing else but write. Schedule specific times to read, research, and revise. The more papers you write, the better you can estimate how long the process takes you. Melissa Toomey always allots herself five

days to get through the initial researching, notetaking, and drafting process for a paper. Melissa Faulkner gives herself the same amount of time but writes into her schedule that, for example, she will do the research notetaking while at her son Brandon's basketball game and finish it up at her daughter Chelsea's cheerleading practice. Because it is important for her to spend time with her family, she made the decision to talk and laugh with her kids on the way to and from practices and games, but while she's at practices, she'll do schoolwork—when she isn't cheering.

You may often feel overwhelmed when you think about dealing with your students, your own work as a student, and your family. Do whatever it takes for you to maintain your balance and sanity. Melissa Toomey only recently decided that she should take an entire day off each week from doing any schoolwork whatsoever. She believes she has made herself a better student; knowing she has a day off coming up soon, she works extremely hard to get there, and after that day off, she feels revived and rejuvenated. If you can't schedule a regular day off, consider a private holiday. When Rich Bullock was in grad school, he and his wife periodically declared "Januarius McGahan Day," and took the day off in honor of the liberator of Bulgaria.

Read actively. Being a busy student and teacher, you need to find ways to read that will help you understand material and remember it long after you have read it.

Generating good reading notes is crucial to initial readings of texts and gives you a way to review the information later. Ask other students in your program to show you how they take notes, and after viewing as many examples as possible, find a system that will work for you, given your learning style. Some students write summaries of text in the margins as they read, some create double-entry notebooks, while others create a form on which they record basic information about each text they read. Such a form might include the following:

- Summarize the chapter read.
- What two questions do I have?
- What three terms should I remember based on the content of the chapter, and what are their definitions?

Whatever strategy you use, it's important to remember that you are building a system that you can consciously change and renegotiate as your learning habits and skills are modified.

Help students manage their time. The syllabus is a key element in any classroom, especially in a writing classroom where assignments are due regularly, so use the syllabus to your advantage by spelling out assignments and rules in detail, making it a place where students can go for quick and concise answers to many of their questions. Students also appreciate having a detailed document to lead them in the right direction when they are experiencing difficulties. Sequences and deadlines help students manage their time.

Outlining assignments on the syllabus before the course starts will also save you valuable time because you will have already planned the fundamental parts of your course. Chapter 2 in this guide to teaching provides detailed advice on what to include in your syllabus. Go over the syllabus with your students, ideally on the first day of class, and discuss exactly what you mean by each item and your purposes for creating such a structure. Leave room for updates, and perhaps even include students in the decision process when making changes.

Although you may change some of your assignments as the term progresses, follow through with whatever policy you have stated. Inconsistency can foster student irresponsibility and reduce your credibility. For example, Melissa Toomey's syllabus states that she does not accept assignments by email. Yet students have sent her their work with notes attached stating that their printer is out of ink or that they forgot to give the assignment in class. Accepting papers after saying she wouldn't do so would undermine her authority as an instructor, and her other policies could also be called into question.

Succeeding as a Graduate Student

Here are some concerns we've encountered, with some advice for dealing with them.

Relating to faculty. As a graduate student, your relationships with faculty are different than they were when you were an undergraduate. Your professors may ask you to call them by their first names. They will probably begin to ask you how things are going. Don't be shocked if they offer suggestions or even offer to help. Take advantage of it! Your professors know the pressures you face and want you not only to survive but to succeed, because your success reflects their own. If you've been admitted into a graduate program, faculty assume you have what it takes to succeed and are interested in helping you do so. In addition, the reputations of universities are formed in part by the quality of the graduate students they produce. Faculty members want to be associated with institutions with excellent reputations. Therefore, they have a vested interest in your success.

Relating to your fellow grad students. Grad school does not have to be competitive. Next to faculty, your fellow graduate students can be your greatest resources and your best sources of support. You have all proven your academic ability by being accepted into your graduate program, so you don't need to compete to see who can be the best of the best. Form alliances, share useful sources, and help one another. Write together. We teach collaboration in the classroom, so why not practice what we teach? This very chapter is the result of an ongoing collaboration between peers. As grad students, first at the same M.A. institution and now with the same Ph.D. program, we have written together, workshopped drafts together,

presented papers together at conferences, and even co-taught together. Although this sort of partnership is not the norm, it's important to find or build your own support system. Even hanging around the teaching assistants' offices or grabbing a beer after class has real benefits: you can build friendships that might lead to collaboration, now and later when you're working in your chosen field, and the act of discussing your course content and your teaching with other graduate students will deepen and enrich your understanding of both.

Publishing. We don't intend to downplay the importance of building your credentials, and we recommend you not feel overly pressured to publish and present at conferences. However, attending conferences even without presenting is an invaluable learning experience. You get to learn about exciting new research and ideas as well as meet people who are important in your field—and they get to meet you. If possible, attend several conferences to learn their routines before you attempt to be a presenter. Seek advice from experienced presenters on how to write a proposal. Investigate which conferences are most respected and well known in your area of interest, whether it is creative writing, literature, TESOL, or composition and rhetoric. Be aware, though, that presenting papers not only adds stress to your already tired psyche and busy schedule but also can get expensive. Even with a student discount, some conferences can cost hundreds of dollars in registration fees, food, and lodging. Some institutions offer financial resources for graduate students' professional development, so be sure to inquire about assistance at your institution.

While publishing is an honor and a desirable goal, concentrate first on writing successful seminar papers; focus on completing your degree. Do not be afraid, however, to submit your work to appropriate journals for publication, especially work that may grow into something larger like an M.A. thesis or Ph.D. dissertation. These submissions can help you develop an area of expertise or specialization and can help to link your name with a very specific topic. Even if your work is rejected, the comments of referees can help you understand what publishable work in your field should contain and may improve your writing just as your comments help students improve their writing. While publication is certainly not impossible for grad

students (plenty of us have done it), it is also not mandatory.

Useful Readings

Bishop, Wendy, and Deborah Coxwell Teague, eds. *Finding Our Way: A Writing Teacher's Sourcebook.* Boston: Houghton, 2005. Print.

Deen, Rosemary. "Notes to Stella." *College English* 54.5 (1992): 573–85. Print.

Dethier, Brock. *First Time Up: An Insider's Guide for New Composition Teachers.* Logan: Utah State UP, 2005. Print.

Fulkerson, Richard. "Four Philosophies of Composition." *The Writing Teacher's Sourcebook.* Ed. Gary Tate, Edward P.J. Corbett, and Nancy Myers. New York: Oxford UP, 1994. 3–8. Print.

Hall, Donald E. *The Academic Self: An Owner's Manual.* Columbus: Ohio State UP, 2002. Print.

Interacting with Students 17

Jimmy Chesire

You are about to enter a college composition class, maybe for the first time. You might be nervous. Good, you should be: I don't think we can do anything well without worrying at least a little. We need a bit of adrenalin to get us going, to keep us going. But we don't want to panic. One reason new teachers worry is that they're adopting a new role, teacher rather than student, and don't know how to act: Should I try to act "professorial," whatever that means? Should I try to be formal, laid-back, distant, a confidant? How do I interact with my students, who so recently—or not so recently—were my peers? Here are a few ideas and suggestions that might help you relax a bit and be yourself—and as a consequence, become a better and more effective teacher.

Being Honest

Be as honest with your students as you can be. Tell them the truth about yourself and the subject at hand. This approach does not mean telling your students everything you feel, think, believe, or desire, nor does it mean telling them your life story. You should, however, try to be open. Often we are so close-minded, so closed off from one another, and why not? As Brenda Ueland says in *If You Want to Write: A Book about Independence and Spirit*, we're well advised to be careful who we trust and open up to. But in your classroom, you have great power and authority. You can afford to take risks, you can dare to reveal yourself, because it is your turf.

If you want to connect with your students, if you want them to trust you, if you want them to do the things you direct them to do, then take some chances to let the real you appear. Be silly if there's a silly moment in class. Be loving and complimentary when you feel like it. Be wise-cracking if that's your bent, but if it is your bent, be sure to make clear to your students that you're joking. When making wisecracks, let them know you're playing and trying to be funny. Let students know if and how and when they can be wisecrackers, and that they can crack wise about you.

Are you scared? Are you lost some of the time? Admit it. Tell your students you're new, that this is your first class, your first year teaching, that you're just learning. They'll appreciate your honesty, and most of them will be relieved because they already know it (or intuit it) and feel embarrassed and uncomfortable when you're embarrassed and uncomfortable. So if you own up and express your concern, they'll understand while being flattered to have been trusted. Then you can both relax.

If you allow it, students will help you and care for you and protect you, too, especially if you tell them you believe they can teach you a thing or two—and that you're open to learning from them. When they do teach you something (and they will), let them know, thank them, and then use that learning in front of them, giving them credit as you do. When your students witness this sort of openness and humility, this sort of graciousness and self-assurance, they'll relax and try harder to do all the work you ask them to do.

Doing the Work

I learned as a TA that one of the most effective teaching techniques was to do the homework assignments you give your students. Do the work you ask them to do. Tell them you are doing it, and tell them why. Explain that you want to keep in close touch with just how complicated and difficult many assignments can be; because when you have trouble doing the work, or can't complete the work in the allotted time, then surely you can understand their challenge—and be sure to give credit to those who are able to do what even you could not.

Early in my TA career, I did every assignment with my students but stopped because it seemed like too much work (which is the whole point—to realize just how much work we're asking them to do). I started again doing all the assignments I give my students, and students appreciate that the teacher is doing the work, that I know exactly what I'm asking them to do, and that I know how hard it is. And they like the forgiveness: "I couldn't get mine typed up, so I'm not going to insist that you type yours up." But mainly they are very impressed, reassured, and wonderfully appreciative of how close I am to the pain and intellectual challenge of the homework I've assigned.

Caring

Look for ways to let yourself really care for your students and learn how to be compassionate toward them. There is a tremendous pressure, in my opinion, to belittle and ridicule our students, to make jokes at their expense, and to laugh at their weaknesses and deficits—as if we teachers are so much more wonderful human beings because of our love of reading and writing. If you witness denigrating stories in your offices, lists of students' mistakes on email, and complaints at faculty meetings, don't be sucked into this morass. Don't make fun of your students, put them down, or laugh at them. Don't get me wrong. I love funny people, I love comedy, I love witty, clever, hilarious people. But there is a big difference between telling funny stories and stories that make the student the butt of the joke.

Try instead to understand how and why your students fell so far behind, and why they don't read. Check out John Holt's wonderful essay, "Making Children Hate Reading." Decide to care about your students and their deficits. Decide to be good and kind. Offer them condolences, understanding, and a second chance. They may have been chastised along the way by a reading or spelling teacher, and it only takes one such teacher to put a child off. Many of my students have told me so.

I love my students and tell them so, especially in the opening days of the term when talking about my university's many strengths. I say things like "I learn a lot from my students and will probably learn a lot from you all." I respect my students and show it by paying attention to them, by taking them seriously, and by looking for reasons to praise and honor them as often as I can for their wit, for their humor, for their compassion, for their kindness to me and to others, for their fine writing, for their clear, incisive thinking, and for their willingness to work hard. I compliment them a lot, only saying things I really mean and believe. I tell my students I like them, that I'm glad they're in my class, that I'm lucky to have them in my class.

Observing Yourself

Discern how you are most effective in the classroom. Perhaps being open, honest, and willing to reveal your vulnerabilities

won't work for you. Find out what does. Notice the things that really get your students reading and writing, and then do more of those things. A number of my peers bring sweets to their classes like donuts or little candies. Their students love the treats and then work harder.

Conferencing one-on-one with students (discussed in Chapter 6) is hard work, but you might love it and students say even ten-minute sessions are valuable. When I discovered how much I enjoyed conferencing, how much my students and I could cover, how much they grew as writers and readers, and how they blossomed as people because of our conferences, I expanded my conferences to thirty minutes per student.

If you discover an approach that works with one class, use it with another. Don't be afraid to do the same thing over and over again. It'll be new to your students, and with the repetition, you'll get better and better at it. If something you find exciting bombs, try it again before abandoning it. Sometimes the idea is good but the term, the students, or your delivery aren't right—but will be another time.

Setting an Example

If you want to be the very best teacher you can be, then make a conscious decision to grow, both personally and professionally. Dedicate yourself to learning—the best teachers believe in teaching, which means we value learning. Actively learning and having a lot of fun in the process will show by your demeanor, and students will see it. They will be excited by your enthusiasm for learning and will be encouraged to follow your lead. Besides, learning is the richest thing, the longest-lasting pleasure, and the most life-extending thing you can do for yourself. You and your students will benefit more from your classes as you take risks and learn and teach together.

Useful Readings

Holt, John. "Making Children Hate Reading." *The Underachieving School.* Boulder: Sentient, 2005, 55–65. Print.

Nathan, Rebekah. *My Freshman Year: What a Professor Learned by Becoming a Student.* Ithaca, NY: Cornell UP, 2005. Print.

Ueland, Brenda. *If You Want to Write: A Book about Independence and Spirit.* St. Paul, MN: Graywolf, 1997. Print.

Teaching for Inclusion **18** and Diversity

Adrienne Cassel

Students who feel comfortable sharing their ideas and experiences with their instructors and other students in their classes will learn more and stay in college longer than students who find their learning environment and their interactions on campus awkward and uncomfortable. But creating a classroom in which all students feel included, comfortable, and respected regardless of physical abilities, learning styles, sex, age, ethnicity, sexual orientation, socioeconomic background, or religion can be challenging, whether you are a graduate student teaching for the first time or an experienced faculty member who has taught for many years. This chapter aims to help you meet the challenge by introducing four key elements of inclusive design and providing ideas for integrating them into your writing course.

Understanding Four Key Elements of Inclusive Design

Simply put, *teaching for inclusion* means you teach so that each student's individual learning needs are met. Sometimes called *culturally responsive teaching*, this approach calls for instruction that honors each student. Inclusive courses, no matter what the subject, contain the following key elements:

1. The instructor demonstrates awareness of his or her own attitudes and biases.
2. Course content reflects various worldviews and perspectives.
3. Assignments are varied to engage students with different learning styles and students with learning disabilities.
4. Materials are accessible for everyone regardless of any physical or cognitive disabilities.

Appraising Your Attitude and Awareness

To create culturally responsive classrooms, begin with an honest appraisal of your own attitudes and biases. Sometimes we think we are encouraging multiple viewpoints and worldviews, but unless we have examined our own beliefs in light of the dominant culture within which we live and work, we may be unconsciously replicating and encouraging the same frames of reference we are trying to avoid.

To begin to discover your own biases, ask yourself, What values do I hold that are consistent with those of the dominant culture? Sociologist Robin M. Williams (Wlodkowski and Ginsberg 11–12) has identified themes that generally reflect the basic values and beliefs held by the dominant culture in the United States. These themes are presented here as questions you might ask yourself to begin examining your own attitudes. Although these questions provide polarized viewpoints, they are not meant to suggest that the only possible responses are "either-or" responses. They are meant instead to provide a springboard from which multiple perspectives and interpretations are possible. As you answer the questions, think about other perspectives that may be equally valid in other cultures or situations, and assess to what degree you allow for these alternative worldviews and approaches to learning in your classrooms. The first two questions include some analysis. Use these examples to help you create your own analysis of the other questions.

- *How do you define success?* In the United States, there is an emphasis on "pulling one's self up by the bootstraps," or the rags-to-riches success story characterized by large financial gains achieved by working hard or by being "rescued" by a well-to-do relative. An alternative viewpoint might be that the highest human value is generosity, and that "conspicuous consumption represents greed and self-interest." Also, the rags-to-riches story overlooks the influence of privilege and ignores the social, political, and economic factors that favor certain groups in succeeding in this way.

- *What do you believe about work?* In the United States, we generally believe that working hard is a virtue; however, that belief devalues the importance of taking time for others and for contemplation and leisure. We often fail to recognize the value of other types of discipline besides the discipline of the workplace.

- *What are your humanitarian mores?* Do you believe people should come together to help the "underdog," or do you believe that people "get what they deserve"?

- *What is your moral orientation?* Do you believe in a definite right or wrong? Should right and wrong be defined in the context of particular cultures? Or, do you believe that "right" and "wrong" are subjective judgments meant to protect the more privileged members of society?

- *Which is more valuable, efficiency and practicality or the quality of the process?* Is it more important to make decisions and act on them or to make sure the opinions of everyone affected by such decisions are heard before a course of action is settled on?

- *What is your view of economic growth and "progress"?* Do you believe that the development of industry, roads, buildings, houses, shopping centers, and the like equals betterment for humankind, or do you believe that honoring the natural world and the inherent cycles is a better way to live?

- *What constitutes "the good life"?* Do you see the good life as the attainment of things that can make you more comfortable, or do you believe the good life is about sharing and giving, even if it involves personal sacrifice?

- *Who controls the government?* Do you believe that every person has a voice in the political destiny of the country or that only those who hold power and its privileges influence politics?

- *Is freedom an absolute good?* Do you believe in freedom at any cost, or do you believe that limiting your own freedom may be a way to show respect for someone else's freedom?

- *What is more important, the individual or the group?* Do you honor being true to yourself, or do you believe the group should take precedence over the individual?

When you look at your cultural values through the various perspectives suggested by these questions from Wlodkowski and Ginsberg, you develop a better understanding of how your worldview can subtly, but profoundly, change the experience your students have in your classroom. For example, simply asking, "Where are you going on spring break?" may unnecessarily make some students uncomfortable. Students who travel on spring break are usually supported by their parents or guardians, giving them the freedom and financial means to make a spring break trip. Many students at the community college where I teach use their spring break to catch up on much-needed sleep or other projects outside of school—or to work extra hours at a job. Taking a trip someplace exotic is not within their means. Instead of asking where they are going on spring break, which assumes that everyone is going some-place, a better question might be "What are you doing over the break?" That question assumes nothing except that they are getting a break, a pretty safe assumption.

Although this variation might seem like a small thing, awareness of these kinds of implied values can have a huge impact on first-generation students and/or students from underrepresented groups who often get through college only if they are lucky enough to find people who are willing to help them interpret, analyze, and maneuver through a system characterized by elitism, process, rules, and complicated traditions. By uncovering your own biases and beliefs, you become more sensitive to your students' biases and beliefs, allowing you to create a classroom environment that is more comfortable for more students.

Revisiting Course Content and Materials

Once you understand how your own values and beliefs shape your teaching, you will be better able to evaluate the content you present and the materials you use in the course. Wlodkowski and Ginsberg suggest first thinking about the course within its discipline. For instance, ask yourself what values are embedded in your discipline that may confuse or disturb some students. How can you encourage students to express alternative perspectives? For example, in writing classes, the focus on teaching traditional genres over alternative forms or genres reveals values embedded not only in the field of writing studies, but also in the entire institution of higher education. The ongoing debate about what authors and works should be included in the English literary canon is just one example of how embedded values shape education.

Another example is the debate over the teaching of a standard form of English and the acceptance of African American Vernacular English and other dialects in spoken language in the classroom. Of course, students must understand and learn to write with the conventions accepted in the professional world, but it is also important that students understand that issues of diversity are inherent in any use of language. One way to honor various dialects and teach students about the discourse communities within their own sphere is to design some assignments that do not require "standard" forms of English. For instance, if you include a literature component in your composition class, you might ask students to write from the viewpoint of a character speaking in a particular dialect in a manner that would be comfortable to that character. You could ask students to write versions of their research or argument essays for various audiences, including younger siblings or friends. When you ask students to generate ideas and text that won't lead to a polished final draft, make it clear that you'll accept their writing in rough draft form, which may be influenced by various spoken dialects.

While it's important to allow students to understand and explore various ways of speaking and writing, it's also important to be aware of the various challenges that students face based on their ethnic background, the area of the country in which they grew up, and their preparation for academic work. If you can identify the challenges facing specific groups of students and learn to work with them beginning where they are—without judgment—you'll be more successful in creating classrooms where students feel comfortable to express themselves.

You should also review your examples. Are the examples that you use to illustrate key points both meaningful and sensitive to the students? Do the examples demonstrate that you value multiple perspectives and ways of viewing the world? One way to incorporate a variety of viewpoints is to first offer your own example and then ask students to supply theirs. Also, consider the models of writing and reading that you assign as part of the course. Do they include materials written by persons of differing backgrounds and ethnic groups? Do they too offer various worldviews? Do they address underrepresented groups in ways that do not trivialize or marginalize those groups?

Understanding Learning Styles

In addition to engaging a diverse student population by providing content that reflects multiple perspectives and experiences, you can also motivate students by designing assignments that appeal to various interests and learning styles. Students learn best when teaching addresses their preferred style. The writing assignments listed below provide additional ideas for designing course work that appeals to each of the four types of learners identified by David Kolb, an organizational researcher (in Sharp, Harb, and Terry).

- *Divergers* learn through interaction and discussion. Freewriting, peer reviews, personal reactions, and opinion papers appeal to this type of learner.

- *Assimilators* learn by observing and reflecting. They like to consult the experts but then discover new ways to tie the old ideas together. They like reading assignments, writing summaries, creating maps and trees, and they actually enjoy listening to well-organized lectures.

- *Convergers* prefer to take things apart and put them back together again. They learn by doing. The key to engaging convergers is to be sure they know why they are doing what they are doing. They like case studies, simulations, and assignments that involve keeping track of problem-solving protocols.

- *Accommodators* learn best through self-discovery. They are risk takers who resent having to follow too many rules. They would enjoy assignments that involve teaching concepts to other students, solving "what if" formulas, and formulating problems.

One of my favorite assignments is for students to post their research projects on blogs they have created themselves. Using blogs for both group and individual projects is an easy way to publish students' work, and blogs also provide an opportunity for students to gain computer literacy skills while participating in an activity that they consider trendy and fun. In addition, the blog assignment has a component that resonates with each of the learning types described by Kolb. For *divergers*, who like interaction and discussion, the blog provides instant access to both. *Assimilators,* who prefer consulting with experts as opposed to consulting with each other, can invite experts to post as part of their project or can cite experts from research. *Convergers*, who like to solve problems, can use the blog assignment as a problem to solve; and *accommodators*, who like to teach to other students, have a perfect venue for doing so. By mixing the types of writing assignments in your courses and providing students with several options for completing their assignments, you will enhance learning in your course and give students tools to succeed in their writing tasks in other classes as well. In addition, assignments such as these encourage authentic assessment: they ask students to perform real-world tasks that demonstrate meaningful application of essential knowledge and skills, the best approach to embracing a diverse student body.

Understanding Learning Disabilities

Complicating the issue of learning styles are students who come to us with diagnosed or undiagnosed learning disabilities. Keeping these students engaged requires going beyond respecting their worldviews, cultural backgrounds, and preferred learning styles. In order for students with learning disabilities to feel respected and comfortable in the classroom, they need to feel that they are able to successfully complete the tasks and assignments. Here are three instructional interventions that consistently help students with learning disabilities (and other students as well) to improve their writing abilities, and thus feel more relaxed and valued in the classroom.

1. Teach writing as a recursive practice. Show students that even the most accomplished writers do not create a successful draft on the first try, and require multiple drafts and editing sessions before they are satisfied with the written product.
2. Explicitly teach critical steps in the writing process and accompany each step with a series of prompts or questions to guide students through the writing task. For instance, in the planning stage, students might be asked to answer a series of questions such as "Who am I writing for?" "Why am I writing?" "What do I know?" "How can I group my ideas?" and "How will I organize my ideas?"
3. Provide frequent feedback based on the information explicitly taught. One way to do this is to give students rubrics that outline the strategies and components that you have identified as most important in their drafts. Students can use the rubrics as guides, and then you can use them to assess their success with the writing task.

Providing Accessibility

In order to meet the needs of all students, course materials need to be available to all students regardless of any physical or cognitive disability. Most campuses have an office of disability services that can help you critique your course materials with student accessibility in mind, but the five techniques listed below will help you get started:

- Provide equivalent print text versions of all materials that are presented as spoken or electronic components of the course.
- If you are using presentation slides, do not rely on color alone to convey information; also use text and shape.

Choose high-contrast colors for text and background and test the presentation by changing it to black and white to be sure it can be easily viewed. Make handouts of the slides on request. (More advice on using media inclusively may be found in Chapter 33 of this guide, "Teaching Media/Design.")

- Provide alternative versions of any material presented in class when students request it. For example, provide outlines of class activities and topics, or allow students to record lectures.

- Encourage students to let you know if they have any kind of disability and then work with students throughout the term to ensure that they are getting the support they need. Most universities have a disabilities office to support students and teachers; many require documentation for granting accommodations.

No matter which group of students you are working with, inclusive teaching means that you let students know ahead of time what criteria you will be using to evaluate their work. Part of teaching for inclusion is to make sure all students have clear and meaningful information for the course. Creating courses where all students feel respected and comfortable can be a challenge, but the rewards go far beyond the classroom. Students will be more engaged and motivated to learn as well as more likely to stay in college and succeed as writers and scholars. As a bonus, inclusive classrooms help to create a more just, equitable, and compassionate world for all of us.

Useful Readings

Corrigan, J.R. "Teaching Writing to Dyslexic Students: A Guide for the Composition Instructor." *Teaching English in the Two-Year College* 24.3 (1997): 205–11. Print.

Dunn, Patricia A., and Kathleen Dunn De Mers. "Reversing Notions of Disability and Accomodation: Embracing Universal Design in Writing Pedagogy and Web Space." *Kairos* 7.1 (2002): n. pag. Web. 13 Oct. 2009.

Sharp, J.E., J.N. Harb, and R.E. Terry. "Learning Styles and Writing Assignments." *The Teaching Professor* (Oct. 1997): 1+. Print.

Wlodkowski, Raymond J., and Margery B. Ginsberg. *Diversity & Motivation: Culturally Responsive Teaching.* San Francisco: Jossey-Bass, 1995. Print.

19 Teaching Second-Language Writers

Deborah Crusan and Carol Cornett

As you read through the stack of your students' first compositions, you may encounter some writing that stands out from the rest, but you can't quite put your finger on what's wrong. You can see that the writing doesn't flow; however, when you stop to decode, you aren't sure how to explain what you see happening on the page in front of you. You may see usages like the following:

- "Living in the cities is wonderful but it depends on how is your living standard."
- "For myself, the people who are college graduates it is better for them to live in the cities, because they will be able to handle that life of urban areas, because they will be getting enough salary to pay the bills and everyday expenses."
- "Teenagers and early twenty people always prefer living in crowded cities or where they can find some action."
- "There are lots of differents between living in cities and living in rural areas, and the most important different is the kind of people you see in each place."
- "My father always give me idea about what should I do."
- "There is not many roads and not many the gas station."
- "I am eighteen years old man."
- "So you can have a fun."
- "I came to the United States so many years but I still can not speak, write English well. Because I always stay at home, don't go outside, and we speak Chinese in my home. Many times I don't know how to speak English. So that shut my mouth."

You might encounter these usages randomly, in a single sentence, in one paragraph, or throughout a paper. If you do, you may well have a second-language writer in your class.

Writing in a second language is a challenging and complex process. Not only are second-language writers attempting to internalize the stages of the writing process, but they also must contend with second-language-processing issues. In some cases, this student should be placed in a class specifically designed for second-language writing. However, the student may well belong in your class, whether

114

through placement, promotion, or lack of alternatives. This chapter briefly describes some characteristics of second-language writers and their writing and offers practical advice on how to help your second-language writers succeed.

Understanding Second-Language Writers

There are no "typical" second-language writers. These writers defy generalization due to their different cultures, religions, ethnicity, language, economics, and development. In your class, you may find an eighteen-year-old with no college experience, a visiting professor doing postdoctoral research, or a student born in the United States who speaks English with peers and in school but speaks another language at home. These students do, however, have some common issues with writing.

Characteristics of second-language writers. Second-language writers differ from their native English-speaking counterparts in two important ways. Most significantly, they use rhetorical strategies from their first languages, often producing writing that seems redundant or repeating the same argument in slightly different ways in subsequent paragraphs. Second, while the stages in the writing process are the same, second-language writers approach each stage differently. Most noticeably, second-language writers are likely to have some or all of the following traits:

- Focus mainly on *what* to write rather than *how* to write
- Worry about vocabulary, constantly referring to a dictionary
- Compose slower and less fluently than native English speakers
- Don't proofread as much or as well as native English speakers
- Concentrate on errors at the sentence level to improve writing
- Make frequent errors, particularly with word usage
- May be unaware of expectations of readers in the United States
- May have little or no experience with or tolerance for peer review
- May have little or no experience with teachers' responses and response styles in the United States
- May be surprised by revision requirements

Common writing problems. Second-language writing may at first appear to be a jumble of errors, but close inspection reveals identifiable problem areas:

- Choice of word or word forms
- Article, pronoun, and preposition usage
- Verb tense, construction, number, and subject-verb agreement
- Sentence word order
- Countable and uncountable nouns and quantifiers
- Sentence boundaries: fragments, comma splices, and run-on sentences

Plagiarism. Even with awareness-building activities, plagiarism remains a problem for English as a second language (ESL) students for several reasons. First, what we call plagiarism in the United States is a practice encouraged in most Asian countries. For instance, Korean teachers give high grades when students imitate classic writers. In China, Confucianism still promotes the use of proverbs to communicate ancient messages about morality and universal truths. Thus, the second-language writer often grows up with a different perspective regarding ownership of text. An additional cause for plagiarism is the second-language writer's lack of adequate vocabulary to paraphrase original textual sources. Because of this lack of language proficiency, second-language writers may fear that they cannot express their ideas effectively in written English; instead, they tend to use what they have read without citing the source. Sometimes, as a last resort, a desperate second-language writer may ask someone else to write an entire paper.

Helping Second-Language Writers

Given what we know about second-language writers—who they are, what they need, and what they do—you can accommodate some of their unique needs, not as intimidating a task as it may seem. If your university offers ESL courses, the specialists teaching those classes can help you plan writing activities. Writing centers and student skills centers can supplement your teaching. Your main focus should be on grammar errors and flawed rhetorical structure, since these represent the most troublesome issues inherent in second-language writing.

Grammar. You shouldn't be an editor, nor are you expected to be an expert in second-language grammar issues. Instead, encourage your second-language writers to take charge of their own learning. Helping them to analyze their errors and to understand why they make them will promote independent learning. Students can keep grammar logs to provide a structure for error analysis. Logs can be a simple table divided into three columns: error, correction, and the grammatical rule that applies to the error. Students record in their logs errors that you highlight in their drafts, by either using electronic tools in a word processor or highlighting by hand. Marking drafts electronically allows the writers to paste errors directly into their log. Although this procedure adds extra work for them, second-language writers do need to keep track of their errors. This process will help them take a major part of the responsibility for analyzing errors and eventually move to self-monitoring, where students independently discover and correct their errors.

You can also devote some conference time to grammatical concerns. However, you should require that students arrive prepared, bringing their draft with highlighted errors and their completed grammar logs. In addition, students can work with second-language writing specialists in university writing centers. Or, you can send them to online grammar resources to work independently on their specific errors. By completing grammar exercises and taking quizzes, writers test their understanding and their ability to apply grammatical rules.

Response. Second-language writers welcome feedback; in fact, they expect it. Sometimes they want to be told how to fix their problems. Strategies that work well with native English speakers often fail with second-language writers. For example, second-language writers fail to discover errors when reading their texts aloud; instead, they will benefit more from frequent conferences and more individualized attention. In general, second-language writers are helped by response

- in the middle stages of the writing process;
- on all elements of their writing—content, rhetorical structure, grammar and mechanics;
- in clear and specific language; and
- on grammatical errors that interfere with comprehension.

Being Flexible

Working with second-language writers may at first seem a daunting task. But don't forget that good teaching for your native English-speaking writers is also good for second-language writers. Yes, second-language writers may need more of everything, but you'll find them grateful for everything you do for them. You'll need to remain flexible, as each student will be unique, with different needs and abilities. One of the most important things you can do is to listen to them; they'll tell you what they need. Their writing will also tell you. As you get to know your second-language writers, you'll appreciate all the ways they enrich the classroom, providing outside perspectives along with linguistic and cultural diversity.

Useful Readings

"ESL Instructors and Students." *Purdue Online Writing Lab (OWL)*. Purdue U, 12 Sept. 2012. Web. 9 Jan. 2013.

Guide to Grammar and Writing. Capital Community College Foundation, 2004. Web. 9 Jan. 2013.

Leki, Ilona. *Understanding ESL Writers: A Guide for Teachers*. Portsmouth, NH: Heinemann, 1992. Print. (Especially Chapters 4, 5, and 9.)

Silva, Tony. "Toward an Understanding of the Distinct Nature of L2 Writing: The ESL Research and Its Implications." *TESOL Quarterly* 27 (1993): 657–75. Print.

TESOL (Teachers of English to Speakers of Other Languages). TESOL, 2011. Web. 9 Jan. 2013.

20 Teaching Multimodal Writing

Carole Clark Papper

Multimodal writing is writing that uses more than one mode of expression, including some combination of words, images, audio, video, links, and so on. It's sometimes called *multimedia writing*. Much written communication today incorporates words, images, sounds, and links; our students now need to see that they can do the same thing in their writing, including their academic writing—and learn how to do it appropriately. If you are interested in exploring this kind of writing with your students, you could create a whole unit specifically focusing on it. You could also expand one of the genre assignments covered in this book to be multimodal.

Determining What Your Students Know about Working with Digital Media

Multimodal writing calls for students to work with digital media, so you'll want to find out how much your students know. The tricky part here is that it's likely that some in the class know next to nothing about working with digital media, while others are quite fluent. For the latter, a little guidance as to the specifics of audience, purpose, and assignment requirements may be all that is needed. For the former, some hands-on, even step-by-step "here's how to do it" instruction will be vital. The good news is that as the teacher, you don't need to be adept at all digital skills. You need to know some basics and where to send students for specific help—perhaps to computing services or a digital learning lab on campus, perhaps to their peers. (Caution here: if you're going to encourage peer-support, try to arrange collaborative working groups with both skills and personalities in mind—avoid putting a student with a tendency to dominate in a group of tech-neophytes, for example. When you set up groups, try to balance proficiency and need, introversion and extroversion, as well as gender.)

Most campuses offer computer support programs for faculty, where experienced staff will help you learn as much as you think you need. And in most classes, there will be students who already do a lot of multimodal composing—engaging them to help their peers is a great way of making the entire enterprise collaborative. During the first week of every class, I ask students about their experience with and interest in using digital media, and I always include questions about their knowledge of word-processing basics. (A complete tech survey is available in the "templates and worksheets" section of wwnorton .com/write/fieldguide/.) Yes, some do not know how to use basic functions to design verbal documents—and this in itself offers a great introduction to the role of design as a rhetorical device.

- *What kind of computer will you be using for this class?* desktop? laptop? iPad? Do you have your own, or will you be using the ones in the school labs? Is it a Mac or a PC? Which operating system runs your computer (e.g., Windows 7, Vista, OSX)?

- *How comfortable are you with basic operations,* such as startup/shutdown, loading software, creating folders and directories, saving, printing? Do you have any trouble entering text, using copy/paste, or undoing typing? Do you know how to find Help or Support?

- *What software is loaded onto your device?* What word processing program will you be using? Does your computer have video- or audio-editing software (e.g., *iMovie* or *Windows Movie Maker*)? If so, which version?

- *How well do you know your word processing program?* Do you use tools like grammar or spell check? Do you know how to track changes or insert com-

ments? Are you experienced with formatting a document to change fonts, adjust line spacing, set margins and tabs, insert headers or footers, create lists and tables? Don you know how to set up notes and works cited or reference lists?

- *Are you comfortable using the internet?* Can you attach files to emails? Do you know how to narrow results on a search site? Do you know how to download files? Have you ever created a webpage?

- *Do you have a digital camera?* Does it also record video?

- *Do you have a way to store and transport media files,* such as a flash drive or portable hard drive?

Adding Multimodal Elements to Writing Assignments

Probably the easiest way to get started teaching multimodal composition is to have students incorporate visual elements into something they've written. You could ask them to add photographs to a narrative, for example. Or they could create audio arguments by using a digital recorder and following NPR's *This I Believe* format (thisibelieve.org). Most students are adept at using social media and at using their phones to snap pictures—but you'll need to encourage them to do so with purpose. For example, a position paper on a campus issue could be enhanced by creating a slideshow of campus shots illustrating the issue. The student could read the written essay aloud while showing the slides—or create an audio file and integrate it into the slideshow. Students who are analyzing visual images (as in Hannah Berry's on pp. 52–57 of the *Field Guide*) could extend their analysis by recording other students responding to a few key questions about the ad or image they are analyzing.

Before working with multimodal texts, students need to learn to think differently about "composition," to imagine it not just as putting words together on a page, but as making something that informs or persuades or engages someone through a medium (or media) other than print. Student writers need to know that they are capable of effectively composing with more than words typed onto a keyboard. They need to feel confident in their ability to create meaning in these unexpected ways.

It's critical to ask students to reflect on what adding audio or visual elements accomplishes: How do these elements alter the essay? How did the students approach it? What did they find difficult? What, if anything, did it enable them to communicate that they couldn't do with words alone? Why?

Some introductory exercises. Students need to be encouraged to take ownership of their own learning, but to do so in an environment where they feel empowered to play with unfamiliar skills. Provide that by encouraging them to experiment in stages. Begin by having the class observe something—such as the *YouTube* video of

the gorilla and basketball experiment (youtube.com/watch?v=vJG698U2Mvo) or a staged interruption of your class, in which someone barges in with unexpected questions or creates a disturbance in some other way—and then question students about what they saw and what drew their attention. What did they notice (or miss), and why? Doing this gets them thinking about how we attend to the visual. You might also distribute pictures (photographs or postcards work best here) and ask each student to study the image he or she's been given and then explain to the class what seems to be going on in the picture, what might be the "story" here. After everyone has explained his or her image, ask them how they came to the conclusions they drew and what evidence in the picture itself led to those conclusions.

Ask them to write a brief reaction to these exercises in seeing and interpreting, and then discuss the relevance of the exercises to the assignment of incorporating visuals into a text. The idea here is to begin thinking about the impact of how what we see or hear can affect us in different ways than what we read.

Then you might try assigning a short narrative essay following regular essay conventions. Once they have written it and revised it successfully, ask them to tell the same story without using any words. They can compose in any other medium, just not the written word. What does this assignment accomplish? It forces them to translate their preferred and comfortable usual way of doing something into a new and—at least initially—perhaps not-so-comfortable form. But somewhere in the process, the task becomes less daunting and difficult. And once they share their "compositions" and explain their processes to each other, they'll see composition with fresh perspective.

Now they're ready to play.

Why Not Just Words?

Students need to realize that whatever mode or media they use—visuals, videos, audio, whatever—it needs to suit their purpose. Their choice should convey something specific, something that would not be as well expressed in another way. It's critical to match the mode to the desired effect. For example:

- Natural sound to establish setting
- Music to create or enhance mood
- Video to depict movement
- Spoken words to add veracity

Natural sound to establish setting. Describing the sounds of a city—New York or Chicago or Los Angeles—can be done with words, but a recording of those sounds can add depth to an essay on urban life because it will capture multiple elements at once: screeching brakes, honking horns, the whine of machinery, the subterranean thunder of a train in the subway, the shouts of street vendors, people talking in a variety of languages at varying volume. Conversely, for an essay set in the calm of a country meadow, broken only by the occasional birdcall, how much more effective it can be to let your audience hear what you hear.

Music to create or enhance mood. Think about your favorite films or TV shows and how important music is to creating a mood, emphasizing some aspect of a character or giving us a sense of where the action is going. Good sound engineers will tell you the score shouldn't intrude, but they'll also admit that a scene can be completely altered by changing the background music. Just think about how iconic some scores have become; without seeing the screen, we only need to hear the first few notes to know a *Harry Potter* film is about to play.

Video to depict movement. Sportswriters can be brilliant at describing action, but even the best written description cannot compete with actually seeing the game. And while the best film and theater critics can almost make you "see" the action they're describing, watching the actual film or play provides a much richer experience than static words on a page can.

Spoken words to add veracity. Writers can always quote what others say, but adding audio files can let those others speak for themselves—and can convey something a written quotation cannot. The idiosyncrasies of our speech—the patterns, intonations, and accents—mark us in unique ways that cannot be conveyed as effectively in a transcript. Listen, for example, to a seven-year-old boy's list of thirty things he believes from NPR's *This I Believe*:

npr.org/templates/story/story.php?story Id=99478226. How much more poignant is the list when we hear it in the child's voice than if an adult had read it? What does the boy's voice add? If you assign your students to compose an oral history, they can transcribe the interviews they do, but if they record the interviews, they can provide an audience with a more intimate experience of the subject.

Guiding Students through the Process of Multimodal Writing

Students know how to compose a traditional written essay, or at least have a sense of many of the things they'll need to do: they choose or are given a topic; consider their purpose, audience, and other aspects of their rhetorical situation; brainstorm, make lists, or generate material in other ways; plan their approach and organization; and then type the words onto a screen or write them on a piece of paper. They might use the available technology to manipulate those words—cut and paste them to shape and reshape the message, add boldface or italics to headings or key points, use grammar- and spell-check—and then save the document to upload or email it to a classmate or teacher for feedback before revising. In a multimodal essay, students begin from the same place. They are still creating a text; and just as in a paper text, they'll want to select the elements that will most effectively achieve their purposes as writers.

Choosing a topic that matters—to writer and audience. It's always important to match the assignment goals to the writers' interests and abilities, but in multimodal composing it's critical. The assignment shouldn't expect students to include all the available multimodal options, only those that will be most effective for their individual rhetorical situation. Assigned topics and requirements for use of media and modes of expression need to be broad enough that students can find solid ground on which to build their personal take on the topic—to feel comfortable with what they're saying and how they want to say it. As with any writing, students need to consider their rhetorical situation:

- *What is your purpose?* What do you want your audience to take away from this piece?

- *Who is your audience?* For whom are you composing this? How will they affect the choices you make about media or modes of expression? What might they already know about your topic? What will you need to include or emphasize to ensure they understand?

- *Consider your stance*—why did this topic engage you, and what's your attitude toward it? And how do you want your audience to perceive you as you present this topic to them?

- *What genre are you using, and why?* Does it allow for (or call for) you to present information visually—or to link to data or other perspectives?

Does the genre have any organizational requirements that would affect where you place links or visuals? Do these elements reflect the proper tone for your genre?

- *What medium and which modes of expression*—words, images (which kinds?), audio (which kinds?), links, presentation slides—will work best for your purpose and audience? You want the modes you select to be the most effective for the message you want to convey and the audience you have targeted.

Exploring the topic and generating ideas and text. Have students begin by assessing what they already know about their topic and determining what they need to discover. Gathering as much information as possible before starting to compose enables them to make good decisions about how best to present their arguments. Which would be more effective: still images presented in a dramatic setting or a short video? Would an audio clip add immediacy and authenticity?

Thinking hard about which media or modes will be best suited to the specific rhetorical situation. Is there a strong visual aspect to the topic? Is it necessary to demonstrate movement through time? How important are actual sounds and voices to the purpose? Is there a need for textual explanation? Using questions like these will help student writers frame their compositions most effectively.

Selecting and organizing material. Selecting and organizing nonverbal material to support the claims being made will depend, in part, on the genre. For example, a narrative organized chronologically could use a sequence of photos over the time involved to good effect. An argument against bullying in schools might want to incorporate one of the videos from the National Bullying Prevention Site at pacer.org/bullying/video. If the assignment is to review or critique a work of art, including images of both the work itself but others by the same artist or of the same type will bring the essay to life.

Keeping track of all the steps. Students will need to think about all the steps specific to multimodal writing: planning, recording, downloading/uploading, editing, publishing. Having them create a project log will help them keep track of progress.

Some Cautions for Teachers

- If at all possible, before you make assignments that require using multiple modes or media, you should do the assignment yourself; this enables you to anticipate and address difficulties that may arise.

- Working in multiple modes and media can take much longer than expected. One way to help students manage their time is by having them lay out a rough storyboard and a timeline, working backward from the assignment due date. Be sure to help them include all the steps and stages of development. Then stay on top of each student's or each group's progress—perhaps by requiring them to keep a project log–and be prepared to intervene if necessary.

- If students are combining video, still images, and audio files, they need to make sure the elements function smoothly together. Edit sound *before* adding it to the video.

- Also, warn students to *back up everything*—to devise a clear (and simple) system for naming and dating drafts and elements of the essay and to save the video, audio, and verbal text at each step. Pay attention to how the student constructs each element separately.

Responding to and Evaluating Student Projects

Whether you're responding to an essay that's all words, a podcast, or a spoken presentation with slides, the basic principles are the same. Our approach to assessment needs to be grounded in our assignments—students need clear and detailed assignments in which our criteria for assessing their work are laid out in advance. So we need to know exactly why we are asking them to do something and precisely what we want them to derive from the experience. Laying all this out in advance enables the evaluative process to become part of the learning.

The guidelines we give should specify the genre, identify the target audience and purpose (or require students to do so), state clearly our expectations for the finished product (including parameters for length and acceptable types of material that may be included), and give specific objectives for the assignment, which should in turn address one or more of the course objectives. Providing students a rubric for evaluation when you give them the assignment (such as the one on p. 125) turns the assessment process into part of the learning process.

Other Things to Consider

Be sure to find out in advance what technology and tech support for multimodal writing are available on campus for your students. At some schools, individual departments make equipment available for students (audio and video recorders, still cameras, computers equipped with software for making and editing movies), while other schools have a central location for such equipment. And still other schools have nothing generally available, so students must provide for themselves. Ascertain what support is available in the classroom where you will be teaching: is there a projector? screen? wi-fi? internet access? Are there outlets enough for multiple students to connect their laptops? What sort of support is available from IT or computing services for students who want to learn software?

Evaluation Rubric

For each of the following items, indicate your comfort level by checking the box under the appropriate number from 5 (maximum) to 1 (minimum).

1. Planning	5	4	3	2	1
Project proposal is clear and specific.					
Storyboard/timeline is detailed.					
Progress log is accurate and thorough.					
Comments—what worked well, what needs to be improved:					

2. Rhetorical Situation	5	4	3	2	1
The purpose is clear.					
Needs of the target audience are addressed.					
The stance is consistent and clear.					
Genre requirements are met, tone is appropriate.					
Medium, mode, and design choices are appropriate.					
Comments—what worked well, what needs to be improved:					

3. Presentation	5	4	3	2	1
Focus is effective for genre and topic.					
Elements are appropriate for subject and genre.					
Use of material is creative and innovative.					
Content and approach are credible.					
Project addresses all points of the assignment.					
Comments—what worked well, what needs to be improved:					

Don't forget to teach or remind students about the basics, like *GoogleDocs,* blogs, and wikis for collaborative work; *Flickr, PhotoBucket,* and *Picasa* for photo sharing (and *Instagram* for smartphone photos); and *PowerPoint, Keynote,* and *Prezi* for slide presentation. If your students want to create and publish videos, have them use *Vimeo* rather than *YouTube;* it is secure, offering password protection and thus restricted access (an important consideration for potential intellectual property issues). There are also a lot of tutorials available online for using presentation software and making films and videos.

Identify what software and what versions of it are available to your students, either on campus-based computers or their own, and what experience they have using it.

Useful Readings

Harding, Matt. "Dancing to Connect to a Global Tribe." *This I Believe.* NPR, 29 Mar. 2009. Web. 3 Jan. 2013.

Matt Harding created a video of himself dancing "terribly," as he says, in a variety of places around the world. He posted it on his website, it went viral, and millions watched and responded. The NPR staff then invited him to create an essay for their *This I Believe* program. Here's a link to a page where you can click on links to the video and to Harding's audio of the essay and read the essay text: npr.org/2009/03/29/102423050 /dancing-to-connect-to-a-global-tribe. Pay attention to how Harding constructs each separately.

Walls, Douglas. "An 'A' Word Production: Authentic Design." *Kairos* 13.1 (2008): n. pag. Web. 3 Jan. 2013.

This playfully constructed multimodal essay warns digital scholars: "We need to understand that meaning is not inherent in our tools (writing, media, ideas, language) nor does meaning reside in ourselves." Note how Walls creates his essay, the very simple tools he uses to convey a serious and complex message: kairos.technorhetoric.net/13.1 /disputatio/walls/index.htm.

Helping Struggling Writers **21** and Readers

Basic writers. Developmental writers. Remedial writers. Students in stretch courses, accelerated learning programs (ALP), integrated reading and writing programs (IRR), developmental reading and English (DRE). Students in our classes whose writing is more problematic than that of most of their classmates. Whatever they are called and whatever course they're in, we all have students who struggle with writing and reading for various reasons. They have trouble reading critically; they have trouble with sentence grammar and punctuation; their writing shows the influence of their home language or oral speech patterns. In many cases, they experience difficulty with college because they lack so-called noncognitive skills or are unfamiliar with the cultures and practices of academic life, including—but not limited to—academic writing. There are ways of helping students with such problems, and this chapter offers some suggestions.

Reading Strategies

Students in basic writing or other remedial writing courses often struggle with reading, and Chapter 41 offers a number of READING STRATEGIES to help them read with greater accuracy and critical awareness. You might start by having students work through the questions in the section on Taking Stock of Your Reading (pp. 396–97), which invites them to examine their own reading process as a first step in improving it. The section on Preparing to Read (p. 398) offers a method to help students read more intentionally by articulating their current knowledge of the topic, their purposes for reading, and what they learn from the reading. Finally, see the advice on Reflecting, Rereading, and Persisting (pp. 404–05), which aims to help students persist when they're called on to read difficult or boring texts. (Chapter 30 in this guide to teaching provides additional tips for using the strategies to good advantage.)

You might also consider having students work with Chapter 8 to ANALYZE TEXTS, either as an in-class activity or as a brief assignment sequence. Doing so might give them additional practice in reading texts closely, analytically, and rhetorically.

Some students' problems with reading stem from lack of practice. Those students may benefit from a program of regular assigned reading—from readings in *The Norton*

Field Guide itself to online newspapers such as the *New York Times*. One way to monitor such assignments is to ask students to respond to the readings in various ways by writing what Wright State TA Adam Kuchta calls Writing Journal Bookmarks. He divides sheets of paper into three horizontal strips and prints a different prompt at the top of each strip. For each reading they do, students pick one of the prompts to write on. Some examples include the following:

- Copy down a favorite one-sentence quotation from the piece. In two to three sentences, explain why you find this quote to be inspiring, interesting, or useful to you as a writer.

- Authors often include visuals (charts, graphs, pictures, tables, drawings, cartoons, etc.) to help make or reinforce their points and make information easier to read. In a sentence or two, describe one visual in this reading. Then explain what information it is communicating.

- Copy one well-written sentence from this reading. Tell how the author's sentence structure or word choice makes this sentence effective.

Sentence Grammar and Punctuation

Although many writing instructors believe that instruction in formal grammar will help students write better, over 100 years of research—by people who shared that belief—have failed to demonstrate the connection. Patrick Hartwell, writing in 1985, began his essay on teaching grammar by quoting from Richard Braddock, Richard Lloyd-Jones, and Lowell Schoer's 1963 work, *Research in Written Composition*:

> In view of the widespread agreement of research studies based upon many types of students and teachers, the conclusion can be stated in strong and unqualified terms: the teaching of formal grammar has a negligible or, because it usually displaces some instruction and practice in composition, even a harmful effect on improvement in writing. (37–38)

Whether or not one believes in the general usefulness of teaching grammar, students need help with the grammar of what they write. Perhaps the best way to deal with this conflict is to adopt the position that faculty at the Community College of Baltimore County have taken: "Whatever pedagogy we use, the goal of our efforts with grammar and punctuation is to produce students who are better editors of their writing and not to produce better grammarians" (Adams). Peter Dow Adams, who directs that college's accelerated learning program, continues: "Agreeing on that goal, we can then have a slightly different and more fruitful discussion. We can explore the question of what a student needs to know to edit his or her writing effectively." Methods of acquiring these editing skills include reading and internalizing the rules of written English the way we learned the rules of oral language: by using it. In other words, by writing—a lot.

More specifically, students can benefit from sentence combining and from copying and imitation.

Sentence combining. This method, whose effectiveness has been demonstrated by research, is simple: the instructor gives students several simple sentences and asks them to combine the sentences into one longer, more complex sentence. Here's an example from *The Writer's Options*, a sentence-combining textbook by Max Morenberg and Jeff Sommers (25):

> The sauce steams.
> The sauce bubbles.
> Its smell fills the room.
> The smell is slightly sweet.

Students may combine those sentences in several ways, including these:

> The sauce steams and bubbles and fills the room with a slightly sweet smell.
> The sauce steams and bubbles, filling the room with a slightly sweet smell.
> Steaming and bubbling, the sauce fills the room with its slightly sweet smell.

This activity can then lead to a discussion of the effects of each version and how each emphasizes different aspects of the sauce's description. Rather than studying sentences as being right or wrong, students work with sentences as flexible units that can take many shapes. *The Writer's Options* and other textbooks take the exercise further, by including paragraphs and essays in which the sentences must be combined to make sense in the context of the whole and also by focusing on—and having students practice—various strategies or structures (for example, coordination and subordination, absolutes, coherence, and tone).

Copying and imitation. Learning to write by copying passages has a history going back to Cicero and Quintilian and has had advocates ranging from Edward P. J. Corbett to Malcolm X. As my colleague Gerald Nelms notes, "The purpose of imitation is to increase your stylistic repertoire—that is, the amount of stylistic options available to you as you make decisions when composing." Corbett offers other advice for effective imitation and copying:

- Copy regularly and systematically—ideally, every day at the same time.
- Read the entire passage before beginning.
- Concentrate on the copying.
- Spend no more than 15–20 minutes at a sitting.
- Write by hand, with a pen or pencil, to slow yourself down and internalize the writer's style.
- Copy slowly and accurately—copy every word exactly as it appears on paper or screen.
- Vary the writers you imitate. (qtd. in Nelms)

Nelms offers one more bit of advice: after each session, spend a few minutes reflecting in writing on the text you have just copied, focusing on its stylistic features, not its content. Does the writer use grammar or punctuation that you don't? Do some words stand out for you? Are some words spelled differently than you expected? If a word is misspelled, is it a typo—or intentionally misspelled? How can you characterize the voice of the text? What other features of the text did you find interesting or unusual? (1–3).

Home Language and Dialect Influence

Often students in basic writing classes write as they speak—and if the features of their home language differ markedly from those of Edited American English (EAE), their writing will be deemed unacceptable in most academic contexts. The instructor's first move should be to acknowledge the legitimacy of the student's home language or dialect, because in sociolinguistic terms, it's every bit as much a language as EAE—though inappropriate in academic settings. Once it's been established that what you're trying to do is extend the student's linguistic repertoire, to help him or her communicate with more audiences and thus to be more rhetorically effective, here are a couple of ways to help students see the differences between their home language and EAE:

Identifying patterns. When you're responding to a student's drafts, pick one or two things he or she does repeatedly—

drop the final "s" from plural nouns, for example—and circle or highlight several instances. Then point them out and have the student find as many more as she or he can. Once the student recognizes the difference between the way the feature works in his or her home language and the way it's done in EAE, move on to another feature, and then another.

Translation exercises. Another way to help students understand the differences between their home language and EAE is to ask them to translate passages of fictional literature written in dialect into EAE and then to identify the differences between the original and the translation. Students may then be able to identify features and recognize the rules governing them as they turn the dialect into standard—and if not, you can help them do so. (You can also ask students to turn passages of EAE into their home language—and then translate it back, and then examine the differences between their version and the original.)

Academic Writing

Writers who are struggling with sentence punctuation, wording, organization, and other basic aspects of writing are likely to have even more difficulty mastering academic writing than other students. So teaching them the conventions of academic writing and offering them many opportunities to practice and revise are crucial.

Chapter 6 in the *Field Guide* offers an introduction to the key features of WRITING IN ACADEMIC CONTEXTS, and the corresponding section in this guide to teaching (pp. 165–67) offers advice on how to go about teaching it—along with references to several useful articles.

"Soft" or "Noncognitive" Skills

A growing body of evidence suggests that students' success in school relies less on intelligence than on a group of traits that include, as journalist Paul Tough describes them, "an inclination to persist at a boring and often unrewarding task; the ability to delay gratification; the tendency to follow through on a plan" (xix). These traits, which are described variously as *grit, resilience, self-efficacy,* and *character,* often make the difference between students who pass and those who fail—or drop out or disappear before the end of the term. Granted, it's not part of our charge as writing teachers to try to change our students' characters, but it's useful to recognize that many students who fail do so not because of their intelligence but because they lack "qualities of motivation and perseverance" and "good study habits and time management skills" (Bowen, Chingos, and McPherson 124).

By teaching writing in sequenced assignments, with careful attention to the various aspects of the processes of writing, we can help these students manage their time. And as we confer with students, get to know them, and praise what they do well while challenging them to revise repeatedly to improve their writing, we can help them be motivated and persevere. Working with them to find appropriate research sources can help them be resourceful. Increasing the amount and frequency of self-assessment and reflection we require can help them better understand their own strengths and challenges as writers, readers, and students. Holding them accountable, by insisting that work be turned in on time in the proper medium and format and that your attendance policy be followed, can help them improve their sense of personal responsibility. And, as successful students and professionals, we can offer our own stories of overcoming difficulties and working for long-term goals.

We can also use informal writing and other writing assignments to help students improve their noncognitive skills. Skip Downing, a student success consultant and longtime community college English professor, offers many journal assignments that can help students become more successful. These include identifying desired outcomes, both short-term and long-term, that will keep them motivated and working (70), analyzing their use of their time so as to learn to manage it to best advantage (106), and developing personal rules for succeeding in college. (Downing suggests these as the first three: 1. show up. 2. do your very best work. 3. participate actively [194].)

Knowledge of Academic Culture

Many students, especially first-generation ones, are struggling because they don't know how academic institutions work, from the odd terms we use (*Registrar? Bursar? Associate Dean? Do I call my teacher "Doctor," "Professor," "Miss," "Ms.," or nothing at all?*) to basic differences between high school and college. For example, I recently set up a conference with one of my first-year students. We didn't connect, however, because I assumed that we would meet in my office whereas she assumed that I would be in the classroom where our class met. Some students believe that if they attend class, they won't fail—even if they do no work. And some expect us to go over each day's assignments in class, while we assume that since all the assignments are listed on the syllabus or posted online, students will look there for them. They see the library as a place where you get shushed or yelled at for talking—not an inviting place to study staffed with librarians eager to help. And so on.

The point is that for many students, and especially those who have nothing but television and movie portrayals of college classrooms and culture to rely on, colleges are mystifying and disorienting—and that can lead students to feel estranged, outsiders. If they are commuting while living off campus and, as is likely, working at a job, they are likely to come to campus for their classes and then leave, further alienating them from the life of the school and from their fellow students. The less students identify themselves as college students and as students at their own school in particular, the weaker their connection to it is—and the less likely they are to persevere.

You can help in several ways. One way is simply to define terms as they come up: "You can pay your technology fee at the bursar's office—that's the office that handles money." Explaining differences between high school and college can be very helpful to confused students; cutting them some slack during the first couple of weeks when they get lost on campus or find out just how difficult finding a parking spot can be can also be useful. Consider holding some question-and-answer sessions early in the term: have students write questions they have about college on an index card and give them to you, and take 5 or 10 minutes to answer them over the next weeks or so. Or you might ask students to write a PROFILE (*Field Guide* Chapter 16) of someplace or someone on campus and then present what they've learned to the class.

Suggested Course Outlines

For teaching a stretch course in first-year writing. Stretch writing courses, which were first developed at Arizona State University, are based on the premise that students' writing abilities develop at different paces: some students need more time and practice than others to gain the competence needed for success as college writers. So stretch courses *stretch* the instruction normally given in a single writing course over two terms. As Jim Garrett, professor of English at California State University, Los Angeles, explains,

> Time and community are two of the three characteristics found in all stretch composition programs. When given more time to write, revise, and discuss writing, students do better with their writing coursework and feel better about their learning experience, especially when that experience takes place within a community of writers. Cohort models, where students stay with the same instructor and same students, lead to effective learning (and writing) communities and allow the instructor to determine pacing and even curriculum appropriate to a specific group of students. The third key characteristic of stretch programs is college credit for all writing classes. College-level work should be rewarded with college-level credit. Since both the stretch version and the unstretched version of ENGL 101 achieve the same learning objectives, stretch courses should be credit-bearing.

Here are sample outlines for the stretch writing course sequence at Wright State University. The two fourteen-week-semester courses ask students to complete the same kinds of writing assignments that are required in our regular first-year course, but provide much more time for repetition (many students need practice runs with unfamiliar genres and assignments and do much better the second time around), work on sentences and editing, and individual conferences. Students are encouraged to revisit relevant chapters in the *Norton Field Guide to Writing with Handbook* as needed, using it as a reference tool rather than simply as a textbook. Norton's online resources are also useful: the companion website (wwnorton.com/write/fieldguide) offers exercises and tutorials, and more. In addition, the *Field Guide* Coursepack can be customized to include a chapter on "Developing Paragraphs."

First Course

Week	In-Class Activities	Assignment
1	Introduce syllabus, course policies, expected outcomes, classroom and electronic composing environments, campus resources. Explain expectations for college courses, including time management. Discuss study skills, introductory writing assignments, and reading exercises.	Ch. 6, WRITING IN ACADEMIC CONTEXTS; Ch. 55, WRITING ONLINE; Ch. 24, GENERATING IDEAS AND TEXT

Week	In-Class Activities	Assignment
2	Additional introductory writing assignments and reading exercises; in-class workshops on reading comprehension and writing summaries; make **Summary assignment.**	Chs. 1–5, "Rhetorical Situations"; Ch. 41, READING STRATEGIES; Ch. 47, QUOTING, PARAPHRASING, AND SUMMARIZING
3	Additional in-class workshops on reading comprehension and writing summaries. Lessons on restating author's thesis in own words; recapping in own words author's points; reducing the original text to main ideas in logical, fluent paragraphs with transitional elements; using third-person voice, present tense, and assertive verbs; avoiding personal judgment and documenting text. Drafting the summary.	Ch. 41, READING STRATEGIES; Ch. 47, QUOTING, PARAPHRASING, AND SUMMARIZING; Ch. 31, GUIDING YOUR READER; Ch. 25, DRAFTING; may also include "Developing Paragraphs" from the Coursepack
4	*Revision, editing, MUGS, conventions, and peer review*: in-class workshop on mechanics, usage, grammar, and spelling (MUGS) conventions for coherence, meaning, and credibility. Review summary assignment, reading comprehension, and academic conventions.	Ch. 27, GETTING RESPONSE AND REVISING; Ch. 28, EDITING AND PROOFREADING; Handbook as needed; exercises on Paragraphs, Sentences, Words, and Punctuation as needed from the companion website
5	Introduce **Short Analysis assignment** (such as an ad, commercial, or short text). Lessons on articulating and assessing author's thesis, purposes, audiences, contexts, bias, and credibility.	Ch. 8, ANALYZING TEXTS or the Visual Rhetoric exercises on the companion website (though having students examine and discuss the text on their own may help them develop confidence in their own critical abilities, which can then be expanded in the longer text analysis to come)
6	Continued lessons, discussion, and exercises on short analysis. Exercises on drawing conclusions about the effectiveness of author's persuasive strategies. Supporting analysis with evidence. Preliminary writing: proposal, outline, or other exercises. Introduce **optional midterm portfolio.**	Ch. 29, COMPILING A PORTFOLIO

Week	In-Class Activities	Assignment
7	Draft the short analysis assignment.	Review Chs. 24, GENERATING IDEAS AND TEXT, and 25, DRAFTING, as needed
8	*Revising, editing, MUGS, conventions, and peer review*: in-class workshop on mechanics, usage, grammar, and spelling (MUGS) conventions for coherence, meaning, and credibility. May include individual conferences.	Use or review as needed: Ch. 27, GETTING RESPONSE AND REVISING; Ch. 28, EDITING AND PROOFREADING; Handbook as needed; exercises on Paragraphs, Sentences, Words, and Punctuation from the companion website
9	Introduce **Text Analysis assignment**. Review summarizing. Review articulating and assessing author's thesis, purposes, audiences, contexts, bias, and credibility.	Ch. 8, ANALYZING TEXTS; Ch. 41, READING STRATEGIES
10	Review drawing conclusions about the effectiveness of author's writing strategies. Supporting analysis with textual evidence. Preliminary writing: proposal, outline, or other development exercises.	Ch. 24, GENERATING IDEAS AND TEXT; Ch. 46, SYNTHESIZING IDEAS; Ch. 47, QUOTING, PARAPHRASING, AND SUMMARIZING; Ch. 48, ACKNOWLEDGING SOURCES, AVOIDING PLAGIARISM
11	Draft the text analysis.	Ch. 24, GENERATING IDEAS AND TEXT, and Ch. 25, DRAFTING as needed
12	*Revision, editing, MUGS, conventions, and peer review*: in-class workshop on mechanics, usage, grammar, and spelling (MUGS) conventions for coherence, meaning, and credibility. Introduction to self-assessment.	Use or review as needed: Ch. 26, ASSESSING YOUR OWN WRITING; Ch. 27, GETTING RESPONSE AND REVISING; Ch. 28, EDITING AND PROOFREADING; Handbook as needed; exercises on Paragraphs, Sentences, Words, and Punctuation on the companion website
13	**Portfolio** or otherwise collect students' work. Self-evaluation with course outcome assessment workshop.	Use or review as needed: Ch. 26, ASSESSING YOUR OWN WRITING; Ch. 29, COMPILING A PORTFOLIO
14	**Portfolio or final collection** prep: final revisions of student work and course evaluations. May include individual conferences.	All chapters previously studied as needed; exercises from the companion website as needed
15	**Finals Week: Final Portfolio Due**	

Second Course

Week	In-Class Activities	Assignment
1	Introduce syllabus, course policies, expected outcomes, info about classroom and electronic environments for composing. Review concepts and ideas from first course, including summarizing and analyzing.	Chs. 1–6, "Rhetorical Situations"; Ch. 55, WRITING ONLINE; Ch. 47, QUOTING, PARAPHRASING, AND SUMMARIZING; and Ch. 8, ANALYZING TEXTS
2	Introduce **Preliminary Research assignment** (such as annotated bibliography, report, I-search, or similar assignment). Discuss topic selection and focus.	Ch. 9, REPORTING INFORMATION; Ch. 43, DEVELOPING A RESEARCH PLAN; as needed: Ch. 24, GENERATING IDEAS AND TEXT
3	Discuss locating and distinguishing academic and professional sources from others, evaluating web sources. Librarians visit class to help students research topics.	Ch. 44, FINDING SOURCES; Ch. 45, EVALUATING SOURCES; as needed: Ch. 41, READING STRATEGIES
4	Lessons on MLA documentation and citation; practice integrating basic paraphrases, quotes, and summarized ideas, and avoiding plagiarism. Preliminary writing: proposal, outline, or other development exercises.	Ch. 47, QUOTING, PARAPHRASING, AND SUMMARIZING; Ch. 48, ACKNOWLEDGING SOURCES, AVOIDING PLAGIARISM (including the exercise and the "Academic Honesty and Avoiding Plagiarism" tutorial on the companion website); Ch. 49, DOCUMENTATION, and Ch. 50, MLA STYLE (with help from the MLA citation drills on the companion website)
5	Draft Preliminary Research assignment.	Ch. 24, GENERATING IDEAS AND TEXT, and Ch. 25, DRAFTING as needed
6	*Revision, editing, MUGS, conventions, and peer review*: in-class workshop on mechanics, usage, grammar, and spelling (MUGS) conventions for coherence, meaning, and credibility. **Preliminary Research Portfolio** due: include copies of all sources and 2–3-page assessment of your work.	Use or review as needed: Ch. 26, ASSESSING YOUR OWN WRITING; Ch. 27, GETTING RESPONSE AND REVISING; Ch. 28, EDITING AND PROOFREADING; Handbook as needed; exercises on Paragraphs, Sentences, Words, and Punctuation on the companion website; Ch. 29, COMPILING A PORTFOLIO
7	Introduce **Researched Analysis assignment**. Review signal phrasing and integrating paraphrases, quotes, and	Ch. 17, TOPIC PROPOSALS; Ch. 8, ANALYZING TEXTS; Ch. 47, QUOTING, PARAPHRASING, AND SUMMARIZING

Week	In-Class Activities	Assignment
	summaries. Preliminary writing: proposal, outline, other exercises.	
8	Draft Researched Analysis assignment.	Ch. 24, GENERATING IDEAS AND TEXT, and Ch. 25, DRAFTING, as needed
9	*Revision, editing, MUGS, conventions, and peer review*: in-class workshop on mechanics, usage, grammar, and spelling (MUGS) conventions for coherence, meaning, and credibility. In-depth self-assessment.	Use or review as needed: Ch. 26, ASSESSING YOUR OWN WRITING; Ch. 27, GETTING RESPONSE AND REVISING; Ch. 28, EDITING AND PROOFREADING; Handbook as needed; exercises on Paragraphs, Sentences, Words, and Punctuation on the companion website
10	Introduction to **Critical Presentation:** Lessons on collaborating, presenting information, selecting media, analyzing and accommodating audience, and incorporating technology.	Ch. 23, COLLABORATING; Ch. 2, AUDIENCE; Ch. 56, GIVING PRESENTATIONS
11	In-class drafting, practicing collaboration, and gathering information. *Revision, editing, MUGS, conventions, and peer review* of **Critical Presentation** assignment. May include individual conferences between instructor and students.	Use or review as needed: Ch. 26, ASSESSING YOUR OWN WRITING; Ch. 27, GETTING RESPONSE AND REVISING; Ch. 28, EDITING AND PROOFREADING; Handbook as needed; exercises on Paragraphs, Sentences, Words, and Punctuation on the companion website
12	Finish and deliver **Critical Presentations**	
13	**Portfolio** or otherwise collect students' work. Self-evaluation with course outcome assessment workshop.	Use or review whatever is needed
14	**Portfolio or final collection** prep: final revisions of student work and course evaluations. May include individual conferences.	Use or review whatever is needed
15	**Finals Week: Final Portfolio Due**	

For teaching ALP, IRR, DRE, or other accelerated learning courses. The Accelerated Learning Program (ALP) concept was first developed at the Community College of Baltimore County, Maryland, and is now being adopted at many other schools. A form of mainstreaming, ALP courses allow students who place into an upper-level developmental writing course to register for certain sections of the regular first-year writing course. At CCBC, these courses include eight developmental students and twelve nondevelopmental students. As the ALP website explains, "These same 8 ALP students also register for a section of the ALP companion course which meets in the class period immediately following the ENGL 101 section. The same instructor teaches both the 101 and the companion course. The ALP section functions more or less as a workshop to provide the support the basic writers need to succeed in ENGL 101."

Other programs, including many in Virginia and North Carolina, use the same ALP format but integrate reading and writing in both the first-year course and the ALP course. To take one example, the North Carolina Community College System's curriculum guide offers the following suggestions for its ALP course, DRE 099:

- Assignments and readings for DRE 099 should complement and be similar in theme to ENG 111 [the regular first-year course] assignments and readings.
- Typically, the assignments for DRE 099 should be shorter than those in ENG 111.

- Writing assignments may include metacognitive reflections on essays composed in ENG 111 or read in ENG 111. These activities will reinforce awareness of both the reading and writing processes.
- Class time may be used to reinforce the just-in-time approach to grammar by focusing on issues reflected in student writing.
- Students should perform close-readings on texts related to ENG 111 material to reinforce reading strategies so they become more comfortable with texts at a career and college-ready level. Students may respond to these related texts using text-to-world connections.

In ALP courses, then, instruction is coordinated and paired with whatever is being taught in the first-year course, and because the ALP courses are smaller, much of the instruction can be individualized. The *Field Guide* can work well in such courses because it includes relatively short chapters on all the topics students are likely to need help with—and is designed to be consulted as needed rather than to be read front to back. So one student may be working on generating ideas and text for an essay (Ch. 24) while another is working on writing a good ending for an essay (Ch. 30), a third is doing an exercise online to better understand how to use semicolons (wwnorton.com/write), and a fourth is studying the chapter on paragraphs that's available in the *Field Guide* Coursepack.

The *Field Guide* can be used as the framework for an ALP course, too. Let's assume that you're teaching an ALP section of a semester-long first-year writing course and using the *Field Guide with Readings and Handbook*:

14-Week First-Year Writing Course

Week	Assignment
1	RHETORICAL SITUATIONS (Chs. 1–6)
2–4	ANALYZING A TEXT (Chs. 8, 41)
5–7	ANALYZING A SECOND TEXT (Chs. 8, 41)
8–11	TOPIC PROPOSALS (Chs. 17)
	ANNOTATED BIBLIOGRAPHIES (Ch. 12)
	REPORTING INFORMATION (Chs. 9, 43–50)
12–14	TOPIC PROPOSALS (Ch. 17)
	ANNOTATED BIBLIOGRAPHIES (Ch. 9)
	ARGUING A POSITION (Chs. 10, 33, 43–50)

In the first-year course, you'd likely focus on the activities in the Genre chapters as outlined above, bringing in Processes, Strategies, and Media/Design chapters as needed and having students read essays in the Readings section of the book as well as those in the Genre chapters.

In the ALP course, then, you could spend more time helping students develop their critical reading skills and formal and informal writing skills. For example, during the two Analyzing Texts assignment sequences, students could first spend time working with a single essay, perhaps "'A More Perfect Union': Why It Worked," Roy Peter Clark's analysis of Barack Obama's speech on race (p. 684), reading, discussing, and writing about it. The questions and activities for "Engaging with the Text" on pp. 690–91 could help them to do so. Then you might assign another speech—perhaps Obama's second inaugural speech—for them to read and analyze briefly in writing. In class, you could also have them compare that speech with the one Clark analyzes.

And there might be material in the *Field Guide* that you would assign in the first-year writing course but not spend much class time on that could become grist for class activities in the ALP course: invention activities in Ch. 24, metacognitive activities in Ch. 26 to help students think about their own writing processes and to take stock of their reading processes in Ch. 41, help with academic research in Chs. 43 and 44—just to name a few.

At the same time, ALP course time could be devoted to issues of paragraphing, sentence control, and punctuation that often bedevil basic writers. You could analyze several readings to study different kinds of paragraphs. For instance, you might compare the rhetorical effects of the brief paragraphs in Brian Stelter's "'We Are the 99 Percent' Joins the Cultural and Political Lexicon" (p. 679) with the longer paragraphs in Diana George's "Changing the Face of Poverty" (p. 667)—and give ALP students additional practice with reading and analysis along the way. And individual students or small groups with similar problems in their writing could be referred to appropriate places in the Handbook (coupled with instruction in how to use a handbook!) and to exercises on the companion website (wwnorton.com/write) or those found in the *Field Guide* Coursepack—which they could do collaboratively or alone while you monitor their progress.

ALP courses, then, provide an opportunity to explore issues students need help with that are rarely possible within the confines and rush of a normal first-year writing course.

For teaching basic writing. The basic writing course outlined below is similar to the Developmental Writing course taught at Wright State University, which meets four days weekly over fourteen weeks. The course includes the following assignments. The first helps students understand their own writing processes, strengths, and challenges by asking them to write a literacy narrative. However, these students also usually need practice and increased fluency in reading; a lengthy unit on text analysis focuses students' attention on their needs as college-level readers. The final major writing assignment introduces students to academic research and documentation—but leaves the heavy lifting of documentation in MLA format for later courses. Students assess their writing and course performance throughout the term.

This course uses *The Norton Field Guide to Writing with Readings and Handbook*, and students are asked to read and respond to several of the readings as ongoing assignments. Students are encouraged to revisit relevant chapters in the *Field Guide* as needed, learning to use it as a reference tool rather than as a content-focused textbook. Two of the three writing assignments for this course—the literacy narrative and profile—are not taught in the first-year writing course that students take after passing this one; the third, analyzing a text, is a feature of that course, but students find text analysis so challenging, and students in this course need so much help in improving their reading and analytical skills, that repeating the assignment is not an issue. Students learn how to use the *Field Guide* in this course and can use it effectively in subsequent courses—and save the cost of an additional book as well.

Since students' abilities and needs will vary widely, some students need more help than others with paragraphing, sentence-level composing, and editing. Norton's online resources are useful and should be assigned to individual students according to their needs: the companion website (wwnorton.com/write/) offers exercises, tutorials, and more. In addition, the *Field Guide* Coursepack can be customized to include a chapter on "Developing Paragraphs."

Week	In-Class Activities	Assignment
1	Intro to syllabus, policies, outcomes; portfolios; computer classroom etiquette; academic integrity; learning survey; tour University Writing Center. Writing: introductory diagnostic essays in class and as homework.	Chs. 1–6, "Rhetorical Situations" Reading: Ch. 57, LITERACY NARRATIVES
2	Intro to learning management system; reading and writing about effective study skills, assessing personal study habits, and creating appropriate study spaces; understanding Wright State information and available resources; responding and summarizing reading.	Ch. 55, WRITING ONLINE; Ch. 24, DRAFTING; Ch. 41, READING STRATEGIES; "Summarizing" from Ch. 47, QUOTING, PARAPHRASING, AND SUMMARIZING Reading, responding, and summarizing: Ch. 57, LITERACY NARRATIVES
3	**Self-Assessment Project: Literacy Narrative** begun; reading others' literacy narratives, understanding reflective narrative; brainstorming topics and details; visit Writing Center.	Ch. 7, WRITING A LITERACY NARRATIVE; Ch. 26, ASSESSING YOUR OWN WRITING Reading, responding, and summarizing: Ch. 57, LITERACY NARRATIVES
4	Drafting: focus on main idea and significant details, thesis and supporting points.	Ch. 7, WRITING A LITERACY NARRATIVE; Ch. 24, DRAFTING
5	Revising and polishing of literacy narrative; addressing specific audiences; creating class rubrics; understanding vocabulary and signal words in context; managing stress through writing.	Ch. 7, WRITING A LITERACY NARRATIVE; Ch. 27, GETTING RESPONSE AND REVISING; Ch. 28, EDITING AND PROOFREADING; Handbook as needed; exercises on Paragraphs, Sentences, Words, and Punctuation on the companion website as needed
6	**Text Analysis assignment** introduced: reading critically, annotating, understanding the larger conversation of popular and scholarly texts.	Ch. 8, ANALYZING TEXTS, or the Visual Rhetoric exercises on the companion website (though for this assignment, allowing students to examine and discuss the text on their own may help them develop confidence in their own critical abilities, which can then be expanded in the longer text analysis to come) Reading, responding, and summarizing: Ch. 58, TEXTUAL ANALYSES
7	Analyzing texts: news editorials, brief arguments: short papers, collaborative work.	Ch. 10, ARGUING A POSITION, and Ch. 33, ARGUING, may provide help with analyzing editorials and brief arguments; Ch. 8,

Week	In-Class Activities	Assignment
		ANALYZING TEXTS, continued Reading, responding, and summarizing: Ch. 58, TEXTUAL ANALYSES
8	Analyzing texts: revising analyses; preparing midterm portfolio; visit Writing Center.	Ch. 8, ANALYZING TEXTS, continued; Ch. 29, COMPILING A PORTFOLIO
9	Analyzing course syllabuses and other course materials: what do faculty expect, even if they don't say so? Intro to scholarly research.	Ch. 21, CHOOSING GENRES; Ch. 44, FINDING SOURCES; Ch. 45, EVALUATING SOURCES; Ch. 46, SYNTHESIZING IDEAS Reading, responding, and summarizing: Ch. 59, REPORTS
10	**Research Project:** Determine topics in groups, develop research strategy, begin researching.	May focus on Ch. 9, REPORTING INFORMATION, or Ch. 16, PROFILES Reading, responding, and summarizing: Ch. 59, REPORTS, or Ch. 63, PROFILES.
11	Work in groups on research project: interviewing experts, organizing research, deciding on appropriate media for presentation of research results.	Chs. 43–48 of "Doing Research"; Ch. 52, CHOOSING MEDIA; other "Media/Design" chapters as appropriate
12	Conferences with research teams; drafting; ethical incorporation of quotes and sources; preparing Works Cited in MLA style.	Ch. 47, QUOTING, PARAPHRASING, AND SUMMARIZING; Ch. 48, ACKNOWLEDGING SOURCES, AVOIDING PLAGIARISM (including the exercise and the "Academic Honesty and Avoiding Plagiarism" tutorial on the companion website); Ch. 49, DOCUMENTATION, and Ch. 50, MLA STYLE (with help from the MLA citation drills on the companion website)
13	**Final Portfolio and Self-Assessment.** Revising projects and preparing project presentations.	Use or review as needed: Ch. 26, ASSESSING YOUR OWN WRITING; Ch. 27, GETTING RESPONSE AND REVISING; Ch. 28, EDITING AND PROOFREADING; Handbook as needed; exercises as needed on Paragraphs, Sentences, Words, and Punctuation on the companion website
14	**Presentations.** Editing of projects and other portfolio contents.	Ch. 56, GIVING PRESENTATIONS; all chapters previously studied as needed; exercises as needed on the companion website
15	**Finals Week: Course Portfolio due.** (Substitutes for final exam.)	

Useful Readings

Adams, Peter Dow. Post to Council on Basic Writing listserv (CBW-L). 12 Sept. 2012. Web. 21 Dec. 2012.

Bowen, William G., Matthew M. Chingos, and Michael S. McPherson. *Crossing the Finish Line: Completing College at America's Public Universities.* Princeton: Princeton UP, 2009. Print.

Braddock, Richard, Richard Lloyd-Jones, and Lowell Schoer. *Research in Written Composition.* Champaign, IL: NCTE, 1963. Print.

Council on Basic Writing Blog. Council on Basic Writing. Web. 21 Dec. 2012.

Downing, Skip. *On Course: Strategies for Creating Success in College and in Life.* 6th ed. Boston: Wadsworth, 2011. Print.

Garrett, Jim. "Stretch Composition." *Composition Conversations.* CSULA, 6 Feb. 2010. Web. 16 Jan. 2013.

Hartwell, Patrick. "Grammar, Grammars, and the Teaching of Grammar." *College English* 47 (1985): 105–27. Print.

Hassel, Holly, and Joanne Baird Giordano. "Transfer Institutions, Transfer of Knowledge: The Development of Rhetorical Adaptability and Underprepared Writers." *Teaching English in the Two-Year College* 37 (2009): 24–40. Print.

Morenberg, Max, and Jeff Sommers. *The Writer's Options: Lessons in Style and Arrangement.* 6th ed. New York: Longman, 1999. Print.

Nelms, Gerald. "Learning through Imitation Copying." 2012. TS.

Roberts, Yvonne. *Grit: The Skills for Success and How They Are Grown.* London: Young Foundation, 2009. *Young Foundation.* Web. 21 Dec. 2012.

Thonney, Teresa. "Teaching the Conventions of Academic Discourse." *Teaching English in the Two-Year College* 38 (2011): 347–62. Print.

Tough, Paul. *How Children Succeed: Grit, Curiosity, and the Hidden Power of Character.* New York: Houghton, 2012. Print.

part 2

Teaching with
The Norton Field Guide

Developing Course Plans **22**
Using *The Norton Field Guide*

The *Field Guide* allows you to create various courses to meet your students' needs—and your own. This chapter offers an overview of some course plans commonly used in first-year writing programs and ways the *Field Guide* may be used in their service. Because writing programs, courses, and term lengths vary from school to school, you may wish to adopt or adapt the following suggestions to your own needs.

Using the Guides to Writing

If you're just starting your career as a teaching assistant or writing instructor, you may benefit from concentrating on the four detailed genre chapters: WRITING A LITERACY NARRATIVE (7); ANALYZING TEXTS (8); REPORTING INFORMATION (9); and ARGUING A POSITION (10). Chapters 7–10 each provide a complete sequence of assignments, beginning with sample readings and followed by tasks that move students from thinking about a topic through drafting, revising, editing, and proofreading. Along the way, students are prompted to get response to their writing from others and to assess their own work. Color-coded links refer them to other sections of the *Field Guide* for detailed

assistance with various tasks if they need more help. This structure permits you to base your teaching activities on the structure of the chapters. Then, as you gain confidence and experience, you can modify your assignments and activities, bringing in lessons and activities from various parts of the book to suit your own purposes.

Creating Assignment Sequences

The *Field Guide* also allows you to create assignment sequences to suit your own instructional goals and your students' particular needs. As a starting point, you may find it useful to show students how to navigate within the *Field Guide*. Show them the Key to the Book located on the front cover flap; each section of the book is listed, with the major topics covered within the section, so they can go directly to the colored pages to find the section they want. A brief menu of the contents is printed on the inside cover for students wanting to get to a specific chapter quickly. Cross-referenced material is highlighted in the color of the section in which it appears, and an icon identifying the section and the page number where the cross-reference may be found are in the margin. Asking students to read "How to Use This Book" will help them see how they can use the *Field Guide* to get the answers to their writing questions; reading it yourself, along with Chapter 1 in this guide to teaching, will help you understand how to help students navigate your own assignment sequences, which may require considerable moving around within the text. Here is a template for an assignment sequence using various chapters to help students compose a text:

1. *Introduce the genre, define key features, and discuss the rhetorical situation as it applies to the assignment.* Ask students to read the writing example presented in that chapter and then discuss it as a class. Introduce the Key Features of the genre as defined in the chapter and as applied to the reading. At this point, you will want to discuss the criteria for your writing assignment, asking students to think about their rhetorical situation. You may wish to assign Chapters 1–6 early in the term to get them thinking about purpose, audience, and the other components of any rhetorical situation. But each of the genre chapters, strategies chapters, and most other chapters include questions that help students focus on their rhetorical situation. You may at this point also want to ask students to read about media and design, in Chapters 52–56, to help them think about the medium they will be writing in and how their rhetorical situation will affect their design choices.

2. *Help students generate ideas and text, do research, and choose a topic.* Each genre chapter offers some guidelines to help students generate ideas and choose a topic to write about. You may ask students to do additional work in Chapter 24, GENERATING IDEAS AND TEXT. If students will be doing research, you might incorporate Chapters 43–51 as appropriate. For smaller projects, choose only the chapters that students need; for a larger project, you might assign students Chapters 43–48.

3. *Teach students to organize, plan, and use appropriate strategies to write a draft.* Each genre chapter offers two or three typical ways of organizing a draft. You might ask students to create an outline (Chapter 24) and then use the advice in Chapter 25 for help with DRAFTING. Along the way, they may need to consult chapters in Strategies for help with DESCRIBING (Chapter 37), NARRATING (Chapter 40), DIALOGUE (Chapter 38), and other writing strategies. If their texts include source material, they should consult Chapter 47 for help with QUOTING, PARAPHRASING, AND SUMMARIZING and Chapter 48 for guidance on ACKNOWLEDGING SOURCES.

4. *Show students how to assess the draft, get responses, revise, edit, proofread, and compile a portfolio.* Chapters 26–29 can be referenced or reviewed as needed and as time allows. These chapters include guidelines and questions that can be applied to any of the genre chapters. If your students will be COMPILING A PORTFOLIO, you will definitely want to spend time on Chapter 29.

A Menu for Designing Assignment Sequences

Here's a quick-reference guide for potential assignment sequences using the chapters in *The Norton Field Guide.* Ask students to read one or two chapters from each column as time and applicability warrant. Other chapters may simply be referenced or reviewed as needed.

Introduce the genre, define key features, and discuss the rhetorical situation:
1–6. Rhetorical Situations
7. Writing a Literacy Narrative
8. Analyzing Texts
9. Reporting Information
10. Arguing a Position
11. Abstracts
12. Annotated Bibliographies
13. Evaluations
14. Lab Reports
15. Memoirs
16. Profiles
17. Proposals
18. Reflections
19. Résumés and Job Letters
20. Mixing Genres
21. Choosing Genres
52. Choosing Media
53. Designing Text
54. Using Visuals, Incorporating Sound
55. Writing Online
56. Giving Presentations

Help students to choose a topic, generate ideas and text, and do research:
21. Choosing Genres
22. Writing as Inquiry
24. Generating Ideas and Text
41. Reading Strategies
43. Developing a Research Plan
44. Finding Sources
45. Evaluating Sources
46. Synthesizing Ideas
48. Acknowledging Sources, Avoiding Plagiarism
50 & 51. MLA and APA Style

Teach students to choose a topic, organize, and use appropriate strategies to write a draft:
25. Drafting
30. Beginning and Ending
31. Guiding Your Reader
32. Analyzing Causes and Effects
33. Arguing
34. Classifying and Dividing
35. Comparing and Contrasting
36. Defining
37. Describing
38. Dialogue
39. Explaining Processes
40. Narrating
47. Quoting, Paraphrasing, and Summarizing

Show students how to assess a draft, get response, revise, edit, proofread, design, and compile a portfolio:
23. Collaborating
26. Assessing Your Own Writing
27. Getting Response and Revising
28. Editing and Proofreading
29. Compiling a Portfolio
49. Documentation
50 & 51. MLA and APA Style
52. Choosing Media
53. Designing Text
54. Using Visuals, Incorporating Sound
56. Giving Presentations

Sample Course Plans

First-year composition courses take many forms. Here are some typical first-year course plans that show how you might use the *Field Guide*.

One-term courses. If your school requires students to take a single first-year writing course, you probably need to move students quickly through several genres. The following course plan begins by introducing students to the notion of the rhetorical situation and then creates a bridge between their past literacy and their current abilities through creation of a literacy narrative. Analyzing a text helps them to become critical readers, an ability they'll need for the next assignments, writing an essay that reports information and one that takes a position. The course ends by asking students to create and evaluate a portfolio of their work.

10-Week Course

Week 1	RHETORICAL SITUATIONS
Weeks 1–3	WRITING A LITERACY NARRATIVE
Weeks 4–6	ANALYZING TEXTS
Weeks 7–9	ARGUING A POSITION
Week 10	COMPILING A PORTFOLIO

14-Week Course

Week 1	RHETORICAL SITUATIONS
Weeks 2–3	WRITING A LITERACY NARRATIVE
Weeks 4–7	ANALYZING TEXTS
Weeks 8–10	REPORTING INFORMATION
Weeks 11–13	ARGUING A POSITION
Week 14	COMPILING A PORTFOLIO

Your writing program's requirements may require you to alter this outline. For example, if your program emphasizes argumentation, in a semester-long course you may need to replace REPORTING INFORMATION with a second assignment based on ARGUING A POSITION. In these circumstances, bringing in a Genre chapter, such as EVALUATIONS or PROPOSALS, can provide variety for you and your students. Similarly, an emphasis on research may lead you to reduce the time you spend on earlier assignments and increase the time spent on REPORTING INFORMATION or ARGUING A POSITION, to make room for instruction in Research.

You may, on the other hand, consider including repetition in your syllabus. Many genres—text analyses in particular—are new to students, so asking them to write in one genre and then move to another gives them only one opportunity to succeed. If they write at least two examples, though, they can cement their learning and produce better essays the second time around. Such a course might look like this:

14-Week Course

Week 1	RHETORICAL SITUATIONS
Weeks 2–4	ANALYZING TEXTS
Weeks 5–7	ANALYZING TEXTS
Weeks 8–11	TOPIC PROPOSALS
	ANNOTATED BIBLIOGRAPHIES
	REPORTING INFORMATION or
	ARGUING A POSITION
Weeks 12–14	TOPIC PROPOSALS
	ANNOTATED BIBLIOGRAPHIES
	REPORTING INFORMATION or
	ARGUING A POSITION

Two-term courses. If your school requires students to take two or three writing courses, you may either require students to write more essays or you may spend more time with each assignment, studying additional readings, asking students to write multiple revisions of their drafts, and including more group work and individual conferences with you. If your courses consist of 28–30 weeks divided among two semesters or three quarters, you can slow the pace even more, offering students additional opportunities to rewrite as well as revise their drafts and prepare lengthier and more detailed self-evaluations. You're likely to find, however, that the demands of doing academic research and creating acceptable arguments dictate devoting as much time as you can to these activities. Here's a two-course sequence based on a ten-week-long quarter:

First Course

Week 1	RHETORICAL SITUATIONS
Weeks 2–3	WRITING A LITERACY NARRATIVE
Weeks 4–7	ANALYZING TEXTS
Weeks 8–9	EVALUATIONS
Week 10	COMPILING A PORTFOLIO

Second Course

Weeks 1–3	REPORTING INFORMATION, including RESEARCH and an ANNOTATED BIBLIOGRAPHY
Weeks 4–7	ARGUING A POSITION, including a TOPIC PROPOSAL and RESEARCH
Weeks 8–9	PROPOSAL
Week 10	COMPILING A PORTFOLIO

A two-course sequence also allows more time to repeat genres; for example, the second course in a 15-week semester might include two sequences that include TOPIC PROPOSALS, RESEARCH, and ANNOTATED BIBLIOGRAPHIES.

Courses that focus on personal writing. If you'd like to teach a course that allows students to develop their personal voices and writing styles, you might design a course that combines several genres, including a profile, which requires a first-hand account and an interesting, often personal angle:

14-Week Course

Weeks 1–2	PROCESSES of writing, focusing especially on GENERATING IDEAS AND TEXT
Weeks 3–4	WRITING A LITERACY NARRATIVE
Weeks 5–8	Writing a MEMOIR
Weeks 9–11	Writing a PROFILE, including lessons on DESCRIBING and DIALOGUE
Weeks 12–14	Writing a REFLECTION

Courses that focus on research. A course emphasizing research might use the Research chapters as a primary focus, moving students through the research process to an essay REPORTING INFORMATION or ARGUING A POSITION:

14-Week Course

Weeks 1–2	WRITING IN ACADEMIC CONTEXTS, examining sample research papers,

	WRITING AS INQUIRY, GENERATING IDEAS AND TEXT
Week 3	Writing a TOPIC PROPOSAL; CHOOSING GENRES
Weeks 3–4	FINDING SOURCES and EVALUATING SOURCES
Week 5	Writing an ANNOTATED BIBLIOGRAPHY
Weeks 6–7	Considering appropriate STRATEGIES—ANALYZING CAUSES AND EFFECTS, CLASSIFYING, COMPARING, DEFINING, DESCRIBING, EXPLAINING PROCESSES, NARRATING, and so on; continuing RESEARCH as needed
Weeks 8–9	Considering appropriate MEDIA AND DESIGN, BEGINNING AND ENDING, outlining and organizing; begin DRAFTING; SYNTHESIZING IDEAS; GUIDING YOUR READER; QUOTING, PARAPHRASING, AND SUMMARIZING
Weeks 10–11	ASSESSING DRAFTS, GETTING RESPONSE AND REVISING; perhaps including additional RESEARCH
Week 12	ACKNOWLEDGING SOURCES, AVOIDING PLAGIARISM; DOCUMENTATION
Weeks 13–14	Further REVISING, EDITING, AND PROOFREADING; may

include publication as print, electronic, or spoken text

Courses that focus on preprofessional writing. A course for students looking for instruction in "practical" writing tasks might look like this one, where students might be encouraged to choose a single topic to research and report on, ultimately composing and presenting a proposal:

14-Week Course

Weeks 1–4	DOING RESEARCH, writing an ANNOTATED BIBLIOGRAPHY, and SYNTHESIZING IDEAS
Weeks 4–8*	REPORTING INFORMATION, including an ABSTRACT— and some attention to the COLLABORATING or MEDIA/DESIGN chapters
Weeks 8–12*	Writing a PROPOSAL, including attention to the COLLABORATING, PROCESSES, STRATEGIES, and MEDIA/DESIGN chapters
Weeks 13–14	RÉSUMÉS AND JOB LETTERS

Courses that focus on textual analysis. If you are using the *Field Guide* in combination with an anthology of literature, you might structure a course that combines analysis of literary texts with analysis of a nonfiction text. Such a course might build on students' familiarity with literary anal-

---

*During the final week of each unit, students might present their findings to the class in the form of a spoken or electronic text.

ysis and then move to the unfamiliar territory of textual analysis:

10-Week Course

Weeks 1–3	Readings from the literature anthology, discussion, and informal writing using the chapters on GENERATING IDEAS AND TEXT
Weeks 4–6	LITERARY ANALYSES (part of ANALYZING TEXTS) with appropriate chapters from PROCESSES and STRATEGIES
Weeks 7–9	ANALYZING TEXTS, with the chapter on READING STRATEGIES
Week 10	COMPARING the two analyses and evaluating their work

Courses that focus on a theme. If your course focuses on readings on various themes, such as work, nature and the environment, government and politics, and so on, you might want students to begin their writing by thinking about the theme, writing informally about readings as a basis for discussion, and then developing essays in response to the concepts they read about rather than writing in a specific genre. You might then ask students to begin by generating ideas and text and do research that leads them to a genre:

15-Week Course or Unit

Weeks 1–2	Read essays and respond in writing as part of a discussion. For example, students may post ongoing responses to a discussion board, share comments at specified times in a chat room, or just talk about their written responses in small groups. This method helps students respond not only to the text but also to other viewpoints and opinions. The READING STRATEGIES and COLLABORATING chapters may be helpful here.
Weeks 2–3	Have students explore topics in relation to the theme using the activities in the chapter on GENERATING IDEAS AND TEXT; and then do some research, first FINDING SOURCES and then EVALUATING SOURCES.
Weeks 4–5	Students choose a genre they will use to approach their topic and refer to the appropriate GENRE, STRATEGIES, and PROCESSES chapters as needed.
Weeks 6–9, 10–13	Repeat this basic structure, either with new readings on different aspects of the theme or on subthemes of the main theme. If you're teaching a 10-week course, repeat only once.

| Week 10 or 14 | Provide time for GETTING RESPONSE AND REVISING and helping students as they work on COMPILING A PORTFOLIO. | Remember that your best resources for course designs are experienced instructors and graduate students in your school. You may also find useful ideas for course plans online. |

The WPA Outcomes Statement for First-Year Composition was adopted in 2000 and amended in 2008 by the Council of Writing Program Administrators (WPA), a national professional organization for faculty who direct college and university writing programs. It offers a clear description of student performance goals for first-year writing courses. The Outcomes Statement is reproduced here, with explanations of how the *Field Guide* helps students meet the specific outcomes.

WPA Outcomes Statement for First-Year Composition*

Introduction

This statement describes the common knowledge, skills, and attitudes sought by first-year composition programs in American postsecondary education. To some extent, we seek to regularize what can be expected to be taught in first-year composition; to this end the document is not merely a compilation or summary of what currently takes place. Rather, the following statement articulates what composition teachers nationwide have learned from practice, research, and theory. This document intentionally defines only "outcomes," or types of results, and not "standards," or precise levels of achievement. The setting of standards should be left to specific institutions or specific groups of institutions.

Learning to write is a complex process, both individual and social, that takes place over time with continued practice and informed guidance. Therefore, it is important that teachers, administrators, and a concerned public do not imagine that these outcomes can be taught in reduced or simple ways. Helping students demonstrate these outcomes requires expert understanding of how students actually learn to write. For this reason we expect the primary audience for this document to be well-prepared college writing teachers and college writing program administrators. In some places, we have chosen to write in their professional language. Among such readers, terms such as "rhetorical" and "genre" convey a rich meaning that is not easily simplified. While we have also aimed at writing a document that the general public can understand, in limited

*The Outcomes Statement may be found on the Council of Writing Program Administrators website at wpacouncil.org/positions/outcomes.html.

cases we have aimed first at communicating effectively with expert writing teachers and writing program administrators.

These statements describe only what we expect to find at the end of first-year composition, at most schools a required general education course or sequence of courses. As writers move beyond first-year composition, their writing abilities do not merely improve. Rather, students' abilities not only diversify along disciplinary and professional lines but also move into whole new levels where expected outcomes expand, multiply, and diverge. For this reason, each statement of outcomes for first-year composition is followed by suggestions for further work that builds on these outcomes.

Rhetorical Knowledge

By the end of first-year composition, students should

- Focus on a purpose
- Respond to the needs of different audiences
- Respond appropriately to different kinds of rhetorical situations
- Use conventions of format and structure appropriate to the rhetorical situation
- Adopt appropriate voice, tone, and level of formality
- Understand how genres shape reading and writing
- Write in several genres

Faculty in all programs and departments can build on this preparation by helping students learn

- The main features of writing in their fields
- The main uses of writing in their fields
- The expectations of readers in their fields

The *Field Guide* supports this outcome in several ways. Chapters 1–6 introduce and define the elements of the rhetorical situation, including purpose audience, genre, stance, and media/design, as well as writing in academic contexts. Fifteen chapters in the Genres section not only offer detailed advice on writing in specific genres, but also provide advice on choosing genres and mixing them when appropriate. Each genre chapter asks students to consider the rhetorical situation in relation to that genre, and each chapter in the Strategies section asks students questions about how the rhetorical situation influences their use of that strategy. Similar questions are included in the Doing Research and Media/Design sections to ensure that students are constantly reminded that their writing always takes place within a rhetorical situation to which that writing must respond.

Critical Thinking, Reading, and Writing

By the end of first-year composition, students should

- Use writing and reading for inquiry, learning, thinking, and communicating
- Understand a writing assignment as a series of tasks, including finding, evaluating, analyzing, and synthesizing appropriate primary and secondary sources
- Integrate their own ideas with those of others
- Understand the relationships among language, knowledge, and power

Faculty in all programs and departments can build on this preparation by helping students learn

- The uses of writing as a critical thinking method
- The interactions among critical thinking, critical reading, and writing
- The relationships among language, knowledge, and power in their fields

The *Field Guide* includes Chapter 22 (WRITING AS INQUIRY) and Chapter 41 (READING STRATEGIES) that directly address this outcome; however, each chapter in the sections on Rhetorical Situations, Genres, and Strategies, as well as several in Doing Research and Media/Design, asks students to critically consider their subjects and the choices they must make as they write. The tasks in Chapter 8 (ANALYZING TEXTS) require students to read texts carefully and critically, while the Guide to Writing in each Genre chapter prompts students to consider these things as they write. Doing Research offers Chapters 44–46, which help students find, evaluate, and synthesize primary and secondary sources, while Chapters 47 and 48 help them integrate their ideas with others'.

Processes

By the end of first-year composition, students should

- Be aware that it usually takes multiple drafts to create and complete a successful text
- Develop flexible strategies for generating, revising, editing, and proofreading
- Understand writing as an open process that permits writers to use later invention and re-thinking to revise their work
- Understand the collaborative and social aspects of writing processes
- Learn to critique their own and others' works
- Learn to balance the advantages of relying on others with the responsibility of doing their part
- Use a variety of technologies to address a range of audiences

Faculty in all programs and departments can build on this preparation by helping students learn

- To build final results in stages
- To review work-in-progress in collaborative peer groups for purposes other than editing
- To save extensive editing for later parts of the writing process
- To apply the technologies commonly used to research and communicate within their fields

Each Genre chapter in the *Field Guide* includes a Guide to Writing that helps students make their way through the process of writing that genre, from generating ideas and text through drafting, revising, and editing to taking stock of their work. In addition, the Processes section offers chapters on GENERATING IDEAS AND TEXT, DRAFTING, ASSESSING YOUR OWN WRITING, GETTING RESPONSE AND REVISING, EDITING AND PROOF- READING, and COLLABORATING—and each provides multiple methods of going about those tasks. Chapter 43, DEVELOPING A RESEARCH PLAN, helps students through the process of creating a research project. And the Media/Design section provides a chapter on CHOOSING MEDIA and three more chapters to help students use those media effectively.

Knowledge of Conventions

By the end of first-year composition, students should

- Learn common formats for different kinds of texts
- Develop knowledge of genre conventions ranging from structure and paragraphing to tone and mechanics
- Practice appropriate means of documenting their work
- Control such surface features as syntax, grammar, punctuation, and spelling.

Faculty in all programs and departments can build on this preparation by helping students learn

- The conventions of usage, specialized vocabulary, format, and documentation in their fields
- Strategies through which better control of conventions can be achieved

Each *Field Guide* Genre chapter describes the key features of the genre, provides typical organizational structures for it, and asks student writers to consider the media and design aspects related to the genre. The four longer Genre chapters, 7–10, offer genre-specific guidelines for editing and proofreading. Chapter 28, EDITING AND PROOFREADING, provides detailed advice, as do the Handbook chapters (which are available on the *Field Guide* website, if you are not using a version of the book that includes the Handbook). Documenting of sources in MLA and APA formats is covered in detail in Chapters 49, 50, and 51.

Composing in Electronic Environments

As has become clear over the last twenty years, writing in the twenty-first century involves the use of digital technologies for several purposes, from drafting to peer reviewing to editing. Therefore, although the *kinds* of composing processes and texts expected from students vary across programs and institutions, there are nonetheless common expectations.

By the end of first-year composition, students should:

- Use electronic environments for drafting, reviewing, revising, editing, and sharing texts
- Locate, evaluate, organize, and use research material collected from electronic sources, including scholarly library databases; other official databases (e.g., federal government databases); and informal electronic networks and Internet sources
- Understand and exploit the differences in the rhetorical strategies and in the affordances available for both print and electronic composing processes and texts

Faculty in all programs and departments can build on this preparation by helping students learn

- How to engage in the electronic research and composing processes common in their fields
- How to disseminate texts in both print and electronic forms in their fields

The *Field Guide* includes a Media/Design section that strongly supports students using digital technologies. Chapter 52, CHOOSING MEDIA, helps students decide which medium or media best meet their needs. Chapter 53, DESIGNING TEXT, offers advice on creating rhetorically effectively designed texts, whether online or in print, and Chapter 54, USING VISUALS, INCORPORATING SOUND, helps students decide when and how to use images and sound effectively. Chapter 55, WRITING ONLINE, introduces students to course management systems and offers advice on managing online writing in college. And Chapter 56, GIVING PRESENTATIONS, includes advice on creating effective visuals. The Doing Research section assumes that most research students will do is electronic and focuses on scholarly library databases and other electronic sources.

That writing is complex is a truism, yet it's worth stating here, because many of these outcomes overlap and in practice are hard to separate out. Many of us teach twenty or twenty-five students in a class, each of whom may have mastered some outcomes before arriving in our class and will struggle with others—but each will have mastered and will struggle with different ones. Our course may turn on a theme that controls what students write about and that affects our teaching. Yet one way or another, we teach (and so the *Field Guide* covers) all of the subjects included in the WPA statement: understanding of rhetorical situations and their components; genres and their requirements; the processes that writers use to think, write, revise, and edit their writing; strategies for developing and organizing texts; the processes and demands of academic research, including citation and documentation of sources; and advice on designing texts in various media. If you're using a version of the *Field Guide* that includes its Handbook, you will have even more detailed information on several of the outcomes.

Below is a grid I use when I'm planning a writing course to help me focus on specific outcomes in my own teaching. As I develop my syllabus, I fill in each day's activities, the assignment that derives from them, and the outcomes I'm emphasizing that day. Once it's finished, I can give copies to my students and discuss the outcomes with them, to show that every activity and every assignment is part of a larger project. I find that students respond well when their instructor makes clear what the ultimate goal of their work is, and that they are often more willing to take it seriously. And it's nice to be able to demonstrate that our courses build on an established, national consensus about what students should know and be able to do when they finish first-year composition.

Week	Day	Subject, Class Activities	Assignment Due	WPA Outcomes Addressed
1	Tue			
	Thu			

Teaching about **24** Rhetorical Situations

Students need to understand that they are always part of a rhetorical situation: Whenever they speak or write, they participate in a context that includes purpose, audience, genre, stance, and medium and design—and they need to address all those elements if their writing is to succeed. The *Field Guide to Writing* offers a general introduction to the rhetorical situation in Chapters 1–5, as well as a chapter that describes the features of writing in academic contexts and genre-specific questions to help students define the rhetorical situation they face when writing in any of the genres. In addition, each Strategies chapter and chapters in Doing Research and Media/Design include questions to help students understand their own rhetorical situation. One way to teach rhetorical situations using the *Field Guide*, then, is simply to ask students to respond to the questions as they prepare to write. You can also ask them to analyze the model essays in the chapters to see how the writers addressed their rhetorical situations. If, however, you'd like to do more, here are some ideas for teaching the rhetorical situation. Although each aspect of the rhetorical situation is considered separately, each one affects the others; each, in fact, cannot be considered apart from the others or emphasized too strongly without comparable consideration of the rest.

Purpose

In its most basic form, purpose in writing is simply the answer to the question "What does the writer want this piece of writing to accomplish?" Usually we write to affect readers in some way: to change their minds, to get them to do something, to make them think or feel something, and/or to share some thought or experience we've had. In fact, we often have several purposes when we write. You might ask your students to list their purposes before they write in order to give them a goal or after they've written a draft so readers can assess how well they achieved their purposes. These purposes might be listed as "primary" and "secondary." For example, a student might write an argument whose primary goal is to get readers to agree with the student's position, but the student may also want to entertain readers and demonstrate the ability to think clearly and do appropriate research.

It's also useful to remind students that their audience has purposes for reading, too: We read instructions to find out how to assemble a bookcase; we read op-ed pieces to understand the arguments over public policy; we read *The Onion* to be entertained. When students write, then, they need to consider why their audience is reading their work. Again, having students identify their audience's purposes helps them see what they need to do to satisfy their readers' needs while meeting their own purposes.

There are questions focusing students' attention on purpose in the guidelines on Considering the Rhetorical Situation sections throughout the *Field Guide*.

Audience

The role of audience can be tricky for students because their writing in composition courses often must satisfy at least two audiences: the audience to which their writing is addressed (classmates, newspaper editors, scholars in various fields, and informed but curious people, to name a few) and the course instructor, whose purposes in reading may differ considerably from the audiences the student writer is ostensibly addressing. A good way to deal with this potential conflict is to discuss it openly: Acknowledge the complexity of your students' tasks and point out ways in which your reading may differ from their chosen audience's. For example, if students are writing a report for an audience of their peers, that audience may well be very interested in understanding the concepts and information presented but forgive organizational problems or formal errors that you as instructor must take into account. If students are arguing a position in an essay for readers of a local newspaper, that audience will likely focus on the writers' perspectives and the force of their prose, while you will be on the lookout for gaps in their logic or misuse of source material as well as even-handedness in their presentation of differing arguments. Such explanations may not make students' jobs easier, but students will understand better how their writing must satisfy your requirements while meeting their other audience's expectations, too.

There are questions focusing students' attention on audience in the guidelines on Considering the Rhetorical Situation sections throughout the *Field Guide*.

Genre

Genre can be either a starting point or a destination. The Guides to Writing in each of the Genre chapters will help students write in a specific genre—narrative, analysis, report, argument, memoir, and so on. Many writing instructors find it useful to teach specific genres: A body of information on the genre can be taught, genre-specific readings can be discussed by the whole class, and student activities and assignments can be coordinated. For example, students can easily work in groups to determine how well one another's drafts achieve the key features of a specific genre.

Sometimes, though, the genre emerges from the writer's needs. Students may study a subject and begin with a topic on which they want to write—but they don't know what they want to write until they've thought, generated text, and conducted research. At some point in that exploratory process, they will choose a goal and with it a genre that will let them achieve it. Chapter 21, CHOOSING GENRES, can help them do this. So in a class of twenty, you might have five students arguing a position, six drafting memoirs or reflections, four writing proposals, and another five reporting information. This approach may seem chaotic, but it needn't be: Students working on similar projects can work collaboratively while you move from group to group, giving help as they need it. No matter what they're writing, they'll need to produce drafts, and at that point you can ask them to read and respond to one another's drafts, perhaps twice: once within the groups (where they can use their familiarity with the genre to assess one another's success) and once by other students (who, with fresh eyes, can respond to the content and clarity better than the students who have been working together).

Each genre represented in the *Field Guide* is described in terms of its Key Features. These Key Features may be approached as textual features—what good examples of the text include or embody—or as features that audiences expect when they read a specific genre. For example, readers of evaluations expect that the object of the evaluation will be described for those who are unfamiliar with it and that the criteria on which the evaluation is based will be identified; if those features aren't present, readers will likely reject the evaluation as incomplete. This approach often motivates students more than the textual approach does, as students often see value in meeting audience expectations but have little interest in crafting a well-formed text for its own sake. The same holds true for the medium and design and stance of a text: Have students think about or do research on what audiences expect of texts in a specific genre so they can meet those expectations.

It's also good to remember that genres are seldom pure. Instead, genres are often combined; for example, someone arguing a position may well include a memoir as evidence, an analysis of a key text on the subject, and a proposal at the end. Therefore, you may wish to encourage students to consult additional Genre chapters in the *Field Guide*, including Chapter 20 (MIXING GENRES), for help as they write—or you could consider creating hybrid assignments, such as a combined evaluation and proposal or memoir and reflection. You might even explore multigenre papers, which Tom Romano defines as "composed of many genres and subgenres, each piece self-contained, making a point of its own, yet connected by theme or topic and sometimes by language, images, and content. In addition to many genres, a multigenre paper may also contain many voices, not just the author's. The trick is to make such a paper hang together" (ix).

There are questions focusing students' attention on genre in the guidelines on Considering the Rhetorical Situation sections throughout the *Field Guide*.

Stance

We can help students convey their stance in their writing by helping them think about their relationship to their subject and audience and by helping them create the appropriate voice to reflect that stance. Ask students to identify the tone they wish to adopt: Serious? Ironic? Playful? Cynical? Scholarly? Optimistic? Neutral or self-effacing? Something else? Have them try out their chosen tone by writing a paragraph and then seeing if readers identify the tone for which they're striving. Or have students find a piece of writing that achieves the tone they wish to adopt and analyze it or imitate it to see how the author creates that tone. Consider having students rewrite a text several ways—either a passage you provide or one of their drafts—to attempt various tones, and then discuss with the class what they did to achieve them.

You can use similar techniques to help students develop voice in their writing. Scholars—like many writers—are split over the nature of voice in writing. In one view, the voice with which we write must be authentic and true to ourselves; in this view, voice can't be taught, but only encouraged. Many students begin with this first position. In contrast are those who believe that our selves, and thus our voices, are socially constructed and don't reflect a coherent self as much as they do our participation in a social group or discourse community. As Toby Fulwiler suggests in "Claiming My Voice," writers can and do move between these poles easily. Writers can learn to adjust their voice to suit both their desire to express their authentic selves and their need to adopt various voices to suit their purpose, audience, and genre. Doing so, however, requires awareness of how the various decisions they make as writers come together to create their voice. Here is a sampling of exercises, adapted from Dona Hickey's *Developing a Written Voice* (1993):

- Have students transcribe a short spoken text from television or radio. Then rewrite it for different audiences and occasions. They can also rewrite their own drafts in the same way.

- Have students write a paragraph using only one-syllable words and sentences one to ten words long. Share some aloud and discuss how the voices differ and what other genres they resemble: children's stories, parables, religious language. Examine some closely to see what features of the prose lend each a distinctive voice.

- Analyze texts that provide good examples of colloquial, informal, and formal voices. See what happens when students rearrange (without altering) the words in some of the sentences. How does the voice change as the word order changes?

- Then have the students write an imitation of one paragraph of the model, maintaining the sentence structure but changing the topic. Ask them to discuss the way they solved the problems of doing so and how the structure limited or enabled their writing.

There are questions focusing students' attention on stance in the guidelines on Considering the Rhetorical Situation sections throughout the *Field Guide*.

Media / Design

As students become familiar with addressing the rhetorical situation of any writing task, you will want to further their understanding by having them explore writing in different media. Students are generally more familiar with print text than with other forms, such as electronic or spoken text—but they may not understand how the design of a print text affects their rhetorical situation. You might present a brief text in several formats—handwritten on notebook paper, typed and double-spaced, printed in two justified columns—and ask students to explore the differences in rhetorical effect each design makes. Asking students to consider how a webpage might be better suited for conveying an argument or how a speech might be more effective for a proposal will enable them to apply rhetorical situations to a broader spectrum of writing situations. See Chapter 33 in this guide to teaching for more ideas and strategies for teaching about media and design.

There are questions focusing students' attention on media and design in the guidelines on Considering the Rhetorical Situation sections throughout the *Field Guide*.

Writing in Academic Contexts

Academic writing presents numerous challenges for students, primarily because they are unfamiliar with the conventions, the language, and the stance required. As David Bartholomae observes, "The student has to learn to speak our language, to speak as we do, to try on the peculiar ways of knowing, selecting, evaluating, reporting, concluding, and arguing that define the discourse of our community . . . . [The student] must dare to speak it or carry off the bluff, since speaking and writing will most certainly be required long before the skill is 'learned'" (605–6).

Nancy Sommers and Laura Saltz suggest that students succeed in this endeavor by taking on the role of novices, "required to become master builders while they are still apprentices" and needing to be willing to open themselves to new ideas, to changing their ways of writing and thinking—of recognizing, "as one freshman put it, that 'what worked in high school isn't working anymore'" (125–34). You will find that some students reach this insight later than others and cling to genres and processes that were successful in high school writing: narratives, five-paragraph themes, and compilations of unsynthesized research, all written as quickly as possible, at the last minute. ("I work best under pressure" is a common first-year myth.)

Because much of the writing students have done before college assumed that the only reader was the teacher and the only purpose was to test their knowledge—an assumption strengthened by recent emphasis on standardized testing—many students have a stunted conception of rhetorical situations. So emphasizing the need to examine in some depth the purpose, audience, genre, stance, and medium of everything they write for their college courses is important—and why sections asking students to Consider the Rhetorical Situation appear throughout the *Field Guide*. For the same reason, slowing down students' writing processes by requiring multiple drafts in carefully sequenced assignments helps students move from superficial, initial impressions to the deeper thinking and development expected of college writers— and disabuse them of the common notion that even complex writing tasks can be done in a single draft, which Margaret Kantz notes "can create a tremendous hurdle for students" (199).

The fact that first-year students are novices, though, should temper our expectations. As Sommers and Saltz point out, first-year students don't know enough about the topics they are studying to step back and analyze them, and so rely on descriptive theses, "the thesis that names or reports on phenomena rather than articulating claims or interpretations" (134). Unsure of how to structure essays

appropriately, they may use the structure of one of their sources, and unable to evaluate the appropriateness of various sources, they use whatever they find (Kantz 189). Through multiple drafts and careful coaching, we can help students improve—but, as in so many things, we need to remember that they are just starting their college careers and are just getting their feet wet in the complexities of academic waters (which can run deep, with strong currents).

Critical thinking. As writing teachers, we are committed to improving our students' critical thinking abilities, and our assignments—from examining their development as writers and readers through literacy narratives to creating multiple-source, research-based arguments—ask students to think critically, defined by Stephen D. Brookfield as "recognizing and researching the assumptions that undergird our thoughts and actions" (50). Critical thinking is a primary value in the academic world—but for students, it can be a much more ambiguous goal. Brookfield notes that some students feel like imposters when asked to critically analyze experts, that "they possess neither the talent nor the right" to do so. Some students feel uneasy when faced with the academic world's emphasis on the contextual nature of truth and on the ambiguous nature of facts, finding the move from dualistic thinking—ideas and people are good or bad, there is a clear demarcation between right and wrong—disorienting and upsetting. And some students, particularly working-class students, sometimes feel that to engage fully in academic life is to betray "the culture that has defined and sustained them up to that point in their life"—a feeling that may be reinforced by friends or family who have not gone or are not going to college (51–52).

While these feelings grow out of students' experience of college, not just our courses, we can help students deal with them. Brookfield notes that asking students to collaborate helps them develop a community of peers that provides support as they engage in the same intellectual journey (54), and John Bean observes that academic writing, which he characterizes as thesis-driven argumentation, is inherently messy, the result of engaging in a process of drafting, revising, getting response, and revising again—and along the way modeling "an interior thinking process" (19–20).

Useful Readings

Bartholomae, David. "Inventing the University." *The Norton Book of Composition Studies*. Ed. Susan Miller. New York: Norton, 2009. 605–30. Print.

Bean, John C. *Engaging Ideas: The Professor's Guide to Integrating Writing, Critical Thinking, and Active Learning in the Classroom*. San Francisco: Jossey-Bass, 1996. Print.

Brookfield, Stephen D. "Overcoming Impostorship, Cultural Suicide, and Lost Innocence: Implications for Teaching Critical Thinking in the Community College." *New Directions for Community Colleges* 130 (2005): 49–57. Print.

Clark, Irene. "A Genre Approach to Writing Assignments." *Composition Forum* 14.2 (2005): n. pag. Web. 13 Oct. 2009.

George, Diana. "From Analysis to Design: Visual Communication in the Teaching of Writing." *College Composition and Communication* 54 (Sept. 2002): 11–39. Print.

Ede, Lisa, and Andrea Lunsford. "Audience Addressed/Audience Invoked: The Role of Audience in Composition Theory and Pedagogy." *College Composition and Communication* 35.2 (1984). Print.

Elbow, Peter. "Closing My Eyes as I Speak: An Argument for Ignoring Audience." *College English* 49 (Jan. 1987): 50–69. Print.

———. "Reconsiderations: Voice in Writing Again: Embracing Contraries." *College English* 70.2 (2007): 168–88. Print.

Fulwiler, Toby. "Claiming My Voice." *Voices on Voice: Perspectives, Definitions, Inquiry*. Ed. Kathleen Blake Yancey. Urbana, IL: NCTE, 1994. 36–47. Print.

Hickey, Dona J. *Developing a Written Voice*. Mountain View, CA: Mayfield, 1993. Print.

Kantz, Margaret. "Helping Students Use Textual Sources Persuasively." *The Allyn and Bacon Sourcebook for College Writing Teachers*. Ed. James C. McDonald. 2nd ed. Needham Heights, MA: Allyn & Bacon, 2000. 187–204. Print.

Romano, Tom. *Blending Genre, Altering Style: Writing Multigenre Papers*. Portsmouth, NH: Boynton/Cook, 2000. Print.

Sommers, Nancy, and Laura Saltz. "The Novice as Expert: Writing the Freshman Year." *College Composition and Communication* 56 (2004): 124–49. Print.

25 Literacy (and Other) Narratives

Brady Allen

Narration tells a story, but narrative is not quite as simple as that. We tell stories many ways, and we tell stories for any number of reasons. A narrative could be a personal anecdote that sets up or that makes an argument, for example, a detailed account of paying too much for your auto repair to demonstrate that computerized engine diagnostics are not as valuable as mechanics who can roll up their sleeves and root around under the hood. We might narrate to relay information; a newspaper reporter might write a straightforward story about a new, technology-based restaurant where customers order their food with a keyboard and monitor and have it sent from the kitchen on a conveyor belt. Or, we might use narration in a business letter such as a claim letter to that auto repair shop when its computer diagnosed a dead catalytic converter but the problem turned out to be bad spark plug cables or a claim letter to that techno-restaurant after your food was ruined by a diner with a cold because there was no sneeze-guard on the food conveyor. Narrative is flexible.

A literacy narrative tells a story about some event that was important to a per-

son's development as a reader and writer. That event may be momentous, or it may be fleeting, noticed only by the writer. It may have happened years ago or fairly recently. Whatever topic students choose, they have many ways of telling their story. Chapter 7 of *The Norton Field Guide* provides students with models and strategies. Here is some advice on helping students tell their stories well.

Sharing Stories

Narrative is the description of an event or series of events. So, while you're teaching narrative, tell your students as many stories as you can. Many of them might be writing-related. Walk into the room on the first day and tell a story—one incoming students will enjoy—about your experiences as a writer, teacher, or former student. You might describe the time your racy love note to the guy or girl you were dating in high school was intercepted by your health teacher—who then used it in her lecture about human sexuality. And ask students to tell their stories aloud in class, too. Ask your students to talk about their past writing experiences, and ask questions that prod them to reveal more detail and significance. This informal discussion is a great way to get you and your students in a storytelling mode together.

Writers write, and teachers should, too. Disprove that annoying old saying about how "Those who can, do, and those who can't, teach." Early on, share your work with them: memoir, fiction, simple narrative accounts. Or tell jokes; that's narrative, too. Point out choices you made and strategies you used in your own writing. It's only fair that you share with them, since they're going to be sharing with you. You'll get a chance to talk about the all-important need to focus on audience. You'll be telling your students that, although you wrote your pieces for yourself in a sense, it's important that the stance, purpose, details, and significance of your work are clear to them, too. Encourage them to discuss your work with you, and you'll all be a lot more comfortable when it comes time to discuss their narratives. You might let them respond to a draft of your writing (don't cheat and show them a revised and polished piece) in a whole-class response workshop (described in Chapter 5 of this guide to teaching). Respond to their suggestions as one writer to another. Discuss your reactions to their comments. In other words, show them that you're not just the teacher, but a writer and a student of writing, too.

Using the Readings and Teaching the Key Features

You can use the readings in Chapter 7 of *The Norton Field Guide* to model key features of literacy narratives, which are also key features of any narrative. Each offers a well-told story, and you might point out what "well-told" consists of. Emily Vallowe discusses the tension between her lifelong self-identity as a writer and her ongoing doubts about that identity. This essays is annotated to show how she weaves the key features of a literacy narrative into her story—and the annotations point out some other features that make it a "well-told" piece of writing. In "Always Living in Spanish," Marjorie Agosín relates with subtlety the story of her family's migration from Chile to the United States and the effects it had on her uses of language. In her final paragraphs, she conveys the climactic reason for her longing for Spanish: "Nothing else from my childhood world remains." Sofia Gomez's piece can illustrate how vivid descriptions might include such details as the Scotch tape on well-used picture books and scary Doberman pinschers. And Agosín's piece also shows how significance can be conveyed by portraying past events through the filter of the present: by writing in Spanish, she can preserve the memories—indeed, keep alive—that which she has lost. You can bring in other narratives to share with your class and invite them to bring examples as well.

Getting Started and Choosing a Topic

So you've told stories to your students, listened to some of theirs, and read some good examples. Now how do you get them started writing in preparation for their own narratives? Narrative writing revolves around five things: people, places, objects, events, and "self." Here are examples of five exercises I give my students within the first week of class to get them thinking, somewhat indirectly, about possible topics for their narratives.

1. Who are some people from your past that impacted your life, taught you, wronged you, interested you, or, maybe, merely amused you? Write a short paragraph each for several of them. You may include one or two people that you're still in contact with or close to, but try to write about three or four that you haven't seen for a while or didn't actually know all that well. Try to touch upon a couple of traits, attributes, characteristics, or quirks for each person. Use specific details.

2. What and where are some of your favorite places? Write a short paragraph each for several of them. Focus on smaller places. (Instead of Pennsylvania, in other words, think of the Summit Diner off Exit 17 in eastern Pennsylvania. Instead of your parents' house, think of your mom's flower bed next to the front porch [where everything was always dead]

or the cardboard box on the aluminum garage shelf where your dad hid [or thought he was hiding] his *Play-boys*.) Try to recall at least five places. In fact, the places don't necessarily have to be your "favorite" places; think of them, simply, as places that you remember. Give specific details for each place.

3. Think of some objects, items, or possessions from your past: things you owned, things you borrowed, or things you wanted but never got, maybe. What about things that were simply in your proximity sometimes? (Some examples: your first baseball glove, your dance shoes, your Britney Spears or Batman poster, a SAFE SEX poster in your school, a family photograph, a Husky pencil, those too-small sweatpants your neighbor always wore that revealed a little too much, your brother's KEEP OUT sign on his bedroom door, an ugly old chair in the living room—anything is fair game here.) List 25–30 things from your past. Now, choose eight of these things and describe them in detail, writing a short paragraph for each one, explaining what its "role" was in your life. How did it affect you? What was its purpose or use?

4. What event . . . ? Write a short line answering as many of these questions as you can. If it's something you don't want others to know, write it cryptically or "in code." What event . . . made you question yourself? Made you question someone or

something else? Made you mad? Made you laugh? Made you nervous? Scared you? Scarred you? Was your most forbidden? Made you proud? Made you feel guilty? Made you happy? Confused you? Excited you? Matured you? Made you lie? Taught you? Made you curious? Made you a little sad? Made you question fairness?

5. So, who are you? Think first about "labels" that might be applied to you (girl, flirtatious, Asian, tall, geeky, upper class, Catholic, auto mechanic, etc.) and describe yourself by looking at yourself from the outside, perhaps through the eyes of another person. What stereotypes are sometimes applied to you because of these "labels"? Second, view yourself from the inside, from *your own* perspective. What are some of the stereotypes that you can dispel? What are some that might be true? What are some things about you that others wouldn't know through a mere surface-level encounter? Flatter yourself, but be honest, too. Finally, think of yourself as a stir-fry dish. What would you be called, and what would be the primary ingredients? Explain.

The key to these exercises is very specific and focused writing prompts that lead students away from obvious "big-picture" topics. Notice how I try to incorporate very short narrative images in the questions themselves.

If you're teaching a literacy narrative, you might want to direct these exercises:

people that affected your literacy, places where you wrote, objects that were connected to your literacy, "literary events," and how *you're* a writer and reader. But "literacy" can be a very broad term, and I think it's a good idea to present it to students broadly. Consider this: Literacy can be drawing or painting, being well versed in the rules or the mastery of a sport or activity, finding the right words to explain to parents why you got home so late past your curfew, repairing a car or building something, making a quilt, or talking trash about a friend. Almost any topic can relate to literacy, one way or another, so more general prompts can help your students who aren't able to think of a topic involving writing or reading alone.

Once students have brainstormed in these five areas, have them do a clustering exercise to see what items match up directly and tangentially from their lists. Good topics are often smaller events (with people, places, and objects) that can be made larger through linking elements and making connections, choosing appropriate details, and finding significance. Letting students know before they choose topics that you're looking for writing that includes connections, details, and significance helps them understand what topics might work or not work so well.

Drafting and Revising

Strong exercises to help students generate ideas and text can make drafting easier.

We might see "drafting" as a very broad term; often, after students have arrived upon topics; revisited their first writing exercises on people, places, objects, and events; and read and done more writing with a focus on the topic they've chosen, most of the preliminary work of drafting is out of the way. Have your students write about the ideas they've generated, and encourage them to add specific details. By doing these activities, they've generated the most commonly omitted details of any narrative, and they are ready to develop a draft.

Ask students to begin their rough draft with "I," to tell the story from their own perspective and to fill in their details where appropriate. Telling the story directly is often the easiest way for students to get it on paper or screen and gives them a text to work with.

When they've completed a draft, consider having students rewrite, starting their second drafts with an engaging line that you pull from the middle or end of their first drafts. You can do this by walking around the class, quickly skimming their drafts, or by looking them over once they've posted them online. You may be met with a little resistance, but explain that there are hundreds of ways they could approach this draft, so why go only with the first? Your strategy in choosing a line for them to begin with is twofold: to find a "hook," an engaging line that gets them right into the heart of the story, and to make them look at the chronological possibilities of narrative.

Organizing, Transitions, and Time Markers

Events happen in some order in life, but our memories can put them in any order we want. Narrative writing can bend time, too, and one of the hardest things to teach about narration is how to make good choices about order and clarity. Here are a few exercises that might help:

- Have students literally "cut and paste" a draft. Not on the computer—have them print it out and then cut and separate each and every paragraph. Have them trade draft pieces with a classmate (preferably one that hasn't seen this draft at all), and have that classmate piece it back together. If the classmate has trouble, it's a sign that the author might need to work on the sequence of events. But also invite students to consider the possibility that stories don't always have to be told in chronological order. Scenes can be reordered or "collaged" to reveal meaning or to make significance clearer.

- Play Stand-Up Comic as a transition exercise. Write out a number of silly, odd, or "confusing" sentences with no context. Lead an exercise where your students have to find ways to connect two nonrelated sentences by using the old standby that many comedians use: "And speaking of . . ."

- For time markers, explain that every *time a sentence or paragraph shifts in time,* a reference should be made to something significant that has already happened in the narrative: Before I went in the Navy. . . . After my sister gave birth. . . . At the same time as the bird flew into the window . . .

- Tell a story in class. Seated in a circle, have each student make up a story, adding one or two lines and building the story from the lines told by the previous speaker. Each new speaker has to start with a time marker: "Three years ago . . ." "Before Megan passed her driving test . . . " "Right after Kenny screamed for rebellion . . ."

- When you read, look for good examples of time markers and save them to show your students, as they will benefit from seeing examples by experienced writers. Ask students to bring examples from their own reading.

Choosing and Maintaining a Stance

Fiction writers often speak of the writer's voice, but writers disagree on a definition of just what "voice" means: Do writers have an "authentic" voice that reflects their true selves, or do they construct various voices to meet various rhetorical demands? You may find that talking about stance avoids this predicament by focusing on the ways writers may alter their stance to achieve their purposes. You can practice in the classroom by having your students rewrite short narrative passages, adopting different tones: angry, passionate, indifferent, cynical. You can also ask students to alter the narrator's point of view, retelling Gomez's story from her parents' perspective or Emily Vallowe's from her kindergarten teacher's point of view. Or go outside the narrative and retell it from another perspective entirely—Agosín's from the point of view of a historian, or Shannon Nichols' from an official at the state Education Department.

If you're brave, you can demonstrate orally. Dust off that old John Wayne impersonation and then try telling the same tale with your bad go at Britney Spears or Jack Nicholson. Ask students to add their own versions.

Find and share examples of writing that has a strong stance and ask students to bring examples. You might also, by analyzing the language of some examples, show that stance and tone are often a matter of word choice and sentence length. For more on the relationship between voice and stance, see Chapter 24 in this guide to teaching.

Adding Detail

Description has to be memorable. Think of a man (or woman) wearing only a coat, opening the coat quickly. What do you remember the most? That detail is probably the most appropriate for your writing. And it's not always the most common or expected detail; it could be the person's navel the size of a half-dollar, or it could be a tattoo of Batman's head on the flasher's left thigh.

Using comics and films. Comic books and graphic novels have some of the clearest narrative drives of any style of writing, and the authors of these works know which details to include and which to leave out. Since narrative writing is often about action and "visual" or sensory stimulus along with some reflection, why not use some comics as models? Students can rewrite scenes based on the dialogue bubbles and comic panels. What details do they need to add to match the comics' imagery and narrative drive without the help of the images and actions in the panels? Conversely, have students rewrite their narratives in comic book form and discuss what happens. They may draw details they can then add to their writing.

A similar activity can be done with film, something a friend and colleague of mine does with great success. For example, play a brief (3–5 minutes or less) scene without any sound. Play it again and have the class discuss details they notice as the scene unfolds. Then have students try to write dialogue that they think fits the details. Play the clip again with sound, and discuss the different interpretations.

Showing, not telling. Stories are told, yes. But the creative writing mantra "Show, don't tell!" is actually valid, if we approach it knowing that we can't and shouldn't get rid of telling altogether. Think of "telling" as the glue that holds the showing together. And what is "showing"? You might demonstrate by give them a one-person show. I sometimes walk into class and play-act like I'm drunk or otherwise not with it: I'll take off my shoes, drop things, and say inappropriate things. When the show's over, I'll have students recreate the scene on paper.

Have your students try one or both of these strategies:

- Use *sensory detail* (taste, touch, sound, smell, and sight) to go beyond adjectives and adverbs. For example, ask students to use *concrete nouns* and *vivid verbs* to portray words like "big" or "angrily."

- Mix *dialogue* or *action* with any necessary reflection. Ask students to add several lines of dialogue to a reflective paragraph or to replace a passage that tells something about a character with a passage in which the character does something that shows what had been told.

Consider, too, these familiar phrases: "Action speaks louder than words" and "A picture paints a thousand words." That's what appropriate detail is all about: pictures and actions transferred through the written word. We can make language move (action), and we can make it vivid (a picture).

Showing students a model—a brief paragraph that tells, followed by a longer revision that shows—can help them see what "showing" is and understand how significance comes about through reflection. An example I wrote can be found in Chapter 30 of this guide to teaching, "Teaching about Writing Processes." But you can also make up your own.

Articulating the Narrative's Significance

Though there are many narrative approaches to choose from, after helping students experiment with tone and details you should present theme or "significance" to the students. Every writing has a theme, which starts, simply, as an abstract noun such as love, fear, or determination. You might help students hypothesize about the theme of their narrative early, so they can choose appropriate details, but remember that their theme or significance may not reveal itself until they start writing or have even finished a complete draft and asked someone else what it means.

In a narrative, the writer is often both a participant (a character) and an observer (a distanced commentator and interpreter). This commentator or interpreter often reveals the significance. A narrative is not a fairy tale, so readers are not looking for "the moral of the story." Steer students away from such endings as, "And so I *learned* never to put glue in my little sister's milk." Also, try to help students avoid vague expressions such as "I learned to strive hard for my goals" or "I learned that nothing can stop me." We are looking for the significance, which is often revealed through the narrator's descriptions of events as he or she looks back at them, revealing a present perspective on a past event: The observer relays the significance while telling and showing the participant's story. Other students who are not as close to the topic are often better at finding significance as opposed to a moral.

Don't force authors to identify a theme too early; perhaps let a classmate lead them in that direction in a workshop.

Evaluating Narratives

How do we grade narratives? Despite the subjective nature of reading and evaluating a narrative, it can be done. You might present your students with a rubric before you actually grade their work. List every single criterion you could possibly use to evaluate it (or show the class your list and see if they have anything to add—see Chapter 9 in this guide on responding to writing for tips on establishing criteria collaboratively). Explain that, depending upon their narrative choices, some criteria might not apply, giving them stylistic options. The rubric I use for narratives appears on the following page. Notice the N/A column? This section is essential because of all the possibilities that narratives present.

Writing and Creative Writing

Despite any tensions between so-called creative writing and other English composition and literature courses, in truth, there's usually little separation beyond preference and politics. All writing is creative in the sense that it wasn't there before the author put it to paper. He or she created it. And each of the divides between modes of studying writing has some sort of bridge over it; for example, narrative writing in a composition course draws a lot

Evaluation Rubric for Narratives

Narrative	Very Strong	Strong	Average	Weak	N/A	*Explanation*
Beginning						
Stance						
Significance						
Details (characters, setting, action)						
Dialogue						
Organization						
Point of view						
Transitions, time markers						
Ending						
Grammar, mechanics (sentence structure, punctuation, etc.)						

from the storytelling features of creative writing or fiction writing. But you don't have to be a "creative writer" in the categorical sense to teach narrative or to write it yourself. Creative writing strategies *can* be employed in composition classes. One book on fiction writing is especially appropriate for classes that teach narratives, especially literacy narratives and memoirs: Stephen King's *On Writing*. This book is a hybrid: On one side it's a compelling memoir or series of narratives on King's development as a writer, and on the other side it's a simple "how to" on telling stories using detail, significance, and other things we've touched on here. As a bonus, many students already know and like King's stories.

Finally, you don't have to be "imaginative" or shuffle around in bunny slippers while mumbling philosophical ideas to yourself to be qualified to write narra-

tive. Imagination evolves from memory, reflection, careful attention to detail, and good storytelling—and these skills, which we all have, are what's important in writing good narratives.

Other Useful Chapters in the *Field Guide*

1–6 RHETORICAL SITUATIONS
15 MEMOIRS
23 COLLABORATING
24 GENERATING IDEAS AND TEXT
30 BEGINNING AND ENDING
31 GUIDING YOUR READER
35 COMPARING AND CONTRASTING
38 DIALOGUE
40 NARRATING
25–28 DRAFTING, ASSESSING, YOUR OWN WRITING, GETTING RESPONSE AND REVISING, EDITING AND PROOFREADING

Useful Readings

Bishop, Wendy. "Crossing the Lines: On Creative Composition and Composing Creative Writing." *Colors of a Different Horse: Rethinking Creative Writing Theory and Pedagogy.* Ed. Wendy Bishop and Hans Ostrom. Urbana, IL: NCTE, 1994. 181–97. Print.

Danielewicz, Jane. "Personal Genres, Public Voices." *College Composition and Communication* 59.3 (2008): 420–50. Print.

King, Stephen. *On Writing: A Memoir of the Craft.* New York: Pocket–Simon & Schuster, 2000. Print.

Mirtz, Ruth. "'You Want Us to Do WHAT?' How to Get the Most Out of Unexpected Writing Assignments." *Elements of Alternate Style: Essays on Writing and Revision.* Ed. Wendy Bishop. Portsmouth, NH: Boynton/Cook, 1997. 105–15. Print.

26 Analyzing Texts

A student reading her history textbook notices that it presents a different explanation for an event than her high school textbook did and wonders which one is correct. She sets the book aside and picks up a magazine, where ads for various creams each say one is perfect for her skin. Flipping to an article in the magazine, she reads about a politician's campaign to save the environment, though she thinks she remembers hearing on the news that the same politician had voted against a bill protecting water quality. This student, like everyone else, is bombarded with information that must be carefully analyzed, not just for its truth or falsity, but also for the ways in which it is designed to influence us, both overtly and covertly. Chapter 8, ANALYZING TEXTS, teaches students to read a text critically and examine it carefully.

Analyzing a Text

Many students arrive in college with limited experience reading nonfiction texts critically. Their high school English curricula probably focused on the reading and interpretation of literature, often characterized as articulating a response to literary texts. In their other courses, they were expected to read their textbooks not as rhetorical documents but as unbiased factual material. As a result, a close, critical reading of a nonfiction text presents a new challenge; they must learn to read in different ways and apply techniques they may have learned in literature study to informative or argumentative texts. Their goal, however, is not response or interpretation but analysis and, possibly, evaluation of the text to determine how the language and structure of the text and its use of aspects of the rhetorical situation attempt to guide readers' thinking. In this assignment, students should not try to create a coherent interpretation of the text as they would in a literature class; rather, they should aim to take the text apart in order to understand its purpose and the ways its author uses textual elements to achieve that purpose. The resulting essay uses evidence students create through analyses of the text to support their assertions about the way the text works—and, often, how well. Here's what first-year graduate teaching assistant Andrea Nay has to say about teaching students to analyze a text:

> First, I must remember that this type of writing is brand-new to many of my students. As Sheena, one of my students, writes, "I think the reason why it's coming so hard is that I never had to do any serious English work." The most important common point I found is that most of my students are quite happy to write their own opinion, but academic analysis comes far more difficult to them. Jana, another student, notes, "I am not good at this kind of analysis because I am an opinionated person and there are not too many places for opinion in this paper." I feel I may have confused some students by starting off the unit having them write me a "Dear Andrea" letter responding to the focus article with their own opinion. That started them, right off the bat, lacing their analysis with their own biased comments. This carried through into their papers, and my workshops and conferences were mainly spent helping them extract their own "rants" from portions of their drafts.

As Nay correctly notes, students are more accustomed to stating their own opinion or reacting to ideas than to analyzing nonfiction texts. Therefore, students often find the task of analyzing a text challenging, so you need to offer considerable help. Modeling, walking the class through analytical techniques, and encouraging even modest progress are all likely to be needed at various points along the way as students try out unfamiliar ways of thinking and writing.

Using the Readings and Teaching the Key Features

You can use readings not only to help students understand how a textual analysis might work but also to help them see what they already know about analyzing texts. You might ask students to discuss the implications of some print ads or television commercials to introduce them to Hannah Berry's analysis of two shoe ads. Berry's essay is annotated to show how she includes the Key Features of a text analysis, and students may benefit from a discussion focused on those features. You might introduce Emily Nussbaum's "In Defense of Liz Lemon" by discussing women as they are depicted in various television shows, both dramas and comedies. You might give students copies of the Gettysburg Address to analyze before reading what William Safire makes of it. And you might introduce Sam Anderson's "Just One More Game . . ." by asking them about their own gaming experiences. Asking students to identify the Key Features of each text—where the writer provides a summary of the text, pays attention to its context, presents a clear interpretation or judgment, and offers reasonable support for his or her conclusions—will help them understand each writer's techniques and the demands of their assignment. After students have read these four analyses, they'll have background to help them see the techniques each writer uses, and they'll begin to exercise their own critical-reading skills.

Choosing a Text to Analyze

Choosing an appropriate text for your students to analyze is your first challenge. A good way to understand some of the difficulties the text will present for your students—and whether or not it's a good one to assign—is to analyze it yourself, using some of the techniques you'll ask your students to use. Guidelines for choosing an appropriate text include the following:

- Look for relatively brief texts. Newspaper editorials are often good choices, as they typically focus on a single, narrowly defined topic and deal with it in a few hundred words at most. Op-ed essays can be useful, though they sometimes are less focused than editorials. Even letters to the editor of newspapers can be fruitful choices, especially when you're introducing the assignment. Other possibilities include sections from college or high school textbooks, parts of longer news or magazine articles, texts of websites, and civic or government documents of various sorts, including speeches (for which audio and video files are often available online).

- Choose a text with a single, clear thesis statement. Many op-ed pieces contain more than one statement that may serve as a thesis for a section of the essay. Some begin with a fairly lengthy introduction, followed by a thesis placed roughly one-third

through the essay. Single-thesis texts may represent only part of the pantheon of possible essay styles, but they function like frogs in biology classes: simple, but still complex enough to be challenging to dissect.

- Look for a text with a structure that can be outlined without undue difficulty and that won't require students to spend too much time figuring out the meaning. Most instructors find that almost any text, even one that seems simple, grows in complexity and depth as students analyze it, and the point of the assignment is the analysis—not mastery of a complex concept.

- Know how much contextual research you'll ask of your students. If you choose a text on a subject of contemporary interest, students will know or be able to find out easily about the context of the information or argument. A document from the past, however, may require students to research the context within which the text was written.

- Consider the emotional response students may have to the text. If you choose a text on a controversial topic, you'll need to deal with students' responses to the text and its stance, allowing them to articulate their response before and during their analysis and drafting. As teaching assistant Sharon Tjaden noted while teaching an analysis, "My students are struggling with separating their responses and their opinions from analyzing this article." The more controversial the topic, the more difficult it is for students to respond objectively.

- Alternately, you might ask students to find a text on their own, though you should design this assignment carefully to avoid being overwhelmed with the work of understanding 20 or 25 texts well enough to determine the accuracy of students' analyses. A good example is an assignment made by Peggy Lindsey, formerly a lecturer at Wright State University. She introduces the assignment by showing a video critiquing advertising, *Killing Us Softly* (one of several useful films by documentary filmmaker Jean Kilbourne; available at www.jeankilbourne.com). After discussing the film, Peggy distributes several print ads and asks groups of students to pick three that are somehow related and discuss how they are related in brief presentations to the class. Students then find on their own ads that "depict similar values or attitudes toward some societal group" to form the basis for their textual analyses. Hannah Berry's analysis of two shoe ads developed from this assignment.

Once you've chosen an appropriate text, you might introduce the textual analysis assignment by modeling some brief analyses of visual texts or advertisements, letters to the editor, or other texts, including texts similar to the one students will analyze. Asking students to participate in these analyses will show them how much they already know about texts and how sensitive they are to nuances of language, arguments, and the ways in which texts attempt to manipulate their responses.

Getting Started

Since this sort of analysis is new for most students, they'll benefit from practice. Consider beginning with brief texts, songs, or videos and providing questions for them to answer about various aspects of the text. Catherine Crowley, a lecturer at Wright State University, asks students to analyze brief music videos by working in groups on the following tasks:

- Write a brief summary of the plot or storyline of the video. Tell who is "speaking" and what information you know about him or her—for example, allegiances, background information, and point of view.

- Discuss the artist's purpose. What is the main idea he or she is trying to get across? Why does the artist want to make this point? What does he or she wish to accomplish? Is the purpose stated directly or implied?

- Discuss the social, political, and/or cultural context of the writing. How does this topic or text fit in with the larger world? In other words, what topics are addressed? For example: Is it a patriotic text meant to inspire people? Does it address poverty and social injustice among immigrant populations?

- Who is the intended audience? What is the artist's stance toward the audience? How do you know this? Who will this video appeal to, and why? Who will it not appeal to, and why not?

- Discuss how the artist portrays his or her ideas. What artistic or technical devices does the video employ? What about the artist's use of language? What about the voice (for example: sarcastic, humorous . . . this may have more than one characteristic). What details add to your interpretation? How do these details influence the message? Give examples.

- *Analysis:* How effective is this video? In other words, does it achieve the artist's purpose? Why or why not?

Doing the Analysis

ANALYZING TEXTS, Chapter 8, provides detailed advice to help students understand what they need to do and how to go about doing it. Once they have developed a tentative thesis, you should direct them to Chapter 41, READING STRATEGIES, where they can find detailed advice on reading carefully along with several methods for analyzing texts. Once they've done several analyses from that chapter, they'll be ready to analyze their text's rhetorical sit-

uation, rethink their thesis, and rough out a conclusion.

Consider asking students to write answers to the questions in the Previewing a Text and Annotating sections of Chapter 41 in the *Field Guide.* You might ask them to annotate the text they're to analyze and compare their annotations with other students'. You might explain that who we are—our thoughts, experiences, and values—are a kind of filter through which we read or absorb information and that we have to recognize this filter and account for it as we begin to analyze. A good approach is to write a first response where we can get all of our reactions out in the open; only at that point can we read the article more objectively. Asking students to play the Believing and Doubting game (described in Chapter 41), either on paper or orally in groups, can help them see the text from at least two perspectives—and get past their own response to the text's ideas, so they can start to develop an analysis. Thus, you can avoid the problem Andrea Nay describes.

You can structure an analysis of the text in several ways. Here are some options:

- Choose the methods of analyzing that the class should complete, or work together with the class to decide which methods are most suitable for the text and the assignment as you've created it.

- Treat each method of analyzing as a separate assignment; for example, each student might be asked to create a topical outline, a *functional* outline, a summary, or a list *of* patterns. Students might then compare their analyses in groups or as part of a class discussion.

- Have students work in groups, each group having as its assignment an analysis of the text based on a specific method or on a subset of that method: one group creates a functional outline while other groups look for patterns: of sentence types, of imagery, of repeated words or phrases, and so on. Then the groups could present their findings to the class for all to share.

- Have students analyze the argument as a group activity (see Analyzing the Argument in Chapter 41 and the advice about exploring the issue strategically and coming up with good reasons in Chapter 10 of the *Field Guide*).

- Give students a quiz on argument fallacies. Many students enjoy ferreting out fallacies as well as deciding whether they are used as fallacies in the rhetorical context of a text, and a quiz really does provide incentive to read and study them. Students may later complain that they're seeing fallacies everywhere, an opportunity for you to smile and nod in response.

Writing an Analysis

The hardest part of writing a critical analysis is moving from analysis to a conclu-sion. At this point, students must shift from collecting information through various analytical activities to creating a coherent essay based on a unifying theme: its response to its rhetorical situation. They have examined the text in three ways: in terms of what the text says, how it works, and what it means. Their analysis essay should include a brief summary that outlines what the text says, but it may then move in one of several directions.

How the text works. In this type of analysis, students focus on the means by which the text gets its meaning across. They may identify a particular strategy of appealing to the text's audience, characteristic use of language, or ways of presenting material (such as metaphors, examples, anecdotes, and explanations). They may draw on their functional outlines to show how the text's organization moves the reader from point to point to a particular conclusion or overall effect.

What the text means. Students focusing on the meaning of the text may focus on their topical outlines to show how the text moves from beginning to ending, building and elaborating on a single overall meaning—or to show that it begins on one topic but diverges from it. They may focus on the logic of individual statements and how that logic either does or does not hold from statement to statement. They may trace patterns of imagery or the writer's use of "loaded" language to show how the writer is writing from a particular stance or slanting the meaning to a particular purpose.

How well the text works. In either case, the analysis may also lead to an evaluation of the text's effectiveness, based on criteria drawn from the elements of the rhetorical situation:

- How effective is this text in meeting its purpose?
- How effective is it in meeting the needs and expectations of its audience or affecting its audience as its author intended?
- How well does it use the conventions of its genre?
- How well does its author convey his or her stance?
- And how well does it employ design in its chosen medium to achieve its aims?

Having students answer these questions about the text's rhetorical situation can help them revise their tentative thesis based on the results of their analysis.

Providing Evidence

Once students clarify their thesis, you may need to help them draw evidence from their analyses to support their assertions. To do this, have students look through their materials for patterns: What shows up more than once, either within a single analysis or across two or more? What relationships can be seen in the information? What do these patterns tell students about the text? How can they fit what they learn together? You may need to help them look for clusters of related information that they can use to create an outline to guide them as they draft their essays. Ways of Organizing a Textual Analysis can help them think about how to structure their essays, and Writing Out a Draft offers several options for drafting, which may have to be done in several stages. Be aware that the novelty of the textual analysis assignment will make it difficult for many students, so schedule ample time for conferences; workshops; Getting Response and Revising activities, both from Chapter 8, and from Chapter 27; and opportunities for students to assess their own writing, using Chapter 29; many students will need several attempts before they fully understand the demands of the assignment.

Evaluating Textual Analyses

Focus on how well students apply the Key Features in their own writing. In addition, you should consider your goal for assigning this task: Some instructors ask students for well-organized, polished final drafts; others, however, use the assignment to improve students' critical-reading and reasoning abilities and are forgiving of structural problems or even surface errors that may increase in frequency when students are thinking hard about their writing's content. For more tips on evaluating text analyses and other student writing, see Chapters 9 and 12 of this guide to teaching.

Literary Analyses

Analysis of literature is the heart of many university English departments, and most universities require students to take one or more literature courses as part of their general education requirements. For those reasons, you may wish to ask students to analyze a literary work in your course. If you do, emphasize that a literary analysis is a form of argument; as in other arguments, students need to make an assertion in the form of a thesis and use evidence from the text to support it. Careful attention to the Key Features, showing examples from your own, other students', or literary critics' work, can help establish your expectations for this assignment.

Using the reading and teaching the Key Features. Allowing students an opportunity to discuss their interpretations of Shelley's sonnet before they read Stephanie Huff's analysis may be a good way of demonstrating the myriad reactions that a literary work may elicit. Huff's analysis may then be read as an example of how a reaction can be shaped into a well-supported analysis by using the Key Features of literary analyses. Also, some students, after years of English classes, have developed a negative attitude toward analyzing literature, believing that it is "much ado about nothing," but for those students, Huff's analysis is a good example of how we can find meaning in the minutest details of a work when we respect authors enough to give them credit—and hold them accountable—for the language they use.

Some tips for teaching literary analyses

Help students choose a method of analysis. There are, of course, many ways to analyze literary texts. One, focusing on the text itself, is likely the most familiar to students from their previous education. The ways of analyzing texts in Chapter 41, READING STRATEGIES, can be helpful in focusing students' attention on specific textual features.

Another, focusing on their response as readers, may be familiar to some students, as the method has become popular in some high school curriculums. To introduce students to it, you might choose the first paragraph in a story or the first stanza of a poem. Write the first word on the board and ask students, "What might come next?" They may be able to guess whether the sentence is likely to be a statement or question, but little else. Add the second word, and repeat the question, then the third, and so on. Students will see that at a certain point, they can guess the shape and likely content of several words to come. As you proceed, add phrases, then entire sentences, to show that as we read, our choices narrow and broaden as we experience the words in sequence. By slowing down the reading experience, we can analyze it and create an interpretation based on our predictions and how the text fulfills or frustrates them.

A third method, analyzing the text as part of a context, can turn the literary analysis into a full-blown research project as students discover the author's biography and other works, the era or culture of the time of the work's original publication, the genre, or some other larger context of which the work forms a part. Analyses based on the other methods will often benefit from some research of this sort; in her analysis of Shelley's poem, Huff might have researched the influence of Plato's allegory of the cave on Shelley's thinking. A context-focused analysis may attract students who are more interested in history, culture, or technology than in literature; at the same time, a danger in this analysis is that the literary work itself may disappear as the student gets caught up in the context. Making sure the student's thesis focuses on the work in its context—and checking early drafts to make sure they relate to the thesis—can keep students' attention where it should be.

Provide questions for revising. Here are some questions for you and peer reviewers to ask about drafts of a literary analysis (adapted from Ockerstrom, 221–22):

- Did the writer's analysis of this work improve your understanding of it? If so, how?

- Identify the writer's thesis. Is the thesis sufficiently focused, clearly worded, and analytical?

- Describe the organization of this essay. Is there a definite organizing strategy?

- Does the writer support the analysis with enough evidence from the work? Where does the writer need more evidence? Where is there too much evidence, or evidence without an explanation? Is this the best evidence to support the writer's analysis?

- Has the writer avoided summarizing the plot?

- Are quotations and paraphrases from the work correctly integrated into the writer's own prose? Are they introduced by signal phrases?

If you are studying literature, you may find some students' apparent opaqueness about literature and inability to analyze it particularly difficult to understand. It's good to remember that when you're very close to a subject, much of it seems self-evident, while to a novice it's challenging and puzzling. For the same reason, you may want to avoid asking students to read and analyze your favorite poems, stories, or novels because you may be disappointed by their responses to your personal preferences.

Be aware of common problems: You're likely to run into the following problems students writing about literature can have:

- *Seeking "the right answer" or assuming that all literary analysis is arbitrary.* Much of students' education consists of learning information and being tested on it, and their goal is, of necessity, knowing the right answers. They may generalize that literature, too, has a correct interpretation that English teachers, for perverse reasons, refuse to tell. Because literature doesn't lend itself to "the right answer," some students may conclude that interpretation is a meaningless game. Explaining how literary analysis makes an argument from evidence to support an interpretation may help correct both misunderstandings. You might also bring up examples from other fields—criminology, biology, history—to show how different analysts can use the same evidence but derive very different interpretations as a way to make the point that literary analysis is not a special case, but an instance of a common human activity.

- *Summarizing instead of interpreting.* Some students retell the story or summarize the action of the poem and think they've interpreted it. Usually, they do so because they don't know what else to do. Walking through an analysis of a brief text in class, or asking students to create topical and functional outlines (from the *Field Guide*, Chapter 41, READING STRATEGIES) can help them distinguish what a text *says* from what it *does*.

- *Failing to support assertions with textual evidence.* Often, students have trouble identifying the parts of the text that can support their thesis—or identifying patterns in the text at all. They're used to reading for meaning, and the interplay between the meaning of a text and the words that convey that meaning (especially literary meaning as opposed to literal meaning) is invisible to them. They might find activities from Chapter 41 of the *Field Guide* helpful here, especially color coding. Students who take in

information best visually may see highlighted patterns in words and phrases that they don't see otherwise. Some students can find evidence but stumble in using it to support their assertions because they have trouble articulating patterns within the evidence. They may benefit from making lists of textual features that they highlight in the same color and writing a sentence describing each list or from annotating the text as they read and reread, perhaps using different colors of ink for each reading's annotations.

Other Useful Chapters in the *Field Guide*

Useful Readings

Booth, Wayne C. "The Rhetorical Stance." *College Composition and Communication* 14.3 (1963): 139–45. Print.

Corbett, Edward P.J., and Robert J. Connors. *Style and Statement*. New York: Oxford UP, 1999. Print.

Hickey, Dona J. *Developing a Written Voice*. Mountain View, CA: Mayfield, 1993. Print.

Reporting Information **27**

Students are accustomed to reading texts that report information because their primary form of reading throughout most of their education has been textbooks. They may also read newspapers, magazines, websites, and books focusing on their various interests. And many of them have written one or more research papers in high school that demanded that they combine several sources of information to create an informative essay. Nevertheless, they may find the assignment sequence in Chapter 9, REPORTING INFORMATION, challenging. They may have difficulty maintaining a neutral stance toward their subject. They are likely to be encountering scholarly research and using the resources of a university library for the first time, and they may find that synthesizing the information they glean from their sources can be daunting. Writing an essay reporting information, though, will give students the experience of in-depth, college-level research and practice in conveying information to an interested audience that will stand them in good stead in other research-based writing assignments in first-year writing courses and beyond.

Using Readings and Teaching the Key Features

You might begin by asking students to write a two-part response to each reading in Chapter 9 of the *Field Guide*, first summarizing its content to show that they understand it and then writing a reaction. Student Michaela Cullington's report on texting offers a detailed examination of a topic many students will find relevant. Because the essay is annotated to show how Cullington integrates the Key Features, it's a good place to start. Nicholas Carr's "Rural > City > Cyberspace," on the other hand, offers a contrasting view of the effects of the internet on our thinking that students will find easy to summarize. "Throwing Like a Girl" relies on detailed descriptions that can be hard to visualize and includes competing hypotheses and opinions, and students may find it a more challenging essay. And Matthew O'Brien's essay on engagement rings offers a straightforward explanation of the economics behind the tradition of giving and keeping the rings. You can use these essays to show the range of possibilities in essays reporting information, in terms of topics and how they are treated. You can then begin a class discussion by asking students to read from their responses. Next, review the Key Features of reports and ask students to discuss how those key features are presented in each of the essays. "Texting" offers a focused topic and accurate, well-researched information; "Throwing" presents detailed explanations of the way our bodies work to throw a baseball; and both "Throwing" and "Rings" use visuals that can lead to a discussion of appropriate design. These activities will lay a good foundation for students to begin thinking about their own report topics and strategies.

Getting Started and Choosing a Topic

Choosing a good topic can be a challenge for students. They may choose a topic that's far too broad to report in a relatively brief essay or that leads to an avalanche of available information that would be hard to sort through. A student interested in a topic relating to domestic abuse or violence within families, for example, found that typing "family violence" into a Web search engine resulted in almost 2 million hits, and "domestic abuse" gave her almost a million. Students may also choose topics that are phrased as arguments or that would be hard to write without becoming argumentative. A student who wants to write an essay exploring how the news media is biased, for example, is making a claim that must be argued. And students

who want to write on topics like abortion or athletes' steroid use will have difficulty not only narrowing their topic but also finding information that is indeed impartial.

For these reasons (and more that your students will reveal as they present their topics to you), it's good practice to spend time with individual students and your class, helping them find and hone good topics. You might ask students to email you their proposed topics or to post them on a discussion board. You can then read over them and either discuss them in class or post your responses online. Students benefit from hearing or reading your suggestions for other students' topics, as many will change or adjust their own topics after hearing your critique of other, similar topics. Getting the topics in advance also allows you to do quick searches on your own to see if topics will lead to enough—or too many—sources of information or if using a synonym or rephrasing the topic will result in better source information. This research can be as simple as using a web search site or a library database, such as *Academic Search Complete*, and it can help you give students good advice on how to proceed.

You can then help students move from a preliminary topic to a working thesis by having them review the rhetorical situation in which they are working and narrow their topic by finding and reading some general sources. Often, students can do this efficiently by interviewing an expert on their topic—for example, a faculty member in the academic field or a local politician, journalist, business leader, mechanic, or farmer. Discussing their topic with an expert can help students limit their topics and point them toward good information, often information more current than is available through the library—and the interaction with a person can engage them with their topic. Then they're in a position to create a thesis and start doing serious research.

Helping Students Research Their Topics

If this assignment serves as your students' introduction to academic research, you may find that their concept of serious research differs from yours. Many students have no clear idea of what constitutes a scholarly source as opposed to a popular source, and careful definitions are sometimes insufficient to help them see the difference. Bringing in or downloading samples of scholarly sources to show students their distinguishing features can be helpful. For example, scholarly sources, unlike many news articles or encyclopedia entries, always list their authors and often their academic affiliations; scholarly sources cite their sources both in the text and in a list of sources at the end, while popular sources do not; and depending on the discipline, scholarly sources include an abstract, while popular sources do not. Students need help finding good sources in the library and online, so provide any help you can. The *Field Guide* offers detailed advice in Chapters 43–45. Here are some suggestions:

- Devote class time to searching for sources. If your school's library will allow you to hold class there, you can work with students as they search for sources in the library's catalog and databases. Often, reference librarians will make themselves available to assist both the students and you as you search. If you're teaching in a computer classroom, you can do this searching there.

- Hold research conferences. Instead of or in addition to working with all your students in class, consider holding research conferences, again where students have access to your library's holdings. I've had success by scheduling three students at a time for thirty-minute periods, helping those three find useful sources.

- Use the services of librarians. The resources available in university libraries grow and change rapidly, and only reference librarians can be counted on to keep up. So enlisting their aid as much as you can will not only help your students find information, it'll help you, too. Invite librarians to visit your class and point out how to access the library's resources. And model good research behavior by asking their help when you're stumped—as you will be.

- Help students rethink their topics if their original topic proves too difficult to find good information on. Sometimes students hit dead ends: There's simply nothing available on their topic, or—as is more often the case—there's too much, leading the student either to become overwhelmed or to think too generally about their topic. In either case, you can help by working with the student to adjust the topic, either making it more specific or more general, or exploring a related issue for which good information is available. For example, a student who wants to report on hypnosis will have trouble finding sources that lead to interesting information; the use of hypnosis by medical professionals, on the other hand, has a wealth of potential sources and the opportunity for further narrowing of the topic to a particular use of hypnosis in medicine.

- Require students to find more sources than they'll use. Like all of us, students practice economy: If you ask for at least three sources in an essay, some students will find and consult three sources. If you ask for eight to ten sources, though, students will find eight to ten, become much better informed about their topics, write better essays (we hope), and be able to choose the best sources, rather than rely on the first ones they find.

Help students organize their research, too. Consider asking them to create an annotated bibliography as part of the assignment, providing full bibliographic information that they can then simply copy and paste into a Works Cited or References page when they draft. Require them to photocopy each source they use—at least the pages containing bibliographic information and those containing information they cite—to label each one, and to include these copies when they submit their annotated bibliographies and drafts. This activity forces them to organize their sources and saves you time when you read their work, as you can quickly consult the sources to see how well they've quoted, paraphrased, summarized, and cited them. Requiring copies of sources also cuts down on intentional plagiarism while showing you instances of unintentional plagiarism—and presents a teaching opportunity.

Organizing, Drafting, and Revising

Reporting information well relies on clear organization, so it's a good idea to ask students to create an outline of their report before they draft it. The *Field Guide* offers three ways to organize a report that students should consider as they plan and offers advice on the various strategies—narrating, defining, comparing, and others—that writing a report may require. Still, you may need to warn students about common pitfalls of writing a report and have students look for them when they're ready to revise:

- *Beginning too generally*: A standard diagram showing how to introduce a report shows a funnel at the top, enjoining the writer to begin with a general statement and gradually zero in on a thesis statement. Students who have learned this technique sometimes take it to an extreme; for example, a student writing on the effect of negative emotions on our physical health began her essay, "Everyone has emotions." See *Field Guide* Chapter 30, BEGINNING AND ENDING, for some other ways of beginning.

- *Turning the report into a how-to manual or argument:* Sometimes students start out explaining a process, but at some point, they begin giving instructions, changing their focus from describing the information being conveyed to what "you" need to do to make something happen. Similarly, students sometimes become engaged in their topic and find maintaining a balanced stance difficult.

- *Scaffolding:* I use this analogy: When someone erects a building, they need scaffolding on the outside to stand on while they do the brickwork, put in the windows, and the like. Once the building is done, however, the scaffolding is removed so we see the structure itself. Statements like "In the following paragraph I will explain . . ." or "In the article 'Legislature Outlaws Visible Underwear,' it states that . . ." are scaffolding that draw attention away from the information being reported to the paper and its writer.

- *Problems with sources:* Some of the most common include not providing citations or signal phrases in the text to show where information came from, citing sources in the text that don't appear in the list at the end, and failing to provide photocopies of cited sources. A problem you may also encounter is the unacceptable paraphrase: a student may follow a source's language, structure, or both too closely. Most of the time, this problem involves a single paragraph or less, but once in a while a desperate student will borrow the structure of an entire source. Examples of unacceptable paraphrase may be found in *Field Guide* Chapter 47, but it's often useful to provide examples from your students' own writing, perhaps by showing the original and the paraphrase side by side, highlighting similar passages.

- *Ignoring conflicting evidence:* When students research topics, they often find sources that offer differing views. They may react in one of three ways: They present both sources' views equally and uncritically, as if no conflict existed; they present both sources' views and end their essay by throwing up their hands and saying something like "It's up to the reader to decide"; or they simply ignore one side's view, presenting the other as if there were no controversy. Instead, they should investigate the sources of the evidence to see if one has greater credibility than the other, and, if that proves inconclusive, present the controversy as a controversy: For example, "Experts disagree over whether or not we can reduce the risk of a shark attack when we swim in the ocean. Source A asserts _____, while Source B says _____." See *Field*

Guide Chapter 41, READING STRATEGIES, and Chapter 45, EVALUATING SOURCES.

Of course, these are the same pitfalls you'll be looking for when you evaluate their finished work, along with their handling of the Key Features of a report. For more tips on evaluating reports and other student writing, see Chapters 9 and 12 of this guide to teaching.

31 GUIDING YOUR READER
35 COMPARING AND CONTRASTING
52 CHOOSING MEDIA
53 DESIGNING TEXT
54 USING VISUALS, INCORPORATING SOUND
25–28 DRAFTING, ASSESSING A DRAFT, REVISING, EDITING AND PROOFREADING

Other Useful Chapters in the *Field Guide*

1–6 RHETORICAL SITUATIONS
17 PROPOSALS (for topic proposals)
43–51 DOING RESEARCH
12 ANNOTATED BIBLIOGRAPHIES
23 COLLABORATING
24 GENERATING IDEAS AND TEXT
30 BEGINNING AND ENDING

A Useful Reading

Connors, Robert J. "The Rhetoric of Explanation: Explanatory Rhetoric from Aristotle to 1850" and "The Rhetoric of Explanation: Explanatory Rhetoric from 1850 to the Present." *Selected Essays of Robert J. Connors.* Ed. Lisa Ede and Andrea A. Lunsford. Boston: Bedford/St. Martin's, 2003. Print.

Arguing a Position **28**

In many first-year writing courses, essays arguing a position are central to the curriculum, and for good reason: As students write in courses across the curriculum, they will be asked to present arguments of one kind or another. Even reports that don't make an overt argument nonetheless represent the writer's version of the information and suggest to readers that that version is reasonable or correct. At the same time, students will be required to read arguments critically and therefore need to know how arguments are constructed. Chapter 10, ARGUING A POSITION, guides students through the process of developing an argumentative essay. Since writing a successful argument is a complex undertaking, you may find that, more than with other assignments, you'll need to assign various sections of the *Field Guide*, either for the whole class to use or for individual students as they generate ideas and text, do research, and draft their essays.

Getting Started

You might introduce the concept of arguing a position with texts in various genres and media, including magazine or television ads and hip hop or rock, to demonstrate that arguments—attempts to influence our thoughts or behavior—are all around us. Indeed, you might ask students to consider the role of corporate logos on their clothes to explore how these symbols may function as arguments. You then need to distinguish between arguments of the sort found in advertisements, arguments around the kitchen table (or on TV news analysis programs), and academic arguments.

Using the Readings and Teaching the Key Features

Having students read the model essays in this chapter is a good way to introduce the Key Features of writing that argues a position, either by teasing out what makes each essay effective or by examining how each writer uses the Key Features. Joanna MacKay briefly outlines the motivations driving the market for kidney transplants and then presents her thesis; MacKay's essay is annotated to show how she includes the Key Features, so you may find that spending some time walking students through her argument will help them understand what an academic argument should include. She offers medical, physiological, and social evidence to support her reasons. In "The Dark Side of Science," Heather E. Douglas relies on reasons and examples to make her case that scientists are responsible for the effects of their research. Lawrence Lessig's essay on electronic piracy states its clear and arguable position in the first sentence. And Andrew Leonard effectively uses a humorous tone and examples from multiple media to argue that holiday advertising is out of control. Each establishes a trustworthy tone in different ways that you may wish to discuss, and each offers careful consideration of other positions, again in very different ways. In any case, students need to be aware of the basic features of writing that argues a position.

To write a good argument, students must choose and refine a topic that is clear and arguable, provide a context for the topic, come up with good reasons and support for each one, appeal to readers' values (which entails understanding what those values are), write with a trustworthy tone, and show that they have considered other positions carefully and are presenting them fairly. The advice that follows covers each of these Key Features, grouped as you might teach them.

Choosing a clear and arguable topic. Students often think that they should choose "big" topics for argument essays, for example, abortion, gun control, or evolution. Such topics are seldom successful.

Opinion on them is so polarized that finding reasoned debate and reasonable sources amid the avalanche of dogmatic and partisan source material available is difficult at best—and students who choose such topics usually begin with strong opinions one way or another, reducing their ability to explore ideas with an open mind. It's better for students to choose issues that they have some personal connection with, as source material on these topics often is more limited and less polarized than with the "big" issues. Even if they choose a major issue, their personal connection to it often helps them narrow it, their knowledge of it aids them in contextualizing it for their readers, and their interest in the topic often leads to a better essay.

The section on Generating Ideas and Text in Chapter 10 asks students to examine their topic from several perspectives and in potentially unfamiliar ways to determine whether it's arguable and worth working on. Within that section, the advice to "explore the issue strategically"—as a matter of definition, classification, comparison, and process (known rhetorically as _stases_)—is particularly useful as students explore their topics. Arguments may be classified in terms of the questions they try to answer: What are the facts of this case? How might this topic be defined? What caused this, or what are its effects? Is it good, bad, or a mix—or better or worse than something else? Should someone do something?

Often, these questions are best addressed in order. Suggest to students that when they write about a topic, they are likely to first *describe* and *define* it. Once they've done that, they can discuss what *caused* it or what its *effects* are, allowing them to *evaluate* it. Then, based on their evaluation, they may *propose* that something be done. For example, Michael Granoff's essay "Course Requirement: Extortion" (pp. 205–7) begins by describing a problem: college textbooks are expensive. He then outlines the cause: used text sales reduce the number of new books sold, so publishers must set high prices and produce new editions often to recoup their costs and make a profit. He then evaluates this cycle, noting that in many fields, the texts are revised and bundled with extras only to keep sales up, not to include new knowledge. His analysis results in a proposal to sell textbooks as software is sold, through licenses.

In some academic writing, however, writers may argue based on a single question—for instance, arguing for a revised definition of an important term, exploring the causes or effects of something, or evaluating it. For example, Carolyn Stonehill's essay "It's in Our Genes: The Biological Basis of Human Mating Behavior" (pp. 564–74) focuses on the causes of humans' attraction to potential mates, from women's need for a "strong, capable man" and men's need for a healthy, youthful woman to the role of the media and humans' capacity for symbolic thought.

The process of exploring a topic leads students to the drafting of a thesis statement, which they then must qualify. Detailed advice on creating an arguable,

appropriately qualified thesis may be found in Chapter 33, ARGUING.

Some students will need to search general sources in order to explore their topics adequately, so you may direct those students to Chapter 44, FINDING SOURCES, for help. You will likely find it useful to check their thesis statements at this point to make sure their topics are appropriate—arguable, narrow or broad enough, and doable in the time available—before they do more research.

Crafting a Good Argument

A good argument is complicated, and taking into account the various aspects that can make an argument succeed or fail can be difficult for students. One way to help them is to deal with these aspects one at a time. Here are some tips for doing so.

Appealing to readers' values. Many students have done most of their writing either for an audience of one—a teacher—or, having been taught formal characteristics of writing, for no audience at all. Their need to define their audience is therefore new to them and deserves your attention as you teach. Insist that they seriously consider—in writing—the questions posed in Considering the Rhetorical Situation, especially those about audience. You may want them to consider one additional question: What kinds of arguments is this audience likely to consider, accept, or reject out of hand? For example, an audience of political progressives is likely to consider an argument suggesting that Social Security creates a safety net that helps all of society but reject an argument suggesting that the pension program reduces workers' freedom to invest their money as they like; a conservative audience will likely do the opposite. In other words, the readers whom students choose to address strongly influence the kind of research they'll do (some audiences will prefer eyewitness testimony over scholarly research, for example) and the nature of the sources they use (conservatives will likely accept conservative columnist George Will's word over that of the more liberal commentator Paul Krugman, and vice versa).

Wright State University lecturer Sarah McGinley puts it this way: "It's not people who agree with you who need reasons to rethink their position (otherwise known as preaching to the choir); it's those who disagree with you that do. By appealing to their values and beliefs rather than only asserting your own, you will be more effective." McGinley offers these suggestions for students to connect the reader's values with their positions:

- If your readers are worried about being safe as they walk home, you can say that legalizing drugs will cut down on street corner dealers.
- If they are worried about how many teens are in jail because of dealing, you can say that legalizing drugs will not just decriminalize dealing but also make it less lucrative and less glamorous. Fewer teens will be tempted.

- If they are complaining about high taxes because of expensive prisons and about police departments being too busy to deal with other crime, you can show how budgets and manpower allocations will change. Legal drugs can also be taxed.

McGinley then asks students to answer these questions:

1. Why do people disagree about your issue? Is it facts, evidence, definitions, philosophies, assumptions, beliefs, and/or culture that causes the disagreement?
2. How do your audience's values, assumptions, and beliefs differ from your own? What aspects of your outlook might threaten or offend them? Does your argument challenge them? What values, beliefs, or assumptions about the world do you and your audience share? How can you find something in common? What can you build on?
3. What audience-based reasons can you work into your paper?

Then, as students draft, they can appeal to their readers' values because they know who they're writing to and what evidence may move those readers. Here are some tips for helping students define and analyze their audiences:

- Have students select two or three different audiences, for example, "classmates," "parents," and "readers of the campus newspaper." Discuss how the rhetorical situation differs for each audience.

- Have students write briefly, perhaps an email or text message to a friend, and then rewrite it for various audiences. Discuss the changes each new audience required.

- Have students explore how readers' purposes can influence their reading. For example, an instructor's purpose in reading a student essay may be to see how well the student demonstrates knowledge and ability to compose; a parent's purpose in reading a student's email may be both to get information about the student's life and to be reassured that the student is doing well physically and emotionally.

Providing background information. Students who already know something about their topic might well use the techniques for GENERATING IDEAS AND TEXT in both Chapter 10 and Chapter 24 to be able to give an overview of the topic. Others may first need to gather background information from general sources as they explore their topics. If your assignment sequence includes a research component, students are likely to come up with sufficient background information as they read their sources; nonetheless, it's a good idea to remind students to look for and take notes on such information as they read.

Coming up with good reasons and support for those reasons. Reasoning clearly is primary to students' success. You should therefore spend some time on the developing of good arguments and the avoidance of logical fallacies. Chapter 33, ARGUING, offers detailed advice on developing reasons and support as well as other aspects of writing assignments. You might have students model essays or evaluate the reasons given in an advertisement. Have students collaborate (see Chapter 23 in the *Field Guide*) on brainstorming and then evaluate potential arguments for one another's drafts. You could write an argument with the class, listing potential reasons for a topic on the board and discussing which ones are suitable for the rhetorical situation you've outlined. Because many good reasons come to us through our reading and research, you should let students know that their reasons may well change as they learn more about their topics.

Doing research to find support. Most of the time, organized, in-depth research to find support is crucial to success in arguing a position. To help students, you should fold into your assignment sequence the activities in Chapter 43 for DEVELOPING A RESEARCH PLAN, Chapter 44 for FINDING SOURCES, Chapter 45 for EVALUATING SOURCES, Chapter 46 for SYNTHESIZING IDEAS, Chapter 47 for QUOTING, PARAPHRASING, AND SUMMARIZING, and Chapter 48 for ACKNOWLEDGING SOURCES, AVOIDING PLAGIARISM. Even if you have assigned these chapters for a previous assignment, it wouldn't hurt to do a quick review. Students' challenge in finding sources to support an argument differs from that of finding information or supporting a textual analysis, so you may need to help them locate balanced sources or a balance among various sources. You may also need to help them evaluate sources to see if the reasons and evidence offered by the sources are themselves questionable. Students may also need to investigate the backgrounds and affiliations of their sources to assess whether the sources are espousing an unstated point of view or philosophy. Some students may choose topics that require interviews or observations for adequate support; they can find help in doing those kinds of research in Chapter 43. Detailed advice on teaching these chapters can be found in Chapter 32 in this guide to teaching.

Refuting or acknowledging other positions. As students do their research, they need to take into account the positions held by those with whom they disagree. In practice, they need to find sources that don't simply echo their own positions, evaluate those sources fairly, and summarize those positions clearly and without bias to show that they understand competing positions. Then they have to deal with those other viewpoints, either by refuting them completely or in part or by acknowledging that they exist, thus presenting themselves as reasonable people who have taken other views into consideration before deciding where they stand. Ways of helping students do this include the following:

- Have students write two drafts of their argument: one favoring their own position, and the other favoring another position. Their goal is to be equally fair and equally passionate in arguing both positions. Refer to Playing the Believing and Doubting Game in *Field Guide* Chapter 41 for guidance.

- Have students look for the beliefs and values underlying opponents' views. Too often, people on one side of an issue can't comprehend how others could disagree, when their view seems so eminently sensible and correct. Moving past the particular issue to the premises underlying people's positions can help students understand differing views.

- McGinley asks students to write op-ed essays, post them online, and then write a letter to "the editor" responding to one of their classmates' posted essays.

- Look for common ground: See if students can find something on which they and their opponents agree, so they can build on that commonality, perhaps by softening their stand or by finding an alternative to polarized positions that both sides can live with.

Adopting a trustworthy tone. As students draft their arguments, they may well need to temporarily ignore the needs of their audience in order to organize and articulate their own views as well as they can. In assessing their drafts and revising, however, they should examine their stance and see whether their tone matches their intent. If they have presented good reasons and done adequate research, their content will be trustworthy. They need to listen carefully as they read their drafts to make sure their tone is confident and reasonable, not strident, angry, or overbearing. Occasionally, students believe that an effective argument bludgeons the opposition into submission, a serious problem with tone. Here are some ways to help students find an appropriate tone:

- Let students play with their voice, rewriting a paragraph from their drafts in an angry voice, a snide or satirical voice, a stiffly official voice, or a slangy voice. Then ask them to decide which of those voices—or combination of them—might best capture their stance and influence their audience.

- Have students read their drafts aloud, or read aloud selected passages from classmates' drafts that may be problematic to the writer. They will quickly hear problems with tone.

- Help students recognize that their voice should be consistently present throughout their draft, including paraphrases and summaries of their source material. If their paraphrases are too close to the original text, the result is a patchwork of voices that diminish the force of the argument—and might be seen as plagiarism. Make sure students can write paraphrases without looking at the original, and use direct quotations when they need specific phrasing from the original.

Organizing arguments. Michelle Metzner, a lecturer at Wright State University, notes that students often find that organizing their arguments is easier if they include their reasons in the thesis statement; for example, "Even though some critics maintain that *All in the Family* is a platform for racist whites, in actuality it is an important part of the television landscape, in that it shows the ignorance of racism, offers a positive portrayal of a Black family, and portrays realistic dynamics between the generations." You might also suggest that students discuss their strongest reason last, where it will carry the most power.

Evaluating Essays Arguing a Position

Evaluating arguments should focus on how well students apply the Key Features in their own writing. Since these features are complex, though, and may be achieved in many ways within a single essay, you may want to break down some into categories. For example, students may include necessary background information but fail to elaborate sufficiently its relevance to their argument; or they may provide convincing support but rely too heavily on a single source. For more tips on evaluating essays arguing a position and other student writing, see Chapters 9 and 12 in this guide to teaching.

Other Useful Chapters in the *Field Guide*

Useful Readings

Fahnestock, Jeanne, and Marie Secor. "The Stases in Scientific and Literary Argument." *Written Communication* 5.4 (1988): 427–33. Print.

Fulkerson, Richard. "Technical Logic, Comp-Logic, and the Teaching of Writing." *College Composition and Communication* 39.4 (1988): 52–64. Print.

Lynch, Dennis A., Diana George, and Marilyn M. Cooper, "Moments of Argument: Agonistic Inquiry and Confrontational Cooperation." *College Composition and Communication* 48.1 (1997): 61–85. Print.

Teaching Other Genres 29

Richard Bullock, Michael Boblitt, and Paige Huskey

Texts are seldom "pure" representatives of a single genre. Instead, most texts combine genres to meet the needs of a rhetorical situation: A report on holistic medicine begins with an abstract and includes an annotated bibliography of articles and books on the subject; an argument against using animals to test cosmetics evaluates several alternatives and ends with a proposal to use computer modeling whenever possible. The Genre chapters in the *Field Guide* all focus on a particular genre but can be combined according to your instructional needs. In fact, Chapter 20, MIXING GENRES, offers advice on combining genres in various ways. Each Genre chapter offers a definition of the genre, a good model, a list of its Key Features, and advice on generating ideas and text and then on organizing that kind of writing. This chapter offers tips on teaching the various genres.

If you're weaving one genre assignment into a larger sequence, you can lead students through the activities in the Genre chapter, folding them into your larger assignment. For example, after choosing a topic in Arguing a Position, students might do extensive research on it, creating an annotated bibliography of

potentially useful sources. If you'd like students to focus on a single genre, such as an evaluation or proposal, simply assign the appropriate Genre chapter. These chapters all include links to other places in the book should students need more detail—help drafting, for instance, or describing, or incorporating source materials. If you know your students need a certain kind of help, you can assign the appropriate chapters; consult the sections at the end of each Genre chapter in this book for suggestions about other chapters in the *Field Guide* that might be useful. Chapters 3 and 22 in this guide to teaching offer suggestions for designing writing assignments and developing course plans and assignment sequences using the *Field Guide*.

Chapter 11, ABSTRACTS

Writing an abstract is an exercise in accuracy and economy. Students need to paraphrase and summarize a report or reading without distorting the information, while condensing it into less than 100–200 words. Creating prose with this precision can challenge students.

203

Using the reading and teaching the Key Features. Three examples illustrate the three types of abstracts students may one day be asked to write, in either their academic or professional field. Discussing how each example accomplishes the Key Features of abstracts will help students understand the different purpose of each type of abstract. For example, students may consider the types of information that are included in the summary of the "Boredom Proneness" study, the language that the authors use in order to remain objective and to convey information concisely, or the sentence structures which aid in brevity. You may also wish to compare the verb tenses in the informative and proposal abstracts to show the differences between an abstract that reports on a completed project and one that has yet to be done and discuss the authors' decisions about what to define (such as the Hopkins Symptom Checklist) and what to assume their readers already know.

Though every abstract should contain these Key Features, certain fields may require a specific format. For example, Philip Koopman, an associate professor at Carnegie Mellon University, suggests that all computer architecture abstracts "for both conference and journal papers . . . should follow a checklist consisting of: motivation, problem statement, approach, results, and conclusions." It may be a good idea for those students who know their intended field of study, rather than drawing exclusively from the "Boredom Proneness" examples, to do some quick research on the Internet to determine any specific guidelines suggested for their discipline.

Some tips for teaching abstracts. Here are some ways you can help them shape an abstract once they've drafted it:

- Revise for completeness. Does an informative abstract include a description of the text's subject, the method used, and the results or findings? A summary of the discussion of the results or findings? The conclusion or implications of the study? Does a descriptive abstract announce the subject of the study and provide an overview of the full paper? Does a proposal abstract announce the subject and summarize the method to be used?

- Revise for objectivity. When students have drafted an abstract, ask them or their peers to look for opinions or interpretations. The abstract must represent the larger text without distortion or bias.

- Revise for conciseness. Draft a wordy abstract and pare it down as a class, looking for unneeded adjectives and passive verbs. Have students work together to decide whether each word in their abstracts is needed. Have them write the abstract as a telegram that costs them $1 for each word. Ask students to reduce the number of words in the abstract by half, and see how close they get.

- Revise for coherence and readability. Having cut the abstract down to its barest bones, what can be done to make it read clearly and smoothly? Have students add transitions where necessary, repeat key words, and make sure each sentence is complete and grammatical.

Other Useful Chapters in the *Field Guide*

1–6 RHETORICAL SITUATIONS

9 REPORTING INFORMATION

41 READING STRATEGIES, for help summarizing

Chapter 12, ANNOTATED BIBLIOGRAPHIES

Annotated bibliographies are useful because the process of writing annotations for several potential sources demands that students understand the sources thoroughly and invites comparing and contrasting of the various sources, which, in turn, makes students more discerning readers and researchers. At the same time, annotated bibliographies present students with several challenges: finding sources to include, creating accurate citations of those sources, and writing accurate annotations. For advice on helping students find and cite sources, see Chapter 32 in this guide to teaching.

Using the reading and teaching the Key Features. After reading the global warming example, students may consider how each entry from the annotated bibliography may or may not be helpful to a person interested in writing a report on global warming. You might adapt the questions from "Decide what sources to include" to the entries listed to guide students in analyzing the appropriateness, credibility, balance, and timeliness of the entries—and even have students find the listed articles in order to assess the accuracy of the entries. After considering the language used and the information included in the examples, students may try rewriting the entries. Where can they add or condense information? How can they alter the wording to change the descriptive annotations into evaluative annotations? Because annotated bibliographies must serve a highly specified purpose in a limited space, it's important for students to hone in on the Key Features, which include a statement of scope, bibliographical information, a concise description of the work, relevant commentary, and consistent presentation. Helping students identify those features in the reading and discussing how the sample annotated bibliography entries communicate them can clarify the assignment's requirements and their writing goals.

Some tips for teaching annotated bibliographies. To write useful and accurate annotations, students must read potential sources carefully. Consider modeling such a reading, perhaps by positing a topic for a bibliography and then giving students an article or essay on that topic. You can then work with them to find the main idea or thesis, identify the writer's purpose and audience, and examine the content carefully to answer the following questions:

- What aspects of the topic are emphasized? What are deemphasized or omitted?
- What does the author assume about the audience's knowledge of or attitudes toward the subject?
- Does the evidence support the main idea?
- Does the writer show bias?
- Would this source be useful for writing about the topic?

Then ask students, working alone or in groups, to write a descriptive annotation—and then an evaluative one. A good way to practice is to identify three websites. Have students work together in class to create citations and annotations for the sites to help them prepare to compile and write their own.

Other Useful Chapters in the *Field Guide*

Chapter 13, EVALUATIONS

Introduce evaluations by pointing out that we evaluate people, places, and things all the time: My English teacher is cool, the guys in the room down the hall party too much, the latest CD from Taylor Swift is better than her last one, this classroom needs to be painted. Implicit in those informal evaluations are criteria or reasons. You might ask students to list the criteria governing each of those evaluations. Then you can point out that formal evaluations work the same way: The writer identifies criteria by which something should be evaluated and then sees how well it meets those criteria and presents those findings as an argument.

Using the reading and teaching the Key Features. Ali Heinekamp's evaluation of *Juno* is likely to strike a chord with students, many of whom are familiar with and concerned about the issues Heinekamp discusses. Moreover, they are probably familiar with movies that do not accurately depict the lives of typical teenagers. As such, students will probably want a chance to react to Heinekamp's message, perhaps applying it to some other, current films or TV shows. While discussing her essay in class, try to steer the students toward the Key Features of evaluations by asking questions such as "What does Heinekamp think makes for a good teen movie?" or "Does Heinekamp provide enough evidence to convince you that Juno is a good role model for teenage girls?" Providing a balanced and fair assessment may be difficult for some students, especially when dealing with controversial issues. Make sure to point out to students how Heinekamp not only included but also remained respectful of sources who disagreed with her position, thus strengthening her own credibility.

Some tips for teaching evaluations

Introduce criteria. Although students can already identify many evaluation criteria, spending class time to identify and clarify the specific criteria for the genre of work they'll be evaluating will help them understand what they need to look for and will allow you to guide them to more rigorous examination. A good approach is to examine together a single example from various perspectives in order to develop a list of criteria. Before you start, ask students to list the criteria they'd use to evaluate it. Then ask them if the criteria need to be revised or expanded.

If you want students to evaluate a TV show or movie, for example, a good way to develop criteria is to show them a brief sample; a music video or even a TV commercial can work well because you can show the same tape several times in a single class period. For each viewing, ask students to focus their attention on a single aspect and write a brief reaction:

- *Purpose.* What is this video or commercial trying to achieve? Does it achieve its purpose? Do you like it? Are you entertained by it? Convinced by it? Why or why not?

- *Plot.* What happens? Does it make sense? Are there jumps or gaps in the narrative? Is there an ending or resolution? Is it convincing?

- *Characters.* Who are the characters? What do we know about them? How do we know?

- *Costume.* What are the characters wearing? Why? How does their dress contribute to the meaning, atmosphere, or overall impression?

- *Setting and background.* Is the film in color? Natural color or manipulated color? Black and white? What do you see in the background? What details do you remember? What else is in there? How does the setting contribute to the purpose?

- *Lighting.* Is the setting brightly lit? Dark and shadowy? How well can you see what's going on in the foreground or background?

- *Sound.* What sounds do you hear? Is there dialogue? Music? Voiceovers? Background sounds? View it again, with the sound turned off: How does the sound—and its absence—affect your experience?

- **Cinematography.** If the screen is like a picture frame, where are important objects or people located within the frame? What are the effects of their placement in the frame and their movement through it? Where is the camera located—at eye level? Looking down from above? Up from below?

You can then ask students to work individually or in groups to put these observations together, first by creating a brief summary or description of the work and then by identifying a small number of criteria—4–6 is typical—that a music video or commercial should meet. For example, a commercial should have the following traits:

- Grab viewers' attention immediately.
- Focus our attention on the product being promoted.
- Entertain.
- Be memorable, so that we remember it and the product it represents.

Follow with a whole-class or group discussion of the way this work meets or doesn't meet the criteria, asking for evidence from their viewings to support their assertions. If you have time, you might ask students to research how others have evaluated similar subjects and to see if their own criteria need to be expanded or changed.

Choose something to evaluate. A common object of evaluation in writing courses is a media work: a movie, a television show, a song or CD or a website. Artwork is also a possibility, as is a work of architecture. You can ask everyone in the class to evaluate the same work, allowing everyone to contribute to the evaluation and discuss it as a class, but you'll then face twenty-five essays on the same topic. You can allow every student to choose whatever he or she wants to evaluate, but then discussion is more difficult because you're faced with one of two scenarios: viewing or listening to twenty-five different movies, TV shows, songs, or websites or evaluating students' essays without having knowledge of the object of the evaluation. There's something to be said for the second position: Students should be able to describe what they're evaluating clearly enough that readers have enough information to know whether or not their evaluation is fair, even if readers aren't familiar with the work. If, however, you'd like to control the range of topics, here are some strategies:

- Create a list of works from which students may choose. Some instructors restrict the items on the list to works they're familiar with or to works they have had success with in the past. Others create lists containing only works within a single genre, such as action movies, situation comedies, hip-hop songs, and fashion websites. The works should be accessible: Films should be rentable or available at area libraries or online; TV shows should be available on DVD, on the web, or currently playing; websites should be up and running (but advise students to save, print, and date the pages they're evaluating, since Web pages are often revised and sites disappear).

- Ask students to choose from the works on your list. You can then assign students to groups according to the work itself or according to the genre, if your list has more than one. The groups can then collaborate on establishing criteria and examining the work or works.

- Alternately, place students in groups first. In a class of twenty-five, four groups of 5–7 work well. Each group should choose one work from the list. By grouping students first, you guarantee that everyone will have others to work with, and you limit the class's evaluations to four works.

- As a variation, you might encourage students to compare two similar works: two situation comedies, two Will Farrell movies, two department stores' websites, two CDs, or two buildings on campus.

Draft an evaluation. Once students have chosen something to evaluate, give them time to obtain the work and watch or examine it several times over several days, probably a weekend, taking notes on different aspects or looking through the lenses of different criteria each time. If they're working in groups, encourage them to view the work together so they can point out observations to one another as they watch and as they discuss it together afterwards. They'll also need class time and your guidance to bring their individual notes together, revise

their criteria in light of their research, and evaluate their subject, possibly comparing it with other, similar works. Their goal is to state a judgment as a thesis statement.

At this point, students are ready to start planning and writing. Review the Key Features of evaluations and ask them to consider the rhetorical situation again in relation to their own project. You might ask them to write answers to the questions posed in Considering the Rhetorical Situation and review Ways of Organizing an Evaluation in Chapter 13, and then have them draft, assess their draft, get response, revise, edit, and proofread, consulting Chapters 25–28 as need be. For help in identifying reasons and evidence, go to Chapter 10, ARGUING A POSITION.

Other Useful Chapters in the *Field Guide*

Chapter 14, LAB REPORTS

Although lab reports are seldom taught in first-year writing courses, students are often required to write them in various science and social science courses, so pointing out this chapter to your students to use as a reference may be helpful to them. If your school has a Writing across the Curriculum program, however, you may be called upon to teach students how to compose lab reports. Disciplines differ in their exact requirements, demanding more or fewer parts or naming them differently, so if you're working with a specific course or instructor, be sure to find out what's required—and emphasize to students that they need to do the same whenever they're assigned a lab report. Also, if possible you should do the experiment yourself to familiarize yourself with the methods, equipment, and expected results.

Using the reading and teaching the Key Features. "The Effect of Biofeedback Training on Muscle Tension and Skin Temperature" by Sarah Thomas offers a good example of the Key Features of most lab reports. Her title is clear and avoids the temptation to begin with "A Study of." She describes her purpose clearly and concisely and notes similar work done by another researcher. Her methods section is divided into four sections, each presenting specific details of the experiment itself. She presents the study's results and discussion, including two detailed charts, and includes a single reference. After students have identified the Key Features of Sarah Thomas's lab report, they may consider the following: What types of information were included in each section? Would they be able to reproduce her experiment if asked? Did her results seem

logical and convincing? Thomas's lab report also offers an excellent opportunity for students to practice writing abstracts, one of the Key Features not addressed in Thomas's lab report. Students could try to condense her report into each type of abstract outlined in Chapter 11.

Some tips for teaching lab reports. Here are some tips that will make it easier for students as they prepare to draft their reports:

Take notes. A lab report succeeds or fails first of all on the accuracy and comprehensiveness of its content. For that reason, students need to take careful notes as they conduct experiments. To help them, consider requiring a lab journal to record each of their actions as they do them and to note carefully their observations as well as their thoughts. They should record their raw data in the journal and use its pages to tease out the implications of their findings. When they are ready to write the report, they'll have collected much of the information they need for the methods, results, and discussion sections.

Draw from the research proposal. If your students write research or topic proposals (discussed in Chapter 17 of the *Field Guide*), they can adapt much from the proposal for the report itself. Research proposals vary from discipline to discipline but typically include an introduction that reviews the relevant literature; a discussion of proposed procedures, needed equipment, and methods of analyzing the data collected; and a discussion of anticipated results—

writing that can be used as the foundation for the lab report itself. Caution students against simply copying and pasting, because it's unlikely that the actual research will match what was proposed. Students will need to revisit their purpose, expand their methods and discussion sections, and change verb tenses to show that the research has been completed.

Use visuals. Students may need to present data in the form of charts, graphs, or tables, so refer them to the *Field Guide* Chapter 54, USING VISUALS, INCORPORATING SOUND, for guidance.

Create an abstract. Once students have finished their lab report, they'll need to write an abstract of it; see the advice on helping students write a good abstract earlier in this chapter and Chapter 11 in the *Field Guide*.

Other Useful Chapters in the *Field Guide*

25 DRAFTING
32 ANALYZING CAUSES AND EFFECTS
35 COMPARING AND CONTRASTING
37 DESCRIBING
39 EXPLAINING PROCESSES
43–51 DOING RESEARCH

Chapter 15, MEMOIRS

Asking students to write about their lives can be rewarding both for them and for you. It's a topic most students find of interest, and they can develop their skills in narrating and describing by writing memoirs. Memoirs are a large genre; literacy narratives are simply memoirs that focus on a particular aspect of students' lives. For that reason, the advice in Chapter 25 of this guide to teaching, "Literacy (and Other) Narratives," will be useful when you ask students to write memoirs.

Using the reading and teaching the Key Features. The reading can help students understand the genre, present a model for their own writing, and provide an example of the Key Features of memoirs. Although few students are likely to have a story like Rick Bragg's, they may remember times when they experienced some strong emotion, when they encountered an unsavory character, or when an experience proved to be the beginning of a significant event in their lives. Discussing "All Over but the Shoutin'" in the context of their own lives can help them see potential topics for their memoirs. The Key Features of memoirs include a good story, vivid details, and clear significance. Helping students identify those features in the reading and discussing how Bragg communicates them can clarify the assignment's requirements and their writing goals. Students often find significance to be a difficult concept to grasp. Discussing the reasons Bragg believes his story is important and needs to be told—and how that importance, both in the short and long term, is conveyed—can help students see how to show the significance of their own memoirs.

Some tips for teaching memoirs

Finding a topic. The first, and probably most important, task in writing a memoir is choosing a suitable topic that has significance for the writer. Given the variety in students' lives, what they might choose to write about is legion; however, many students don't understand the implications of *significance*. They may gravitate toward big topics that so many others share—prom, graduation, the state wrestling tournament—that they're drained of uniqueness and are hard to write about well and originally. Alternately, students may want to write about recent events—prom and graduation, yes, but also serious car accidents or postgraduation breakups—that they don't have enough distance from. Your first task, then, is to encourage students to consider significant and unique events in their lives, ideally events that took place at least two years ago, and events that only they may know about. Here's a short list of such topics from my life; you might create such a list yourself to share with your students:

- The day I looked in my sixth-grade teacher's car and found out she smoked
- When one of my grad school professors, seeing me struggle writing an essay on a comic novel, gave me permission to use humor, saying, "You're writing about a funny book; write a funny paper!"
- Seeing my father cry for the first time

In other words, a significant event can be a realization, a new perspective, or a memory revisited—something important for the writer but perhaps unknown to anyone else. Occasionally you'll encounter a student who insists that nothing of any importance has ever happened to him or her. It's helpful to sit with such students and ask them as many questions as you can think of about their lives and interests, seeing why, for example, they like to hunt or what it was like to move to a new high school their senior year. Usually, those conversations lead to several significant moments, and your next task may be to convince these students that you'd like to know more about them—and so would others.

Drafting the memoir. Students sometimes think they need to give readers a great deal of background information or start their memoir far earlier in the day or week than they have to. When they write a first draft, they may need to work up to the event that they're focusing on. When it's time to revise, however, ask them to consider just how much or how little background readers need to understand the circumstances and shape their stories so they can draw readers in, keep them interested, and express the significance clearly.

Here is the next challenge you'll face: helping students understand that a memoir need not be a completely factual record of an event in their lives. Like other narratives, it must be shaped—omitting some details, emphasizing others, possibly even altering events—to both tell a good story and express the significance of the event for them. You should also help them focus not only on telling the story but also on exploring its significance; in a memoir, *introspection* is just as important as *retrospection*. You might ask students to rewrite the memoir from multiple perspectives to see which point of view seems to work best.

Other Useful Chapters in the Field Guide

Chapter 16, PROFILES

Profiles introduce students to firsthand research by asking them to observe people, places, or events; interview key people; and organize their findings into a report that readers will find interesting and engaging. Students typically visit their subject one or more times, taking careful notes on what they see, hear, and experience, and then shape those notes and their memories into a detailed, focused account.

Using the reading and teaching the Key Features. The reading presented in the *Field Guide* is particularly useful for dis-

cussing the Key Features of the genre. Students will be amused by Christian Danielsen's description of Daniel Meyer's quest for a Guinness world record. You can help students understand the concept of finding an angle by asking them what they know about Meyer as a person besides his desire for a record (probably not much, as Danielsen focuses on Meyer as paperclip man). This discussion can also show students how Danielsen uses engaging details to draw his readers in, this demonstrating three Key Features of profiles: a clear focus, an angle, and engaging details.

When discussing the assignment, you may want to clarify to students the difference between firsthand and secondhand accounts. Be sure they understand that reading a newspaper article and then relaying those facts in a profile would be considered secondhand since they did not witness the event with their own eyes and ears or do the research themselves.

Some tips for teaching profiles

Finding a topic. Students may choose to profile people in the area who have interesting occupations or hobbies or who have distinguished themselves in one way or another. They may profile places, ranging from areas in parks or other public places to buildings or structures, from retail stores to factories. Or, they may profile events such as a concert, a poetry reading, a rodeo, a stock car race. Encourage students to choose topics with which they aren't familiar; they need to be able to see their topic through fresh eyes, without the preconceptions that previous experience or familiarity brings. Guide them, too, to subjects that are clearly focused: "the lake" or "the campus" or "the supermarket" are all too broad and won't yield the sharp detail that makes a profile interesting. Also, make sure students choose topics they can gain access to. Students who choose a hospital operating room or a lawyer's office, for example, are unlikely to be allowed in; certain people—the mayor, a convicted felon—may be unavailable for interviews; and if the subject is located away from the campus area, students without cars may have difficulty getting to it. Finally, discourage students from choosing illegal or dangerous topics, such as drug deals or a gang leader; you don't want them to risk harm, and as a college teacher you don't have any confidentiality privileges, like lawyers and doctors, and don't want to know things that you'd have to share with law enforcement authorities. The best advice? Approve each student's topic before allowing them to pursue their research.

Doing research. Profiles require field research, placing demands on students that academic or web-based research doesn't. Specifically, they have to schedule appointments and interviews and times when they will observe their subjects. It's especially important to have students create a research schedule as outlined in the *Field Guide* Chapter 43, DEVELOPING A RESEARCH PLAN, to help them structure their time so they can get their research done with ample time to draft and revise their profiles—and, if need be, do addi-

tional research. Research will consist primarily or entirely of firsthand observing and interviewing; those two sections in the *Field Guide* Chapter 44, FINDING SOURCES, can help.

If they've done good research, students will have a lot of notes and evidence to sift through. Help them find patterns: A good angle or point of view offers a new way of seeing the subject, rather than simply confirming what most people already know about it.

Organizing and drafting. Once students have examined their research material and settled on an angle, they need to decide how to organize their profile and whether they have enough information. They may consider creating an informal outline (from *Field Guide* Chapter 24, GENERATING IDEAS AND TEXT) and then seeing how much information they have for each topic they want to cover. If some of their research is thin, they can do additional fieldwork—visit the event or scene again, do a follow-up interview—or do some research for background and more information on the topic. For example, if they were writing on the Circleville, Ohio, Pumpkin Festival but the festival is over, they could interview one of the organizers, see what's been written about the Pumpkin Festival itself, or look for information on agricultural festivals and fairs to see how Circleville's festival is part of a long American tradition. Warn students to focus on their subject rather than on themselves as researchers or observers; some students draw unnecessary attention to themselves by statements like "Then I asked her . . . ."

Other Useful Chapters in the *Field Guide*

Chapter 17, PROPOSALS

A proposal is a kind of argument, but proposals present students with some unique challenges in terms of choosing a topic, justifying the need for the proposal, and shaping their proposal for their audience.

Using the reading and teaching the Key Features. The reading offered in the *Field Guide* is useful for pointing out to students the Key Features of proposals. In addition, you may want to mention areas where the writers could have chosen a different stance or solution in an effort to help students understand the choices they will need to make as they write their own pro-

posals. For instance, one of the Key Features of a proposal is a well-defined problem. In his essay, Granof defines the problem as "outrageously expensive textbooks" for college courses and compares their cost to those of "hardcover best sellers and other trade books," which sell for far less. He doesn't stop there, however; he then describes the effects on textbook sales of the used book market, which causes publishers to set textbook prices high in response—and to publish new editions every few years, whether new understandings in the field dictate them or not.

You will also want students to note the appropriateness of Granof's tone, another Key Feature of proposals. Granof states his concerns and solutions calmly and matter-of-factly, basing his proposal on logical examination of the problem and avoiding emotional appeals (with the possible exception of the word "outrageously").

Other Key Features of proposals include a recommended solution and a call to action. Point out to students that Granoff first states his solution in a brief statement: "A textbook's value, like that of a software program, is not in its physical form, but rather in its intellectual content. Therefore, just as software companies typically 'site license' to colleges, so should textbook publishers." He then explains the implications of this proposal in several paragraphs of detail, showing that he has thought carefully about his proposal—and so helping to make it convincing (another Key Feature).

Some tips for teaching proposals

Choosing a topic. The problems for which students can best propose solutions are often specific, local issues in their community or on campus. The broader or more abstract the problem, the harder it will be for students to write about because they'll have trouble identifying a specific audience and specific solutions. If they choose something local—for example, the lack of weekend tech support for computer equipment in the dorms—they not only can discuss the problem in specific terms, they also can find out who is responsible for technical support on campus, analyze the rhetorical situation as it applies to them as students writing to a university administrator, and direct their proposals to that person. They can also evaluate the problems to see whether they need a proposed solution: Will the problem go away by itself, be solved too easily, or be seen as trivial by readers?

Defining the problem. Make sure, through conferences or topic proposals (also discussed in this chapter) or both, that students' proposals are clear, focused, and significant and that they know to whom their proposal will be addressed. Approving their topics before they start can forestall many problems.

Doing research. Students may not initially have a solution (or they'll have one that may or may not be feasible) but will need to research the problem to find out its dimensions. If this research involves interviews or observations, it's important for students to recognize that field research places demands that academic or Internet-based research doesn't. Specifically, they have to schedule appointments and interviews and times when they will observe their subjects. It's especially important to have students create a research schedule as outlined in the *Field Guide* Chapter 43, DEVELOPING A RESEARCH PLAN, to help them structure their time so they can finish their research with ample time to draft and revise their proposals—and, if need be, to do additional research.

Drafting. Proposals often consist of two arguments: one to frame the problem, and a second to support the preferred solution. You may want students to explain why the issue is a problem, to help them understand that problems are not necessarily self-evident; after all, one person's problem may represent another's happy status quo. Then, have them write about a proposed solution or solutions. Although the finished draft may or may not present alternative solutions—that may be a function of the problem itself, or may reflect a particular audience—students should anticipate and think about alternatives to show that they've weighed their preferred solution against other possibilities.

Other Useful Chapters in the *Field Guide*

Chapter 18, REFLECTIONS

Reflections—essays in which the writer shares his or her thoughts on a subject—are challenging to teach because their subject matter, form, and style are nearly limitless. Reflections are places for writers to play with ideas, unlikely juxtapositions, unconventional organization, and innovative language—all in the service of exploring a line of thinking about a subject. That's also what makes them fun for students to write, read, and share, because they can compose with a freedom few have had permission to experience in their writing in school.

Using the reading and teaching the Key Features. The reading provided in the *Field Guide* is a wonderful example of just how playful and yet serious reflections can be. Foer begins his essay with a meditation on how "strange it is that dogs live in New York [City] in the first place" in the context of a proposed health board regulation that dogs be leashed at all times. He poses questions about whether dogs can live a good life in the city—and then describes his own dog in less than flattering terms, ending with "I love her." He explores their

relationship and the reasons people love dogs and other pets, but then turns to the flip side: that while we love animals as companions, we also eat them. In tracing the complexity of the relationship between people and animals, Foer shows how intriguing he finds the idea, and includes many specific details (not just about his own dog but also about dog, and human, behavior in general—two Key Features of reflections. And while his focus shifts incrementally from topic to topic, his essay has a structure.

You may want to have your students, either as a class or in small groups, draw an outline or some type of visual map of Foer's essay. In this way, students will better understand how Foer's reflection is structured to help readers make connections and follow his logic. Ask students to try to rearrange Foer's essay in a way that it still makes sense, but perhaps leads to a different conclusion. Explain to students that, although structure is a key feature of reflections, there are many options with which they will probably want to experiment. Chapters 30 and 40 in the *Field Guide* can give students more ideas for organizing or structuring their essays.

Some tips for teaching reflections

Choosing a topic. Here, the topic is less important than what students do with it. Sighing and other bodily emanations, observations ("My mother, my grandmother, and my sister all share a way of standing with their arms folded"), interesting facts ("40,000 Americans are injured by toilets each year"), speculations ("What if dogs could talk?")—all are grist for reflections. Students may be able to write about their topics using their own knowledge of them. However, most reflections are enriched if the writers do some research, deepening their understanding of their topic and gaining additional insight and perspective on it. Asking students to do some research on the topic of their reflection is a good way to improve the quality of your students' drafts while lessening the chance that they'll rely on their (often not inconsiderable, but sometimes painfully sophomoric) wit.

Organizing. Since reflections are by their nature idiosyncratic, their organization can take many forms. The charts presented in the *Field Guide* may be helpful, but students may benefit from these tips, too:

- Provide several examples of reflections. "My Life as a Dog" offers one kind of reflection, but showing students several different models can help them see both common elements—some kind of organizational scheme, and an overall focus and unity to the essay, even if it wanders—and the breadth of possibilities open to them. Consider giving them one example from a Dave Barry piece to show how discursive and tangentially relevant some pieces of a reflection can be, as long as the writer can tie up the loose ends by the end.

- Have students write a draft as a PowerPoint presentation. As odd as it sounds, asking students to turn their essay into a series of slides may help them achieve a better organization by showing them how the pieces—the individual slides—fit together (or don't). If the slides just stop, students can see that some sort of conclusion is needed. And they can easily move the slides around to play with different organizational patterns.

- Caution students not to turn their reflections into arguments. As students write, they may switch from reflecting and playing with ideas to arguing a point. In group work, ask readers to watch out for such a shift, which may reflect not a loss of control but a new understanding of the subject or a new commitment to a particular position. If so, the student may not need to revise the reflection but instead may need permission to switch genres to reflect his or her new learning.

Reflections are by nature playful (though they are often serious in intent and tone), so you and your students may find the rewriting activities in the *Field Guide* Chapter 27, GETTING RESPONSE AND REVISING, helpful as students revise their drafts. See also Paul Heilker's "Twenty Years In: An Essay in Two Parts."

Other Useful Chapters in the *Field Guide*

Chapter 19, RÉSUMÉS AND JOB LETTERS

Although usually reserved for courses in business or technical writing, instruction in creating résumés and application and thank-you letters is often greatly appreciated by students, many of whom are seeking part-time or summer work and may be clueless about presenting themselves effectively on paper. This chapter offers help in teaching these important documents.

Using the reading and teaching the Key Features. Although the examples in the *Field Guide* are useful for illustrating the Key Features of résumés and application and thank-you letters, you may also want to have students spend some time reviewing numerous types and styles of all three. Viewing samples written for various purposes and audiences will help students develop a large inventory of active verbs and better understand how to effectively relate their own qualifications in a succinct, organized fashion using a design that highlights their noteworthy information (all Key Features of résumés). Stu-dents may benefit from learning that employers, on average, spend no more than a minute reviewing each applicant's résumé to determine if the person is worthy of an interview or further consideration. An easy way to have students test out their résumés is to have them exchange with a classmate and scan each other's drafts for one minute. When the time is up, have them hand back their résumés and share with each other everything they can remember reading. This activity will help students understand the importance of being concise and presenting information effectively.

When discussing application letters, point out to students that in addition to using a businesslike format and presenting qualifications succinctly, students will want to stay primarily focused on how they can best meet their potential employer's needs. For instance, Praeger writes, "Since your internship focuses on public relations, my experience in the field should allow me to make a contribution to your company." This is more effective than if he had said, "Since your internship focuses on public relations, I can expand my current knowledge and expertise."

You might present thank-you letters as one more way of demonstrating your qualifications for the job—and, maybe even more important, of showing people you might work with that you are agreeable, have good manners, and are a person who will get along with coworkers and supervisors. If the job has attracted many applicants, a thank-you letter will jog the interviewer's memory. Even more, perhaps, than the application letter and résumé, the thank-you letter can separate the writer from the pack—and that's a good reason to write with the same care and attention to detail as in the application materials.

Mention to students that writing centers, job centers, and libraries are wonderful resources, too. Many offer advice, handouts, and even miniworkshops—all free of charge! In addition, the following websites provide numerous samples and can be helpful for teaching résumés and application letters:

jobchoicesonline.com
owl.english.purdue.edu
career-advice.monster.com
msn.careerbuilder.com

Some tips for teaching résumés and job letters

Choosing content. When putting together a résumé, some students need to choose among their many activities to keep to a single page. Help them distinguish between personal information or hobbies that employers are unlikely to care about and activities that show their abilities to good advantage. Some students who didn't have jobs or pursue activities in high school may have trouble filling a page. These students may benefit from such activities as clustering and looping (in *Field Guide* Chapter 24, GENERATING IDEAS AND TEXT) or from doing research on potential employers or

careers (Chapter 16 in the *Field Guide*, PROFILES, offers useful advice on this kind of research, as does Doing Field Research in Chapter 44). You may need to confer with such students to help them see that activities they may see as irrelevant, such as volunteering at their church or helping the local T-ball coach, can be presented as valuable activities that show their skills and character.

Drafting, revising, editing, and proofreading. Readers of résumés and application letters expect specific information in a specific order; résumés are highly stylized documents that don't invite much creativity (with the possible exception of job seekers in "creative" fields, such as advertising). Help students phrase their educational and work experience using action verbs to show what they *did*: Offering a list of such verbs, asking students to find action verbs in sample résumés, and revising some entries with the class can help them see what to do. It's useful to emphasize to students that application letters are arguments: The writer is presenting an argument that he or she should be considered for a job. As such, application letters need to present reasons and evidence, just as in any other argument. In both résumés and application letters, students should make their points in parallel form. Finally, plan on spending considerable class time on editing and proofreading all three documents. These documents should be flawless, without a single typo or misspelling, because busy employers look for ways to make the number of applicants they must evaluate manageable, and evidence of carelessness is a good reason for rejection.

Designing. To make their print résumé and letters each fit on a single page, students may also need help in manipulating design elements, including font size and use of white space. *Field Guide* Chapter 53 offers design advice. The documents should be printed on good-quality white paper with a laser printer—special "résumé papers" or folders aren't likely to impress potential employers, and in fact may annoy some. Consider going over how to address a business envelope and fold the documents to fit inside, skills that students used to email may not have mastered.

Other Useful Chapters in the *Field Guide*

1–6 RHETORICAL SITUATIONS
24 GENERATING IDEAS AND TEXT
28 EDITING AND PROOFREADING
53 DESIGNING TEXT

Chapter 20, MIXING GENRES

Outside the classroom, most writers mix genres most of the time. A quick scan of op-ed articles shows a common pattern: begin with a brief narrative or two to draw readers in and provide a context; offer some information; present an argument, often including brief evaluations along the way; and end with a proposal. Reports often alternate between general or abstract information and examples or anecdotes, and proposals often result from a combination of reports and evaluations. So this chapter can help students move from genre-specific to more complex and interesting writing. A good way to begin is to show them lots of examples and have them identify the various genres embedded in the texts. Then you can discuss how mixing genres may help them achieve their purposes with their particular audiences better than a single genre can.

Using the reading and teaching the Key Features. Going through the Quindlen piece will help students understand the basic concept of mixing genres. You might move the discussion along by asking them what Quindlen's purpose was in including the various genres (why incorporate stories and reflections instead of making a sustained argument?) and then asking them to explore how she fits them together—how she uses transitions and other devices to move the reader from textual analysis to report to reflection, all the while building her argument. You can also ask students to discuss how her essay includes the Key Features, finding examples from the text in addition to those mentioned. You might then have them flip to Chapter 10 to see how well Quindlen achieves the Key Features of ARGUING A

POSITION, Quindlen's primary genre. Finally, you might have them do the same with a new text, to show how the Key Features work in other essays as well.

Some tips for teaching MIXING GENRES. There are at least three ways you and your students can use this chapter: as a resource, as an assignment framework, and as a basis for a multigenre project.

Use MIXING GENRES as a resource. As students develop a piece of writing in a specific genre, they may find that drawing on other genres can help them write what they want to write. You might suggest that students browse the Some Typical Ways of Mixing Genres section to see if any of the suggestions there would help them as they write. All students will likely benefit from reading ARGUING A POSITION, as it suggests that arguments may be embedded in much of their writing—and so looking at Chapter 33, ARGUING, might also be helpful. But if students are writing in other genres, they may find the other suggestions in this chapter useful.

You might also use these suggestions as the basis for a rewriting and revising exercise. Chapter 27, GETTING RESPONSE AND REVISING, offers the option of rewriting a draft by starting over in a different way; you might ask students to rewrite all or part of their drafts, following the suggestions in this chapter.

Using MIXING GENRES as an assignment framework. You might ask students to start an assignment with this chapter and create an essay that uses more than one genre. For example, you might ask students to write a proposal that includes an evaluation, or a report that includes a memoir. This can be done in at least two ways: Students may weave a personal narrative about a topic into their report on it, or they may make the process of searching for, organizing, and reaching conclusions about their topic itself the focus of the narrative. Some students will be familiar with a version of this assignment developed by composition theorist Ken Macrorie known as the I-Search paper. To do this sort of mixed assignment well, students will need to use at least two of the *Field Guide*'s Genre chapters, and you will need to help them sort out the requirements of both genres, the processes they should follow, and the proportions of each genre that their draft should contain. They'll need to keep in mind that one genre should be primary, both to make the draft itself coherent and to help them (and you) proceed.

Creating a multigenre project. Multigenre projects could as easily be called multiperspective projects. Rather than integrating several genres into a single, focused, coherent document, multigenre projects include several discrete texts that are meant to be read together to form an overall impression or message—much like a museum exhibit, in order to help museum visitors understand an artistic movement, might display several artists' work, their letters describing their art, preliminary sketches, and a catalog by the curator. Writing teacher and author Tom Romano offers this definition:

> A multigenre paper arises from research, experience, and imagination. It is not an uninterrupted, expository monolog nor a seamless narrative nor a collection of poems. A multigenre paper is composed of many genres and subgenres, each piece self-contained, making a point of its own, yet connected by theme or topic and sometimes by language, images, and content. In addition to many genres, a multigenre paper may also contain many voices, not just the author's. The trick is to make such a paper hang together. (xi)

Indeed, making the paper hang together is the biggest challenge students face with this project. A practical and useful resource to consult, on making diverse pieces cohere as well as on other challenges college writing teachers face in developing multigenre project assignments, is my colleague Nancy Mack's essay, "The Ins, Outs, and In-Betweens of Multigenre Writing."

A somewhat different version of multigenre writing is presented by Cheryl L. Johnson and Jayne A. Moneysmith in *Multiple Genres, Multiple Voices*. They suggest asking students to "create an argument that explores alternative perspectives by using multiple genres written from different points of view. Genres might include a letter, a dialogue, a report, or even a poem—in addition to the traditional essay" (2). Such a "multivoiced argument" must "be aimed at a specific audience," and the parts "would work together to convey a central, significant point" (3). In the process, students come to understand multiple viewpoints and often become engaged in their writing in ways they don't with traditional argument essays.

Other Useful Chapters in the *Field Guide*

Chapter 21, CHOOSING GENRES

Much of the time, choosing the appropriate genre is easy: we apply for jobs with application letters and resumes, we create memoirs or literacy narratives to relate events in our days or our lives, or we're assigned to write in a specific genre: "Create a topic proposal and annotated bibliography for your project in this course"; "Write an essay arguing whether or not the 1964 Civil Rights Act usurped powers reserved to the states."

Sometimes, though, the best genre or combination of genres to use isn't clear, and often the assignments students must write are presented in vague terms or with the expectation that students understand what is meant, when they don't. This chapter provides brief summaries of the genres presented in the *Field Guide,* along with terms that may signify which one students are meant to write. It then examines two ambiguous assignments to help students interpret them correctly.

Some tips for teaching CHOOSING GENRES

- Ask students to bring in sample assignments, from their own courses or their friends' and roommates', and spend time analyzing them by identifying the key terms within the context of the assignment itself and the course. For example, you might explore with students the difference between *Discuss why* (explore the causes of something) and *Discuss how* (describe the details of a process), to help them understand the need for careful reading of assignment prompts.

- Provide some assignments that you've made up—both clear and ambiguous— and ask students, in groups or during a whole-class discussion, to determine which genre each one calls for.

- Have students create an assignment and then have other students decide what genre it's asking for.

Other Useful Chapters in the *Field Guide*

Useful Readings

Bartholomae, David. "Inventing the University." *When a Writer Can't Write: Studies in Writer's Block and Other Composing Process Problems.* Ed. Mike Rose. New York: Guilford, 1985. 273–85. Print.

Bazerman, Charles. "The Life of Genre, the Life in the Classroom." *Genre and Writing: Issues, Arguments, Alternatives.* Ed. Wendy Bishop and H. Ostrom. Portsmouth, NH: Boynton/Cook, 1997. 19–25. Print.

Elbow, Peter. "The Cultures of Literature and Composition: What Could Each Learn from the Other?" *College English* 64.5 (2002): 533–46. Print.

Freedman, Aviva. "The What, Where, When, Why, and How of Classroom Genres." *Reconceiving Writing, Rethinking Writing Instruction.* Ed. Joseph Petraglia. Mahwah, NJ: Erlbaum, 1995. 121–44. Print.

Heilker, Paul. "Twenty Years In: An Essay in Two Parts." *College Composition and*

Communication 58.2 (2006): 182–212. Print.

Johnson, Cheryl L., and Jayne A. Moneysmith. *Multiple Genres, Multiple Voices.* Portsmouth, NH: Boynton/Cook, 2005. Print.

Koopman, Philip. "How to Write an Abstract." Home page. Electrical & Computer Engineering, Carnegie Mellon U, Oct. 1997. Web. 13 Oct. 2009.

Mack, Nancy. "The Ins, Outs, and In-Betweens of Multigenre Writing." *English Journal* 92.2 (2002): 91–98. Print.

Ockerstrom, Lolly. *Teaching with a Purpose.* Boston: Houghton, 1992. Print.

Romano, Tom. *Blending Genre, Altering Style: Writing Multigenre Papers.* Portsmouth, NH: Heinemann, 2000. Print.

Trupe, Alice L. "Academic Literacy in a Wired World: Redefining Genres for College Writing Courses." *Kairos* 7.2 (2002): n. pag. Web. 13 Oct. 2009.

Young, Art, and Toby Fulwiler, eds. *When Writing Teachers Teach Literature.* Portsmouth, NH: Boynton/Cook–Heinemann, 1995. Print.

30 Teaching about Writing Processes

For many students, writing a text is an activity that has typically taken place the night before it's due. Some students believe that they write best "under pressure." Few have been required to think on paper about their topics, been given guidance in fleshing out their ideas with memories or research, or been asked to revise, except to "fix" errors pointed out to them on their drafts. If they have been asked to write using a full range of writing processes, they may have experienced them as rigid, even lockstep: First, you brainstorm; then you write an outline and then a draft; then you revise it, edit it, and turn it in. Many students may not understand how writers create good writing or how they can use the activities in this chapter flexibly to accomplish what they need to do. See Chapter 3 in this guide to teaching, "Designing Writing Assignments," for suggestions of ways to create sequences of assignments incorporating these processes along with various genres and strategies. Remember, though, that the best way to encourage students to use the processes of writing is flexibly, honoring their needs and acknowledging what works for them. Here are some suggestions for teaching using the processes of writing:

- Give students choices, but ask that they experience several strategies, so they can make informed choices about what works for them—and so they have alternatives if one method doesn't work.

- Ask students to describe how they write an academic essay. Invite them to describe it in a flowchart, diagram, list, or narrative, and then compare various students' processes to show how they can differ.

- Suggest that students write in brief sessions with breaks between to make writing part of their daily routine: freewriting on their topic one day, outlining the next, writing a beginning that evening, and so on. Or tell them to stop when they feel their creative juices drying up—in the middle of a paragraph or the middle of a sentence, if need be. They should quickly jot down a few notes about how and why they want to continue—and then do something else for a while.

- Suggest that students set intermediate deadlines for themselves, for example, an outline by Wednesday and a rough draft by Friday. If their personal deadline is several days before the actual deadline, they then have time to improve their draft before submitting it. One way to enforce the deadline is to make an appointment for a conference with you or with a tutor at the campus writing center.

- Include time during class for students to write, share their writing, and talk about it. Teachers demonstrate what's important by their use of class time.

- Write with your students. Teachers also demonstrate what's important by what they do—and if you do assignments with your students, you can then talk with them as one writer to another about what you did, what worked for you, and what didn't.

This chapter offers advice and tips for teaching each chapter in the Processes section of the *Field Guide*.

Chapter 22, WRITING AS INQUIRY

For many years, educators and others have advocated such concepts and abilities as lifelong learning, self-motivated learning, discovery learning, creative thinking, curiosity, risktaking, and other traits that characterize bright, interesting, creative people. At the same time, schools, motivated by poor funding and the demands of the No Child Left Behind law and various state mandates, have focused their attention on the teaching of "basic skills," often through rote memorization, while neglecting the subjects (literature, music, the arts, and even lab sciences) that traditionally have been seen to foster creativity and a spirit of inquiry.

College writing courses often offer students opportunities to use their creativity to inquire about themselves and their world, simply because they are asked to write various essays about topics they may have never encountered or considered—and because they have considerable latitude to explore and research their topics. This chapter offers advice to students on moving from doing the minimum necessary to complete the assignment to engaging with their subject. In a way, this chapter functions as a companion to Chapter 24, GENERATING IDEAS AND TEXT, in that it asks students to expand their thinking about their topics and to explore the implications in unexpected and unfamiliar ways, generating ideas and notes that may lead them to better understanding of their topic, strategies for approaching it, and possibly new ways of REPORTING on it or ARGUING A POSITION related to it.

Starting with questions. If students are exploring a subject but haven't settled on it yet, ask them to explore it by answering some of the questions in Starting with Questions. They may be able to freewrite or do other writing activities (see Chapter

24) to pull knowledge from their own minds, but they may also need to do research to answer the questions. Either way (or both!), they can come to understand the subject better and make an informed decision about if they want to pursue the subject, if they need to expand or limit the scope of their thinking, or if they want to pursue a possible topic that hadn't occurred to them beforehand.

If students have settled on a topic, the questions can provide direction for them as they research and consider the topic. If the topic or the genre seems to invite certain strategies (an essay REPORTING INFORMATION, for example, will likely include DEFINING and EXPLAINING, and possibly COMPARING AND CONTRASTING), ask students to answer the questions relating to those strategies. Those answers might open up new possibilities for rethinking, further focusing, and revising their topics—or let students know that their original ideas are on target.

Keeping a journal. Artists maintain sketchbooks; scientists keep logs; people in many professions maintain journals, daybooks, or diaries—all places where they can jot down ideas and play with them. To encourage students to develop a spirit of inquiry, you might ask them to keep a journal, at least for a specified period of time, to see what they learn from the experience. You might ask them to keep a double-entry notebook, which is described in Chapter 8 in this guide to teaching, "Using Readings to Teach Writing." Or you might ask students to keep a journal, which is described in Chapter 22 of the *Field Guide*, WRITING AS INQUIRY.

You can give credit for or assess the journals in several ways. You can simply give completion credit—so many entries equals an A, so many a B, and so on; or you can grade for length. You can assess the journals according to criteria you set up, such as "more speculating, synthesizing, and questioning than personal responses or summary," but you invite both arguments with students and a stifling of their playfulness if *you* do the assessing. Better to ask the students to assess their own journals, and a good way to do that is to ask them to highlight the kinds of thinking in the journals (observations in pink, questions in blue, summaries in yellow, speculations in green, and so on) and then look at the proportions of each color. They will usually make adjustments on their own.

Keeping a blog. A blog can function like a journal, but with one big difference: It's not private. Unless a blogger limits access—to the writer alone or to a group of friends or classmates—blog posts can be read and commented on by anyone who finds them. That can be a good thing, as others may bring up ideas or offer suggestions that can further students' understanding or stretch their inquiring into new areas. But some students will likely resist sharing exploratory thinking with others, so it's a good idea to make creating and using a blog voluntary.

Chapter 23, COLLABORATING

Students may not enter into collaboration willingly. Some students have endured bad experiences with group work, others took seriously their teachers' admonitions to "Do your own work," and still others simply do not trust that the advice given by their peers is trustworthy and may think the teacher, as the bestower of the grade, is the only voice that matters. For those reasons, you need to lay some groundwork to make collaborating a successful part of your writing class.

First, you need to establish and maintain an atmosphere of trust and safety in your classroom so students will willingly share their ideas and work with one another. Early in the term, perhaps beginning on the first day of class, do some activities to help students get to know one another. You might pair students to interview one another and introduce their partner to the class, ask students to describe themselves in such a way that someone standing across the room could pick them out and then have students find each other, or do other ice-breaking activities to help students see one another as individuals. Ask students to share some writing with one another and with the class, with the simple rule that no one responds, except to clap at the end. Put students into groups and have them respond only positively to one another's writing, discussing three things they like about the draft.

How you assign students to groups is both a matter of pedagogy and a matter of taste. For informal activities, you might simply ask students to get into groups of four or five, letting them choose their partners. When you assign more serious group work, such as responding to drafts or doing collaborative projects, you're better off assigning students to groups. Instructors commonly divide students in various ways: They may want each group to include a mix of writing ability or to reflect the class's ethnic, racial, gender, or other diversity; sometimes you may need to create groups to separate students who do not work productively together.

The physical arrangement of groups can affect their functioning. If you're teaching in a room with moveable desks, insist that each group member's desk faces everyone else's equally; if the students are sitting in a row, the quality of their interaction will suffer because the students on the end can easily opt out of participating (and, indeed, may be unable to hear or see). If you're in a classroom with stationary furniture or teaching in a computer classroom, you may need to arrange the groups so that students are seated in two rows or working across a computer table—or allow students to sit on the floor or in the hall. If possible, move groups to the corners of the room, with one or two groups in the middle, to provide as much space between the groups as possible.

When you assign group work, establish clear rules about how students should behave: They should focus on the work and not on personalities, modulate their voices so the groups can work productively without disturbing one another or classes in other classrooms, and, in general, treat others as they want to be treated. When students read one another's work, give them advice on how to be good readers:

- Let the writer lead you by asking questions or requesting that you focus on certain parts of the draft.

- Be positive—look for what works well, rather than for mistakes—but be honest. Try to balance criticism and praise.

- Focus on the writing, not the writer. Describe what the *writing* says and does, rather than saying, "*You* do this or that."

- Be specific and constructive. Offer suggestions if you can; for example, "I'd like to know more here—maybe a couple of examples," or "What if you rearranged this sentence to say . . . ."

You can also help groups function by assigning roles. For example, one student might be the timekeeper, in charge of making sure that each student's work is given equal time; another might be the moderator, charged with seeing that every group member has opportunities to contribute and that one person does not dominate the group. Another student might be the recorder who takes notes on the group's work and reports the group's results to the class. Give the class a specific time period in which to work and call out the time periodically to remind students how much time remains. Consider giving students *less* time than you anticipate their task taking; for example, if you think the group work should take thirty minutes, give them twenty or even fifteen. You can always give them more time if they need it; and if they don't, you can move on.

Reporting results is itself a powerful way to keep groups working. If you assign a specific set of tasks that must result in an oral report to the class or a completed worksheet or text, students will be more likely to approach the work responsibly. It's also useful to have a backup activity— also leading to a product—for the groups that finish their first task far sooner than you had planned!

To keep groups working, walk around the room, monitoring their conversations, or sit at a desk in the middle of the room, where you can look at one group or a book while listening to another. Some groups will get to work and do exactly what you want, even if you never go near them; other groups will work when you're in the vicinity and lapse into conversation once you're on the other side of the room; and some groups will require you to sit with them to direct their activities. If you are needed for five minutes to clarify the task or your expectations for it, that's okay; however, if the group won't work unless you're sitting with them (fortunately, a rare occurrence), the group isn't functioning and should probably be disbanded, with its members assigned to other groups.

Chapter 24,
GENERATING IDEAS AND TEXT

Often the biggest challenge for generating ideas and text is convincing students to loosen up and give the activity a chance. Some students may see such activities as inefficient, preferring to jump directly to drafting prematurely; others may have tried such activities in the past and felt that they weren't helpful. Here are some ways to help convince students to try the activities:

- Stress that freewriting, brainstorming, and other generating activities won't be graded—or that you'll grade on length or amount of elaboration, perhaps with a three-point system: 3 = lots of writing, playful and thoughtful; 2 = goes beyond the minimum; 1 = meets the minimum requirement.

- Offer choices, so students may select a method that matches their abilities and ways of thinking. People who tend to think in words may prefer freewriting or listing, for example, while visual thinkers may prefer clustering or even sketching a picture. Some students may feel at home writing on a computer, while others need to use pen and paper.

- Encourage students to create outlines or numbered lists, or to move from these activities to the Organizing sections of the Genre chapters in the *Field Guide*. Rosemary Deen, in "Notes to Stella," says, "Structure pulls material out of the mind. You pluck something out of the mind's plenty that you would otherwise not pay attention to because you need it to complete your structure" (62).

- Make it clear that if the activity doesn't work, you won't force students to do it. At the same time, if their subsequent writing lacks content or is poorly organized, you should reserve the right to ask students to return to these activities to help as they revise.

Chapter 25, DRAFTING

Although DRAFTING stresses that drafting is exploratory and tentative, some students find the task daunting. They don't know where to start, they reach a certain point and grind to a halt, or they fear loss of control over their ideas as their prose leads them in directions they hadn't anticipated. These students need encouragement and comfort: If they can't think of a way to begin, suggest that they start somewhere in the middle. If they hit a wall, suggest that they revisit activities in Chapter 24, GENERATING IDEAS AND TEXT, that worked for them before, or that they stop trying to write that section and begin another section or paragraph. If they find that their writing is leading them to a topic or a perspective on their topic that they hadn't planned, they can decide to see where the new topic leads, planning to rewrite the beginning to fit their new ideas; or they can try to figure out where in the draft their thinking abandoned their plan and try again to write what they'd planned. Before they do, however, they should consider carefully whether their new ideas are indeed a distraction or represent better ideas than they came up with earlier.

If writers are blocked and cannot write a draft, you can suggest some ways to get them going:

- *Revise your standards.* Some writers feel a need to perfect each sentence before moving on to the next. Many student writers feel such pressure to avoid error that they can't write anything. These writers need to be reassured that there'll be plenty of time to clean up their prose later, that their first priority must be getting text on the page or screen so they'll have something on which to work.

- *Write a letter.* Suggest that blocked students write a letter explaining what they want to say in their draft. By the time they've finished, they'll have a draft that they can rewrite to meet the demands of the genre in which they need to write.

- *Say it out loud.* Ask blocked students to explain orally what they want to say in their draft, to you, to another student, or into a tape recorder. Once they're done, they'll have rehearsed it and can usually put it into writing.

Chapter 26,
ASSESSING YOUR OWN WRITING

Donald M. Murray observes that "the writer's first reader is the writer" (58). The advice in this chapter of the *Field Guide* begins with that premise: Before students have others read their writing, they should read and assess it themselves. Students are more likely to take these activities seriously if you assign them.

- Ask students to highlight or color-code their formal and informal writing (for example, yellow for highlighting, green for responding, pink for questioning, and so on). This activity can lead to good class discussions about what students characteristically do when asked to respond to readings or speculate about concepts—and what college faculty expect of them.

- Have students answer the questions in the sections on Considering the Rhetorical Situation in this chapter and also those questions in the genre chapter they're working from to prepare them for revising and rewriting.

- Ask students to answer the questions in Examining the Text Itself as another way to help them see how their writing measures up.

- Have students analyze their own writing using the analysis techniques in Chapter 41, READING STRATEGIES: writing outlines of what their draft says and does, identifying patterns in their writing, and analyzing the argument.

Chapter 27, GETTING RESPONSE AND REVISING

You can use the advice in this chapter to encourage students to move from "fixing" their drafts—usually meaning that they change only what you have marked in your responses—to more global revision of their texts. This process isn't easy for some students, who struggle to get one draft written and honestly can't see how they might have written it differently. So encouragement and modeling with your own writing—perhaps by revising or rewriting a paragraph in class, thinking aloud as you make changes—can be helpful, as can your responses to students' writing. See Chapter 9 in this guide to teaching for tips on responding to students' writing.

Here's an example of how you might model the thoughtful revising behavior you want from your students. Students' initial drafts may briefly sketch anecdotes or descriptions that need to be fleshed out so readers can understand what they're saying and why they're including it. In the following paragraphs, writing teacher Brady Allen revises a childhood memory from an initial anecdote to a memoir that also makes an argument. Allen introduces the memory in general terms:

> My teacher said I'd done the assignment wrong, that I'd crossed the line, that my drawing was dirty. I had an argument with her about not being fair with me, and I was scared to death because she was so intimidating. She was big and mean looking, But I stood my ground, and I made her rethink things.

The underlined parts are all labels or vague descriptions that offer little information. Look now at his revision that adds details to bring the memory to life:

> I stood in front of Mrs. Jones, and I clutched my artwork in my hand. It was a drawing of an apple—only my apple was upside down and had a head and face, arms and legs, and a stem where a penis might be. I had scribbled a title along the bottom: "You Are What You Eat." My classmates had thought it was funny.
>
> Mrs. Jones was perched atop her thick-heeled shoes, staring down through her glasses across the bridge of her nose. Her forehead was wrinkled and she was grinding her teeth. She frowned at me; it was a staredown.
>
> I felt a fat bead of sweat slip from my underarm, slide down my side, and disappear into the band of my Fruit of the Looms. But I stood my ground and looked into her unblinking eyes.
>
> "That was not the assignment," she said, finally.

Here the specific details—the showing—give credibility by creating a scene and characters readers can see, hear, and sense. Allen doesn't stop there, however; he adds another layer, of reflection, which takes the narrative beyond a simple anecdote to an argument for students' rights to protect their creativity. At important points, he adds reflections, which are underlined here:

> Mrs. Jones was perched atop her thick-heeled shoes, staring down through her glasses across the bridge of her nose. Her forehead was wrinkled and she was grinding her teeth.

Looking back, I see that it was something of a façade. She was a fifth-grade teacher built to terrorize, sure, but I think she was only trying to be scary. I would get to know her better throughout the rest of the year, and I remember her as a woman afraid of losing control. We all know how a soft-spoken teacher can be usurped by class clowns, especially rowdy fifth-grade boys. She wanted to avoid that, and frowning over her nose from atop her tall shoes was her means.

So she frowned at me; it was a staredown.

I felt a fat bead of sweat slip from my underarm, slide down my side, and disappear into the band of my Fruit of the Looms. But I stood my ground and looked into her unblinking eyes.

I'm not sure why I really felt the need to stand up to her. I knew the drawing was "obscene." That's part of why I drew it that way after all. I know I didn't really have any concept of censorship at that age, but I think even then there was something inside me that knew my artistic freedom was in jeopardy. Somewhere in the back of my mind I knew I had to defend my art. Something told me that my creativity, my urge to expand the boundaries of the assignment, was more important than the petty "perversity charge" of my teacher. My creativity hadn't hurt anyone, had it? No. It was a simple apple with human anatomy. I mean, come on.

"That was not the assignment," she said, finally . . . . "*Your* apple has body parts. *Appendages*," she said. I recall that she made the word appendages sound like it was a pile of maggot-infested crap. *Ah-peeen-daaageees.* Like merely having an appendage went against some strict religious doctrine.

"I know, but. . . . Look at my apple." I held the paper up, and turned it upside down so that the apple itself was right side up. I recall my hand shaking slightly, the paper rustling softly. "My apple has the same bad spots—it looks the same as the one on the table. I just added to it."

"Did I tell you to add to it?" Her nostrils flared, and I could see her jaw working where she was still grinding her teeth.

I said nothing. Just locked with her eyes.

"Did I?" she asked again.

"No."

"You'll stay after school and wash my boards for the rest of the week. Okay? You'll take the second bus home. Do you understand?"

"Yeah, I guess."

" 'Yes,' not 'Yeah, I guess.' "

"Yes."

"So, what have you learned from this?"

I thought about this for only the briefest of moments, and then I said, "That you've got no imagination."

I thought she was going to wear her teeth down to the gums, the grinding got so bad. I thought I was going to catch some hell. She poked me in the chest with one meaty finger. But what Mrs. Jones did after that surprised me: she smiled slightly and said simply, "Maybe you're right."

With these additions, Allen moves beyond the perspective of the classroom anecdote itself to his current, adult interpretation of this childhood drama. He shapes the narrative by telling, showing, and reflecting on it and so shapes readers' interpretation as well. You can create similar, multiple revisions to illustrate how to revise to improve a text's focus, argument, organization, clarity—or anything else.

Rewriting is useful for at least two reasons: When students rewrite a draft in a completely new way, they are forced to see their writing with new eyes, making various changes to fit a new rhetorical situation; such revision can be challenging in a way few students have experienced previously. And that makes it fun to do: since students already have a "serious" draft, asking them to play with it lets them explore various alternatives without risk. In the process, they often discover ways of integrating some of their rewrites into their original and sometimes decide to focus their attention on the rewrite, abandoning the original. You can assign rewriting in various ways: You can have students do quick rewrites in class, you can have them work collaboratively on one another's drafts, you can have them rewrite a single paragraph of their choice (or yours), or you can require that they produce a completely new draft that's at least as long and as carefully thought through as the original.

Chapter 28,
EDITING AND PROOFREADING

For many students, what they were taught to call "revising" is really editing and proofreading. And some of them have been taught that editing and proofreading are the only parts of the writing process that really matter. You should try to convince students that they can put off serious editing and proofreading work until the final stages of writing a text—that there's no point in fixing a sentence or phrase that might be revised out of the text. Also, as students revise, they'll see problems or straighten out sentences or spellings, so many editing and proofreading issues will disappear as they go over their work. But once their texts are in the overall shape they think is best, they need to go over the texts carefully, making them as clear and correct as they can for the simple reason that readers are often intolerant: They judge a writer's ideas and personality by the correctness of their prose.

Some versions of the *Field Guide* do not include a handbook, but Chapter 28, EDITING AND PROOFREADING, offers advice for students on major questions they need to ask about their paragraphs, sentences, and words. In addition, you may ask students to look for patterns of errors in their writing, as they might in analyzing the writing of others (see *Field Guide* Chapter 41, READING STRATEGIES). From this exercise, students can compile a record of their error patterns, allowing you to provide focused, detailed instruction in the correct forms. You may also assign worksheets on such problems; several are available on the Web, and more may be available in your campus writing center. These records can also help students edit, using them as checksheets to make sure those errors don't appear in their work.

When you see a student's early drafts filled with mistakes, don't panic. Often, students who are struggling with new concepts and unfamiliar genres can't successfully manage the rules of language at the same time. Some students who speak dialects of English compose in their home dialect first. In both these cases, as students gain control over content and organization, many of the errors and non-standard usages will likely disappear—and what's left is where you should focus your teaching.

Chapter 29, COMPILING A PORTFOLIO

Chapter 10 of this guide to teaching, "Teaching with Writing Portfolios," offers detailed advice on assigning, maintaining, and evaluating writing portfolios and is a good place to start. When you ask students to create portfolios, you can use the questions in Considering the Rhetorical Situation either as a way to help students choose the sort of portfolio they'd like to create or as a framework for defining the kind of portfolio you'd like them to create. In other words, you may wish to offer students considerable freedom or carefully define for them the portfolio's purpose, audience, included genres, desirable writer's stance, and range of media and design options.

Students usually find a list of required and optional pieces useful, and you will, too, since the first requirement for any required piece in a portfolio is simply, "Is it in there?" As Chapter 10 notes, asking for all drafts and source material for essays helps students assess their progress while helping you read their material efficiently. Similarly, asking students to organize their portfolios carefully helps them see what the portfolio contains while aiding your reading and evaluating.

For many instructors, students' reflections on their portfolio contents is very important in assessing their growth as writers and potential for independent work once they leave the writing course. Ask students to read the Sample Self-Assessment and discuss it, identifying the various elements of a good self-assessment and the evidence Nathaniel Cooney uses to support his statements; note how the assessment itself demonstrates Cooney's writing ability as much as any other piece in his portfolio.

Electronic portfolios. Kathleen Blake Yancey, author of several books and articles on electronic portfolios, compares print portfolios to catalogs and electronic portfolios to galleries: they have "a central entry point"; they "[include] both text and image, using the one modality to explain and juxtapose the other"; and they "make multiple contexts part of the display," using links within the portfolio and out to other sites and pages "to show multiple and complex relationships" (91–93). In other words, e-portfolios offer students opportunities to construct and display knowledge that crosses genre and media boundaries and makes connections among a wealth of ideas, concepts, facts, and images. You can help your students create such connections.

As is noted in Chapter 29 of the *Field Guide*, several excellent, easy-to-use tools are available with which students can create complex and visually appealing electronic portfolios. If you want to ask your students to create e-portfolios, your first task is to find out what tools are available to you. If you'd prefer that your students follow a standard format, tools such as Epsilen.com are best; if you want to give students maximum freedom to exercise their creativity, a program like *Google Sites* (sites.google.com) may be preferred—but you also need to balance those values against ease of use. The preformatted tools restrict students' freedom, but they can be very easy to use, allowing students to put together an e-portfolio in a few hours, while the more flexible tools may require you to spend more time teaching students how to use them.

Once you've made a tentative decision on a tool, you'll need to try it out by creating at least a rudimentary portfolio of your own. You'll quickly learn how easy or difficult it is to create a homepage and links to other sites; upload documents and images; change, edit, or reformat your pages; and post the finished product. You'll need to know how to help students perform those actions as they create their own e-portfolios, and having a portfolio of your own gives you a model both to show them and to use as an example of how to add to, edit, and revise their own.

Most online tools offer Webinars or tutorials that you and your students can learn from. Dr. Helen Barrett's website, Electronicportfolios.com, offers a wealth of advice and how-to that will help you develop an e-portfolio using various tools, as well as links to other helpful sites.

A literacy portfolio. This is a special portfolio that nicely accompanies the literacy narrative assignment in Chapter 7 of the *Field Guide*. You can assign it as a way to create a bridge between the literacies students bring with them to your classroom or the literacy instruction they've had before reaching you and the expectations of college writing. The assignment itself is deceptively simple: "to put together a portfolio that chronicles your development as a reader and writer." As students collect materials from their past and organize them for presentation, they often make striking discoveries, find books or papers they'd long forgotten, and connect various significant literacy events. And as they share their portfolios with other students, they learn that others have had similar experiences and enjoyed some of the same books, and they see possibilities for adding to and reorganizing their own portfolios—and they get to know other students in the class. Most students find this a very rewarding experience. Here are some tips for making the assignment work:

- *Create one yourself.* As is generally true, doing what you're asking students to do will help you explain it to them while providing you with a model for them to see. You can use your portfolio to show them what they might include in theirs and various ways of compiling the material: plastic sleeves for essays, photo album pages for individual sheets, two-pocket folders for bulky items, and even boxes or baskets for oddly shaped items.

- *Assign the portfolio early* and give students several weeks to work on it. Some students need to travel home to get material; some need to get their parents to dig papers and picture books out of closets, attics, and basements. They'll also need time to organize what they find and annotate each item.

- *Offer options.* Some students have little to collect, because of frequent moves around the country, house fires, or simply a disinclination to keep old schoolwork. Such students may compile portfolios of current writing, writing done for work, or even remembered writing—brief descriptions of pieces of writing or reading they remember as significant but that they don't have. (One schoolteacher who had lost everything in a fire created a moving portfolio composed entirely of the memories he had of important papers in his life, from his daughter's birth certificate to his divorce papers.) Some students who have few artifacts of their reading or writing have many of other kinds of literacy, including artwork, sports, auto mechanics, and music—allowing alternate forms of literacy to dominate some portfolios may draw otherwise disengaged students to participate in this project (and enrich the portfolios of other students, too).

- *Share the portfolios.* You should share your portfolio with them as an introduction to the assignment. Most instructors spend class time flipping through the pages and explaining each item orally; you might ask students to do the same, perhaps assigning two or three students to share theirs at the beginning and end of each class period. Alternately, you can ask students to bring their portfolios on the due day and place them on their desks; they can then circulate around the room, reading one another's portfolios and discussing the contents with one another. If students scan materials and create an online literacy portfolio, you can ask that students visit one another's sites during or outside class. It's useful to close the sharing activity with a brief writing activity, asking students to reflect on what they learned about one another's literacy—and their own.

Useful Readings

Armstrong, Sonya L., and Eric J. Paulson. "Whither 'Peer Review'? Terminology Matters for the Writing Classroom." *Teaching English in the Two-Year College* 35.4 (2008): 398-407. Print.

Boynton, Linda. "See Me: Conference Strategies for Developmental Writers." *Teaching English in the Two-Year College* 30.4 (2003): 391–402. Print.

Brookfield, Stephen D. "Overcoming Impostership, Cultural Suicide, and Lost Innocence: Implications for Teaching Critical Thinking in the Community College." *New Directions for Community Colleges* 130 (2005): 49–57. Print.

Cambridge, Darren, Barbara Cambridge, and Kathleen Blake Yancey, eds. *Electronic Portfolios 2.0*. Washington, DC: Stylus, 2009. Print.

Dawkins, John. "Teaching Punctuation as a Rhetorical Tool." *College Composition and Communication* 46.4. Rpt. Josephine Koster Travers, *Teaching in Progress*. 2nd ed. New York: Longman, 1998. 438–55. Print.

Hartwell, Patrick. "Grammar, Grammars, and the Teaching of Grammar." *College English* 47.2 (1985): 105–27. Print.

Krause, Steven D. "When Blogging Goes Bad: A Cautionary Tale about Blogs, Emailing Lists, Discussion, and Interaction." *Kairos* 9.1 (2004): n. pag. Web. 13 Oct. 2009.

Micciche, Laura R. "Making a Case for Rhetorical Grammar." *College Composition and Communication* 55.4 (2004): 716–37. Print.

Murray, Donald. *A Writer Teaches Writing*. 2nd ed. New York: Houghton, 1985. Print.

Perl, Sondra. "Understanding Composing." *College Composition and Communication* 31.4 (1980): 363–69. Print.

Sommers, Nancy. "Revision Strategies of Student Writers and Experienced Adult Writers." *College Composition and Communication* 31.4 (1980): 378–88. Print.

Tobin, Lad. "Introduction: How the Writing Process Was Born—and Other Conversion Narratives." *Taking Stock: The Writing Process Movement in the '90's*. Ed. Lad Tobin and Thomas Newkirk. Portsmouth, NH: Boynton/Cook–Heinemann. 1–14. Print.

Yancey, Kathleen Blake. *Teaching Literature as Reflective Practice*. Urbana, IL: NCTE, 2004. Print.

31 Teaching Writing Strategies

Defining. Analyzing causes and effects. Comparing and contrasting. Writers constantly employ these and other strategies as they write, whether they focus primarily on a single strategy or combine several strategies in order to achieve their purposes. Other strategies—for creating effective beginnings and endings, guiding readers, using dialogue, and reading critically—are useful in many writing situations. The chapters in this section of the *Field Guide* are designed to help students as they write and read, so encourage them to refer to the Strategies chapters as they plan and draft their work. They may find that one strategy, such as analyzing causes and effects or classifying, becomes the major strategy they use when writing some essays; for others, they will combine several strategies—narrating an anecdote, defining a key term, comparing several things, and so on.

Each of these chapters offers guidance in deciding how to use the strategy and a brief example, followed by ways of organizing a text using the strategy and an outline of the rhetorical situations in which using each strategy is a good idea. If students are writing a text that primarily uses one strategy, they can follow the sug-

gestions in that chapter as they plan and draft. If they're combining strategies, they may choose among the options to suit their needs as writers. Students may find the section on Starting with Questions in Chapter 22, WRITING AS INQUIRY, useful in helping them think through the implications of using a particular strategy. See Chapter 5 in this guide to teaching for suggestions on integrating the Strategies chapters into sequences of assignments leading to a finished text. You may find yourself discussing these strategies with students more often during one-on-one conferences, as their varying topics and approaches to those topics will dictate their need for specific strategies. Here are some additional pointers for helping students use these strategies effectively.

Chapter 30, BEGINNING AND ENDING

Chapter 30 explains several ways for students to begin and end their essays. You might ask students to draft several opening and closing passages and then compare them to see which most effectively achieves their purposes. Some students may need to play with several opening paragraphs in order to find a direction for their papers and to develop momentum for further writing. Some may need to wait until they've finished a draft to write a beginning, so they can write knowing what they're introducing. Others might benefit from drafting the ending first, to help them work toward a goal. Students might also share their drafts in groups to see how each affects an audience. Some additional tips for helping students with beginnings and endings include the following:

- *Use Considering the Rhetorical Situation to help students choose an appropriate beginning and ending.* Ask them to consider the general questions in this chapter in light of their understanding of the genre in which they're writing—and refer to the questions on the rhetorical situation in the Genre chapter for more specific ways to think about them.

- *Encourage them to think in terms of content, not paragraphs.* Many students believe they need an opening paragraph and a concluding paragraph. That's often not enough space to provide a useful introduction or a satisfying conclusion. One teacher I know suggests devoting the first page to the beginning, with the thesis at the bottom of the page, and the last full page to a conclusion. Showing models of multiparagraph beginnings and endings can help, too.

- *Consider an essay a journey to a new place—not a round trip.* Students taught rigid formats may write essays in which the first and last paragraphs are virtually interchangeable. Note that beginnings and endings serve different purposes—and so should contain different information, even when the conclusion restates the main point, so that readers feel satisfied.

Chapter 31, GUIDING YOUR READER

The advice in Chapter 31 helps students in the creation of titles, thesis statements, and topic sentences and presents advice on using transitions effectively. It's a good idea to refer students to this chapter repeatedly as they plan and draft their texts. Here are some ideas for helping students write good titles and thesis statements:

Titles. Have students write five, or ten, or twenty possible titles and choose the one that they like best. Have other students choose from their list or compose a thesis based on the titles. Have students come up with a title as they work on generating ideas and text to help them focus their thinking. See if key phrases in their thesis statements can be combined or modified to act as a title. Explore the differences between titles in newspapers, popular magazines, and scholarly works by sharing examples from all three media and having students analyze them for structure, content, and intent: Do they try to entice the audience to read the piece? Provide a concise summary of the content? Entertain? Something else? Have students find several titles that they like or that make them want to read further and then discuss what qualities of the titles make them effective.

Thesis statements. Chapter 31 outlines a process for generating good thesis statements, so you may assign your students to follow the three steps outlined in the chapter. In addition, students may benefit from the following advice:

- Thesis statements are tentative. As students write, their drafts may head in a direction different from their original thesis, and it's okay to change the thesis statement accordingly. They do need to be sure that every other part of the draft relates to the new thesis, though.

- A good thesis statement is meaningful for its intended audience and suggests that the writer will have something interesting to say about the topic. Have students ask of their thesis statements, "So what?" For example, while an audience of undergraduates may be uninterested in a thesis like "It snows too much in the Midwest"—it's hard to see what there is to say about such a topic— they're likely to find a thesis like this more meaningful: "Financial aid to college students, including Pell grants, should be eliminated to reduce the influence of the federal government."

- The thesis of an essay that makes an argument should state a position that others could oppose or challenge. If it doesn't, there's no argument. For example, the statement "Beef tastes best when grilled" can't be argued because it's a matter of taste.

- Sometimes a template can help students compose a thesis. Here are three models from the website of the Writing Center at the University of Wisconsin–Madison:

  A. Although most readers of _____ have argued that _____, closer examination shows that _____.

  B. _____ uses _____ and _____ to prove that _____.

  C. Phenomenon X is a result of the combination of _____, _____, and _____.

Topic sentences. Topic sentences in paragraphs—sentences that state the main idea of the paragraph—function not only to signal to readers what a paragraph is about but also to help readers move from paragraph to paragraph, idea to idea. Help students by beginning the first sentence of a paragraph with a summary of the previous paragraph, by repeating key terms or restating the previous paragraph's content in a word or phrase, combined with "This," as the example by Deborah Tannen ("This episode . . .") does. You can ask students to find such signal phrases in their reading and analyze how they function in the text. Students can trade papers and underline the topic sentences in each other's paragraphs. You can also help students write effective paragraphs by pointing out that the various approaches for organizing in the Strategies section of the *Field Guide* can be applied to single paragraphs as well.

Transitions. To clarify for students the need for transitions in their writing, remove all the transitions from a brief text and show it to students, asking them how the various ideas and sentences relate to one another and then inserting transitions where they think best. Now show the original with transitions, and compare the results. If you use PowerPoint, you can create a series of slides—the first showing the first sentence of the passage, the second showing the first two sentences, the third showing the first three, and so on—to dramatize the reader's journey through the text and show how transitions help guide the reader's understanding. Have students exchange papers and circle the transitions in each other's drafts.

Chapter 32, ANALYZING CAUSES AND EFFECTS

Analyzing causes and effects is challenging, because there are seldom definitive, clear chains of causes and effects and because in many cases the task requires writers to reason backward from an effect to the probable causes of it or speculate that a certain cause will probably lead to certain effects. Both are abstract and tricky, and speculating about possible or probable effects is particularly difficult for many students, as their arguments may quickly devolve into conjecture, fallacious reasoning, or "common sense," which is often anything but. They're better off using this strategy to analyze the causes of a specific event for which evidence exists. If they need to analyze the plausible effects of something, they need to be aware that their analysis must be grounded in evidence: analogous situations, similar events, testimony by experts.

If you're asking students to ARGUE A POSITION (Chapter 10) but focusing their argument on analyzing causes and effects, you might ask the class to work together to identify promising topics. Then discuss each one to see if it has these characteristics: it will be interesting for the audience to whom the students are writing; it's researchable—information on possible causes is available; and its causes are arguable.

A danger of the cause-and-effect strategy is oversimplification: arguing that B follows from A, when in reality B might also result from the influence of C, D, and E. Emphasizing the classification of causes and effects as plausible, probable, or likely—not statements of fact—can help students see the need for selecting and interpreting as well as making an argument. To emphasize the interpretive nature of cause-and-effect analyses, students should take extra care to include signal phrases that introduce their sources, as the credibility of their sources will help them make their case. A signal phrase like "Jonathan Pope, former director of the Institute on Applied Behavioral Sciences and author of seven books on the subject, states that . . ." makes it clear that the source is authoritative—important in any argument, but especially so in one of this nature.

Chapter 33, ARGUING

Almost any writing you assign may be construed as an argument. Arguing a position, evaluations, and proposals are obviously arguments. Textual analyses argue that a text should be looked at in a certain way, and reports argue that the information they provide accurately describes their subjects. But literacy narratives, memoirs, profiles, and even reflections also may contain arguments: that the slice of life they portray is true, if only for the writer. So you may find that students need to refer to this chapter often to help them write in various genres for myriad purposes. Ways you can help them use this chapter include this advice:

- Helping students develop a topic into a claim is crucial to their success. You'll do them a favor by steering them away from topics that are overwhelming and very difficult to limit or say anything new or interesting about (e.g., abortion, gun control, euthanasia, gay rights, and lowering the drinking age) and toward topics that

have some connection to their own lives (e.g., the cost of higher education, parking on campus or public transportation options, Ritalin use among children, whether or not the school should have a football team, and on-campus child care).

- Make sure students present adequate context for their arguments. Many who have been taught the five-paragraph theme will think that a threadbare introductory paragraph is all their argument requires, when much more is needed. A wise high school teacher told one of my students that the introduction should be at least one full page long—sometimes much longer—to establish the need for the argument and the terms under which it is being argued.

- Consider having students identify a real audience for their arguments (a specific individual or organization, a local or national newspaper or magazine in which it might be published), carefully research that audience, and then submit their final drafts to that audience.

- One way to help students build toward a solid, researched argument is to design a sequence of assignments. For example, you might help students come up with a topic idea, which they then research, finding 8–10 sources of information with help from the Research section. They might complete an Annotated Bibliography of those sources, evaluating their potential usefulness to their argument. Using the REPORTING INFORMATION chapter as a basis, they might then write a report that outlines the nature of the argument, describing all sides' positions as carefully and objectively as possible. Use their improved understanding to help them focus and qualify their claim and create a thesis and good reasons, and then they can look through their sources for useful evidence to support those reasons. Then they can write a draft of the appropriate argument (which might be an essay ARGUING A POSITION, an EVALUATION, a PROPOSAL, or an essay MIXING GENRES), using their understanding of the various positions to fairly deal with positions counter to theirs.

- You can help students deal with positions different from their own by asking them to explore the reasons behind those positions. Have students state their opponent's claim (in the text example, "iPods and other MP3 players harm society") and reasons ("because they isolate users from other people") and then explore the unstated assumptions underlying that "because" ("isolation is bad"). If students can understand that people hold different positions because their basic assumptions or beliefs differ, they may find more appropriate methods of arguing— and of building common ground.

- When you discuss fallacies with your students, you might point out that at the heart of most fallacies are a few common problems: a tendency to overgeneralize or jump to conclusions based on little or even no evidence; the abuse or exaggeration of legitimate reasoning processes, such as causal analysis or comparison; and the substitution of emotion (fear, prejudice, pity, pride, etc.) for thinking. Give some examples of common fallacies, and then have students find fallacious reasoning in newspapers, magazines, advertisements, and commercials; have them share these with the class.

You may notice that both ARGUING and Chapter 10, ARGUING A POSITION, avoid terminology often taught in courses focusing on argument. As is true throughout the *Field Guide*, rhetorical terminology is kept to a minimum, because students need to know what to do; they don't necessarily need to identify it by its formal term. For example, philosopher Steven Toulmin's characterization of arguments identifies three elements common to all complete arguments; the basic Toulmin scheme diagrammed in Reasons shows students that they need to support their reasons with evidence that is based on an underlying, unstated assumption, but they don't need to grapple with Toulmin's term for that belief, *warrant*. (Claim, however, is a common term that is worth having students understand and use.) Many texts ask students to think in terms of *logos*, *ethos*, and *pathos*; however, *logic and evidence, convincing readers you're trustworthy,* and *appealing to your readers' emotions* get the same point across without using what is, after all, our jargon.

Chapter 34,
CLASSIFYING AND DIVIDING

To help students understand this strategy, you might present several items—names of cars or popular singers, fast-food menu items—and ask students to classify them into groups, identifying the characteristics of each group and why each item fits into it. Alternately, you might present large categories—automobiles; music; fast food—and ask groups of students to divide each one into subcategories. In both cases, ask students to articulate the criteria they use to classify or divide. Your goal here is to help students see that classifying and dividing can be done in various ways; for example, automobiles might be classified by make, function, color, performance, or "coolness," to name a few categories. When possible, students should devise categories that are clear and distinct—or be able to justify a scheme that permits something to be part of more than one category. In their writing, the categories should relate directly to their purpose; if I'm writing about emissions controls on trucks, for example, whether pickup trucks seat two, three, or five is likely irrelevant, unlike their gas mileage and tailpipe emissions.

If you're asking students to ARGUE A POSITION (Chapter 10) but focusing their argument on proving that something is a member of a class, you might begin by giving them some sample assertions (W. Mark Felt, Deep Throat, was a hero; a nearby deserted factory should be declared a hazardous waste site) and then asking the class or groups of students to identify the characteristics of the class (What are the characteristics of a hero? Of a hazardous waste site?). They could then see that the task of arguing is to demonstrate that their topic has or doesn't have each of those characteristics.

A common pitfall of the classifying and dividing strategy is to confuse it with the goal of the essay, to assume that classification or division of something is inherently interesting and worth writing about, rather than a way of understanding a topic. Describing the characteristics of red state and blue state voters, for example, might be useful for analyzing two main political currents in the United States, but the essay needs a clear purpose to go beyond mere listing. Students may also need help in making sure that each category they identify is described consistently, using similar criteria to place items in each category and devoting similar amounts of text to each category.

Chapter 35,
COMPARING AND CONTRASTING

When comparing and contrasting two items with the purpose of showing the superiority of one over the other, students will sometimes be unfair in their characterizations of one item, noting only the strengths of one and the weaknesses of the other; you should urge them to acknowledge the strong points of both items because maintaining a judicious, fair stance will increase their credibility for readers.

If you're asking students to ARGUE A POSITION (Chapter 10) but focusing their argument on comparing and contrasting two or more things, you might give them terms that they may see as very different. Ask them to identify the differences—and then ask them to identify similarities, too. For example, "conservative" and "liberal" are often viewed as opposites. Yet both stand for philosophies of government; both imply ethical stances; both advocate policies on a wide range of issues. This sort of discussion can help students see that their comparisons need to be even-handed.

You might extend discussions of comparing and contrasting by asking students to create analogies, perhaps by starting with clichéd analogies—"My love is like a red, red, rose," "He dropped like a sack of potatoes," "Her face turned as red as a beet"—and seeing how students might revise them to make them fresh and new. Students might practice block and point-by-point organizations by drafting information both ways and discussing each method. Some students will benefit from creating charts or illustrations that help them see the points of their comparison.

Chapter 36, DEFINING

How you define something determines how you—and, potentially, your audience—

see it. Helping students see that definitions aren't static or universally agreed upon, that how we define the words we use strongly influences our thinking, is important. To illustrate, you might give students a short list of contested terms—stem cells, character, inheritance tax—and ask them to find out how various people and institutions define them. Then you can discuss how the definitions lead to certain arguments and perspectives. You might also discuss what linguist George Lakoff calls "frames" that define social issues. For example, one way of framing the issue of taxation is to talk about the need for "tax relief," which implies that taxation is something from which we need to be relieved; a different way of framing the issue is to talk about taxation as "paying our dues as Americans," which implies that paying taxes is a patriotic act. The frames we use, Lakoff says, define our thinking (Powell).

It's also useful to point out that for most purposes in writing, a bare-bones dictionary definition isn't sufficient; ask students to examine the examples of definitions in the chapter to demonstrate how far beyond *Webster's* they go. This is also a good time to note that regular dictionaries are only one source of definitions; to get useful definitions, students may have to look in specialized dictionaries, etymological dictionaries, textbooks, encyclopedias, and scholarly books and articles. To underscore this fact, you might ask groups of students to find definitions of a single term in several different reference works and compare their findings. You might also ask students to choose a term to define in each of the ways described in the *Field Guide* and explore how each might serve a different purpose.

Chapter 37, DESCRIBING

Describing plays an essential part in many genres and media. Students, however, often need to be nudged to provide descriptive details rather than labeling or classifying. For example, an acquaintance may be described as a geek, or a music CD as cool—but those labels tell us little, other than the writer's overall evaluation. Ask questions: How do you know this person is a geek? What does this person wear, say, and do that makes him or her geeky? Why is this CD cool? What about the music and lyrics makes this CD cool? Or have students write out a description of someone sitting near them (providing guidelines, of course, to avoid negative or hurtful descriptions). Collect them and hand them out randomly; then ask students to silently find the person being described.

In addition to the suggestions presented in this chapter, you might also show students various ways of using description by adapting a technique first presented by Young, Becker, and Pike.

Think of your subject as a **particle** (as if it were a static object sitting still, by itself):

- **Describe it as something standing alone.** What features make it different from others? (Young, Becker, and Pike use as their example a particular, old oak tree: "'Old Faithful' contrasts in size and age with the surrounding trees.")

- **Describe it as a specific variation of its concept or idea.** How much can it differ from others like it before becoming something else? (The oak "is shedding its leaves more slowly than the other trees. Although still stately, it has passed its lifetime peak of mature, vigorous health.")

- **Describe it as part of a larger context.** How should it be classified? What is its typical position in a time sequence, as a person may be a baby, an adult, or a senior citizen? What is its position in space—as a tree may be part of a forest, or grow by itself in a yard? (The oak "is composed of roots, trunk, and branches, leaves, and reproductive system [not readily discernible, thus an unknown for this inquirer]; each part is composed of subsystems [again, not discernible and thus unknowns]. Since all trees have roots, trunks, branches, and so on, this oak probably differs from other kinds of trees most clearly in the particularities of its subsystems. . . .")

Think of it as a **wave** (as if it were moving, growing, changing, and dynamic):

- **View it as something that changes over time.** What physical features distinguish it from similar objects or events? What is its core or center? (The oak "is now old, nearly leafless, with one broken limb and numerous scars where others have fallen off. Ten or twenty years ago it was the same tree, but not at its inception as a seed. Then it was only potentially a tree. When it falls and rots or is cut up into lumber, it will lose its identity.")

- *View it as a dynamic process.* How is it changing? ("It is clearly rotting; some of the branches are already dead and other show signs of decay.")

- *View it as part of a larger, dynamic context.* How does it interact with its environment? Does it have clear borders, or does it blend into its context? (The oak's "subsystems support, feed, and repair each other by means of a physiological network. The state of the system differs from hour to hour [e.g., in the regulation of moisture loss] and from day to night [in the handling of carbon dioxide]. Some parts of the system can be lost, either temporarily [leaves] or permanently [some branches] without destroying the system.")

Think of it as a *field* (as if it were a network of relationships or a part of a larger network):

- *View it as an element of larger classification systems.* How are the parts organized: in time, in space, in relation to one another? (The oak "is a member of a class of trees called hardwoods, . . . part of a larger class system that includes all trees. . . . It dwarfs the second-generation trees around it.")

- *View it as an element of larger physical systems.* How do particular parts of the system vary in how they interact with the larger systems of which it's a part? ("As part of a scene, its branches stand out sharply against the sky . . . , but from a distance its dark trunk merges almost indistinguishably with the trunks of surrounding trees. . . . It shelters wildlife; it draws raw materials for growth from the earth in which it is rooted and in turn enriches the earth with its fallen leaves.")

- *View it as an abstract system within a larger system.* How does it fit into the larger system? What features and components make it a part of the larger system? ("A system in itself, it fills a place in a larger system, a niche in the ecology of the area. . . .")

Chapter 38, DIALOGUE

To show students how dialogue can tell readers much about speakers and help writers achieve their purpose, ask students to analyze some dialogue, considering questions like these, adapted from *The English Teacher* website (Danielson): What dialogue gives clues to the speaker's occupation? Nationality or ethnicity? Social class or position? Personality? Character? Intelligence or education? Where does the dialogue refer to or advance the text's narrative or argument?

Your students may attempt to write dialogue containing dialects of English. Writing dialect is tricky: done well, it can clearly convey the speaker's heritage and social class; done poorly, it can seem condescending or inappropriate. If some of your students wish to try to capture a speaker's dialect, offer these suggestions:

- Write out the dialogue in Edited American English first, so that the meaning is clear.

- Select a few key characteristics of the dialect to use, and revise the dialogue to include them consistently. Actual dialect can be difficult to transcribe, partly because many dialectal differences involve differences in pronunciation that are hard to capture without a special alphabet (for example, the regional differences between *pin* and *pen*), and partly because actual speakers aren't consistent in their use of dialectal features. In addition, some dialects contain features that students may not know without linguistic study that may well be inappropriate for your class (such as verb tenses in African American Vernacular English).

- Ask students to do their best to use the dialect they actually heard the speakers speak, rather than falling back on stereotypical dialect.

Chapter 39,
EXPLAINING PROCESSES

If students explain a process that is familiar to them, a potential pitfall is inattention to the needs of their audience, because their familiarity with the process leads them to take for granted steps and explanations that someone unfamiliar with the process needs in order to complete it. One way to demonstrate this problem in class (and have some fun, too) is to ask students to write out instructions for making a peanut butter and jelly sandwich. Take to class bread, peanut butter, jelly, a knife, and a disposable tablecloth (this gets messy), and, following their instructions literally, make some sandwiches. They'll quickly see how unstated steps can lead to unintended consequences—and they can eat the evidence. Also, you'll be able to demonstrate that to explain a process well also requires describing, narrating, defining, and even classifying.

In addition, the more complex the process, the more readers need some orientation in the form of an introduction that identifies the process and its purpose and briefly summarizes the primary stages of the process. Readers will keep this overview in mind as they go through the details of the process. The ending of a process explanation may vary: it may simply end with the end of the process, with a brief summary of the process or its main stages, or with some commentary on the process.

Students' purpose also affects how they explain processes. The chapter focuses on explaining how something is done to inform readers, and explaining how to do something by writing a set of instructions. If the process is complex, you might suggest that students break the process into stages, with steps within each stage, to make the overall task easier. Doing this also lends itself to a series of illustrations, one or more for each stage, or a flowchart.

Chapter 40, NARRATING

Narrating is a strategy used by writers in virtually all genres. You can demonstrate this fact by showing students how narrating is used, not only in Chapter 7, WRITING A LITERACY NARRATIVE, but in the readings in many other chapters as well. Here's a partial list:

- ANALYZING TEXTS: William Safire includes several brief narratives in his analysis of the Gettysburg Address, using several time markers: for example, "Then," "Finally," and "Lincoln, thirteen years later."

- ARGUING A POSITION: Lawrence Lessig's "Some Like It Hot" presents narratives of the emergence of piracy in various mass media.

- LAB REPORTS: The "Procedures" section of lab reports, including this one by Sarah Thomas, consists of a narrative outlining how the experiment was conducted.

- MEMOIRS: Rick Bragg's "All Over but the Shoutin'" narrates a story of his final encounter with his father.

Additional teaching issues and suggestions related to this strategy are covered in detail in Chapter 25 of this guide to teaching, "Literacy (and Other) Narratives."

Chapter 41, READING STRATEGIES

Many of the students you'll encounter in first-year writing courses have extensive experience in reading for meaning. They have read textbooks to learn facts and concepts and have read literature, often for plot and theme. However, they have far less experience or training in reading nonfiction texts critically, examining the words and sentences of the text and exploring the contexts within which it was produced and reading to determine whether information is correct, dated, incomplete, or biased—in other words, whether it's a good source or not. The activities in this chapter are designed to help students read more critically as they ANALYZE TEXTS (in Chapter 8 of the *Field Guide*) or FIND and EVALUATE SOURCES (in Chapters 44 and 45). Here are some suggestions for using these activities to good advantage:

- When you introduce the rhetorical situation, have students read a brief text and analyze it as the activity on Previewing a Text in Chapter 41, READING STRATEGIES, asks, killing two birds with one stone.

- Ask students to submit responses to texts they read to make sure they're reading accurately and responding appropriately and not, for example, reacting to something they've misread or misunderstood. You might ask students to submit two-part informal writings for assigned readings: one paragraph of summary, to show that they understand the piece, and another paragraph of response, to show that they've thought carefully about it.

- Ask students to annotate a text collaboratively, perhaps writing on an overhead transparency or using the Comment feature of their word processor. Then each group explains to the class why they annotated as they did, and the groups compare notes to see what everyone agrees are the most noteworthy passages of the text.

- If your class is analyzing a single text, divide the class into groups and ask each group to analyze it using one of the methods described in Chapter 41: One group creates a topical outline ("What it says"); another creates a functional outline ("What it does"); a third color-codes repeated words and phrases, and a fourth counts parts ("Identifying patterns"); and a fifth creates a flowchart of the text's structure. Then the groups share their work with everyone, creating a pool of information from which individuals can draw as they develop their own analyses. You can do the same with the questions in Analyzing an Argument.

Chapter 42, TAKING ESSAY EXAMS

Along with Chapter 19, RÉSUMÉS AND JOB LETTERS, students appreciate having this chapter available as a reference, and you may find it a useful one to teach, for a few reasons: It's immediately relevant to most students, since most of their course requirements include timed exams and some of them will include essays; and it's an opportunity to help students transfer their learning in first-year writing to other coursework.

The biggest challenge in teaching this chapter is convincing students that the processes they've been asked to follow in your course—analyzing the question, generating ideas and text, planning, drafting, revising, and editing—will help them write better essay exams as well. Their tendency, by and large, is to assume that because their time is limited, they must write as much as they can as fast as they can in hopes of answering all the questions on the exam. But the advice in this chapter can help them see that they can write better answers if they break down the task—answering a prompt—into several processes, budgeting time for each one.

To do this, you might bring in sample questions from your own undergraduate courses and ask your students to bring in some, too. Together, you can analyze the questions using the advice in the chapter and project possible strategies for answering the questions together. Working alone or in groups, have students write essay questions and analyze them—and possibly answer them. If several students are in another class together, ask them to work together to speculate what that class's instructor might ask.

You might also have students write an in-class essay exam, ideally on a subject related to your course, and coach them as they write: Post a schedule on the board (10:00–10:05—analyze the question;

10:05–10:10—brainstorm parts of the answer; 10:10–10:15—organize the parts into an outline; and so on), monitor students (in other words, look over their shoulders) to see that they're following the process, and call out the time and what they should be doing. Then, after they've finished, ask them to write a self-assessment: What did they do well in this exam? What could they improve? How? What factors (anxiety, inadequate preparation or sleep, no breakfast, worries about other things, and so on) affected their performance? What can they do to improve their exam-taking abilities next time? Then, or during the next class, discuss their tests and self-assessments to help them develop a plan for being successful essay exam takers.

Useful Readings

Bunn, Mike. "How to Read Like a Writer." *Writing Spaces: Readings on Writing.* Ed. Charles Lowe and Pavel Zemlianksi. Vol. 2. 2011. *Writing Spaces.* Web. 28 Nov. 2012.

Connors, Robert J. "The Rise and Fall of the Modes of Discourse." *Selected Essays of Robert J. Connors.* Ed. Lisa Ede and Andrea A. Lunsford. Boston: Bedford, 2003. 1–12. Print.

"Developing a Thesis Statement." *The Writing Center: University of Wisconsin: Madison.* 2004. U. of Wisconsin: Madison, Web. 16 Oct. 2009.

Danielson, Leif. "Teaching Dialogue Analysis." *Teacher2b.com.* N. p., n.d. Web. 16 Oct. 2009.

Elbow, Peter. "Reconsiderations: Voice in Writing Again: Embracing Contraries." *College English* 70.2 (2007): 168–88. Print.

Hoeft, Mary E. "Why University Students Don't Read: What Professors Can Do to Increase Compliance." *International Journal for the Scholarship of Teaching and Learning* 6.2 (2012): n. pag. Web. 28 Nov. 2012.

Powell, Bonnie Azab. "Framing the Issues: UC Berkeley Professor George Lakoff Tells How Conservatives Use Language to Dominate Politics." *UC Berkeley News.* UC Berkeley Public Affairs Office, 27 October 2003. Web. 16 Oct. 2009.

Qualley, Donna. "Using Reading in the Writing Classroom." *Nuts and Bolts: A Practical Guide for Teaching College Composition.* Ed. Thomas Newkirk. Portsmouth, NH: Heinemann, 1993. 101–26. Print.

Salvatori, Mariolina. "Conversations with Texts: Reading in the Teaching of Composition." *The Writing Teacher's Sourcebook.* 4th ed. Ed. Edward P.J. Corbett, Nancy Myers, and Gary Tate. New York: Oxford UP, 2000. 163–74. Print.

Young, Richard, Alton Becker, and Kenneth Pike. *Rhetoric: Discovery and Change.* New York: Harcourt, 1970. Print.

32 Teaching Research and Documentation

Why do we ask students to do research? Research helps students become better thinkers, investigators, critics, and writers. Asking them to find, evaluate, and synthesize the ideas and words of others helps them form and express their own ideas. Ultimately, such activities will help them become better students, able to examine concepts and arguments from a thoughtful, informed perspective, and better citizens as well, less vulnerable to emotional appeals and attempts to mislead them.

Students who have experience with researched essays often conceive the assignment minimally: Pick a topic for which there's lots of information (such as abortion or gun control); do as little research as possible, often looking only for sources that agree with the position they already hold or finding one source that presents "the" opposing view so they can have a "con" to balance their "pro"; string quotes and paraphrases from the sources together to create a draft that meets length requirements; write an introduction and conclusion that could be interchangeable; and make sure the finished paper looks neat. Your task in teaching researched writing is to help students understand that

doing research involves much more. Good research engages the researcher, and that engagement carries over into the writing. Academic research requires examining sources that may hold various points of view and seeing why they agree or disagree, and then creating a text that carefully articulates those various perspectives, drawing from them thoughtful conclusions.

Research assignments can appear daunting at first: find, read, and use several sources of information to write an essay of 5–10 pages. Breaking the assignment into a series of smaller tasks, though, makes it manageable for students and for you. Here's a sample sequence using the *Field Guide*:

- Make a list of possible sources (Chapter 43, DEVELOPING A RESEARCH PLAN; and Chapter 44, FINDING SOURCES).
- Compose an annotated bibliography (Chapter 45, EVALUATING SOURCES; and Chapter 12, ANNOTATED BIBLIOGRAPHIES).
- Summarize the positions taken by several sources (Chapter 47, QUOTING, PARAPHRASING, AND SUMMARIZING).
- Draft a tentative thesis (Chapter 31, GUIDING YOUR READER).

- Make an outline (Chapter 24, GENERATING IDEAS AND TEXT).

- Write a draft (Chapter 46, SYNTHESIZING IDEAS; Chapter 25, DRAFTING; Chapter 47, QUOTING, PARAPHRASING, AND SUMMARIZING; and Chapter 48, ACKNOWLEDGING SOURCES, AVOIDING PLAGIARISM).

- Assess and get response to the draft (Chapter 26, ASSESSING YOUR OWN WRITING; and Chapter 27, GETTING RESPONSE AND REVISING).

- Document sources (Chapter 49, DOCUMENTATION; and Chapters 50, MLA STYLE, and 51, APA STYLE).

- Revise (Chapter 27, GETTING RESPONSE AND REVISING; and Chapter 28, EDITING AND PROOFREADING).

Research assignments usually form part of a genre-based or inquiry-based assignment, such as essays reporting information or taking a position. For that reason, much of the advice in this chapter is generic, to be adapted as needed for the particular kind of task your students face. The sections below offer advice on using the chapters on Research and Documentation.

Chapter 43, DEVELOPING A RESEARCH PLAN

Helping students choose a topic. Students typically start with big topics, often a single word or phrase: stem cell research, gay marriage, or legalizing marijuana. The *Field Guide* offers advice on narrowing a topic to make it manageable, but you can add to the advice in various ways.

Help each student with his or her topic. A research project typically stretches over several weeks, so it's worth your while to make sure students are working on topics that are unlikely to cause them trouble down the road. Three ways you can do this: (1) *Ask for a topic proposal.* Have students write out a formal or informal description of what they'd like to research and why. You can collect these on paper or via email and respond to them individually, or have students post them to an online discussion board, where they can read one another's proposals and your responses. For help with topic proposals, refer students to *Field Guide* Chapter 17 (PROPOSALS). (2) *Hold a workshop in class.* Students, especially those who are having trouble coming up with a topic, benefit from hearing other students' topics and from hearing how you respond to them. Ask students in your class to briefly describe their topics (or read their topic proposals aloud) to you and their classmates and then respond, perhaps asking other students to chime in as well. After responding to seven or eight, you'll find students revising their topics before their turn comes. (3) *Hold topic conferences.* You can also ask students to come to individual conferences to discuss their topics. Again, asking them to write a topic proposal and either bring it with them or submit it to you ahead of time will help them clarify what they want to do and help you respond appropriately.

Encourage students to choose topics in which they have an interest and a personal connection. Their own interest in a topic will lead them to invest time and energy in the research and writing and will likely produce a better text in the end than a topic they've chosen because they think it's expected or it's easy or it's one they wrote on in high school.

Guide students away from topics on issues like abortion, legalizing marijuana, gun control, and others that are subjects of ongoing, hot debate in society. Although these are important issues, two problems can make these topics very difficult for students: There's so much information available, so many arguments from so many passionate people, that students may be overwhelmed and unable to sift through the mass of data to core arguments; also, students who choose such topics often have a definite position and have difficulty seeing other points of view, let alone treating them fairly.

Also, steer students away from topics on which they're likely to have trouble finding information. Topics on legal or medical cases or sensitive corporate or government information, for example, require access to sources that they're unlikely to have. If you can hold topic conferences or workshops where you have access to your library's online catalogue and databases, you can quickly determine if a topic is likely to be a dry well or to require access to sources that can't be obtained within the time constraints of the course. Also, don't let students choose topics that might lead to harm; a colleague once had a student who wanted to do field research by going underground at a crack house—not a good choice.

Don't let students write on topics they wrote on in high school or wrote on for another course. Aside from issues of recycling—if they simply rework a paper done previously, they aren't doing the work of your course—most schools forbid submitting papers to more than one class unless both instructors agree to it.

Helping students see their biases. Ask students to explore not only what they already know about their topics, but what their opinions and beliefs on it are as well so they understand their potential biases. This process is important so students approach their research task knowing that they need to balance sources that bolster their position with sources that offer other viewpoints. You might also help students see multiple perspectives on their topic by asking them to consider what other positions—more than one—people might hold on their issue: Ask questions like, Can you be in favor of X in some circumstances but against it in others? Is there a middle ground between two extreme positions?

Emphasizing the need for organization. Students sometimes collect, photocopy, and download source material willy-nilly, forcing them to sort through piles of material to find sources they need. Ask them to follow the advice in Keeping Track of Your Sources and bring their source material to show you. Emphasizing that the advice in the *Field Guide* on organizing their material is important as a start, but you may want to ask students to try some of the following methods for keeping on top of their research material.

Filing. Simply having one place—a computer folder, a notebook, a two-pocket folder, or even a paper bag—devoted solely to research material on one assignment will help your most organizationally challenged students. Be flexible, since people need to organize in different ways to suit their personalities and ways of working. Asking students to bring all their research to class or conference on a flash drive or in some sort of container can be helpful to them. In class, they can then organize the material if they haven't already done so: Bring markers, sticky notes, a stapler, scissors, a three-hole punch, and transparent tape so students can help one another categorize, annotate, and organize their notes and research.

Double-entry notebooks. Show students the double-entry system for taking notes: In a spiral notebook, they write on the left-hand page direct quotations, paraphrases, and summaries of source material as well as observations or interview notes. On the right-hand page, they write reactions, insights, questions, and connections—the thinking they need to do about their sources that will help them integrate the material into their own work.

Annotations. Students are generally unused to annotating source material—and if it's from a library, of course, they shouldn't write on it! But when they photocopy material or print it from the web, they should underline or highlight important passages and write notes in the margins or on sticky notes to help their understanding and to identify useful material. Refer students to Annotating in *Field Guide* Chapter 41, READING STRATEGIES, for advice.

Research portfolios. If students are keeping notebooks or folders with their research material and notes, and if you ask them to submit their source material when they submit their finished essays, they have most of the raw material to create a research portfolio. In a research portfolio, students present a record of the processes of thinking, researching, and writing that led from the initial assignment or topic idea to the finished product. The students then can reflect in writing on those processes, how well they worked and what they might change in the future. Reviewing their research portfolios needn't consume much time: Have them place their materials on their desks and, while they're doing an activity in class, quickly flip through each student's material. Place on each portfolio and in your gradebook a quick evaluative mark (check plus, check, check minus) plus give a brief oral description of what the mark means (very well organized, acceptable, needs work) and you're done.

Chapter 44, FINDING SOURCES

By and large, first-year students rely for their research efforts on the internet and their local public library. These are useful places to find general sources for their preliminary research, but they need to learn to focus their search efforts on more scholarly sources for their college work.

Consulting reference librarians. Because electronic research tools evolve so quickly, librarians have more up-to-date knowledge of where to look and how to search than anyone else. In many students' minds, librarians are the people who shushed them when they whispered and wouldn't let them borrow the really interesting books, so they need to understand that librarians in academic libraries are not only helpful, they're indispensable to thorough research. Here are suggestions for introducing your students to the services of your school's research librarians:

- *Invite a librarian to your class.* Many librarians have prepared workshops during which they describe what the library offers and how to access it.

- *Meet in a computer classroom or lab.* If you can arrange meeting in a classroom with access to the library's catalogue and databases, the librarian can demonstrate how to use them, and then your students can start searching while you and the librarian circulate, offering advice and troubleshooting.

- *Investigate your library's services.* Some libraries offer guided tours, workshops, searching scavenger hunts, and other services that bring students to the library, where they learn how to use its services.

Encouraging students to interview experts. Specialists in the subject on which they're

writing can help students focus their topics, offer ideas they hadn't considered, provide the most current information available, and point them toward valuable sources they might have missed in their own searching.

Permitting students' research to influence their topic choice. While it's good to set a deadline after which students cannot change their topics—desperate students sometimes use a last-minute topic change to substitute a plagiarized paper for the one they're having difficulty writing—giving them the opportunity to allow their research to influence their treatment of the topic reinforces the concept that research is a learning process.

Chapter 45,
EVALUATING SOURCES

Evaluating sources is really a twofold activity: Students first evaluate sources as they find them, quickly discarding obviously unsuitable ones and moving on; but next they need to evaluate the remaining sources carefully for their suitability and relevance for their needs. Students often use whatever they find, whether or not it's appropriate. To keep that tendency in check, consider asking them to complete a worksheet on which they answer questions about each source: You might select a few questions from *Field Guide* Chapter 45 and staple the worksheets to photocopies of the sources they plan to use.

Some students may misread their sources. While the ways of misreading are many, a common concern, especially with historical topics, is reading sources not as informational texts but as stories. Students may read for plot and character, as they were taught in their literature courses, not as arguments written for specific purposes. They may try to structure their own essays the same way, writing a narrative of their examination of their sources rather than a report or argument.

Students also tend to believe that what their sources say is the truth—after all, if it's in print, it must be the truth, right? After years of reading textbooks, which are not usually open to questioning, this attitude is understandable. Consequently, students may have difficulty when they encounter two or more sources that contradict one another. They often cannot reconcile the differences and therefore assume that one or the other is wrong, when each may represent a different argument, written at different times for different audiences, rather than statements of fact. As Margaret Kantz writes in "Helping Students Use Textual Sources Persuasively," "[F]acts and opinions are essentially the same kind of statement: they are claims. . . . [T]he only essential difference between a fact and an opinion is how they are received by an audience" (195).

You might give students a list of statements that either are true but disbelieved by many people or that are false but believed by many (Snopes.com, a website that debunks urban legends, is a good source of both). Ask them to label each as fact or claim; and then, after you reveal which is which, use their reaction as a springboard to discussion. You might also present students with some sample sources and have them play Peter Elbow's Believing and Doubting game (described in *Field Guide* Chapter 41), either individually or in groups. Or present headlines from news articles that carry bias from various perspectives and have students rewrite a current headline to change its bias by substituting new words for the originals.

You may find it worth your while to spend part or most of a class period on evaluating websites. Students find searching the Web very attractive and comfortable, so they often rely on unrefereed websites rather than scholarly sources. Show them some websites and have them evaluate their credibility, using either the questions in the *Field Guide* or on one of the many websites that offer guidelines on evaluating websites. Discuss what features make some websites seem to be credible—or not.

Chapter 46, SYNTHESIZING IDEAS

In its simplest form, synthesizing ideas in college writing means using two or more sources to support one's claims. At its most complex, it means seeing novel relationships among ideas and so creating new knowledge or art. While most of us would be thrilled if our students regularly came up with such insights, in most situations students need to come to grips with synthesizing the ideas contained in their sources. This chapter offers advice on doing that.

One assignment that may help students see relationships among ideas is the *synthesis journal* as described by college writing and reading instructors Karen Irene Burrell and Patricia J. McAlexander (1998).

Building on composition theorist Ann Berthoff's double-entry notebook (in which students take notes on one side of a page and write responses on the other), Burrell and McAlexander advocate expanding Berthoff's notebook to include five sections, arranged graphically on a sheet of paper into four boxes surrounding a central box:

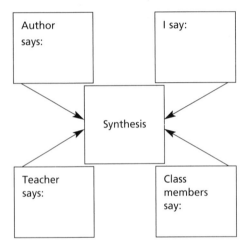

After reading a passage or brief essay, students fill in the top two boxes, summarizing the text and writing a personal response to it. The teacher then gives a brief lecture and students take notes in the "Teacher says" box. Then the students discuss the text with one another and place their notes in the "Class members say" box. At this point, each student uses the "Synthesis" box to explore how the ideas in the other four boxes might relate. According to Burrell and McAlexander, the way students complete this assignment offers insights into their ability to synthesize information in their reading—before they begin writing essays.

The synthesis journal can also introduce students to their need to read source materials carefully and critically if they are to synthesize the ideas in those materials appropriately. You might combine work on synthesizing with advice and activities from Chapter 8, ANALYZING TEXTS; Chapter 41, READING STRATEGIES; and Summarizing from Chapter 47.

Discerning relationships among ideas ultimately requires insight and creativity, so students may not "get it" easily. Karen Craigo, an instructional assistant at Bowling Green State University, offers suggestions on helping students understand synthesis through an examination of what is often presented as synthesis but isn't. Here are some of her near-misses:

• Including two sources in a paragraph, but not relating them to one another—simply placing them side by side.

• Using connective words (agrees, endorses, supports, affirms, concurs, disagrees, rejects, and so on) simply to introduce a source, when there is no obvious relationship between two sources' ideas.

• Getting the relationship between two sources' ideas wrong—for example, saying they agree when they don't.

• Relying too heavily on a single source, so that synthesis (which depends on multiple perspectives) cannot take place and the source may replace the student writer's own voice. (Craigo)

It's important to note that the ability to synthesize sources—or not—often determines whether or not a source "fits" or can usefully be included in a text. Students often think they're using their time and research most efficiently by using all the sources they've found, whether or not they work, or by using only the sources they've found on a first pass, even though they may be insufficient. When teaching them to synthesize, you need to emphasize that they must read their sources carefully and use the sources they need to express their ideas clearly and appropriately.

Chapter 47, QUOTING, PARAPHRASING, AND SUMMARIZING

Quoting. Many students need help integrating quotations smoothly into their own prose. A useful minilesson on doing so might include not only the uses of signal phrases but also the use of a colon at the end of one's own sentence (For example: *My father's first reaction to seeing my grades was swift and surprisingly gentle: "Go to your room; we'll discuss this later."*) and incorporating brief quotations grammatically and gracefully into a sentence, including omitting words and using brackets and ellipses. As an in-class exercise, give students a brief text along with three or four excerpts from sources that support the text's assertions; have students incorporate the source material into the text. You might combine this activity with advice on acknowledging sources: what needs to be acknowledged and what doesn't.

Paraphrasing. Paraphrasing correctly can be challenging for students and accom-plished writers alike, so spending some time working with your students on creating good paraphrases is often useful. Consider having students paraphrase a brief text and compare their versions, demonstrating that the ideas in a text may be expressed in various ways. Have students read a text and then create a paraphrase without looking at the text itself until it's time to see whether everything in the text is included accurately in the paraphrase.

Deborah Healy has her students tease out the ideas in a passage, then points out phrases they should avoid when they paraphrase it, and then shows a good example that demonstrates how the grammar, wording, and order of ideas should change.

The original text
Named for James Brady, the White House press secretary who was shot and wounded by John Hinckley Jr. during the attempted assassination of President Ronald Reagan in March 1981, the Brady Bill establishes a national waiting period and background check for the purchase of a handgun. (Bender 137)

Main Ideas
Brady Bill = named for White House press secretary James Brady
Brady was shot during an assassination attempt on President Reagan
Brady Bill provisions = people who want to buy handguns have a waiting period and check on their backgrounds

Phrases to avoid from the original
Named for James Brady, the White House press secretary who was shot and wounded by John Hinckley Jr. **during the attempted assassination** of President Ronald Reagan

in March 1981, **the Brady Bill establishes** a national waiting period and background check for the **purchase of a handgun.** (Bender 137)

A good paraphrase
Bender explains that people who want to buy handguns in the US now have a waiting period and a background check as a result of the Brady Bill. The bill was named after White House press secretary James Brady, who was wounded during an assassination attempt on President Reagan. (137).

Also, giving students access to online plagiarism detection tools such as *Turnitin .com* can help them see for themselves where they are using the language of the original text.

Summarizing. Students may find summarizing correctly a difficult task. Some will produce paraphrases; others will distort the original beyond recognition. Some tips for helping students produce effective summaries include the following:

- Have students identify the thesis of the passage and restate it in their own words. That sentence becomes the first sentence of their summary.

- Have students highlight or underline the main ideas in a text (you might model this activity using the highlighting function in your word processing program or on an overhead slide); then ask them to turn over their highlighted text or start a new document and draft a summary of it without looking. Then have them compare their summaries, working together to create a "best" summary.

- Have students write a summary for one audience and then rewrite it for a different audience. Discuss the changes they made and the reasons for the changes.

- Have students write a paraphrase, then a paragraph-long summary, then a three-sentence summary, then a one-sentence summary of the same material. Impose word limits to see how concisely they can summarize a passage.

Chapter 48, ACKNOWLEDGING SOURCES, AVOIDING PLAGIARISM

Most plagiarism in first-year writing courses grows out of ignorance or desperation, not dishonesty. Many students have a limited or mistaken concept of what constitutes plagiarism, for example, that it means only using someone else's exact words, and sometimes a certain minimal number of them. Quite a few students honestly believe that anything they find on the Web is fine to use without attribution. Some cultures have concepts of what constitutes intellectual property that differ from ours, and though nonnative students who have studied in the United States for several years may know our rules, some students who have recently arrived in the United States don't. (See Chapter 19 in this guide to teaching for more advice on teaching second-language writers.) Some students have no intention of plagiarizing but, faced with an assignment they don't think they can do, download an essay from the Web or from their roommate's computer and hope for the best. Only a few students deliberately set out to mislead instructors by turning in plagiarized work, and some of them do so because they see so much unattributed or copied writing or "sampled" music all around them. Still, all students need to know what is considered plagiarism in academic writing, as academic audiences define it—and how to avoid it. Here are some tips for preventing plagiarism, which is much better than dealing with suspected plagiarism in submitted essays:

- Emphasize that using the words *or ideas* of others without attribution constitutes plagiarism. Show examples, including unattributed paraphrases. Send students to websites that discuss plagiarism. Make sure they read and understand your school's academic dishonesty policies.

- Create writing assignments that make plagiarizing difficult. Slightly alter your requirements each time you teach a course, so that students' work will differ from previous courses' essays. Ask students to choose topics—or shape assigned topics—to some personal interest in the subject, both to increase interest and to individualize their research and writing. Require some recent sources; some student papers have been circulating for several years,

so their sources are suspiciously dated, but even papers whose Internet sources predate your introduction of the assignment should raise a red flag.

- Monitor students' generating, researching, and drafting activities by collecting drafts and holding conferences. Establish deadlines for changing topics, so desperate students can't find and submit a plagiarized essay at the last minute.

- Remind students that you know about and have visited online term paper mills, such as *WriteWork.com* and *Schoolsucks.com*.

- Consider using online plagiarism detectors such as *Turnitin.com* or *EVE2*. Some instructors use these programs only when they suspect plagiarism; some insist that all students submit their final drafts for checking. I prefer to use *Turnitin* as a teaching tool, asking students to run their rough drafts through the program in order to see where they might need to revise to avoid plagiarism. (Note too that some instructors and students question the ethics of *Turnitin*'s policy of maintaining a library of student work without the students' permission.)

If you suspect a student of plagiarizing, be as certain as you can that the work is indeed plagiarized before making accusations, by checking the paper's sources, submitting the work to a detection program, or simply searching in *Google* for unusual or key phrases. In my school's writing program, simply showing the suspect essay to other instructors who have taught the course recently gets surprisingly good results; students often recycle writing done just the previous semester, apparently assuming that writing teachers never talk amongst themselves. If you find that a student did indeed submit plagiarized work—or if you strongly suspect it but can't prove it yourself—check with your writing program administrator for your school's policies for dealing with plagiarism and, if necessary, for help before confronting the student.

You may also want to acquaint yourself with the ongoing debate over plagiarism, academic dishonesty, and intellectual property. Good sources for information on plagiarism and on this debate—and several good links—include Penn State's *Plagiarism Detection and Prevention: An Instructor Guide* (tlt.its.psu.edu/plagiarism/instructor-guide) and several bibliographies of articles on plagiarism by Syracuse University professor Rebecca Moore Howard (rebeccamoorehoward.com/bibliographies).

Chapter 49, DOCUMENTATION; Chapter 50, MLA STYLE; and Chapter 51, APA STYLE

Very few students in first-year composition classes will be majoring in English or the other humanities disciplines that use MLA style. Most will major in a social science that requires APA or a business, scientific, or engineering field that uses some other citation method. For that reason, students should learn that citation systems are indeed *systems* with shared features. Whatever system they use to cite sources, it will demand that they include similar information to show where they got their information and to permit others to find the information if they want. The systems differ in how that information is presented, the order in which it is presented, and the punctuation used to separate items within each citation. The *Field Guide*'s advice on documentation is color-coded to make those systematic similarities clear to students.

That's not to say that you shouldn't try to teach MLA and APA or some other system. Teach the system that you're comfortable with or that your program prefers. If you teach the basic concepts well, students will be able to adapt the principles to other systems as they need to.

Some tips on teaching documentation:

- Give students sample texts to document. Students will likely be familiar with single-author texts and popular magazines and can find the appropriate documentation information fairly easily. Many students have never seen an academic journal, however, and may need help understanding how they differ from other periodicals.

- Focus attention on documenting websites. Show students how to cite various websites and how to find the necessary information—and how to cite the page if the information (such as the posting date for the page or site) can't be found.

- Tracking down the source of some Web documents can require sleuthing: Show students how to backtrack to a home page by deleting sections of the URL. For example, a webpage discussing the health effects of drinking water containing perchlorate, chemical used in rocket fuel, has the following URL:

councilonwaterquality.org/science/health_effects.html

Deleting everything behind the final slash yields:

councilonwaterquality.org/science/

This page offers several links to scientific data on perchlorate, while removing *science/* leads to the homepage of the Council on Water Quality, an industry-funded public interest group. Backward searches can be important since search engines often find online source materials that turn out to be—but aren't labeled as—student essays (and sometimes high school student essays rather than credible sources).

- Give students a brief text that includes source material that needs to be cited, and have them add in-text citations and create a Works Cited page for it.

- Give students a "cheat sheet" containing examples such as excerpts from a paper you've written showing various citations. Sometimes students get lost in a long text.

Useful Readings

Bishop, Wendy, and Pavel Zemliansky, eds. *The Subject Is Research*. Portsmouth, NH: Boynton/Cook, 1981. Print.

Burrell, Karen Irene, and Patricia J. McAlexander. "Ideas in Practice: The Synthesis Journal." *Journal of Developmental Education* 22.1 (1998). Print.

Craigo, Karen. "Tell 'Em What It Ain't: Teaching Synthesis through Anti-Synthesis." BGSU: Academics. Bowling Green State University, 24 Mar. 2003. Web. 24 Sept. 2009.

Howard, Rebecca Moore. "Plagiarisms, Authorships, and the Academic Death Penalty." *College English* 57.7 (1995): 788–806. Print.

Kantz, Margaret. "Helping Students Use Textual Sources Persuasively." *College English* 52.1 (1990): 74–87. Print.

Mellon, Constance A. "Library Anxiety: A Grounded Theory and Its Development." *College and Research Libraries* 47.2 (1986): 160–65. Print.

Price, Margaret. "Beyond 'Gotcha!': Situating Plagiarism in Policy and Pedagogy." *College Composition and Communication* 54 (2002): 88–115. Print.

Sidler, Michelle. "Web Research and Genres in Online Databases: When the Glossy Page Disappears." *Computers and Composition* 19 (2002): 57–70. Print.

Zwagerman, Sean. "The Scarlet P: Plagiarism, Panopticism, and the Rhetoric of Academic Integrity." *College Composition and Communication* 59.4 (2008): 676–710. Print.

33 Teaching Media / Design

Email, text, or tweet? Smartphone photo or *YouTube* video? Poster, *PowerPoint,* or *Prezi?* Print essay or multimodal composition? Our students face media and design choices every day and need to be familiar with many options, so it makes sense to help them make informed choices and use media they choose appropriately. The five chapters in Media/Design offer help with choosing media, designing text, using visuals and incorporating sound, writing online, and giving effective presentations.

Chapter 52, CHOOSING MEDIA

The first step is understanding what media are available. This chapter offers an overview of the various possibilities and how they might be used effectively. Because the decision to use one or more medium depends on the rhetorical situation, you might guide students to reflect on which ones that will best meet the needs of their audience, purpose, and stance and the genre in which they're writing. Of course, as instructors we can specify particular media, and we may want to nudge students to try new media, or require that they do.

Although students occasionally go wild with media, creating multimodal compositions that are daunting in their complexity and sometimes dizzying in their assault on the senses, more often students are surprisingly conservative and need to be nudged to add other media or modes of expression to their written texts. You might ask them to start by inserting an appropriate photograph into their text; or they might collect images that would make their case or provide the information they're writing about and create a visual version of their draft—and then combine words and images into one composition.

Certain genres invite various media or modes of expression. For example, literacy narratives and their accompanying portfolios can include photographs and various other artifacts, from childhood writings to beloved picture books. Reports might include photos, drawings, charts, or videos of speeches or processes. Profiles invite podcasts of interviews or videos of the essays' subjects. Charts and graphs are often used in arguments to make data easier to present—and those charts and graphs often find their way into slide presentations of those arguments as well. As you consider the genres you want your students to explore, consider too the media they might use to compose in those genres.

Chapter 53, DESIGNING TEXT

This chapter presents basic design principles that may be applied to many media, from print texts to blogs, presentation slides to charts: consistency, simplicity, balance, and careful use of color and contrast. These principles can serve as the cornerstone of instruction in designing text and can easily be used also as items in rubrics, to help students evaluate the media they encounter and produce and to help you evaluate their productions as well.

In general, the best advice to give students about designing text is: exercise restraint. Computers give us the ability to create texts in an abundance of fonts and colors, warp and distort the fonts, add illustrations and backgrounds, and—if the text is delivered as well as created electronically—include text and images that flash, fade in and out, and march across the screen before settling in. However, under most circumstances, those effects are more irritating to readers than helpful. Add to that the unfortunate fact that the current rules for MLA and APA formatting preclude not only such typographic pyrotechnics but also simple but useful options for using boldface type and white space to aid readers. Therefore, students' text design options are likely to be limited by disciplinary standards.

Still, you can teach students how a well-designed document can improve readers' understanding of the content. Technical writer Beth Conney Lisberg likens good document design to the principles informing well-designed public parks. Each, she says, should pay attention to these five principles:

1. *Navigation.* Make it easy to find the various components of the text, such as its main sections, visual components, and bibliography using headings that show a hierarchy of importance, along with pagination and headers or footers.
2. *Circulation.* Use components that unify the text: an introduction that provides an overview of what's to come, information boxes, consistent heading styles and structures.
3. *Space.* Allow space for readers to take notes, locate headings, and notes—and to add emphasis where appropriate. Create white space with margins and spacing between paragraphs or sections, and distinguish space by setting off special information in boxes or other visual tools such as charts, graphs, or lists.
4. *Equipment.* Include the correct tools, such as charts, tables, infographics, good illustrations. When appropriate, create tables of contents.
5. *Safety.* Provide no unpleasant surprises. Give texts visual consistency.

Lisberg's analogy provides both a rhetorical justification for working with text design and easy-to-grasp ways of thinking about the roles visuals, white space, headings, and consistency play for readers.

Design options for writing assignments.
One way to introduce students to design is by incorporating design elements into other writing assignments. For example, you can expand the ANALYZING TEXTS assignment (*Field Guide* Chapter 8) by asking students to analyze the effectiveness of the design on the text's overall message. How does the design appeal to the intended audience? Does it reflect the writer's stance? Will it help achieve the desired purpose? You might also consider offering students the opportunity to redesign one of their essays, choosing a different font, adding images or pull quotes, setting off key information as a list, or turning a narrative or report into a photo essay or cartoon. Many students will find it an exciting challenge.

You can also invite students to revise something they've written in a different medium—to turn a print analysis or argument into a slide presentation, or to adapt an essay as a classroom presentation. Such assignments offer you the opportunity to then ask how the message changes as the medium changes. Which version meets the demands of the rhetorical situation better, and why?

Chapter 54, USING VISUALS, INCORPORATING SOUND

This chapter gives a solid base for students' use of photos, charts, video, and audio elements in their writing. It focuses more on the nuts-and-bolts of using those elements, offering advice on the best ways to incorporate, format, and label visuals and sound—and to use them ethically.

Both the logistical and ethical issues are important, as students may know how to forward photos in email and texts and post videos on their *Facebook* pages—but because so many images and videos are shared willy-nilly, they are unaware of the need to identify sources and provide citations for such items or to get permission to use some of them. They also are often ignorant of the mechanics of creating links within documents and the ethics of cropping photos or editing video or audio recordings. If you're asking or permitting students to incorporate images or sound in their writing, then, you should plan to spend time helping students make sure these elements work. You should also become familiar with the legal concept of "fair use" (the right to use copyrighted material without permission or payment for certain education-related purposes) and share appropriate information with your students. One excellent resource for this purpose is Stanford University Libraries' *Copyright & Fair Use* website (fairuse .stanford.edu), which offers a wealth of information, resources, and tools for determining whether a work is covered under the fair use doctrine. Another useful resource is the Center for Social Media's *Code of Best Practices in Fair Use for Media Literacy Education*, at centerforsocialmedia.org; the site describes the document as "a code of best practices that helps educators using media literacy concepts and techniques to interpret the copyright doctrine of fair use."

Chapter 55, WRITING ONLINE

Students are said to be more computer-literate than instructors, and in some ways, especially when social media are involved, that's true. But students often arrive at college with limited knowledge of the alternatives for online writing available to them, very little experience or understanding of computer file management, and little or no knowledge of learning management systems like *Blackboard* or *Desire2Learn*. This chapter offers an overview of online genres and their requirements, advice on managing files, and help dealing with online course tools.

Of course, you have multiple options for creating an online presence for your courses, too. Your school likely has a learning management system (LMS), which may or may not meet your needs. Many of the commercial systems are designed for content-focused courses and make commenting on student drafts difficult—restricting instructor comments to the end of a text, for example. Some online plagiarism-detection programs—*Turnitin* is a good example—include sophisticated writing course–focused LMS's as part of the program, but to use them you need to accept the premises of plagiarism detection and their use of student work. Some instructors adapt *Facebook* to instructional uses, creating a group page for the class and having students post writing there; others create class wikis, websites, and blogs—or simply work through email. You have choices, in other words, and those choices determine what your students'

online experience in your course will include and what they'll need to know to function in it.

Managing files will likely be a challenge for some students. If your school provides students with online storage that they can access anywhere on campus, expect that many first-year students won't know about it or won't use it—and will come to class and say, "My draft is at home on my laptop." Flash drives also will be left at home, and files will disappear into the chaos of their computers—or into the ether when their hard drives crash or, as has happened to my students, their roommates sit on their laptops. So plan on taking time, both at the start of the term and later, when students will have amassed several drafts of several papers, to walk through effective file management with them.

If you're using an LMS that provides dropboxes into which students can post their drafts but doesn't automatically list the files under the students' names, it's important that they name their files consistently—if the files can be listed alphabetically, you can save time in recording students' work and grades. For example, when I used one system available at my school, I had students name each of their files "Lastname_Genre_Draft and number" (Wellington_Profile_D2)—only to find out that if the last name wasn't capitalized, it went to the bottom of the list.

Teaching students about universal design. It's important that electronic texts be accessible to everyone. Programs can magnify text and read it aloud or convert it into Braille, and adaptive devices allow people with various physical disabilities access to the full range of the web's capabilities. These are all examples of *universal design,* the principle that all products (including buildings and sidewalks, not just websites) should be designed to be usable by everyone. Here is some advice you can give students to help them put this principle into practice.

- *Follow basic design principles.* A clear organization; consistent design and layout; concise, precise language; and freedom from errors will benefit all visitors to your site.

- *Use clear, simple language.* Be as clear and precise as possible. Use simple words (for example, "use" instead of "utilize") to enable speech synthesizers and Braille devices to recognize the words more easily.

- *Provide introductions to special features and acronyms.* Introduce lists in your text: "The following list provides six ways to make your site accessible." Spell out acronyms, abbreviations, and initials the first time you use them: "Yellow Springs High School (YSHS) is the home of the Bulldog Marching Band."

- *Integrate links into your text.* "This site includes photos of the Thurber House" is better than "To see photos of the Thurber House, click here" because screen readers pull out links and create a list of them. A list of "click here" links isn't helpful.

- *Use "alternative text" tags for all images and image maps.* "Alt" tags contain text descriptions of images or image map contents. Some browsers display this informative label when you move the cursor over the image, allowing page visitors to decide whether or not to wait if the image is too large to appear quickly. More important, adaptive software will read these descriptions to visually impaired visitors, thus making page contents more comprehensible.

- *Pay attention to color.* Many people have problems perceiving or distinguishing certain colors (especially red/green and blue/yellow contrasts), so relying on colors for any aspect of your site's message may not work. The safest combination: black text on a white background. Fairly safe: any primary color (except yellow) on a white background, or any two colors that contrast highly with each other.

- *Avoid flashing, scrolling text, and other animation tricks.* For the most part, blinking or moving text or graphics should be reserved for personal pages, like a blog that you maintain for close friends but don't intend for the world at large. Pages designed for general access should exclude most animated or psychedelic features. They not only tax eyesight and make content less effective, but can also cause real problems for visitors with seizure disorders.

- *Test your website for accessibility.* The International Center for Disability

Resources on the Internet (ICDRI) provides an online accessibility testing program (icdri.org/test your site now. htm), and Web Accessibility in Mind (WebAIM) offers another, along with articles and resources on web accessibility, at webaim.org.

Chapter 56, GIVING PRESENTATIONS

Presentations in most classes are often accompanied by visual aids in the form of *PowerPoint* slides or *Prezi*. As you may know or remember, moving from the student's desk to the instructor's place in a classroom—let alone behind a lectern or in front of a microphone—can be daunting. For that reason, it's useful to provide (or at least offer) coached practice sessions, perhaps in small groups in your office, before asking students to present to the class or a larger group. Some of the problems students encounter when asked to present orally include the following:

- *Stage fright.* Many students are terrified of speaking in front of a group. Opinions vary on how instructors should deal with such students, ranging from insisting that they do the assignment just like everyone else to offering alternatives, such as videotaping their presentation and showing the tape or writing out their presentation, with copies for everyone in the class. You might offer different degrees of exposure: sitting at their desk, using a lectern, or sitting at a table rather than

standing in front of the class. If the course includes a significant oral component, consider creating a series of assigned presentations, each one more formal, to allow frightened students to acclimate slowly. In fact, most speakers get more comfortable the more they speak in front of a group, so offering more, rather than fewer opportunities to speak can be helpful.

- *Reading the script or the slides.* Even though students should prepare for a talk by writing a script and an outline, they should be discouraged from reading a script when they present. The student who stands clutching a sheaf of papers, reading every word, is painful to watch and listen to. Encourage students to speak from outlines or notes, but if they need to read—as some speakers (including me) do—help them write the speech for oral delivery: mark pauses; shape sentences to resemble speech; include stage directions, such as when to change slides or even (in extreme cases) when to smile. Encourage them to rehearse before a friend or a mirror. If students are using slides, remind them to follow the advice in the *Field Guide* and keep the slides simple, to act as enhancements or outlines of their spoken texts; doing so will discourage their copying the entire text of their speech onto slides and reading them.

- *Talking to one's shoes.* Inexperienced or shy students often avoid eye contact with the audience, mumbling with head down. Others stand woodenly, sometimes hiding behind (and often clutching, white-knuckled) a lectern. Coach such students to look out at the audience, speak to the back row, and use gestures; and encourage them to write stage directions to that effect on their scripts or notes.

- *Talking or changing slides too fast.* Many students habitually speak very quickly and, with the added nervousness and desire to be finished that come with speaking publicly, they may be impossible to understand. Again, coaching can help, along with notes to themselves on their outlines: SLOW DOWN. In addition, students need to monitor the pace at which they change slides, to make sure they're visible long enough for their audience to read them.

- *Ignoring the audience.* Many speakers pay no attention to the reactions of their audience. Advise students that one reason to look at their listeners is to gauge their reactions: Are they nodding? Smiling? Looking puzzled? Ignoring the speaker? Their reactions can tell speakers if they should speed up, slow down, or restate something audience members clearly don't understand.

Making your expectations clear. Your students' presentations will be better if you clearly identify what you expect them to do. Answer these questions when you present your assignments:

- What is the purpose of the presentation? What is its goal?

- Who is the audience? If it includes people in addition to the class and you, who are they?

- Will students be given a list of topics from which they can choose, or will they choose a topic on their own?

- What tone is appropriate? Are humor, parody, or satire permitted, or should this be a serious event?

- How long should the talk be?

- How should presenters dress: formally? informally? in a costume?

- What criteria will be used to evaluate the presentation?

- Are visuals, props, or handouts required? permitted? How will they be evaluated?

- If groups collaborate on a presentation, must every member be an active participant in the actual presentation, or can some students be writers and others performers?

Scheduling enough time. Requiring students to present something to the class can take a lot of time. If you have 25 students, each one responsible for a 10-minute presentation, you need to allot 250 minutes of class time, not including the minutes between each presentation for setting up props, loading slide shows into the computer, and passing around handouts. In most schools, that's close to two weeks of class. Also, consider the effect on you and your students of watching five presentations each day for five days straight; it would be difficult to be the presenters on that last day. For those reasons, consider spreading oral presentations or teaching demonstrations or speeches through the term, perhaps one or two each class day.

Another option that lets all your students present in a single class period is to ask them to present to one another in small groups. Each group then chooses one presentation to show to the whole class, with other group members introducing the speaker and explaining why the group selected that presentation as its show case.

Useful Readings

Coombs, Norman. *Making Online Teaching Accessible: Inclusive Course Design for Students with Disabilities.* San Francisco: Jossey-Bass, 2010. Print.

Gurak, Laura, et al., eds. *Into the Blogosphere: Rhetoric, Community, and Culture of Weblogs.* U. of Minnesota, 2005. Web. 16 Oct. 2009.

Hill, Charles A. "Reading the Visual in College Writing Classes." *Intertexts: Reading Pedagogy in College Writing Classrooms.* Ed. Marguerite Helmers. Mahwah, NJ: Lawrence Erlbaum Associates, 2003. 123–50. Rpt. *Visual Rhetoric in a Digital World.* Ed. Carolyn Handa. New York: Bedford, 2004. 107–30. Print.

Kramer, Robert, and Stephen A. Bernhardt. "Teaching Text Design." *The Technical Communication Quarterly* 5.1 (1996): 35–60. Print.

Lisberg, Beth Conley. "The Architecture of Designing Documents." *1999 Proceedings.* Society for Technical Communication, n.d. Web. 16 Oct. 2009.

Reynolds, Garr. *Presentation Zen.* N.p., 26 Aug. 2009. Web. 16 Oct. 2009.

Selfe, Cynthia L., ed. *Multimodal Composition: Resources for Teachers.* Creskill, NJ: Hampton, 2007. Print.

7 Things You Should Know about WIKIs. *EDUCAUSE Learning Initiative.* EDUCAUSE Learning Initiative, July 2005. Web. 16 Oct. 2009.

Williams, Robin. *The Non-Designer's Design Book: Design and Typographic Principles for the Visual Novice.* 2nd ed. Berkeley: Peachpit, 2004. Print.

part 3

Teaching
the Readings

Literacy Narratives **34**

DANIEL FELSENFELD

624 *Rebel Music*

On Engaging with the Text

1. This question draws students' attention to the significance of Felsenfeld's literacy narrative, an important feature of this genre but one that students have difficulty identifying in reading and writing literacy narratives. By asking students to specify where in the essay the significance is made clear, students need to read the text closely and identify the phrases that indicate what they see as crucial to the narrative. For Felsenfeld, this literacy narrative identifies the moment when he discovered that he wanted to become a composer, a moment in his youth he perceived as a rebellion. As he writes, "My passion for this 'other' kinds of music felt like the height of rebellion: I was the lone Bolshevik in my army. . . . Rebels sought to break the mold, to do something that was exclusively 'theirs,' to be weird by way of self-expression. And since I was the only one I knew listening to symphonies and concerti, operas and string quartets, I felt I was the weirdest of them all." You might ask students how familiar they are with classical music, and then play one of the pieces Felsenfeld names. After the music, lead a discussion on whether they would classify this music as "weird." Ask them what music they would identify as rebel music. Finally, you might ask students if they have a clear sense of what profession they want to enter, and if so, if they recall when they made that decision and what led them to that decision.

2. Students should understand that writers' tone and word choice create a stance or attitude toward the subject they treat in a piece of text. They should be able to identify Felsenfeld's deep respect and love for classical music and his profession by the central experience in this treatment of "rebel music." The phrases leading up to the significance of the literacy narrative will get them to see that classical music for Felsenfeld was "rebel music" because he had not yet been exposed to it in home or school except in small doses when he took piano lessons—lessons he treated with little respect. You might lead a discussion on how his stance would

277

have been different had he focused on his experiences with pop bands of the 1980s such as General Public, the Thompson Twins, David Bowie, and the Clash. Ask students which bands they listen to today and which they find boring and banal. Then ask them what makes a genre of music or a performer's treatment of it exciting, or what makes it dreadful. By focusing on how writers reveal their stance toward a subject, students are made aware of the need to make clear through their use of words and tone their own attitudes toward the subjects they write about.

3. By asking students to explain how music literacy is similar to print literacy, they begin to understand that learning a literacy is a habit developed through exposure to and lots of practice in reading and writing. By focusing on the different genres in this book (and those even outside this book), you can help students begin to see that there isn't one literacy but many literate practices of reading and writing depending on the genre. If you have students compare the different genres that Felsenfeld describes in his literacy narrative, you can help them see that music literacy, like print literacy, is also made up of many literacies. Ask students to think about other practices that they may associate with literacies (e.g., math literacies, scuba diving signals, various sports and their ways of speaking and doing, visual literacies in print and digital ads, digital literacies for blogs, games, and websites). Ask them how they learned one or more of

these literacies and how the lessons they took away could help them in reading and writing genres that are new to them.

4. Increasingly students are reading and writing digital texts in which visuals play a significant role. (Visuals, of course, play an important role in print and in TV media as well.) Have students decide which point(s) they think would be useful to highlight in Felsenfeld's literacy narrative. For these points, have students locate a visual that they believe expresses the key sentiment. Lead a discussion on how they read visuals and how they expect audiences for Felsenfeld's text might read them.

5. *For Writing.* This writing prompt asks students to consider the various literacies they control in addition to reading and writing and to pick one to focus on to explain how they developed it. Responses to question 3 serve as a good heuristic for starting this writing assignment. By writing a narrative on a literate practice other than print literacies, students can begin to understand that they are already a master of many literacies and that a literacy develops over time through experience and practice. Defamiliarizing the familiar makes this a significant assignment.

For Further Discussion

1. Daniel Felsenfeld explains that because he lived in the suburbs of Orange County, California, in the 1980s, he had not been

exposed to classical music in any substantive way until one of his friends shared audiotapes of various classical composers with him. Why do you think he would have had so little experience in that city? What kinds of music do you expect he would have been exposed to frequently? In what city or cities, do you think he might have grown up with classical music and why? What genres of music did you grow up with where you lived? Were these the most popular in your hometown? Or were you exposed to these genres through family or friends?

2. Learning a literate practice often involves a sponsor,* someone who either helps you gain experience in it or someone who sets up obstacles to it. Who were the sponsors in Daniel Felsenfeld's journey in learning classical music and becoming a composer? Identify those who helped him and those who hindered him. Discuss the roles that people have played in your learning one literate practice. Who were they in your life and how did they either help or serve as an impediment on your way to mastering that literacy?

TANYA MARIA BARRIENTOS

629 *Se Habla Español*

On Engaging with the Text

1. This question focuses students' attention on the title of Barrientos's literacy narrative. In so doing, it helps students to learn how titles create a framework and a set of expectations for readers. Students might notice that the title signals a shift in Barrientos's attitude toward Spanish, from the "*yo no hablo español*" of her youth to the "*se habla español*" of her adulthood—a shift that is the focus of this essay. This awareness should help them as they generate their own titles. Also, by asking students to consider whether the impression set forth by

the title is supported by the essay, you can help them examine how a focus is maintained through an essay. You might ask students to generate alternative titles for Barrientos's essay and lead them in a discussion of how these variations subtly, and sometimes not so subtly, create different expectations for reading an essay.

2. This question draws students' attention to the anecdote with which Barrientos begins her essay, and asks them to consider how it functions in terms of generating interest and setting up expectations for the rest of the essay. The opening

---

*Deborah Brandt, *Literacy and Learning: Reflections on Writing, Reading, and Society* (Hoboken, NJ: Jossey-Bass, 2009), print.

anecdote sets up the problem Barrientos treats in her literacy narrative and provides a context for it. You might direct students to the section on beginnings in Chapter 30 to help them respond to this question. Focusing on rhetorical strategies for opening an essay can help students consider the various ways they can generate beginnings for their own writing.

3.   This question focuses on one of the key features of a literacy narrative, namely, an indication of the significance of Barrientos's literacy narrative. Students should notice that this essay holds both personal and broader sociocultural significance. Considering the role significance plays in an essay helps students to consider how writers signal the importance of their topic. You might recommend that students review the discussion of significance in literacy narratives in Chapter 7 to help them articulate the significance of Barrientos's essay.

4.   In this question, students are asked to consider the contribution Barrientos's use of Spanish phrases makes toward indicating her stance. In incorporating the Spanish phrases, Barrientos honors her heritage and demonstrates her respect for it. Asking them to think about how her stance might be different if she had translated those phrases helps students to consider the ways in which a rhetorical stance is constructed by the choices a writer makes. As such, students can become more sensi-

tive to the choices they make in their own writing.

5. *For Writing.* This writing prompt encourages students to consider the relationship between language and identity, and the ways in which the different languages we speak (and write, for that matter) are intimately tied up with, and help construct, our identities in different contexts. By writing an essay that reflects on the ways they speak and its relationship to their identity in different situations, students can develop a greater sensitivity to the power of language and a greater control over the genre of literacy narratives.

For Further Discussion

1.   Tanya Maria Barrientos's literacy narrative reveals the close ties between language and culture. She points out that early in her life she rejected everything Spanish, saying, "If I stayed away from Spanish, stereotypes would stay away from me"; now she wants to embrace her Guatemalan heritage by learning to speak, read, and write Spanish fluently. Discuss the relationship between language and culture. How does Barrientos's story give credence to Frances Christie's observation that "learning the genres of one's culture is both part of entering into it with understanding, and part of developing the necessary ability to change it"?*

*Frances Christie, "Genre as Choice," *The Place of Genre in Learning: Current Debates,* ed. Ian Reid (Geelong: Deakin, 1988), 22–34, print.

2. What are some of the barriers to literacy that Tanya Maria Barrientos identifies in her literacy narrative? Who has helped her and who has directly or indirectly served as obstacles? Discuss the roles that different people can play in one's journey toward literacy.

AMY TAN

633 *Mother Tongue*

On Engaging with the Text

1. This question draws students' attention to the opening of Tan's literacy narrative and the way it establishes her ethical creditability. In doing so, it helps students understand how writers gain their readers' trust and how in their introductions writers can forecast their topic and its treatment. You might direct students to the discussion of beginnings in Chapter 30 to help them consider the way in which Tan draws her readers into her essay and prepares them for her topic.

2. By examining how Tan classifies different "Englishes," students can become more aware of classification as a rhetorical strategy—a strategy treated in Chapter 34. This question also helps students think about the complexities of language, and its various forms, by making them see that English is not one language but many. Finally, asking students to locate examples in the text to support their response helps them practice finding and providing evidence to support their claims.

3. This question asks students to consider how Tan's audience affects the language choices she makes, and indirectly speaks to the relationship between the context of an essay—where it is published—and the audience for whom it is written. Tan is writing for scholars and teachers in English studies in one of the Englishes she reserves for outside the home, though she includes examples of the other Englishes to support her points. You might ask students to review the crucial role of audience as detailed in Chapter 2 to help them respond to this question. Further, directing students to support their answer with quotations from the essay will help them read the text carefully and learn to supply textual examples as evidence for their responses.

4. Titles set a focus for reading and writing an essay. In this question, students are asked to consider Tan's title and the way it frames her literacy narrative. Tan's title

evokes two meanings of "mother tongue": one's home language influenced by cultural heritage, and her own mother's tongue. Generating different titles can serve as a useful heuristic for writers as they craft their own essays. Thus, asking students to generate different titles for Tan's essay will give them practice with this strategy and will also help them better grasp Tan's main points.

5.   *For Writing.* In this writing prompt, students are asked to explore the languages they speak. It may not have occurred to them that they already possess several different languages, even if they are monolingual. By reflecting on the various discourses they already possess, they can be led to see that they are already proficient in learning languages and have the necessary tools for acquiring new discourses. The writing task also provides them with experience in reflecting on different contexts, a useful skill for writers.

For Further Discussion

1.   Scholar Deborah Brandt has defined literacy sponsors as "any agents, local or distant, concrete or abstract, who enable, support, teach, model, as well as recruit, regulate, suppress or withhold literacy— and gain advantage by it in some way."* How did Amy Tan's mother serve as a literacy sponsor for her? Who else in Tan's essay might be considered a literacy sponsor?

2.   In her literacy narrative, Amy Tan considers how the different Englishes spoken with her mother and others in her life found their way into her fiction writing. In so doing, she raises questions about the relationship between spoken and written language. Discuss how spoken language can shape written and, conversely, how written can shape spoken language, using Tan's experience as support.

MALCOLM X

640   ## Literacy behind Bars

On Engaging with the Text

1.   The relationship between literacy and freedom is complex, as Malcolm X's literacy narrative suggests. This question asks

students to think about that relationship and the ways in which literacy is central to attaining and maintaining one's freedom as well as to building and sustaining a free society. You might ask students to begin by

*Deborah Brandt, *Literacy in American Lives* (Cambridge: Cambridge UP, 2001), 19, print.

defining the key terms *literacy* and *freedom*. Based on the various definitions they offer, lead a discussion that explores the relations between literacy and freedom.

2. This question asks students to analyze Malcolm X's stance in his literacy narrative. Students should be able to recognize his reverence toward his subject—reading and writing—both by how he speaks about it and the pains he took to learn it. His writing does convey, to use Malcolm X's words, the impression of one who "went to school far beyond the eighth grade." You might direct students to the discussion of stance in Chapter 4 to prepare them for this question. By asking students to identify specific words and phrases that convey Malcolm X's stance, you can help them not only understand this rhetorical device more firmly but also provide them with practice in supporting their observations with textual evidence.

3. This question asks students to explore the rhetorical strategies of objective and subjective descriptions. You might recommend that students review the differing purposes of objective and subjective descriptions as outlined in Chapter 37. Asking them to consider the types of descriptions Malcolm X incorporates and reasons for these will help students develop a keener awareness of the kinds of rhetorical decisions writers make as well as the effects of those decisions. You might also help them see the connections between rhetorical purpose and description by leading a class discussion on this relationship in Malcolm X's narrative.

4. Significance is a key feature of a literacy narrative, and among the more difficult for students to grasp. This question asks them to consider the significance of Malcolm X's literacy narrative and how it relates more broadly to learning to read and write and the power associated with literacy. Malcolm X makes clear that literacy opened a whole new life for him and fostered a sense of freedom he had never before experienced. Understanding the broader implications will help students to consider the significance of their own literacy narratives beyond their immediate personal significance.

5. *For Writing.* This writing prompt asks students to focus on the roles various kinds of literate practices have played in their education. As students consider other kinds of discourse tasks—exams, lectures, discussions, essays, or blogs, for example— they may be guided to see the interrelationship between reading and writing, for, as they should discover, these literate practices are integral to one another.

For Further Discussion

1. Socrates said, "Wisdom begins in wonder." How does Malcolm X's observation that "If I weren't out here every day battling the white man, I could spend the rest of my life reading, just satisfying my

curiosity—because you can hardly mention anything I'm not curious about" relate to Socrates' point about wisdom? What role can reading play in both "wonder" and "wisdom"?

2. What is Malcolm X's purpose in this literacy narrative? Who is his audience? How are his audience and purpose related in this essay?

AMBER WILTSE

645 *How Do You Go from This . . . to This?*

On Engaging with the Text

1. Students are asked to examine the effectiveness of the beginning and the ending of Wiltse's multimodal literacy narrative. Doing so helps students consider the ways in which literacy narratives open to draw readers in and close by echoing the beginning and the main point. They come to understand that the beginning and ending of an essay must frame the narrative it offers. Students should recognize that the beginning question—"How do you go from this . . . to this?"—depends on the two photos of Wiltse at the opening of the narrative, the one at birth and the one today. They should also recognize that the final photo of Wiltse and her brother hugging at Wiltse's high school graduation powerfully illustrates her conclusion that literacy "can be a useful tool for making and solidifying relationships." Both visuals are central to her narrative of coming into literacy.

2. This question requires students examine the digital literacy narrative video so they can hear the different songs and styles of music Wiltse incorporated into her video, everything from top pop songs to movie soundtracks. Students will probably be familiar with the songs. If you have internet connection in your classroom, play the video and ask them to name the songs and to explain what tone they create. Focusing on the audio choices Wiltse made will help them understand the need to fit sounds to images and words. They may have suggestions for other songs that Wiltse could have used in various places in her video. If they have suggestions, have them bring in the songs and match them to the video. Of course, doing this task creates a video that is far more complex but students will begin to see that different audio selections set up different expectations and meanings.

3. Wiltse establishes that reading was important to her mother, brother, and herself with her description of how the three of them shared the Harry Potter books. She makes the point that both the Harry Potter books and films is "a special bond I share with my family" and that the series "is the

way my brother and I stayed connected as we were starting new eras in our lives." Students should understand that literacy plays a social role, connecting family, friends, and acquaintances. They should see the significance of Wiltse's final point that literacy "can be a useful tool for making and solidifying relationships."

4. Wiltse chose text from a literacy narrative she wrote for another course to incorporate into this digital literacy narrative. Students should see that the text tells the narrative while the visual images support and hold the textual narrative together. In a text only narrative it would be much more difficult to create the mood as set by the music, demonstrate the closeness of her family and her relationship with her brother as set by the images, and make less of an impact with the phrasing that pops out the point while the images and audio that support these points allow time to think about them. Students should be led to see the pros and cons of text only essays and multimodal essays.

5. *For Writing.* The writing prompt asks students to create multimodal literacy narrative with a clear focus—on a person, technology, powerful childhood book, or an activity. Students may need help in drafting the video before attempting to create it. Teach them how to story-book their idea which will include text (written or spoken), images (moving or still or both), and audio (sounds or music). Once they have sketched

out their idea and received peer feedback on it, you can help them use a simple video program to pull it all together. (Some if not all of your students may have already posted something on *YouTube,* and could act as useful resources in the classroom to help others learn how to make a *YouTube* video.)

For Further Discussion

1. Amber Wiltse reveals that her mother and brother were partners with her when it came to reading books but that her father joined them when it came to watching movies. How might movie-watching be a form of literacy? What do viewers needs to learn about the various genres of films (e.g., sci-fi, romantic comedies, dramas, documentaries) to be able to understand them? What kinds of literacies were in your home as you grew up? What kinds of reading and films did your family enjoy? Did you share in literacy practices together? Does your own narrative support or challenge Wiltse's point that books and films serve to connect people?

2. Who is the targeted audience for Amber Wiltse's literacy narrative? How do the images, audio, and text offer evidence of the intended readership? What if Wiltse were to rework this multimodal literacy narrative for an older, retired generation of baby-boomer grandmothers and grandfathers? What changes would she have to make to reach this audience?

35 Textual Analyses

TORIE BOSCH

651 *First, Eat All the Lawyers*

On Engaging with the Text

1. This question asks students to identify the intended audience for Bosch's essay and to point to a paragraph that makes the audience clear. Students should notice that Bosch uses first person plural (we and us) when she is talking about white-collar workers, and thus her intended audience. She also shows how contemporary zombie apocalypse films and books portray the destruction of the white-collar skills "not through technical advance but throughout total system collapse" where blue-collar skills are the only ones valuable and viable. Students can point to several paragraphs that use the first person plural and/or the central point of Bosch's essay to show they understand the intended audience is the white-collar, university educated worker.

2. Bosch's main point is that zombie films today are in response to the economic crash; they offer, as she says, "an outlet to more realistic fears of personal economic collapse." Students should see that she uses direct quotations from novels, and descriptions of scenes from films to support this point by crafting white-collar horror stories. With zombie stories destroying all that white-collar workers hold dear—education, non-manual labor, financial advisors, and fine neighborhoods—they turn white-collar values upside down by making leaders and valuable workers the blue collar.

3. This question asks students to consider the effectiveness of the title and whether the effectiveness is contingent on knowing the allusion to Shakespeare's *Henry VI, Part 2.* Of course, since the main point is the destruction of the white-collar class and value system in these zombie stories, the title makes clear sense—eat the lawyers as representative of the class under attack. However, the title is made even more powerful should readers recognize the allusion to Shakespeare, which requires an advanced education and the fine tastes usually associated with the white-collar class.

286

4. This question works in concert with question 2. Students should recognize that these long quotations from two popular zombie novels serve to support Bosch's thesis and main points by specifically detailing the destruction to the values and activities associated with the white-collar class. You might spend time discussing with students when long quotations are appropriate and when paraphrasing may be a better option. Shirley Rose offers a useful way to think about long quotations as an indication of deep respect for the author or as a way to distance oneself from an author with whom you don't agree.* Ask students to paraphrase one of the quotations and to discuss how the paraphrase is less powerful than the direct quotations in this case.

5. *For Writing.* For this writing prompt, students are asked to analyze a specific successful television show and to use data from at least three episodes to support their analysis. They might focus on the meaning of the show's underlying message and how its portrayal fares better or worse than another show, website, or book that offers a similar message. This assignment will help them learn how to analyze a text (whether visual, video, or print) and how to use data from the text to support their analysis.

For Further Discussion

1. The economic crash of 2008 had a long reach and reverberated globally. Discuss what evidence you see that tells you whether or not we are in economic recovery. What values do you believe the white-collar class holds? Do you think that white-collar values need to be adjusted? Why or why not?

2. Select a satirical and highly critical cartoon (e.g., *Family Guy, Simpsons, South Park,* or *Futurama*) and explain why the show is so successful and still on the air. What is the underlying message of the show? Who is the intended audience? Who might be offended by the show? How does the message of the show relate to the message of contemporary zombies?

---

*Shirley Rose, "'What's Love Got to Do with It?' Scholarly Citation Practices as Courtship Rituals," *Language and Learning Across the Disciplines* 1.3 (1996): 34–48, print.

LAUREL THATCHER ULRICH

656 *Well-Behaved Women Seldom Make History*

On Engaging with the Text

1. Students are asked to examine the way Ulrich begins and ends her essay to see effective methods for opening an analysis that grabs audience attention and for ending a text to create a frame for the analysis. Ulrich begins with an anecdote concerning the phrase "well-behaved women seldom make history" that has taken on a life of its own in all sorts of merchandise. The ending returns to the importance of texts in making history. In her words, "People do not only make history by living their lives, but by creating records and by turning other people's lives into books or slogans." Discuss with students the fragility of certain histories that have left no material record. Ask them what that means about history. How thorough is a history? What does it mean to have gaps in the historical record?

2. Students are asked to find two examples Ulrich offers as support for her point that some people (her focus is on women but of course it relates to all sorts of people) are erased, ignored, or left out of history because there is little left in the records about them or because they were not seen as important enough to record. She points to several women who illustrate this point, women who are remembered because there has been a record of some kind that makes their lives available to historians: Martha Moore Ballard, Rosa Parks, and Mae West. Discuss with students what made their stories available to historians. Why were they, as opposed to someone else, written about in histories? How do we recoup others whose voices are lost?

3. By asking students to identify the purpose of Ulrich's textual analysis and how the purpose relates to the thesis, they can begin to understand the ways in which the rhetorical situation helps to construct the text. In this essay, Ulrich describes the complexities of creating histories, and how many voices are left out of the historical record. Her scholarship recoups women who have been previously ignored, silenced, or erased from history. But others can use it to recoup voices from different classes, ethnicities, abilities, races and so on. In short, History with a capital "H" is not possible; history is always the combination of multiple histories and still is never complete. By showing the fragility of the tissue webs that history presents of the past, students can begin to understand that they must always read history against the grain, asking who is missing and who has been silenced. Where can we find other voices to add to the narrative?

4. This question asks students to locate three pieces of evidence that Ulrich offers

to support her analysis. In responding to this question, students learn that crafting an analysis of a text requires that they share with readers the specifics that led them to argue a particular point about the text. They need to understand that not everyone reads texts in the same way and thus audiences need to understand how the writer has interpreted the text because they may not have seen the same thing in it. Ask how many students are aware of the many men and women of color who, like Parks, refused to give up their seat at the front of bus and were arrested? Ulrich offers the explanation and direct quotation from E. D. Nixon, former president of the Montgomery NAACP, that Parks was selected as the representative of this action over others because "she's moral, she's reliable, nobody had nothing on her, she had the courage of her convictions."

5. *For Writing.* Students are asked in this assignment to locate three objects on which Ulrich's slogan—"well-behaved women seldom [rarely] make history"—appears and to analyze the meaning of the slogan on each object. Ulrich describes how the slogan has been used by various merchandizing companies for different reasons, depending on how the phrase is assumed to be understood. Students' analysis of the phrase on these objects (which they should understand are texts) will help them see how meaning does not reside in the words themselves, as Bakhtin taught us.* They are offered a series of questions as a heuristic to help them in their analysis.

For Further Discussion

1. Define *history* and share your definition to discuss the various responses. (You can freewrite a response or work in small groups, with each group coming up with a definition.) Discuss the common saying that history is typically written by and for the victors in a conquest. If this is the case, what does this mean for the ways in which we should read all histories?

2. Consider the following questions: Why does history matter? What ends do histories serve? What is the relationship among the past, present, and future? Why should we care about histories, who they are written for, and whom they serve?

*Mikhail Bakhtin, "Marxism and the Philosophy of Language," *The Rhetorical Traditions*, ed. Patricia Bizzell and Bruce Herzberg (Boston: Bedford, 1990), 944, print.

DIANA GEORGE

667   *Changing the Face of Poverty*

On Engaging with the Text

1. This question asks students to identify George's central thesis—namely, that media representations of poverty are inadequate. More specifically, they are too narrowly focused, create the impression that poverty is an individual problem requiring individual solutions, and suggest that poverty is easily recognizable. Students will gain valuable insight into how writers treat complex, multidimensional issues as they engage with this question.

2. Asking students to consider George's beginning and the audiences for whom her text is written helps them to develop a repertoire of rhetorical strategies for beginning an essay (as discussed in Chapter 30) and of targeting one or more audiences (as discussed in Chapter 2). Since students may not be familiar with bell hooks, you might describe some of her scholarly work to help students see the relevance of the quote and the scholarly audience that would be drawn in by it. To help students consider other relevant audiences for this text, you might ask them who would benefit from this information regarding representations of poverty and who could use it most immediately.

3. In this question, students are asked to analyze one of the images George treats in her textual analysis, considering it in light of George's phrase "emotional overload." Students may need some help in unpacking this phrase, so you may want to devote class time to discussing it before they examine the visual. Responding to this question will give students valuable practice in examining visual texts, practice that should serve them well in writing their own textual analysis. This question lends itself well to both small group and whole class discussions. Seeing how their peers tackle visuals and "read" them can provide students with strategies for approaching other visual texts.

4. Focusing on the purpose of George's textual analysis will help students learn how to ferret out purpose, a skill useful both in writing and in responding to peers' writing. You might recommend that students review Chapter 1 in preparation for responding to this question. Students should learn that while an essay may serve one major goal, it can serve other purposes when read outside its original context and by different audiences. In this case, George's text serves one purpose for an academic audience when it appears in an academic book but can serve a very different one for an audience of advertisers, or charity workers, or funding agency decision-makers or even writing students in a writing course.

5. *For Writing.* This writing prompt directs students to conduct a textual analysis of

the visual and verbal text in an ad focusing on a specific political or social issue. Through this assignment, students will gain valuable experience in reading visual and verbal texts closely, and in supporting their analysis with textual evidence.

For Further Discussion

1. Diana George argues, "I would suggest that the way poverty continues to be represented in this country and on tapes like [Habitat] videos limits our understanding of what poverty is and how we might address it." According to George, what are the limitations of the visual representations of poverty? How does her description of various media demonstrate those limitations? How might these limits be addressed by other kinds of print and video images?

2. In her analysis of the representation of poverty by nonprofits, Diana George analyzes pictures, written texts, and videos. How does her analysis of these different media support and strengthen her argument about the ways in which poverty is represented, and the shortcomings of those representations?

BRIAN STELTER

679

"We Are the 99 Percent" Joins the Cultural and Political Lexicon

On Engaging with the Text

1. This question asks students to focus on the appropriateness of the title for this textual analysis and to compare it with the title for the online version of the text. Examining a title to see how it functions in relation to the text and how it prepares readers for the main point of a text will help students come to understand the importance of titles for anything they compose. The online title is a dated and location-specific phrase since the occupation of Wall Street and other spaces is now long over, and so it can confuse and possibly mislead readers who either were unaware of the occupations held across the country or who are not familiar with the issue to which occupiers were responding. You may need to explain the term "lexicon" as "the vocabulary of a language, an individual speaker or group of speakers, or a subject," to use the *Merriam-Webster Dictionary* definition. Ask students how the terms "cultural and political" are useful adjectives for "lexicon" and what difference it makes to use these terms versus not using them as in the online title.

2. Students need to understand the important role contextual information plays in a textual analysis. This question helps them come to see that explaining the origin, the circulation online and

elsewhere, and the meaning of the phrase "99 percent" offers a base on which Stelter can analyze how the term has been used. Ask students to consider the different ways the term has been used and to account for those difference in terms of speaker, situation, audience, and purpose.

3. Stelter identifies several different political slogans that have had staying power in our political and cultural lexicon (e.g., "give me liberty or give me death," "no taxation without representation," "we shall overcome"). Ask students if they know the origin of these and when they have heard them used. Ask them as well if they are familiar with the slogans "59 cents" or the "stop the draft" from the 1960s and 1970s. Students are asked to compare the earlier slogans to the recent "99 percent" slogan and to discuss whether they think it will have staying power for the future. This question offers an opportunity to discuss how ideas are circulated and why some phrases have traction while others are lost over time.

4. This question asks students to examine and discuss the evidence Stelter uses to support his claim about the cultural and political power of the slogans "99 percent" and "1 percent." Examining how writers use evidence and the types they use to support claims is an important exercise for students so that they can think about what kinds of evidence are available and how they can use these different types in their own writing. Stelter uses political and advertising examples, numbers ("seven-

fold" increase on *Google*), direct quotations from professors and politicians, and digital and print publications. Ask students to read the *Vanity Fair* article by Joseph E. Stiglitz "Of the 1%, by the 1%, for the 1%" (pp. 746–53) and to discuss how pointing to this article helps Stelter to support his claim.

5. *For Writing.* This writing assignment asks students to analyze a slogan by examining how it originated, how it circulated over time, and when it has been used, especially most recently. The prompt offers a series of questions as a heuristic to help students locate and generate information to support the analysis. You might also ask them to consider if the slogan's meaning has varied over time or place, or whether different speakers have interpreted the meaning differently. This assignment gives students a chance to hone their skills at analyzing texts and at providing evidence.

For Further Discussion

1. Brian Stelter ends his essay with a quotation from a protester: "As they lost physical ground for their local movements, protesters told each other online, 'You can't evict an idea.'" To what degree do you think this is true? Where else have you seen an idea remain in circulation long after the event that prompted it was over? How do ideas continue to circulate? What does the staying power of some ideas suggest about the author-ity of language? In what ways does this function of language help us understand the devasta-

tion of those who have been silenced or ignored?

2. Xeni Jardin, editor of *Boing Boing*, a blog with strong impact, calls attention to one of the problems with the term "99 percent," namely, it does not offer the "many shades of gray" in economic disparity. It includes everyone from those who are penniless to those who live a comfortable and privileged life. The 1 percent refers to multibillionaires who sway politics and other venues. What do the 99 percent share? What distinguishes people of different economic classes within the 99 percent? Can you come up with a better phrase to capture the great disparity in economic wealth in the United States?

ROY PETER CLARK

684 *"A More Perfect Union": Why It Worked*

On Engaging with the Text

1. This question asks students to identify the four patterns Clark uses to show how Obama's text works and why it was so successful. As such, this question offers students a way to think about conducting and composing a textual analysis. Point out to students how Clark uses the four strategies as an organizing scheme. Since Clark uses rhetorical strategies to construct his list and analyze Obama's speech, this question gives you a good opportunity to discuss the power of rhetorical strategies not just in textual analysis but in other kinds of writing as well. By asking students to identify evidence used to support each strategy, they are learning the power of evidence and the kinds of evidence available to them as writers. Clark provides quotations and textual examples from Obama's speech as evidence of each strategy and he points to other speakers who have used each strategy successfully. Discuss with students how using direct quotations from texts offer powerful evidence of one's reading of a text (even if the audience disagrees with the reading).

2. Students are to explain Clark's stance toward the speech. It shows up in the title and throughout the essay as one of admiration and respect for this particular speech by Obama. Asking students to identify phrases that reveal the stance helps them to understand that they need to include clear signal phrases that reveal their attitude toward the subject of their writing.

3. Clark notes that in just hearing the speech some of its rhetorical features are more difficult to notice; as he says, "when received in the ear, these effects breeze through us like a harmonious song." However, he also notes "Like most memorable pieces of oratory, Obama's speech sounds

better than it reads." Discuss with students how having read Clark's analysis prepared them for listening to Obama. Ask them to talk about Obama's delivery style and how that helped or didn't help him get his points across. This question offers you an opportunity to discuss the difference between written text that is delivered orally and written text that is delivered in print. Which presentation do the students prefer and why?

4. Students should see that Clark references Martin Luther King Jr. to explain how Obama uses allusions as a rhetorical strategy in ways similar to Dr. King's famous "I Have a Dream" speech. Both frame "racial equality in familiar patriotic terms." Provide students with a printed text of Dr. King's speech and have them listen to an audio version of it. Ask them if they see additional similarities in the style, intent, or delivery of speeches that King and Obama make on race.

5. *For Writing.* The writing prompt asks students to produce a multimodal textual analysis on a political, cultural, or social speech that examines specific patterns in the speech. For this assignment, students are asked to link their text to relevant sites that deal with the speech, information in the speech, or even reviews of the speech as evidence for the points they are making. Thus, this writing prompt helps students to develop a multimodal text, an increasingly frequent medium, and it helps them with a particular method for analyzing a text.

For Further Discussion

1. Roy Peter Clark notes that those who have praised the brilliance and power of Obama's speech focus on "the orator's willingness to say things in public about race that are rarely spoken at all, even in private." Why does talking about race remain so difficult today, fifty years after the civil rights movement? How can you explain the reticence of folks from all walks of life to speak freely about race? What other subjects are taboo, and how does that affect those who are within the groups of these subjects (e.g., ability, sexual identification, mental illness)? How would speaking more openly about these subjects help to achieve Obama's "expressed desire to move the country to a new and better place"?

2. Examine the quotation Roy Peter Clark provides at the beginning of his textual analysis. What does DuBois mean by "double-consciousness"? Is it only an experience of race or do you see other aspects of identity that embody a "double-consciousness"?

ELEANOR J. BADER

693 *Homeless on Campus*

On Engaging with the Text

1. This question asks students to identify the purpose of Bader's report and to select examples to illustrate that purpose. Students should be able to see that Bader's goal is to call attention to the plight of homeless college students as she repeatedly notes that part of the problem is that "they are neither counted nor attended to." By focusing on purpose and how it's signaled, students become sensitive to the multiple purposes that reports serve. They also gain valuable practice in supporting their observations with textual evidence.

2. In this question, students' attention is focused on Bader's thesis, and how it is articulated in her report. Students should notice that Bader's thesis is implied: Homelessness is a serious problem on college campuses. By asking how else the main point could be made explicit, students learn to consider the various ways in which a thesis can be signaled in a text. You might direct them to Chapter 31 on

thesis statements to help them respond to this question.

3. Students are asked in this question to tackle the complex issue of homelessness and the role education plays in it. In focusing on the final quotation in the essay, students can be led to see how a writer can use an ending to open up a space for further discussion of an issue treated in a report. Through their discussion, students should become aware that Bader does not offer a quick-fix solution in her report. This awareness should help students realize that some issues cannot be resolved simply or easily, and that identifying the complexities of an issue is a valuable contribution.

4. This question focuses on the rhetorical strategy of narrating as a powerful way to support certain kinds of ideas. In this text, Bader piles narrative upon narrative to evoke the seriousness of the issue of homeless college students and to put a face on that issue. You might recommend that students review Chapter 40 on narration to help them respond to this question. In

asking them to consider other kinds of support, you can help students see that narration is only one in a range of possible strategies for substantiating ideas.

5. *For Writing.* This writing prompt gives students an opportunity to research student services on their campus and write a report on one of those services. This assignment helps students hone both their research and their report-writing skills. The alternative, to develop a website on student services, would give students practice in creating digital texts.

For Further Discussion

1. Eleanor Bader notes that "for all the anecdotes, details about homeless college students are hazy." Discuss why this might be the case. How is it that homeless college students tend not to be on the radar of private and government organizations?

2. Who is the audience for Eleanor Bader's report? What role can this audience play in addressing the problem Eleanor Bader reports on?

LINDA BABCOCK AND SARA LASCHEVER

699 *Women Don't Ask*

On Engaging with the Text

1. This question asks student to identify the topic and thesis of Babcock and Laschever's report and to relate these to the title of their report. By examining the topic in relation to the thesis, students can learn the difference between a topic (what the essay is about) and a thesis (a statement of the writer's position or main point about the topic). Students should be able to see that the title "Women Don't Ask" focuses on one part of the topic (the difference between how men and women negotiate) and the thesis (that women tend to accept whatever they offered whereas men tend to negotiate for more). Having students examine titles helps them to see how writers select titles for different reasons and why some titles are more appropriate or effective than others. Learning about titles also help students begin to understand that every text needs a focus, and the title often (though not always) identifies the focus.

2. Students should be able to see that Babcock and Laschever do not rely on anecdotal evidence such as that given by the associate dean at Carnegie Mellon University that "more men ask. The women just don't ask." This statement led Babcock and Laschever to raise a number of questions and to conduct several studies to test the veracity of the statement. Thus, this question gives you an opportu-

nity to discuss different kinds of evidence, and the ways anecdotal evidence often can't support claims. The authors do a study on the starting salaries of male and female MA graduates of the university, which led them to design a study of men and women playing Boggle for an ambiguous sum of money, which led them to develop a larger online survey and to interview 100 people in various professions in the United States, Great Britain, and Europe. The findings were consistent across different studies: "men [ask] for things they want and initiat[e] negotiations much more often than women—two to three times as often." Ask students whether they were surprised by these results, or by results showing that younger women are just as passive as older women when it comes to accepting what is offered rather than negotiating.

3. Students are asked to indicate what the report says about the economic effect of not negotiating a better starting salary. Students should be able to understand that over time, as men and women get raises, men will advance much more quickly having started with higher salaries from the beginning. Ask students to comment on the authors' observation that "the salary differences between the men and the women [in their study] might have been eliminated if the women had negotiated their offers."

4. In this question, students are asked to identify the intended audience for the report. The intended audience is economists but another viable audience is women who will learn how they should be speaking up for what they want. By asking students to point to phrases that make clear who the intended audience is, this question helps them see that well designed studies offer important evidence for scholars, especially for those in the social sciences such as economists. It also shows them how to anticipate and fulfill what a targeted audience expects in a report.

5. *For Writing.* This question asks students to replicate one of the research studies that Babcock and Laschever report on to collect and analyze data to see how men and women negotiate on their campus or in their area. Students won't be able to get access to university information on the salaries of students; however, they could conduct the Boggle study, the online survey, or interviews.

For Further Discussion

1. In the 1960s, women averaged about 59 cents for every dollar a man made. Today, the gender pay gap is smaller, with women on average women earning about 77 cents per dollar as compared to what men earn, though that gendered figure varies by race, region, and occupation. How do you think the gap should be bridged? What is one step that might be taken according to the studies conducted by Linda Babcock and Sara Laschever? What other measures would lead to more equal distribution of pay?

2. Examine the footnotes that Linda Babcock and Sara Laschever post in their report. What function do these notes serve? In what ways do they offer additional support for the main point the authors are making?

JONATHAN KOZOL

705 *Fremont High School*

On Engaging with the Text

1. This question offers students an opportunity to explore the complex problem of unequal educational opportunities in the United States. You might lead a class discussion on how Kozol's report challenges the American dream—the commonplace notion that everyone has an equal opportunity to succeed and that anyone can "pull themselves up by their bootstraps."

2. Asking students to consider the purpose of this report helps them understand that reports can serve a variety of purposes beyond simply disseminating information. Kozol clearly seeks reform of public education to make educational opportunities equally available to all children in the United States. Students should be able to identify Kozol's audience as those who are in a position to contribute to educational reform. In so doing, students learn how audiences and purposes are intertwined. You might recommend that students review Chapter 1 on purpose and Chapter 2 on audience to prepare them for responding to this question.

3. Kozol draws on a variety of evidence to support his claims: textual evidence from newspapers, interview data from students and teachers, and his own observations. By examining Kozol's use of evidence, students learn that claims can be supported in different ways depending on the genre and that these are strategies they can use in their own writing. Asking them to consider the accuracy of Kozol's information makes them aware of how evidence, such as direct quotations, demonstrates that information given in a text is well-researched.

4. Focusing on how Kozol ends his report offers students an opportunity to learn one effective way of ending their own essays. You might ask students to review Chapter 30 on endings to prepare for responding to this question. Given Kozol's purpose—to reform and improve public education for all children—Kozol clearly believes there is an answer to Mireya's question, though he admits that he has yet to find a "good answer." You might lead a class discussion in which students explore some of the possible answers to Mireya's significant question.

5. *For Writing.* This writing prompt offers students an opportunity to conduct a research project on a public high school in which they collect and analyze several types of data (textual evidence, interviews, observations), then compare their findings to what Kozol reports about Fremont High. You might recommend that students review Chapter 38 on interviews and Chapters 43, 44, and 47 on research strategies to help them undertake this project. This assignment would also lend itself well to a collaborative project in which students could work in small groups, dividing up research and writing tasks.

For Further Discussion

1. What does Fortino mean when he says, "You're ghetto—so you sew"? What observation is he making about social mobility? How does this brief statement get at the heart of the problem with public schools such as Fremont High?

2. What are some of the ways Jonathan Kozol shows that students at Fremont High School are "short-changed"? How do the conditions at Fremont High School compare with those of your high school? How do you account for any differences?

ALINA TUGEND

714 *Multitasking Can Make You Lose . . . Um . . . Focus*

On Engaging with the Text

1. This question asks students to examine the effects of multitasking as explicated by Tugend and to consider why Tugend focuses on effects with little attention to causes. Students should be able to see that the purpose of Tugend's essay—to report on how multitasking leads to a loss of focus and efficiency—directs Tugend to treat the effects. Asking students to consider the possible causes of multitasking gives them practice in speculating on and identifying causes. Of course, multitasking is supported, if not encouraged, by increasingly sophisticated technologies that permit switching from one task to

another quickly, but students may also identify increasing pressures from school and work to do more in less time, and increasing numbers of tasks to do (e.g., email, tweet, read websites, listen to voice mail, and so on). You might lead a class discussion on the various causes students identify.

2. Asking students to examine Tugend's focus—the effects of multitasking—should help them understand how a tight focus leads to a readable report. The claim of her title—that multitasking can make you lose focus—offers an indirect lesson on why a tight focus is necessary in an essay; just as Tugend recommends learning "the art of

single-tasking," writers need to learn the art of focus in writing.

3. Tugend defines several terms (e.g., "multitasking," the topic of her essay; "prefrontal cortex," a technical term; "e-mail voice," another author's term). By examining the various kinds of terms defined, students learn that different occasions require the definition of terms. You might direct students to Chapter 36 on defining to help them with this question.

4. Tugend's stance toward multitasking is respectful, academic, and serious, though she injects lighthearted remarks at points. Directing students toward Tugend's stance should help them understand that every piece of writing exhibits a stance, even pieces that report information. You might lead a class discussion on how this essay would differ if Tugend assumed a different stance toward her subject (e.g., skeptical, ironic, or critical). You might also direct students to Chapter 4 on stance to prepare for discussing this question.

5. *For Writing.* This writing prompt asks students to conduct their own study of multitasking to test the claims Tugend makes in her report. This research project will offer students practice in conducting field research and in analyzing observation and interview data. You might recommend that students review Chapter 37 on describing and the section in Chapter 44 on field research to help them undertake the research and writing for this project.

For Further Discussion

1. How does Alina Tugend support the claim she makes in her title about the effects of multitasking? What evidence does she provide? Do you think her evidence is accurate and well-researched? Why or why not?

2. What is your view on multitasking? How often do you find yourself juggling two or more tasks at once? In what ways, if any, do you relate to the examples of multitasking Alina Tugend supplies? Do you think it possible for people today to learn single-tasking? Why or why not?

LAURA SULLIVAN

719 *Escape from Alcatraz: A 47-Year Manhunt*

On Engaging with the Text

1. This question asks students to examine the quotations Sullivan inserts and to explain how they are used. Learning when to use a quotation versus when to paraphrase or summarize can be a difficult process for some stu-

dents.* If they take a close look at how, when, and who authors choose to quote, students can gain a fuller understanding of how to use quotations in their own writing. Students will notice that Sullivan quotes former and current staff at Alcatraz as well as the daughter of the then acting warden. These serve as powerful, illustrative evidence for what happened on the evening John Anglin, Frank Morris, and Clarence Anglin escaped.

2.   Students are asked to examine the online version of this article to discuss what the visuals and the audio add to the report. Students will need to go online to respond to this question. You might show the multimodal text in class as a starting point for discussion. Having examined both, students are asked what other visuals and audio they would include. This question thus helps students to study a multimodal report so they can understand some of the techniques authors use online and can then incorporate them into their own multimodal writing.

3.   By asking students to examine the captions on pictures, they can learn the benefits of creating clear labels for visuals they may use in their own writing. The labels in Sullivan's report offer historical and biographical information that help the reader understand each image and its relation to the report. Students sometimes assume that readers will know what a visual means.

They need to understand that meaning doesn't reside in the visual any more than it does in words. You might ask them to come up with alternative labels for the pictures and then compare all of the students' responses for the whole class. This activity would lead into a good discussion about meaning and interpretation.

4.   This question asks students to speculate on what happened to the three inmates who escaped Alcatraz. What clues, if any, do the students find in the wanted posters and in the label that accompanies these? Why is the U.S. Marshals Service holding the cases of these three men open? Do you think the disappearance of these men will ever be explained?

5.   *For Writing.* This writing assignment asks students to find an unusual room on their campus or in their neighborhood that they can report on in a multimodal essay. Students gain valuable experience doing research by observing the room, studying early pictures, conducting interviews, and working with librarians and/or archivists to find out all they can about the room. Questions are given as heuristics to help students think about the kinds of information they can collect to write a report. Creating a multimodal report will help students gain experience with the kind of writing, visuals, and audio that best serves the information they wish to convey.

*For a good discussion of using citations, see Shirley Rose, " 'What's Love Got to Do with It?' Scholarly Citation Practices as Courtship Rituals," *Language and Learning Across the Disciplines* 1.3 (1996): 34–48, print; and Shirley K. Rose, "Citation Rituals in Academic Cultures," *Issues in Writing* 6.1 (1993/1994): 24–37, print.

For Further Discussion

1. Today Alcatraz is a public facility open to tours. Why do you think that the holes, spaces, and materials are still present? What role could the public play in helping to search for these three inmates?

2. How do you think the inmates managed to escape? What preparations were required to complete the escape? What do you speculate happened to the three inmates? What leads you to that speculation?

ALEX WEISS

727 *Should Gamers Be Prosecuted for Virtual Stealing?*

On Engaging with the Text

1. Students are asked to identify the thesis of this essay, and they should clearly see that Weiss disagrees with the judge's ruling that convicted a teenager for stealing something in the virtual world of *RuneScape*. He cites the gaming blog *Kotaku* and his own experience. Students should find these creditable sources for this argument and should applaud Weiss for not just resting on his own experience. Having students examine a thesis and the evidence used to support it helps them to develop an awareness of how various positions can be argued effectively. They may or may not agree with Weiss's view that "attempting to bring real-world law into virtual realms—and putting monetary value on time spent immersed in a virtual world—seems dangerous." However, this prompt offers a good starting point for discussing the argument.

2. This question asks students to think about legal policies and issues regarding behavior in the virtual lands of online games. Have the students explain what needs to be made legal or illegal. Have students consider how the policies will be enforced. Their responses could be used to generate a broader set of online laws to govern all virtual interactions that happen over the internet.

3. Asking students to examine a writer's stance helps them to consider how they will display their attitude toward their subject in arguments. They should realize that disdainful, sarcastic, or condescending tones and stances are inappropriate for presenting an argument. In this case, Weiss clearly has a great deal of respect for online gaming as he himself is a gamer. He treats the subject and this court case with reverence, offering a fair and balanced argument. Students should be able to select a sentence or phrase that reveals this stance.

4. Students should be able to see that the question posed in the title is central to Weiss's thesis. Weiss answers "no" with his text but others may answer "yes" as

did the Dutch Supreme Court. This question asks students to expand on their responses to question 1.

5. *For Writing.* With this writing prompt, students are offered an opportunity to consider an issue related to emerging technologies, perhaps an issue that plagues them right now. Students will need to research how others have treated the issue to find out the various positions on it. They will then need to explain the issue in appropriate detail so they can argue for how they think it should be handled and who they think should be involved in solving it. In this prompt, students are reminded of some of the key features of an argument, features they have focused on in responding to the questions.

For Further Discussion

1. Should gaming—whether digital, online, or board games—be subject to real-life laws for actions taken in virtual worlds? Why do you think this issue has come up now? What makes an online game different from a board game? Should, for example, players in a Monopoly game be held legally responsible for stealing from the bank? How is this different from stealing in *RuneScape?*

2. Gaming and creative play is becoming a robust scholarly area. Researchers from a variety of disciplines have taken up the topic to explore its potential for health and social impact and for developing meaningful learning in and out of school. As of now, games are being developed to treat all sorts of issues—as educational tools, as health and living tools, as training tools for employees, as global communication tools, and so on. Such work calls for multiple transdisciplinary teams of scholars working together to design, test, and run the games. Research gaming to find out about some of these projects. A good starting point is the Center for Games and Impact at Arizona State University (gamesandimpact.org). What uses do you envision for gaming?

NICHOLAS CARR

731 Is Google *Making Us Stupid?*

On Engaging with the Text

1. Drawing connections between Sergey Brin's observation and Carr's essay helps students learn to consider the larger context and conversations of which the texts they read are a part. You might lead a class discussion and ask students to consider whether Brin's point that other search engines are a "single click" away is suspi-

cious in light of what Carr asserts about Google's efforts to corner the market on information flow. Students should be able to see that if Carr and those he cites are correct, the Internet—whether for good or bad—is radically transforming our cognitive functions and so it's important that we pay attention to its effects.

2. Directing students to examine the effects of the Internet as Carr outlines them in his essay helps them learn how writers analyze effects. Students should be able to recognize that Carr draws on several kinds of evidence to support his claim about how the Internet is changing how we read, write, and think: personal anecdotes, interviews with academics, scholarly textual evidence, and historical precedents. By considering how Carr's examples of changes wrought by earlier technologies function, students will learn how examples can serve as powerful pieces of evidence. You might recommend that students review Chapter 33 on arguing for help with this question.

3. This question asks students to locate instances where Carr offers opposing viewpoints. Students should be able to note that Carr shows how technological changes, beginning with Plato, have throughout history run the spectrum from sharp criticisms and dystopian warnings to unwavering support and utopian visions. Carr's balanced presentation invites us to take a middle road—critical and skeptical. Asking students to support their view of the effectiveness of this approach gives them useful practice in supporting their own claims.

4. Asking students to pay attention to the beginning and ending of Carr's piece helps them learn a strategy for opening and closing their own essays. Given the date that the film 2001 first aired (1968), Carr is appealing largely to an educated baby boomer audience who are concerned with the explosion of technology over the last two decades. The quotes Carr includes from the film play on the fear some have of technology displacing humans and signals his critical, though even-handed, approach to this subject.

5. *For Writing.* This writing prompt directs students to explore Carr's topic—how technology is (or is not) affecting the way we think, read, write, and live—and to craft an argument that supports their position on the topic. Since most of these students have grown up with the Internet, they no doubt have a good deal of experience with it that would yield material for their essay, so the prompt suggests they include a reflection on the topic. You might recommend that students read Chapter 10 on arguing a position and Chapter 18 on reflections to prepare for this assignment.

For Further Discussion

1. Nicholas Carr observes that "for all that's been written about the Net, there's been little consideration of how, exactly,

it's reprogramming us. The Net's intellectual ethic remains obscure." What do you believe the internet's "intellectual ethic" should be? How can that ethic be accomplished?

2. What is Nicholas Carr's stance toward his topic? Point to two or more passages that support your response. Is this stance appropriate for the purpose of this essay? Why or why not?

JOSEPH E. STIGLITZ

746 *Of the 1%, by the 1%, for the 1%*

On Engaging with the Text

1. This question asks students to examine the reasons Stiglitz gives to support one of his claims in his argument. Students should be able to see that Stiglitz offers three main reasons: (1) "growing inequality is the flip side of . . . shrinking opportunity"; (2) "many of the distortions that lead to inequality . . . undermine the efficiency of the economy"; (3) "a modern economy requires 'collect action'." Students will find evidence throughout to support the claims Stiglitz makes. The question asks them to focus on one kind of evidence: statistics. Stiglitz uses statistic to describe the proportion of wealth the 1 percent controls (40 percent), the percentage of unemployed young people (20 percent), the ratio of those on food stamps (1 out of 7), the ratio of those searching for a full-time job (1 out of 6), and the small percentage of twenty-year-olds who voted in the last election (21 percent). Students should see that these numbers underscore the growing disparity between the 1 percent and the remaining U.S. citizens.

2. Students are asked to explain one of the economic theories Stiglitz points to that is meant to explain the vast inequalities in wealth, marginal-productivity theory. Stiglitz offers an explanation of the theory early in his essay, writing, "in a nutshell, this theory associated higher incomes with higher productivity and a greater contribution to society." Ask student to discuss this theory and its implications for our economy. Is it necessarily true that someone who makes more than someone else works harder than the other person? What have reality television shows, blogs, and news stories on some of the wealthy suggested about this theory? Why do some people buy into it?

3. By asking students how the main point at the end of the essay relates to the beginning, students gain a good understanding of how openings and closing can work together to make a complete argument. Stiglitz alludes to the fall of past empires, ruling classes, and leaders. You might ask students to discuss some of the falls of the "mighty" in history and to dis-

cuss similarities they see between those falls and the current economic situation. Of course, this ending echoes the beginning when he calls attention to the growing disparity in wealth across the economic classes. As he notes, "America lags behind any country in the old, ossified [Western] Europe . . . . Among our closest counterparts are Russia with its oligarchs and Iran." The aristocratic ruling classes in both countries were overthrown. Ask students what they think will happen if the growing disparity isn't corrected.

4. This question asks students to identify the stance in this argument and to find two passages that illustrate that stance. Students should see that Stiglitz is serious and reasonable in his stance. He points several times to history which asks readers to think back to times and places in a similar economic situation. He offers statistics, quotations, and plausible reasons for his claims. Students may not agree with Stiglitz's argument but they should see that he is trustworthy. They can check each piece of support he offers to see if it is correct.

5. *For Writing.* This writing prompt follows from the response to question 3. If students answer that question, they will have begun brainstorming their position for the argument called for by this assignment. Students will need to identify a time and place in history and do research on it to get details and support for their argument. Have them explain the reasons why

the government that they are focusing on fell. Encourage them to use a range of sources, including quotations, statistics, and examples. This prompt thus gives students an opportunity to hone both their research, writing, and argument skills.

For Further Discussion

1. What is the allusion in the title of Joseph E. Stiglitz's essay? How does it call to mind Lincoln's famous line from his Gettysburg Address (November 19, 1863) "government of the people, by the people, for the people"? Of course, it is the contrast between the two very different groups of "people"—the 1 percent who control most everything (and especially 40 percent of the wealth in the United States) and the ordinary citizen (what is being called the 99 percent) to whom Lincoln referred. Discuss the two contrasting phrases and explain why Stiglitz echoed Lincoln. Explain how the title supports Stiglitz position in this argument.

2. Discuss Joseph E. Stiglitz's argument in relation to Brian Stelter's textual analysis, "'We Are the 99 Percent' Joins the Cultural and Political Lexicon" (Chapter 58, p. 679). How do these two essays speak to each other? If we view writing as a kind of conversation, as Kenneth Burke theorized,* what might be the next contribution to this discussion?

*Kenneth Burke, *The Philosophy of Literary Form* (Berkeley: U of California P, 1973), 110–11, print.

GRANT PENROD

Anti-Intellectualism: Why We Hate the Smart Kids

On Engaging with the Text

1. Focusing students' attention on the kind of evidence Penrod supplies to support his argument—web sources, print sources, and poetry—should help students think about some of the available ways they can support their own arguments. You might direct students to his Works Cited page as a strategy for identifying and describing the kinds of support Penrod uses. Asking them to consider how persuasive Penrod's argument is gives them practice in evaluating arguments, and in using reasons and evidence to support their own claims. You might recommend students review Chapter 44 on finding sources to help them with this question.

2. This question focuses on Penrod's title and what it signals about his intended audience. This is an interesting question. The "We" in the title signals those who hate smart kids and his ending supports this initial read of his title: "For the sake of smart kids, we all need to 'lay off' a little." However, because his essay offers a reasoned argument for why "anti-intellectualism" exists, it is equally appropriate for the intellectuals who are his subject. By discussing his title and its relation to the intended audience, students can discover how much work a good title can accomplish.

3. This question offers students an opportunity to discuss one of the reasons Penrod offers for anti-intellectualism. In supporting whether or not they agree with Penrod's reasoning, students gain useful practice in building an argument.

4. Like the previous question, this one asks students to take up one of the reasons Penrod offers in support of his position—the role of media in fueling anti-intellectualist sentiments. Students are asked whether they agree with this claim, and to come up with evidence to refute it. Students should be led to see that counter-arguments can be used both to counter and to bolster positions.

5. *For Writing.* This writing prompt asks students to think about the way students were classified in high school, and to write an argument about one of those groups that examines the factors that motivated the stereotyping of the group. This assignment will give students an opportunity to explore deeply a topic that they know well, and to come up with reasons and evidence to support their perspective on it.

For Further Discussion

1. Grant Penrod begins his essay with a series of specific examples to set the stage for his argument that anti-intellectualist tendencies are pervasive today. Discuss his examples. How do they help prepare readers for his argument?

2. Grant Penrod includes a poem toward the end of his essay. What does the poem contribute to his argument? How does it relate to his final statement: "For the sake of smart kids, we all need to 'lay off' a little"?

DAVID SIROTA

759 *Kenneth Cole Gets Schooled*

On Engaging with the Text

1. This question asks student to identify Sirota's thesis and the support he supplies. Students need to learn how to set a focus for an argument that lays out their position and then to decide from among various kinds of support what is the strongest for their subject and position. Clearly, Sirota believes that Kenneth Cole's advertising campaign is "wrongheaded and ideologically extreme [in its] crusade against public schools, teachers and unions." He draws on information he learned from Cole's company, quoting his spokeswoman; he references social science studies on education; he explains the fallacies in the ad campaign; and he draws on Gotham Schools, an online site for conversations about issues related to teaching and public schools. Students should find this evidence very effective.

2. For this question, students need to go to the online site for this essay. You might show it in class if you have students who have limited access to computers or internet. Students are asked to follow the hyperlinks in the argument and to discuss their function, their relevance, and their importance to Sirota's argument. Focusing on the hyperlinks helps students to see when and how it can be effective to connect to other texts, images, and videos.

3. By examining the title, students learn one of many ways titles are generated for arguments. Sirota title, "Kenneth Cole Gets Schooled," is a double entendre, meaning that Cole focuses on schools and that he later learns that his ad campaign that bashed public teachers, unions, and schools was inappropriate. The company removed it, issuing the statement "We misrepresented the issue—one too complex for a billboard—and are taking it down." Is it the complexity or the position that Cole assumes in his ad campaign that is at issue here? Have students discuss the statement issued by Cole's company and what they see as the finer points in debate here.

4. This question asks student to think about Sirota's ending and to explain the claim it makes. They are to consider Kenneth Cole's message, who that message benefits, who it hurts, and whether bashing public school teachers and unions is an ethical or even useful thing to do. You might use this question to launch a whole

class discussion of this argument and the point of view it represents.

5. *For Writing.* This writing prompt asks student to respond to Sirota's essay by either defending Sirota's position or refuting it. Students are likely to have strong opinions on this ad campaign. However, they should understand that how they frame the argument and support their claims varies according to the audience they target. What needs to be said to teachers is very different than to politicians or parents and so on. Students are to compose a multimodal argument, using resources available to them, such as images, video, audio, graphs, and so on. This assignment helps student learn how to argue in an online environment.

For Further Discussion

1. Compare David Sirota's essay with Natasha Singer's profile, "On Campus, It's One Big Commercial" (pp. 837–47). What role does advertising play in our society and culture today? Should you become more vigilant about looking at ads closely? How influential are ads? Does it matter? Why or why not?

2. Examine and analyze the visual on p. 760. What does Kenneth Cole mean by the question, "Shouldn't everyone be well red?" What can "red" refer to apart from a play on words for "read"? What political or social group would likely sympathize with Cole's ad campaign? Why?

JODY ROSEN

765 Born This Way: *Lady Gaga's New Album Is a Pop Rapture*

Engaging with the Text

1.   Students are asked to identify Rosen's target audience, and they should be able to note that Lady Gaga fans would be the proper reader, though given Rosen's description of her music and his comparison of Lady Gaga with Bruce Springsteen, this evaluation may open up new audiences. There are several places in the essay where the target audience is made clear by the references to activities and sounds with which Gaga fans would be familiar. The strongest signal of audience, perhaps, is the end where Rosen writes of the album: "You stop thinking about Gaga's newest dress or Tweet or *success de scandale*—you stop puzzling over Gaga in the cultural sense—and surrender to the music's crude power."

2.   This question asks students to judge the opening claim Rosen makes about Lady Gaga's album being "bigger, more emphatic, and more campy than anyone's." Those who have already listened to *Born This Way*

may or may not agree with this assessment. For those who haven't, students are asked if Rosen offers enough evidence to support this claim. They should see that he offers specifics about the musicians who play with Gaga on the album, and vivid descriptions of songs and sounds and lyrics that are meant to support his evaluation. Again, students may or may not agree with Rosen's examples but they should see that he does offer specific details as support. This question helps students come to understand that detailed support is necessary for readers to see an evaluation even if they do not agree with it.

3.   Rosen compares Gaga to Bruce Springsteen, providing evidence of similar American lyrics and pointing to his sound of the 1980s. With this question you can help students understand that for those who have not yet heard the album, such comparisons help readers to understand the evaluation and its claims. For those who have heard it, such comparisons offer evidence of those claims. This question then offers students

311

a clear example of a role comparisons play in a text and demonstrates just how specific and on target the comparison needs to be. Rosen is not just offering a sweeping vague reference to Springsteen; Rosen specifically spells out what he sees as Gaga echoing his words and sounds.

4. Asking students to focus on the stance of an evaluation is an important lesson for them. Here they should understand that Rosen clearly admires Lady Gaga's most recent album, *Born This Way*, by the positive statements he makes about the lyrics, music, and arrangements. An evaluation, like other kinds of writing, calls for a strong ethos so that readers trust the criteria and the assessment even if they do not agree. Rosen demonstrates his familiarity with the current and past music scene in the examples he uses and in the details he offers. Such efforts show him to be knowledgeable. The other aspects of ethos—good intentions and trustworthiness—are also apparent here. You might ask students whether they believe Rosen has the readers' best interests at heart and whether they find his evaluation trustworthy. Ask them to point to specific phrases or sentences that lead them to their responses.

5. *For Writing.* This writing prompt asks students to write an evaluation of a recently released album that they find on *Billboard*, though they may be aware of another web or media source for this information. For this writing task, stu-

dents will need to establish their ethos by showing they are knowledgeable about the music, artist, and current musical work in the genre, so encourage them to select music they already know something about. They also need to write for an audience that is familiar either with the type of music (e.g., pop, classical, soul, rap, rock and roll, country, and so on) or with the artist. Have the students listen to the album several times to come up with criteria that will allow them to make a positive, negative, or neutral evaluation of the work. Let them know that they might need to do some research on the musicians listed on the cover if they are not well known.

For Further Discussion

1. What kind of music do you frequently listen to? What is it about the artists or the genre(s) that keeps you coming back? Jot down what you consider to be the top or most important song right now. In small groups, brainstorm a list of criteria to evaluate your selections then defend the selections.

2. Do you think there is a nostalgia for the 1980s with albums such as Lady Gaga's coming on the market? What other artist do you hear echoing the disco era? What do you make of the fact that many artists from the 1960s through the 1980s (you grandparents' and parents' eras) are still performing and still drawing a

large crowd? (Consider Mick Jagger, Paul McCartney, Bruce Springsteen, and so on.

Who else would you name as iconic still today?)

MICHIKO KAKUTANI

770 *The End of Life as She Knew It*

On Engaging with the Text

1. This question focuses on the way Kakutani begins her review of Joan Didion's *The Year of Magical Thinking*. Rather than begin with the book, Kakutani opens with a biographical statement on Didion and her work. Since Didion's book is a memoir, this opening seems entirely appropriate for preparing the reader for a review of the memoir. Students should become aware of one strategy for opening a review of a book—making the opening reflect the genre of the book. You might recommend that they read Chapter 30 on beginnings to help them respond to this question.

2. Focusing attention on how Kakutani weaves quotations from Didion's memoir into her review should help students see one of the ways quotations can be used as both support and illustration. You might direct students to Chapter 47 on quoting as a rhetorical practice to help them answer this question.

3. Kakutani's descriptions—"devastating new book," "stunning candor and piercing details," "[a]t once exquisitely con-

trolled and heartbreakingly sad"—reveal her unabashed admiration of Didion's memoir. By asking students to identify passages such as these, you can give them valuable practice in mining texts for implicit assessments. In turn, students can learn how their descriptions should support their overall evaluation of a subject.

4. This question asks students to consider the purpose of Kakutani's review. You might remind students that writers typically review books to help readers decide whether or not to read a particular work. Kakutani's evaluation implicitly says, "Yes, read this work." The penultimate paragraph captures the memoir and points up its universal appeal: "It is a book that tells us how people try to make sense of the senseless and how they somehow go on." By focusing on the purpose, students can understand the implicit question readers of reviews hold. "Should I get this book?" This central question should help students write their own reviews.

5. *For Writing.* This writing prompt directs students to pen a book review. Students

may need help in realizing that different genres of books—how-to, novel, textbook, biography—demand different kinds of criteria. This assignment should help students learn how to develop relevant criteria for assessing a book's strengths and weaknesses, and use textual evidence from the book to support their assessment.

For Further Discussion

1. Michiko Kakutani ends her review of Joan Didion's memoir with a "tragic coda." How effective is this ending?

2. What is Michiko Kakutani's stance in this review? Point to specific passages in the text that reveal her stance.

DANA STEVENS

775 ## The Help: A Feel Good Movie That Feels Kind of Icky

Engaging with the Text

1. This question asks students how Stevens achieves a balanced and fair assessment. They should be able to see that while Stevens praises the film with one phrase she often critiques it within the same sentence with another one. For instance, she writes, "It's hard to actively hate The Help, a movie so solicitous of audience's favor that it can't help but win it some of the time"; or after praising a few bits of the film notes, "But after a while all this emotional dexterity starts to resemble emotional manipulation. The Help is a high-functioning tearjerker but the catharsis it offers feels glib and insufficient, a Barbie Band-Aid on the still-raw wound of race relations in America." Given her balanced critical and positive remarks on this film, ask students if they are more or less likely to see the film. Why or why not? Discuss what positive, negative, and balanced reviews regarding a movie, product, album, and so on lead students to do in relation to the subject.

2. Asking students to examine the title of Stevens's evaluation should reveal to them one strategy for titling a work, which would be to hint at the central point of the essay—a "Feel-Good Movie That Feels Kind of Icky." Here Stevens signals that the review of The Help will be neither fully positive nor fully negative. Discuss with students how titles can help readers expect what an evaluation will be. Ask them what other title they might give this movie review.

3. Students are asked to identify the thesis of this evaluation. Clearly, for Stevens there are too few moments that treat race relations in any substantive or realistic way. As she notes, the movie treats race and racism as if it were "a

quaint artifact" of the past. She argues that it would be a stronger contribution if it "contained more moments in which Skeeter's good will wasn't enough" so that viewers "might recognize a moment we've actually lived through, rather than being encouraged to congratulate ourselves on how far we've come."

4.   Central to Stevens's evaluation is the ambivalence she experiences regarding how seriously race is or is not taken in *The Help*. Students should be able to note that the last two paragraphs of the evaluation develop this question with great care. This question asks them to go beyond the review and to consider how they think the movie will be received and how, if there is a debate as Stevens predicts, the sides of the debate will be defined. By asking students whether they think the debate would be a "valuable contribution," they will need to consider what the outcome may be and whether it will move the country forward regarding race relations.

5.   *For Writing.* This writing prompt asks students to review a movie, whether in theaters or on DVD or online, about which they have mixed feelings, just as Stevens's does. Help students brainstorm a list of films they have recently seen or plan to see within a week, and then to make a positive and a negative column for the movie. They can then explore what makes the movie neither a hit nor a dud. This assignment also offers students an opportunity to draft a balanced evaluation and to draft a title that reflects the two reactions to the one movie. Have students write their titles on the board, and then have the other students discuss what they think is the topic of each review's ambivalence.

For Further Discussion

1.   Discuss the central point the author offers in her last paragraph: "Do we [as marginalized groups] count ourselves glad to make any inroads we can, or do we demand rich, nuanced, subtle representations right from the start?" How should we focus on underrepresented groups of people? What do you think needs attention now?

2.   Compare Dana Stevens's review of *The Help* with Roy Peter Clark's textual analysis of President Obama's speech on race in his essay "'A More Perfect Union': Why It Worked" (pp. 684–91). In what ways do their perspectives on race compare? Discuss the common theme in both that we need to open up the hard discussion to explore race and race relations in nuanced detail.

779 *Fast Food: Four Big Names Lose*

Engaging with the Text

1. Students are asked to identify the criteria *Consumer Reports* used to evaluate fast food chain restaurants. The criteria are easy enough to find—they're listed in the title. Nearly 37,000 readers rated the chains according to the following four criteria: the quality of the food, the value for the price, the politeness of the staff, and the speed of orders. Lead a class discussion on what students value in a dining experience at a fast food restaurant chain. Do the students find the four criteria resonate with their criteria or would they like the restaurants to be judged differently? You might also point out how the writers of this evaluation organized their text by the responses readers gave on the survey.

2. This question asks students to examine the two charts on pp. 785 and 788 to determine the usefulness and helpfulness of the charts in summarizing the evaluation and in permitting a sense of the ratings at a glance. Ask students if and how they will use the information in the charts.

3. With this question, students are expected to connect the information on how healthy fast food chains are in terms of their menus and the implied argument to "eat healthily." Increasingly, chains are adding lighter, more health-conscious fare; yet consumers continue to select the higher calorie choice. Given this behavior, *Consumer Reports* offers tips on making better, healthier choices at these chain restaurants. Hold a discussion with students about the kinds of choices they make at restaurants when they go out. Ask them why they think the clients surveyed here make poor choices when it comes to food.

4. Students are asked to examine the headings *Consumer Reports* uses to guide readers and to explain how these function. This question is meant to help students become savvier navigators of text. Students will see that not all readers will read the whole essay. Some readers may skim the evaluation only for information they are interested in, so the headings point out shortcuts. But the headings also reveal how the evaluation is organized and thus help readers anticipate information that will be included. Discuss with students how they have used headings in past pieces of writing and how they might use them in future.

5. *For Writing.* The writing prompt offers students experience with gathering information via a survey and with analyzing survey results. Students may need guidance with creating a viable survey and they should be encouraged to pilot it before gathering their primary data. Having a small sample of friends or classmates take the survey will help them find out which

questions work and which are not clear. After students have completed the assignment, ask them to share their results and to talk about what surprises they found and what they personally thought about the hangouts other students chose.

For Further Discussion

1. Create a healthy menu for a restaurant that either exists or one you design. Support your chosen menu by describing the health benefits of each item.

2. Look at the tables on pp. 785 and 788 and write a set of instructions describing how one should read the table and what information the table reveals. Explain the logic of these tables and how they are organized.

ROBERTA SMITH

790 *An Online Art Collection Grows Out of Infancy*

Engaging with the Text

1. This question asks students to explain how Roberta Smith achieves a balanced and fair assessment of the *Google Art Project*. By having students point to specific sentences that show she is being fair and offering both strengths and weaknesses of the project, students can see how they can phrase pros and cons reasonably.

2. Students are asked to click on the hyperlinks in this evaluation to see where they go and to compare and contrast each site. This activity helps students understand why authors make choices to hyperlink sections of their online texts. Understanding the reasons for these links will help students write their own multimodal documents.

3. Ask student to share the information they gathered by visiting the *Google Art Project* site. Have them explain why they picked a particular museum as a favorite and what they look for when they visit a museum. Then have students share with the class information they learned when they clicked on the Details link.

4. The question asks students to identify the target audience for this evaluation and to point to a section in the essay where the targeted audience is made clear. Of course, students will say that "anyone" can click on this multimodal evaluation but they need to understand how authors make choices for what to include, what examples to give, what links and pictures to embed, and so on when they write, especially multimodal pieces.

5. *For Writing*. This writing prompt asks students to evaluate a website that they admire or one that they dislike. The trick will be for them to provide a fair and balanced evaluation on a site they feel strongly about. They are then asked to write a multimodal evaluation that includes useful links, visuals, screen shots, and so on. This assignment gives students a valuable lesson in digital writing, something they will be doing increasingly in school and the workplace.

For Further Discussion

1. What are the drawbacks of viewing artwork on the internet versus viewing it in person? What are the advantages? How would you try to ameliorate the cons of each?

2. Rewrite one paragraph of Roberta Smith's review so that it includes information that is currently available via a link. Explain the difficulties in rendering visuals and information from other sites into a written text. What are the costs and what are the advantages of multimodal texts versus print texts?

DAVID SEDARIS

Us and Them

On Engaging with the Text

1. This question asks students to focus on Sedaris's title and to identify the "us" and the "them" in the memoir. The "us" is, of course, Sedaris and his family—but also those who, like his family, lead lives that are shaped by TV; the "them" refers to his neighbors, the Tomkeys, who don't own a television and so become a fascinating, almost obsessive subject of scrutiny for the young Sedaris. In asking students with whom we are meant to sympathize, you may have to help them disentangle the two perspectives in the memoir—that of the naïve young Sedaris and that of the wiser mature and ironic Sedaris who recounts the story. By focusing on the title, students can learn how a title sets up a framework and set of expectations for reading.

2. In this question, students are directed to assess whether Sedaris's memoir is a good story—one of the key features of a memoir. You might refer them to Chapter 15 on memoirs for a discussion of the criteria for a good story. In responding to this

question, students should be able to identify the central conflict, something signaled by the title. By asking students to refer to the text in their response, you can help them develop skills in supporting observations with the textual evidence.

3. This question draws students' attention to two concrete details in Sedaris's memoir—the two handwritten signs. In asking what the significance of these are to his memoir, you can help students understand that they embody the main point that Sedaris wants to make about his neighbors and himself, and as such, capture the significance of his memoir—the lesson he learned about himself. By responding to this question, students can learn to identify significance—a key feature in a memoir—and by extension learn one strategy for signaling significance in their own writing.

4. Students are prompted in this question to identify Sedaris's stance, a key aspect of the rhetorical situation. You might point them to Chapter 4 on stance

319

to help them prepare for responding to this question. Students may need some help in recognizing the dual perspectives—the naïve and mature—that Sedaris constructs so that they can fully understand his irony throughout the memoir.

5. *For Writing.* This writing prompt directs students to consider a past experience that taught them something about themselves. As such, it provides a focus to help them identify a specific topic and engage specific rhetorical strategies of description and narration.

For Further Discussion

1. David Sedaris observes of the Tomkey family, "They had no idea how puny their lives were, and so they were not ashamed that a camera would have found them uninteresting. They did not know what attractive was or what dinner was supposed to look like or even what time people were supposed to eat." In this observation, Sedaris is being ironic, and making a broader commentary on the role of television in our lives. What is Sedaris's point here? Discuss how television influences, whether directly or indirectly, your life and the choices you make.

2. David Sedaris ends his memoir with a description of his family sitting before the TV watching a western and the ads that accompany it, viewing "one picture after another, on and on until the news, and whatever came on after the news." How does this ending reflect the main point of his memoir? How else might he have ended his memoir?

JUDITH ORTIZ COFER

806 *The Myth of the Latin Woman*

Engaging with the Text

1. For students to answer this question, they need first to identify the thesis so they can select two details that support the major point of the essay. By asking students to identify details as support, they can come to understand that readers look to details to see a claim from the author's point of view. Cofer includes many details to support her message of the ways in which Latinas are poorly understood and grossly stereotyped, so students should be able to locate two of these without much difficulty.

2. Students are asked to examine how Cofer ends her essay to see one of many strategies for closing a memoir. She concludes with a poem she wrote in which she calls Latinas "God's brown daughters." The significance is two-fold. On the one

hand, by writing a prayer that talks about Latinas praying to a God not of their heritage—"an Anglo God/with a Jewish heritage"—she frames Latinas as morally good, an antidote to the typical stereotyping by Anglos. On the other hand, she also makes clear the point that Latinas are misunderstood in part because of a language barrier as well as a cultural one. The Latinas in her poem "fervently hop[e] . . . He [God] is bilingual." It is, of course, ironic since He is understood as "omnipotent" within Christianity, a religion that developed and spread through many other languages—Hebrew, Aramaic, Greek, and Latin.

3. This question asks students to identify the purpose of this memoir. Understanding that all writing serves a purpose—whether intended or not—is an important lesson for students. In this memoir Cofer works hard to dispel misunderstandings, misrepresentations, and stereotypes of Latinas in Anglo culture. Her purpose underscores every vignette in her memoir but it is most explicitly stated toward the end: "My personal goal in my public life is to try to replace the old pervasive stereotypes and myths about Latinas with a much more interesting set of realities."

4. Students are asked to consider the role dress plays by examining the two very different readings of how Latinas dress in their homeland versus in an Anglo space.

Have students provide examples of how they or groups they know read other people. How, for example, were groups identified in their high school by their clothing? How accurate were the identifications? What do they think should be accomplished by "reading" groups by dress? And how might they separate dress from how humans should be treated and understood?

5. *For Writing.* This writing prompts asks students to consider their own ways of dressing and how style gets read by others. They then write a memoir that recalls one or more instances of being read by another group that rendered an accurate—or an inaccurate or unintended—*reading* of them.

For Further Discussion

1. How can Judith Ortiz Cofer and others dispel and replace "old pervasive stereotypes" apart from writing memoirs and poems and giving readings? What other social groups suffer under misinformed stereotypes? How might these groups use Cofer's methods?

2. Come up with a list of clothing that you would never buy or wear and explain why. What is your reasoning behind these choices? Did Judith Ortiz Cofer's memoir have any impact on how you now consider the role of clothing?

ILIANA ROMAN

814   *First Job*

Engaging with the Text

1.   Students are asked to identify the significance of this memoir, especially to its author. Having students identify a phrase or section that makes the significance clear teaches them a strategy for articulating the significance of a memoir. Roman begins her memoir with the irresponsible action she took while in high school and then recounts all of her efforts to redress that action by working hard and getting an education. This route is important to her because it follows her father's good example of hard work and serves as an important example for her children who she hopes will not become "deadbeats or . . . be in gangs." She wants them to admire her as she admires her dad and so far they are on a promising path. The message of this memoir is the rewards of hard work.

2.   This question asks students to consider the author's stance in the essay and the way it relates to the lesson Roman learned about having to "sell yourself a little bit, in order for [customers] to believe you." From examining how authors establish a stance toward their subject, students can come to understand that readers make judgments about authors according to the way they express their attitude in the writing. This question, then, gives you an opportunity to introduce students to the rhetorical concept of "ethos" that is measured by how well an author makes clear that she is trustworthy, of good will, and well informed.

3.   Asking students to examine the organization of this memoir and to discuss its effectiveness helps them learn a strategy for ordering their own memoirs and essays. Typical of many memoirs, this one is organized in chronological order, and effectively so because it is a story of how she recovered from an early misstep through hard work and determination. Have students discuss other ways she might have organized her memoir.

4.   Having students examine beginnings in relation to endings can help them understand the concept of framing an essay. Roman begins by telling us about her parents, focusing on her dad and how hard he works. After showing her own efforts to follow in her father's footsteps, Roman ends with a description of what that hard work and devotion has earned her—a successful life and her own beauty salon. She tells us that she "made a promise to my dad that I would do this right. . . . He did so much for me. I do not want to let him down." Thus she begins and ends with her dad and the lessons he taught her about the importance of hard work.

5.   *For Writing.* This writing prompt asks students to consider a time in their life when they made a wrong decision and its impact on their life then and today. The

decision may have led to a bad outcome or good. This assignment helps them to consider and write about consequences in a memoir. Encourage students to work on vivid details and to review strategies for explaining cause and effect.

For Further Discussion

1. Compare Iliana Roman's "First Job" with Judith Ortiz Cofer's "The Myth of the Latin Woman." Both authors cope with similar stereotypes and misunderstandings. What are the differences between the efforts each author articulates in her memoir to overcome being poorly understood and grossly stereotyped?

2. To what degree do parents or guardians have an effect on what you do in life and how you do it? Do you follow your guardians' example or did you choose a different path? What force do you believe is the strongest influence in your life at this moment?

ABIGAIL ZUGER

822 *En Route*

Engaging with the Text

1. This question asks students to examine how Zuger begins her memoir. Studying openings helps students develop different strategies for beginning their pieces of writing. Memoirs need to be able to draw in their reader with an interesting or provoking opening. Zuger begins with a flashback of some 30 years ago when she was a new intern dealing with a patient who had a mysterious condition that may or may not have been related to her drug habit. Students need to determine whether Zuger's opening is effective for her memoir. They then are asked how else she might have begun, giving them again a way of understanding the range of possibilities in opening a piece of writing.

2. Asking students to study how Zuger compares and contrasts two doctors in her essay helps them understand how this rhetorical strategy can be used to make a claim. In this case, she claims that "neither would last a moment in my world" because both approaches to medicine, though different from one another, are equally flawed. Zuger is establishing a medical perspective that understands people as people, not as diseases. Treating people with respect is what establishes a strong doctor-patient relationship—a point made, as Zuger tells us, in 1925 by Dr. Peabody when he said to a Harvard class, "The secret of the care of the patient is in caring for the patient." Zuger's patients are people who have made bad choices but aren't bad people, a fact that would be missed by

one of the doctors who refused to treat those patients who engaged in acts he did not approve of; her patients are also people who have contracted difficult diseases such as AIDS, a fact that would be missed by the other doctor who seemed to have little understanding of current medical treatments. Students should be able to articulate how the information on these two doctors clarify and support Zuger's claim.

3. Asking students to attend to the significance of a memoir helps them understand that in telling one's story, an author needs to have a significant piece of information or a lesson to pass on. Students should see that how doctors—or anyone—treat other people has a lot to do with the relationships they establish and the way they themselves are treated. Her message: treat a patient "like a person, not a patient."

4. This question asks students to identify Zuger's targeted audience. Again, students need to understand that while anyone might pick up an essay to read, the essay itself is never written for a generic "anyone." Memoirs, like all essays, are targeted at a specific audience. This memoir is best suited for medical staff, especially doctors, though any professional would benefit from Zuger's lesson.

5. *For Writing.* This writing prompt asks students to identify a time in their lives when they learned that every person deserves to be treated with respect and humanity. Students may need to be prodded to come up with a specific event or lesson that led them to understand this point or to think about a time when they didn't treat someone with dignity and respect. They then write a memoir about the event to get the message across to a specific audience that everyone deserves to be treated humanely.

For Further Discussion

1. Bellevue Hospital was the first public hospital in the United States and is well known for its contributions to a breakthrough treatment for AIDS, the "Triple Drug Cocktail" or HAART. How does knowing this fact affect your reading and understanding of Abigail Zuger's memoir?

2. What other group apart from doctors would benefit from the message of this memoir? How would the memoir need to be revised to reach that group as a target audience? What details would need to be included and which might be left out of Abigail Zuger's memoir?

SULEIKA JAOUAD

831 *Finding My Cancer Style*

Engaging with the Text

1. This question asks students to examine the visual images that accompany the text to see how they function. By having them create titles that explain the relationship between the text and the images, students learn how best to use visuals in their own writing and how those visuals need to relate in some way to the written text.

2. Students are asked to identify the purpose of this memoir and to pick a section in it that makes the purpose clear. This multimodal memoir and Jaouad's entire blog serve a purpose for her as a way to reflect on and cope with her illness. By sharing her experiences, she is also helping other to find ways of coping with their disease.

3. Asking students to identify the result from chemotherapy that most haunted Jaouad will get them to consider how she handles the loss of her hair. What steps does she take throughout treatment to control the fear and to try to stay in charge of her hair—and her body? Students can point to specific sentences to show how they understand the central fear, and in so doing, are reminded that an essay requires a center or a few focal points to anchor its meaning.

4. By asking students to identify vivid details in this memoir and to discuss how they both bring the story to life and make clear its significance, students learn the purpose of details beyond decorating an essay. They can play an important role in making the memoir valuable and in bringing out its message and significance.

5. *For Writing.* This writing prompt asks students to identify a difficult time in their life—an illness, an injury, deep disappointment, marital stress, and so on—and to write a multimodal memoir about how they coped with it, or how they helped someone else cope with a difficult situation. This assignment gives students an opportunity to select visuals (photos, drawings, videos) and music to set the mood of the memoir and to communicate its meaning. Students gain valuable insights about how to construct a multimodal text, a skill they will find valuable in their personal and professional lives.

For Further Discussion

1. Suleika Jaouad made choices to reduce her fear about losing her hair. How do you read the ending where she explains that once again she is bald and that this time she designs her hair tattoo herself? What do you think about this ending? What is Jaouad trying to convey by making this announcement?

2. There are are advantages and disadvantages to multimodal memoirs. What does a multimodal memoir allow a writer to do that print alone doesn't? Conversely, what does print allow for in the text that is less likely to be apparent in a multimodal essay? Which do you prefer? Why?

NATASHA SINGER

On Campus, It's One Big Commercial

Engaging with the Text

1. This question asks student to identify the purpose of this profile, a task that should remind them that all writing serves an intended purpose. The purpose of questioning particular business practices and how embedded they are in our social practices should lead to a vibrant and lively discussion. Some students may disagree with Singer's critical take on these business practices, arguing that they are well aware of advertising ploys. However, it might be useful to ask the class how many are wearing clothes with logos from the manufacturers and ask them to consider the effect of wearing logos, something they should be able to answer after reading this profile.

2. Students are asked to identify three phrases in the profile that make clear it is a firsthand account. This essay is filled with such cues, including vivid descriptions of move-in day, interviews, and dialogue.

3. Asking students to examine openings helps them to develop different strategies for how to begin their essays. This opening makes clear that the writer was present on move-in day at the University of North Carolina and introduces one of the corporations that will be examined in the profile. Singer establishes a setting and a clear topic—the role of corporate practices on college campuses—right at the onset.

4. The questions in this prompt are meant to ignite a strong discussion about the growing trend of blatant corporate practices that try to turn college students into consumers of specific products. This question pairs well with question 1 and provides an opportunity for deeper discussions about how companies attract and retain their customers. Students certainly have been surrounded by these kinds of advertising practices on their high school campuses and elsewhere. To start off the discussion, have students brainstorm and write on the board some of the advertising methods they have already been exposed to and their responses to them.

5. *For Writing.* This writing prompt invites students to profile a campus activity or event at their college. College campuses offer a plethora of social, academic, political, religious, and other kinds of events for students to choose from. A side benefit of this assignment is that it will make students aware of all their campus has to offer. Students are reminded to take an interesting angle and to use engaging details and dialogue. Recommend that they audiotape interviews so they can concentrate on the people they are interviewing and can revisit the dialogue later.

For Further Discussion

1. Examine the photographs that accompany this profile. Why do you think Natasha Singer selected these images for her essay? What other images might she have included? What do these images convey separately and together?

2. Divide the class into two groups, one that would ban all corporate connections and the other that would invite any corporate sponsor to their college. In small groups, brainstorm a series of claims about your position to build an argument that supports your side. As a whole class, debate your position using the claims created in your small group work. After debating your position, have you changed your views on corporate-sponsored events?

NATHANIEL RICH

848 *Marlen Esparza: Going the Distance*

Engaging with the Text

1. This question asks students to examine the dialogue that Rich uses by focusing on the people he interviews. They will see that these are not random quotations but meaningful statements said by those who are closest to the story of Marlen Esparza's long path to becoming a highly successful boxer. Let students know that Esparza did win a bronze medal at the 2012 Olympics in London. Ask students if they are surprised that she won, especially after examining what her parents, her coach, and others have said. What quotations make clear why she deserves to win an Olympic medal?

2. Ask students to identify why Esparza is an interesting subject to profile. In addition to the fact that women's boxing appeared as an event for the first time at the 2012 Olympics, students will see that Esparza is admirable as an athlete and an

individual for her unwavering determination. Ask students to list and discuss the obstacles Esparza had to overcome to train to be one of the world's best female boxers. What lesson can students learn from Esparza?

3. Rhetorical stance—the writer's attitude toward the subject—is crucial for readers to trust what the writer says. Clearly, Rich admires Esparza. His description of her, the events he includes, the quotations he chooses, and the tone of the opening and closing are some of the places students will identify to reveal Rich's stance.

4. Students are asked to identify two passages in which Rich compares Esparza to other people and to explain the significance and effectiveness of these comparisons. In one place, Rich compares Esparza's current record—69–2 wins with a 97 percent winning percentage—to the winning percentages of three highly successful male boxers: Cassius Clay, Floyd Mayweather Jr., and Mike Tyson. To date, Esparza's record surpasses those of these three outstanding male boxers. Rich later quotes one of Esparza's mentors, who compares her to four other highly successful male fighters—Leonard, Ali, Frazier, and Foreman—noting that he "put her in that caliber of fighter." Rich also compares her against the contemporary amateur male fighters she trains with to show that she outshines them. All of these comparisons are favorable and make a connection to fighters the readers interested in boxing would know.

5. *For Writing.* This writing prompt asks students to identify a leader on their campus whom they can profile. Students may need guidance on identifying social, political, or academic groups where leaders emerge. This project will help them learn more about their college campus—whether it is a virtual campus or a traditional one. Have them brainstorm potential interview questions they can ask their profile subject and those who know the leader. Recommend they audiotape the interviews so that they can select the best quotations to use to make a case about the profile subject.

For Further Discussion

1. What are the pros and cons of male and female boxing? What life lessons do successful boxers learn from their training? What do you expect Marlen Esparza will take away from her training and her experience at the 2012 Olympics?

2. Why do professional female boxers "rarely make more than $10,000 for a title" while male boxers "can earn millions for a title bout"? Although male and female salaries are still not equal, the disparity is rarely this large in occupations other than professional sports. What makes one group more "worthy" of monetary recognition? What steps could be taken to even the professional playing field?

ROB BAKER

858 *Jimmy Santiago Baca: Poetry as Lifesaver*

On Engaging with the Text

1. Focusing on how Baker begins his profile of Baca helps students learn a powerful strategy for opening an essay. The opening anecdote foreshadows the life-altering changes Baca experienced as he shed lifestyles "just as a snake sloughs its skin." Students should be able to see that learning to read and write saved Baca from a wreckless life and contributed to building a new life as an author and later a teacher. You might direct students to Chapter 30 on beginnings to prepare for answering this question.

2. Asking students to identify engaging details—one of the key features of a profile—helps them become aware of the need to draw readers in with specific details. Focusing on how these details create an impression of Baca helps students become aware of how details coalesce to create a dominant impression of a subject. Such awareness helps students learn to read with a writer's eye, a strategy they can apply to their own writing.

3. Students will probably notice that the focus in this profile—how reading and writing turned around Baca's life—would appeal to English teachers. Directing students' attention to the audience helps them understand how the main point and the specific information supporting that point are carefully crafted to appeal to a specific group of readers. By considering how the profile would need to be revised to appeal to a different audience, students gain practice in addressing different readers. You might direct students to Chapter 2 on audience to help them respond to this question.

4. A full appreciation of Baca as a poet rests on an understanding of his past. Students should be able to identify the background Baker includes to create a meaningful profile of Baca. You might lead a class discussion on how this information gives them a greater understanding of Baca as a writer and on what would be lost in this profile if that background were not included.

5. *For Writing.* By directing students to select a person with an interesting career, job, or hobby as a subject, this prompt offers a focused assignment. Of course, students will need to determine what is meant by "interesting." You might have them consider "interesting to whom" and "interesting for what purpose" as they work to identify a person to profile. The answers to these questions should help them not only locate a subject but also identify an audience. In completing this assignment, students also gain experience in using dialogue and detail in their writing.

For Further Discussion

1. Rob Baker notes that "Baca's writing explores his fractured family and personal life, his prison experiences, and his ethnicity." In other words, Baca writes about what he knows—his own life. What lesson about writing can you draw from this observation that might help you as a writer?

2. Identify passages where Rob Baker quotes Baca. What central theme do these quotations circle around? How is this theme related to the main point of this profile?

ALEX WILLIAMS

863 *Drawn to a Larger Scale*

Engaging with the Text

1. Asking students to examine titles for meaning helps them to learn one strategy for titling profiles and other essays. Here "drawn" has two meaning—drawn as in *drawing* and drawn as in *pulled toward*. Both meanings fit the essay that profiles Scott Campbell and how he moved from a small Louisiana town to college to becoming a celebrity tattoo artist, and finally an artist with his own shows and museum exhibits. Ask students how else Williams might have titled the profile and what would have been gained or lost with a different title.

2. This question asks students to identify Williams's stance in this profile. Rhetorical stance plays a critical role in clarifying the writer's attitude toward the subject. Having students point out a phrase where the stance is clear helps them see how writers establish stance and tone in a piece.

3. Williams paints a vivid picture of Campbell through the details he uses to describe him. Just one of the engaging sections is his physical description of Campbell: "dirty blond hair," "ink stained forearms," looking "like a kid in Salvation Army vintage who sells Minor Threat albums at Bleecker Bob's." Yet, as Williams notes, this is a misleading image because Campbell wears expensive clothes and sports a Rolex watch on his wrist. Have students discuss how engaging details helps readers understand the subject of a profile.

4. This question asks students to speculate on Campbell's success. It is a response to the question Williams asks in his opening: "How did a 32-year-old college dropout from the bayou of Louisiana, with no formal training in art—well, to be frank, no training at all—end up with a one-man show in a New York gallery and a client list that includes Robert Downey Jr. and Orlando Bloom?" Students need to go

beyond the narrative of how he moved from his hometown to eventually end up in Brooklyn, the current hotbed of artists. Have students discuss to what degree being in the right place at the right time is serendipitous.

5. *For Writing.* This writing prompt encourages student to write a profile of an artist in their community. Students could visit the Art Department in their college to gather community artists names, or to write on one of the professors or students in that department. They could also start with a medium. What mediums are they interested in: paint, sculpture, needle-work, yarn, tattooing, performance? Iden-tifying a medium may help direct students to a particular group of artists. This assignment helps them to become more familiar with their community or the col-lege community they are now living in.

For Further Discussion

1. How would you to define art? Based on your definition, is Scott Campbell an art-ist? Is tattooing an art? If so, how does that answer change—or does it change—your definition of art?

2. Why do you think tattoos have become so popular over the last fifteen years? What role do tattoos play in estab-lishing an identity? Do you think tattoos will wane in popularity over the next fif-teen years? Why or why not?

BILL PENNINGTON

867 *Defying the Odds: Victor Cruz*

Engaging with the Text

1. This question asks students to iden-tify the purpose of this profile. This profile of Victor Cruz provides a powerful lesson about tenacity and success.

2. Asking students to examine begin-nings and endings together helps them develop strategies for opening and clos-ing profiles and other essays. Pennington begins and ends with Pamela Marsh-Williams, the associate dean for under-graduate advising at the University of Massachusetts. The opening recalls the second time Cruz had been tossed out of UMass because of his grades. The ending quotes Marsh-Williams again, closing with her remarks on the refocusing and hard work Cruz had to undertake to complete his college program. Students should notice the parallel and the progress between the events recounted in the piece's opening and its closing.

3. Have students discuss Cruz's role in helping the Giants win the 2012 Super Bowl. What does this achievement add to the profile Pennington wrote about Cruz? What do students expect Cruz will do this upcoming football season?

4, This question prompts students to examine the multimodal presentation of this profile and to explain what the hyperlinks and images contribute to the profile information. What information do the six interviews add that is not found in the main text? Understanding digital multimodal forms is becoming increasingly important in students' professional and personal lives, and this kind of task helps students learn ways of presenting information beyond just text.

5. *For Writing.* This writing prompt asks students to write a multimodal profile of an interesting teacher or student in their school. Students are asked to collect images, video, audio, and to write text that provides background and engaging details to showcase the subject of the profile. Working with images—whether still or on video—requires securing permission from subjects. Help students develop a permission sheet that those they photograph can sign if the subjects agree to have their images used in a multimodal assignment. This assignment offers important experience in designing and writing a multimodal profile in a digital space.

For Further Discussion

1. Locate two current stories on the web about Victor Cruz. Explain whether Cruz is still understood as a successful and crucial player in his league and on his team.

2. What is the most important lesson of Victor Cruz's story? Beyond sports, where else would this lesson serve us well? Discuss the tough road taken by Cruz and explain how this might have helped Cruz in ways a straight road would not have.

41 Proposals

MICHAEL CHABON

876 *Kids' Stuff*

Engaging with the Text

1. This question asks students to examine the background Chabon's supplies for his proposal. Having students identify phrases that lay out the background helps them understand the role of background information and offers them a strategy for providing it.

2. Students are given an opportunity to grapple with one of Chabon's claims in this profile and the way that he supports it. They then can form and express an opinion based on their own experience and understanding of the problem. This question should lead to a lively class discussion.

3. For this question, students are asked to name the four principles Chabon recommends for creating great comics for children. These are discussed on page 883, where he also offers an explanation for each principle. The overall support for these principles comes from personal experience and from the way they "hold true as well for the best and most success-

ful works of children's literature." Have students discuss their view on his principles and his rationale.

4. Students are asked to identify the purpose of this essay—one aspect of the rhetorical situation that guides every piece of writing. This proposal began as a talk given at the 2004 Eisner Awards, the "Oscar awards of the comics industry." Given the original venue, the intended audience is clearly defined as those who work within the comics industry, a group capable of taking action on Chabon's proposal. Chabon obviously sees the great value of comics for children and adults, and clearly wants to get the comic book industry back to its earlier popularity.

5. *For Writing.* This writing project asks students to research children's games that have lost steam over the last couple of decades and to propose a way of rescuing a game from obscurity. Gaming and creative play is becoming an important area of study and students should look at research studies in this field to help them develop a

proposal. This assignment will help students conduct research in the library, online, and through in-person interviews.

For Further Discussion

1. The number of children's books that are published has been increasing over the last decade and has become an important literary genre. Where do children's literary books and comics intersect? What do they share? How are they different?

2. Game designers increasingly are devising games for a variety of learning outcomes. What role do you think online comics and gaming could play in teaching?

DENNIS BARON

886 *Don't Make English Official—Ban It Instead*

On Engaging with the Text

1. This question focuses students' attention on how Baron opens his essay. Baron begins by outlining in clear terms two sides of the debate over making English the official language of the United States, thus establishing the problem. In responding to this question, students should be able to identify the opening as establishing a well-defined, though very complicated, problem—one of the key features of a proposal. By considering alternative ways Baron might have opened his proposal, students will gain experience in brainstorming beginnings. You might direct them to Chapter 30 on beginnings to help them with this task.

2. Here students are asked to state explicitly what Baron leaves implicit—his main point that the Official English legislation is as damaging, as foolish, as inef-

fectual and absolute as the Ban English proposal. In considering Baron's purpose, students can be led to see the proposals can serve a variety of different purposes. In this case, the purpose of this proposal is to draw attention to, and gain support for, the position against the Official English proposed legislation.

3. Students are asked to examine the reasons Baron offers to build a persuasive case for his position. Students should realize that Baron offers outlandish reasons as a way to signal his opposition to the official English-only position. By focusing on the reasons and the relationship to the main point, students can learn one strategy for supporting a case, and in the process, come to appreciate the power of satire.

4. This question asks students to consider what genres are available to Baron to make his case. Students might point to

arguing a position or reporting information as two possibilities. You might lead a class discussion about what would be lost and what gained if a different genre had been used.

5. *For Writing.* This writing prompt directs students to identify a hotly debated national or local issue, and to write a satiric proposal to address the issue. To prepare for writing this proposal, students will gain useful research experience by accessing appropriate web and print sources to uncover the various positions on the issue.

For Further Discussion

1. How does Dennis Baron end his proposal? How effective is this ending? How does it relate to his opening?

2. What is Dennis Baron's tone in his proposal? How effective is that tone?

MEGAN HOPKINS

Training the Next Teachers for America: A Proposal for Reconceptualizing Teach For America

On Engaging with the Text

1. Hopkins proposes three major changes to Teach For America in the second paragraph of her proposal. Students should be able to recognize that she fleshes out each of these recommendations in the rest of the proposal, where she also entertains possible objections. By examining how Hopkins builds a compelling argument in support of her recommendations, students learn how establishing one's credibility (e.g., the fact she taught for Teach For America), anticipating opposing views, and offering well-supported reasons create a persuasive argument.

2. This question focuses students' attention on how Hopkins ends her proposal, thus, teaching them one strategy for ending an essay. In quoting from the Teach For America mission statement, Hopkins demonstrates that she believes strongly in the goal of Teach For America and that her proposal should be understood as a call for improving a significantly worthwhile endeavor. By asking students to consider how Hopkins's porposed solutions contribute to this goal, students can be led to see how drawing a connection to a larger purpose or mission can be an effective strategy for persuading readers of the importance of the actions they propose.

3. Given that this piece was originally published in *Phi Delta Kappan*, a journal aimed at educators and education policy makers, students should be able to iden-

tify the audience for this proposal easily. Further, since proposals ought to be aimed at those who can play a part in carrying out the call to action, students will no doubt recognize that educational policy makers and teachers are the most appropriate readers. This question helps students learn how the purpose of an essay is one aspect that controls the audience.

4. Anticipating questions and objections is the hallmark of a good proposal. Students should notice that Hopkins effectively anticipates questions by supplying highly developed discussions of each of her recommendations. Students should also be able to identify the section on "challenges to implementation" in which Hopkins outlines potential objections. You might lead a class discussion on the power of anticipating objections in a proposal, and how failing to address them weakens one's argument.

5. *For Writing.* This writing prompt asks students to write a proposal for reforming

education from their perspective as a student. This assignment gives them an opportunity to identify one or more problems in education and ways to address these based on their lifelong experience's in the educational system. In completing this assignment, students will thus gain valuable practice drawing on their own experience to analyze and solve problems.

For Further Discussion

1. Megan Hopkins begins her essay by summarizing her experience with Teach For America, the subject of her proposal. What role does this beginning serve in the proposal? How else might she have opened her essay?

2. Why is Teach For America an important program? What does it do for students and what does it do for those who teach in the program? Should this program be maintained, in your opinion? Why or why not?

PETER SINGER

902 *The Singer Solution to World Poverty*

On Engaging with the Text

1. This question focuses students' attention on the purpose of Singer's proposal—to alleviate world poverty by encouraging people with disposable income to donate

to worthy charities. By asking students to point to specific passages that reveal his purpose, you can give students valuable experience in close reading and supporting observations with textual evidence.

2. Students are asked in this question to examine and assess the effectiveness of Singer's opening. The Brazilian film *Central Station* and the hypothetical situation of Bob and the train switch serve as ethical touchstones throughout the essay, constant refrains that focus attention on the ethical question of supporting worthy charities. This question asks whether students find this technique persuasive, and in so doing, calls attention to a rhetorical strategy they can use in their own writing.

3. This question engages students in a philosophical debate that is central to Singer's proposal—namely, that people should give away anything above and beyond what they need to meet the basic necessities in life. Students should be able to see that although Singer advocates this as the ideal, he "accept[s] that we are unlikely to see, in the near or even medium-term future, a world in which it is normal for wealthy Americans to give the bulk of their wealth to strangers." You might ask students: If this is the case, then what does Singer reasonably expect would be the outcome of his proposal? What does he hope for?

4. By asking students to identify the counterarguments Singer anticipates and deals with in his proposal, you can help them see the value of strengthening an argument by addressing potential objections. In most cases, Singer poses the counterarguments in the form of a ques-tion—a powerful rhetorical strategy. In analyzing these moves, students can develop a useful rhetorical strategy for dealing with counterarguments. You might direct them to Chapter 10 on argu-ing a position to prepare them for res-ponding to this question.

5. *For Writing.* This writing prompt directs students to identify a social prob-lem and to consider how the actions of individuals could help alleviate that prob-lem. Students may need some help in see-ing how specific local actions can help alleviate larger problems. Class discussion of one or more issues and a brainstorming session on local actions would be useful.

For Further Discussion

1. Peter Singer ends his essay by claim-ing that "we are all in that situation" that the hypothetical Bob was in when he had to decide whether to flip a switch to save a child from a runaway train or not flip it to save his precious car. In what ways are we all in that situation?

2. Peter Singer describes himself as a "utilitarian philosopher"—"that is, one who judges whether acts are right or wrong by their consequences." How well does his proposal fit this definition? Does he base his argument on consequences? Point to specific places in the text that reveal this philosophy.

JOHN BOHANNON

910 *Dance vs.* PowerPoint: *A Modest Proposal*

Engaging with the Text

1. Asking students to examine how Bohannon begins his multimodal "modest proposal" and to discuss its effectiveness will help teach them one strategy for opening a multimodal proposal. Stating the effectiveness of the purpose helps student realize the role of rhetorical purposes in writing

2. This question asks student to explain why they think Bohannon waited more than five minutes into his proposal to state the thesis. Help student understand the various points at which a thesis can be articulated and how the expectations for audience reaction can control when writers decide to announce their main point.

3. Students are asked to consider the satiric problem Bohannon describes by considering the differences between static images and words on a *PowerPoint* and live performance. Ask them to describe how Bohannon uses dance and why it is an effective way to express complex ideas. What would be lost if his point were delivered in print text only?

4. This question helps students understand the role of stance—a writer's attitude toward his subject—as an important strategy for communicating an idea. Using dancers on stage to help him explain the uses of dance for a PhD student demonstrates the power of mixing art and scholarship.

5. *For Writing.* The writing prompt asks student to develop a multimodal proposal on a serious problem that can be approached in an unusual or unexpected way, and to write a satirical proposal. Lead a class discussion on Swift's modest proposal. Have students compare it to Bohannon's proposal. Identify the features and strategies of writing a satire through exaggeration. Students are asked to use a combination of text and visuals to help communicate their proposal. This writing task gives them valuable experience in crafting a multimodal essay.

For Further Discussion

1. Why do you think John Bohannon chose this title? What is he alluding to? How does this allusion help readers understand his proposal?

2. How might art (in addition to dance) help scholars think through research problems and projects? Brainstorm other art mediums apart from dance that could help a writer work through a scholarly research project—painting, sketching, knitting, crocheting, sculpting, stain glass work, and so on. Select one of these and design a prompt to complete an art project related to a research problem.

42 Reflections

DAVE BARRY

Guys vs. Men

On Engaging with the Text

1. As one of the first in a long line of verbal ironies on which Barry relies to create humor in his essay, this verbal irony serves as a forecast for the entire reflection. While students may recognize this first contradiction and perhaps others, they may need some guidance on the nature of verbal irony as a figure of speech. After introducing the concept of verbal irony, you might ask students to locate other instances of this figure of speech in Barry's reflection and explain what point he is making in each instance. This question and class activity will help students learn how humor and irony function in a text and will encourage them to try this strategy in their own writing.

2. Barry's reflection can be read as one extended definition of "guy." By asking students to point out the characteristics of "guys" that Barry identifies, this question helps students learn how an extended definition operates in writing, and gives them valuable practice in mining a text for

details. You might direct students to Chapter 36 on defining to help them respond to this question. You might also lead a class discussion on whether or not students agree with Barry's portrayal of "guys," and discuss what other characteristics they may have identified. This activity gives students a chance to support their positions with textual evidence.

3. Asking students to locate and analyze specific examples that Barry includes in his reflection helps them learn how examples function to support a point, a strategy that they will find useful in their own writing. You might place students in small groups to share the examples they found and to discuss what each example contributes to Barry's reflection. Students can then vote in their group on the best representative example and present it to the class.

4. Students should be able to easily identify Barry's stance as humorous and ironic. Indeed, many may expect this if they are familiar with Barry's work. Of

340

course, Barry's purpose is to produce laughs while making observations on life—some truer than others. Hence, students ought to find Barry's stance appropriate for his purpose. You might ask students to review Chapter 1 on purpose and Chapter 4 on stance to prepare them to respond to this question.

5. *For Writing.* This writing prompt directs students to select a specific group of people, animals, things, or places on which they write a reflection. Narrowing in on a specific group encourages them to find a focused topic for their writing. In identifying the distinguishing characteristics of the group they select, students learn a valuable strategy for defining subjects and concepts. Depending on their topic, students will need to decide on an appropriate tone, as not all topics will lend themselves to a humorous treatment. For those that do, students may need some guidance in how to incorporate humor, which can be challenging to use effectively.

For Further Discussion

1. Dave Barry details what makes a "guy" distinct from other "men." How might women be similarly classified? Jot down characteristics that distinguish a "woman" from a "girl."

2. How does Dave Barry defend "making gender-based generalizations"? Why do you think Barry offers this defense? What does it contribute to the portrait he is painting of "guys"?

GEETA KOTHARI

922 *If You Are What You Eat, Then What Am I?*

On Engaging with the Text

1. This question draws students' attention to two rhetorical strategies—specific details and description—to help them ponder the larger issue of the relationship between cultural identity and food. Asking students to point to specific details and descriptions helps them develop a writerly sense for using these strategies as well as practice in using textual evidence to support their observations. You might direct students to Chapter 37 on describing to prepare them for responding to this question.

2. In focusing attention on Kothari's title, students can become more aware of the important role titles play in drawing readers in and setting up expectations that will guide their reading. You might suggest that students review Chapter 31 on how titles function to help them develop a list of criteria by which they can judge the effectiveness of Kothari's title.

3. This question asks students to examine how Kothari begins her essay to determine how it functions and whether it is effective. Students should notice that Kothari's opening anecdote establishes the central conflict for her reflection—the clash between Indian and American cultures that Kothari experiences. You might direct students to Chapter 30 on beginnings to help them evaluate Kothari's opening.

4. This question is designed to provide students with an opportunity to think about the ways in which cultures connect, and how those who stand between two or more cultural worlds struggle to define themselves. You might lead a discussion on this topic by asking your students what cultural worlds they inhabit, and how they view themselves in relation to those worlds.

5. *For Writing.* This writing prompt offers a focused topic by directing students to reflect on the kinds of food they have grown up with and the role this food has played in their own sense of cultural heritage and identity. North American students may need to be reminded that "American" food is an ethnic food, and they may want to examine the specific region of the United States where they grew up for foods that mark that place, and their sense of themselves.

For Further Discussion

1. Geeta Kothari claims that parents "are supposed to help us negotiate the world outside, teach us the signs, the clues to proper behavior: what to eat and how to eat it." In what ways and to what degree did her parents succeed in teaching her these lessons?

2. Food, as Geeta Kothari shows, offers one cultural marker. Discuss other aspects of life that signal culture and cultural identity.

ALEX HORTON

928 *The Ides of March*

Engaging with the Text

1. This question asks student to examine the title and explain its effectiveness. They may need to be told that Julius Caesar was assassinated on the Ides of March in 44BC and *ides* comes from the Latin *idus,* which means "the middle of the month." Ask students to consider the point being made by Horton with a title that identifies the day Brian Chevalier was killed—March 15, 2007. Is an allusion to Caesar appropriate?

2. Horton includes quotations from other soldiers, including the squad leader, offering an anecdote about Chevalier (or

Chevy, as his buddies called him). Students are asked to explain what the quotations contribute to the reflection on Chevy. Together they offer a vivid portrait of the kind of man Chevy was and the love and respect his squad had for him.

3.   Students are asked to explain why Horton went to Antietam National Park on March 15, 2011. Referring to Caesar's death and to those who lost their lives on September 17, 1862, Horton reveals that he is very much still mourning the loss of his fellow. Asking students to consider the purpose of this essay helps them understand the rhetorical force of this reflection, one that pays homage to the many who haunt him, but who no one should forget. In the words of his squad leader, Richard Kellar, "As long as we don't forget him, he will live longer than all of us."

4.   This question asks students to examine Horton's conclusion and the way he ended his essay. Horton points to the heaviness of coping with death and the loss of a friend who will never experience spring again. The sentiment in the final quotation supports Horton's use of the term "the best" to describe men like Chevy.

5.   *For Writing*. The writing prompt asks students to identify a time that stays in their mind as a moment of significance. How many, for example, remember exactly where they were when they learned of the events of 9/11? They are then asked to write a reflection on the meaning of the date they chose and to use quotations

from those who also shared the experience of that date. Reflections, like other genres, must indicate the significance of the subject, and so this prompt asks students to consider and convey the significance of the events that happened on their chosen date. This assignment pushes students to think critically about events in the past.

For Further Discussion

1.   Like the soothsayer in Shakespeare's play *Julius Caesar* who warns Caesar to "Beware the Ides of March," Alex Horton sends his family an email with a link to an article on the place in Iraq they were heading because he could not tell them directly; he writes simply, "Beware the Ides of March." Little did he know that this was the day a member of his squad would die. What is the effectiveness of the allusions to Caesar here and in the title? What do these allusions say about Horton's feelings for his departed friend?

2.   What role do blogs play in personal and professional life? What function do you think Alex Horton's blog *Army of Dude* serves for him and for others who have been in service? Locate and analyze the function of a blog. It can be one you already know about or one that you research. Who writes the blog, and who are its readers? What is the blog's purpose, and how does it achieve that function?

JOAN DIDION

932   *Grief*

On Engaging with the Text

1.   This question focuses on the central theme in Didion's reflection and how this theme connects to her organization. Didion's exploration of grief raises unexpected questions about how to deal with this powerful emotion. She returns to strategies she used in the past for coping with the uncertainties and finding meaning. Students should note that recalling these moments highlight her central point that nothing can prepare you for dealing with grief.

2.   In focusing on Didion's tone, students should be able to note the quiet seriousness of her prose, and detect her stance toward the subject of her reflection—namely, the grief over her husband's death. You might direct students to Chapter 4 on stance to help them identify the tone and discuss its appropriateness for her message.

3.   This question addresses two related features of the rhetorical strategy of description—specific details and dominant impression. Students should notice that Didion piles domestic details one upon the other in a list, referring to them as the "fragments" that mattered to her. You might direct students to Chapter 37 on describing to help them respond to this question. By asking them to point to specific details in the text, you can also help them develop a strategy for supporting their observations with textual evidence.

4.   Students are directed in this question to consider the rhetorical purpose of Didion's reflection. Doing so can help them understand that a reflection can serve a variety of different purposes. Didion's purpose is not explicitly stated in this piece, but students should be able to recognize that her reflection serves her own journey toward understanding and coping with the grief over the loss of her husband.

5.   *For Writing.* This writing prompt asks students to recall and ponder a strongly felt emotion on which they can write a reflection. This focused topic should help students concentrate on discovering concrete details to help them describe how that emotion affected them.

For Further Discussion

1.   In the first part of her reflection on grief, Joan Didion spends most of her time reflecting on how she pondered meaning in life. Where did she find meaning as a child and later as an adult? What does this reflection contribute to your understanding of how she has come to cope with grief?

2.   It is not until the very last sentence that we understand that what triggered Joan Didion's reflection is her husband John's death from "cardiac arrest at the dinner table." What effect does this suspension of detail until the end of the piece have on you as a reader?

ARMANDO MONTAÑO

936 *The Unexpected Lessons of Mexican Food*

Engaging with the Text

1. This question leads students to analyze how Montaño coped with his struggles over his biracial identity and how food—what he cooked and where he ate—became a strategy for dealing with these struggles. Montaño recalls how he was viewed by both the Mexican and the Anglo sides of his family as always being of the other. He also recalls a story of traveling with his father through Texas and being turned away at a motel because of his father's dark complexion. How does a child make sense of the motel owner's refusal to serve his father? Lead a discussion on how these personal anecdotes of racial discrimination set a backdrop to Montaño's narrative about the significance of cooking Mexican food.

2. Asking students to identify the purpose of the reflection helps them to understand that reflections, like all writing, center around a rhetorical purpose. Having them locate a passage where the purpose is most explicit shows them one example of how to make the purpose evident in a piece of writing. Montaño's purpose is to reflect on a way he has learned to deal with his biracial identity—by cooking "food that doesn't have to be Mexican or American."

3. This question offers an opportunity for discussing how readers can vary in their conceptions of a topic and their reactions to a writer's treatment of a subject. These comments are reader responses, the kind a writer works to imagine as he or she drafts. (If your students have trouble finding the comments on *Salon*, tell them to scroll down past the related stories, slideshows, and videos.) Use this question as an opportunity for discussing audience and strategies for accommodating differences among readers.

4. Students are asked to examine some of the engaging details Montaño includes in his reflection. Montaño is especially vivid in his descriptions of cooking ingredients, those he recalls from his childhood and those he recalls from his own independent efforts at making a meal. Ask students to discuss the details they chose from the essay and to explain how they are especially engaging. What are the features of engaging details? How do they help a writer tell a story? What does it mean for a writer to recall with such vividness details from his or her past?

5. *For Writing.* This writing prompt asks students to write a multimodal reflection that focuses on a feature of their own identity—racial, ethnic, religious, or some other feature—and a specific activity that calls it powerfully to mind. Students should be encouraged to include visuals, sounds, and videos to help them discuss the feature with vividness and to help them recall specific incidents.

For Further Discussion

1. Brainstorm details (sights, sounds, smells, tastes, touches) of a memorable family meal. In a small group, share your details with each other and work on gathering more details. Then write a descriptive paragraph on the meal using these details. What did this exercise help you understand about writing descriptions?

2. How do borders as sociopolitical spaces privilege some and disadvantage others? Define "border." How are borders formed? Who controls them? What happens when they are redrawn? How does Armando Montaño's essay help you understand borders in a new way?

DAVID RAMSEY

I Will Forever Remain Faithful: How Lil Wayne Helped Me Survive
944 *My First Year Teaching in New Orleans*

Engaging with the Text

1. Students are asked to examine how Ramsey organizes his mixed genre text. They should recognize the headings come from song lyrics by Lil Wayne. They will also notice that Ramsey goes back and forth between analyzing Lil Wayne and his rap songs and telling stories about his students that relate in some way to the lyrics of the heading of the section or to his analysis of Wayne. Examining organization is important because there are many ways to organize written work, some more effective than others in certain rhetorical situations. This analysis helps students see that writers make decisions about how to organize their writing in relation to the subject, the readers, the purpose, and the stance.

2. This question asks for students to explain what Ramsey means when he notes that New Orleans natives often say "this is New Orleans" to explain "absurdity, inefficiency, arbitrary disaster, and transcendent fun" to those who come from outside of the city. Students should see these conditions in relation to Wayne's lyrics and his expressed love of New Orleans no matter its difficulties.

3. By asking students to examine the purpose of this essay, they will understand how writing is often driven by an agenda. Ramsey's purpose is to share a successful pedagogical practice he used when he was teaching middle school in New Orleans, and to show how the students were able to work with Lil Wayne's lyrics. Wayne gets New Orleans and the students get Wayne. Ask students which musical artist they would select to connect to most of the students in their high school. Which lyrics and which musical style would best fit?

4. Asking students to examine dialogue and how it functions in a particular essay helps them understand the ways dialogue can be used to communicate ideas, details, and tone. Most of the dialogue here is from

347

Ramsey's students, with some quotations from interviews with Wayne. The dialogue helps establish the scene of the school and the dialectical relation of Wayne's lyrics and Ramsey's students' lives. Not all students make it but despite the problems, there are those who do. Ramsey realizes that New Orleans is much more than the place where Hurricane Katrina took place with devastating force. New Orleans is "the best city in the world," the reason Lil Wayne "will forever remain faithful to New Orleans."

5. *For Writing.* This writing prompt directs students to select a favorite music artist and to write an essay about the importance of that artist in their thinking and in their relationships with family and friends. As a way to learn one strategy for organization, the prompt asks students to use lyrics from the artist (as Ramsey does) to organize their essay. After brainstorming on the lyrics, their importance, and their relation to those who matter in the writer's life, they are instructed to use their responses to create a thesis that they can either state explicitly or implicitly in their essay. This assignment thus gives students good practice with strategies for analysis and for organization.

For Further Discussion

1. Many essays mix genres. This is one of the reasons you find the same essay identified by different genres in different textbooks. What genres do you identify here? Do you find the essay more or less powerful because of the mixing? Why do you think "pure" essays of only one genre are rare, most often showing up only in writing textbooks?

2. How does David Ramsey's pedagogy resonate with the practice of writing itself and the need to identify a rhetorical situation? Put another way, how are teaching and learning actions that involve a rhetorical situation? What is the role of purpose, audience, context, and stance in teaching?

ALISON BECHDEL

955 *Fun Home*

Engaging with the Text

1. This question asks students to analyze Bechdel's book title by considering the dual meaning of "fun home" and the irony of it. Examining titles helps students understand that titles often do work beyond announcing a topic. In this graphic essay, Bechdel's titles serves as an assessment of her childhood in which the fun house played a strong role. Her experience of it is surreally akin to a fun house in an amuse-

ment park. It also is an ironic comment on the funeral home and her interactions with her family. Students are also asked to identify the purpose of Bechdel's text, an important activity for understanding the role purpose plays in writing. Her memoir reflects the confusion she felt growing up and her surprise when she learned about her father being gay, something that would have helped her to cope with her own sexuality during her childhood.

2. Students are asked to pay attention to the work graphic images do in communicating ideas. The details in the images (and in the text, for that matter) create a dominant impression of Bechdel's family as creative, artistic, and literate—but nonetheless isolated and isolating. Understanding how images function in communication is important for both print and digital texts.

3. By asking students to pay attention to how Bechdel guides her readers through her graphic text, they come to learn strategies writers use to help readers navigate the ideas, claims, arguments, and points of the text. Students should realize that clear guideposts prevent readers from getting lost in a text.

4. The focus in this graphic mixed-genre essay is on growing up in the Bechdel family and the ways in which they did and did not interact with each other. While many panels show the disconnect—mother on tape recorder, mother at the piano, father on tape recorder and at the typewriter—the last is the most explicit, with each family member in a different room with

the text: "Our home was like an artists' colony. We ate together, but otherwise were absorbed in our separate pursuits. / And in this isolation, our creativity took on an aspect of compulsion" (967). Students should be able to notice the contradictory forces of the experience.

5. *For Writing.* This writing prompt asks student to write a graphic narrative in which they communicate an experience they had earlier in life. In selecting the experience, students need to be able to identify the significance of it—what they or others learned. Students can either draw the graphic images or take images from other sources. This assignment helps student focus on images in an important way since the images here are much larger physically and metaphorically than the written text. Such experience will help students draft both print and digital texts.

For Further Discussion

1. Why do you think Alison Bechdel included the two anecdotes of her father offering "help": the first when she wrote a poem and the second when she colored an illustration from *The Wind in the Willows*? What do these two anecdotes reveal about Bechdel's relationship with her father?

2. What purpose does the newspaper clipping of Alison Bechdel's father's obituary serve? Why do you think she chose to put the clipping in her graphic text? How else might she have conveyed the information it contains?

ANU PARTANEN

969   *Finland's School Success: What Americans Keep Ignoring*

Engaging with the Text

1. This question asks students to identify some of the major differences between the way schools are run in Finland and in the United Sates. By asking students to identify at least three differences and to point to phrases that reveal them, students will become more attuned to how Partanen makes her points in this essay.

2. In examining the title and its implied question, students understand that titles do more work more than just announcing the subject. The answer to this question is the focus of the essay—the reasons Finland's schools are so successful.

3. Students are asked to examine Partanen's ending for her essay. She ends it with the topic she began with—education in America. Students can learn a strategy for closing an essay by circling back to the beginning. Lead a discussion on Partanen's last sentence: "More equity at home might just be what America needs to be more competitive abroad." What do students think about this point? What does she mean by "more equity at home"? How would this state of affairs affect the U.S. economy?

4. This question asks students to look at the evidence Partanen uses to support her argument. She draws on a variety of highly respectable sources. Asking students to explain how sources are used will help them learn strategies for incorporating sources into their own writing. You might lead a discussion on what makes a source creditable and convincing.

5. *For Writing.* This writing prompt asks students to respond to Partanen's essay and her main point that the Finnish system of education would improve schooling and the economy in the United States. Students are asked to read Jonathan Kozol's essay "Fremont High School" (p. 705) to prepare their argument. Encourage students to understand arguments as ongoing conversations, and to use Kozol's points as sources to support their argument.

For Further Discussion

1. What surprised you when you read Anu Partanen's essay? Which would you find more motivating—competition or cooperation? Why? Where did you learn this road to motivation?

2. U.S. private schools are increasingly becoming more expensive and are now becoming for-profit businesses. What do you think about private education versus public education? How do you explain the disparity among schools both private and public? What does this disparity create in the general population? Who benefits, and who is hurt by it?

SOJOURNER TRUTH

977 *Ain't I a Woman?*

Engaging with the Text

1. This question asks student to look at Truth's opening and closing. The opening serves as a way to get the crowd's attention and offers a question about Truth's subject. The closing serves as a vernacular goodbye, thanking her audience for listening to her and telling them she has nothing left to say. Both are appropriate for an oral delivery. The opening shows students a strategy for beginning a text and grabbing an audience and the ending shows a similar strategy for acknowledging listeners. Students thus gain strategies in ways of beginning and ending oral presentations and texts.

2. Students are asked to examine the repeated phrase "Ain't I a Woman?" that Truth uses when she compares what she can do with what men can do to show how they are equal in what they bear and suffer. This repetition pounds home her point that men and women are equal. Having students generate another sentence will indicate that they have understood what Truth was doing.

3. Students are asked to identify Truth's thesis and tone. Truth had suffered discrimination as a slave, as a black woman, and as a woman. She spoke up to support women's rights, specifically at the Ohio Woman's Rights Convention but her powerful speech also makes clear that black and white women deserve equal treatment to white men and equal access to the vote. Her tone is forceful for a woman and former slave, a tone more typically expected from a white man. Truth most likely thought that since she as a black women would be seen as less than human by white men and those in power, she could cross gender and racial lines and if challenged point to her age. She makes the point that she is an old woman in her final years with her first sentence which begins "Well, children," and with her last sentence "...now old Sojourner ...." The tone clearly relates to her point that she has endured what every man has endured and has been equal in the struggles.

4. This question asks students to identify the audience for this speech and the rhetorical stance Truth assumes. Clearly, the target audience is made up of those who can do something about unequal treatment of women and people of color—white men. Even though the speech takes place at the Ohio Woman's Rights Convention, the women present were fighting for the same rights and were powerless to take any action. Truth's stance is serious and strong; she clearly feels quite impassioned by this topic.

5. *For Writing.* This writing prompt asks students to write a brief speech about a position they were denied unfairly, or perhaps they could write about someone else they know who has suffered

discrimination. They are then asked to come up with a repetitive phrase along the lines of "Ain't I a Woman" that they could use in their speech as an anchor that will function similarly to Truth's use of the phrase. This prompt gives students a chance to draft a speech to practice honing in on an important point in a brief span of time. It also gives them practice in using a particular rhetorical device.

For Further Discussion

1. What is the situation with gender and racial equality today? What are the ongoing problems with both social identity markers? Where do we see evidence of the problems?

2. Rhetorical scholar Walter Ong called oral practices in a chirographic culture a second orality. He claimed writing-based cultures had a different cognitive make up than those who were in oral cultures without writing.* Today scholars are discussing third orality to describe the discursive practices on the web in social media, email, blogs, websites, gaming, texting and so on. Discuss on the kinds of oral residue you see in the writing on the internet. What effect do you believe a third orality will have on how we communicate?

MICHAEL KIMMELMAN

979 *A Ballpark Louder Than Its Fans*

Engaging with the Text

1. This question asks student to identify features of two other genres in Kimmelman's essay. In addition to evaluation of the new Marlins Park stadium, Kimmelman profiles and creates an argument about the ambience of older baseball stadiums versus the new corporate ones. Students should understand that most essays mix genres and that this is a valid and useful strategy for communicating ideas.

2. Students are asked to explain the comparison Kimmelman makes between the Marlins Park's home-run display versus the Mets' home-run apple display, and the video game *Call of Duty*, a widely popular, sophisticated war game, versus a jack-in-the box. Examining strategies for creating comparisons will help students understand how a writer draws comparisons to things the audience is probably familiar with to help readers understand what it is the writer is describing. Kimmelman's comparison highlights the

*Walter Ong, *Orality and Literacy: The Technologizing of the Word* (London: Routledge, 1982), print.

futuristic style of the new stadium that will likely attract many young people.

3. Asking students to identify the target audience of an essay helps them recognize how target audiences help writers make choices about what details to include and what to leave out. Kimmelman is targeting U.S. baseball fans in this piece. International audiences can learn something about the cultural connections between baseball and Americans by reading it but some of the evaluation points may be missing for an audience who is outside of the United States.

4. This mixed-genre essay is multimodal in that it incorporates visuals and links to support the claims Kimmelman makes in his treatment of Marlins Park. Having students click on the links and study these visuals helps them to see how one writer models strategies they can use to incorporate links and images in their own writing. They also are asked to think about the benefits and drawbacks of incorporating these pieces into a written text. Lead a discussion on whether links and visuals are necessary or appropriate for every kind of writing.

5. *For Writing.* This writing prompt asks students to research a sports facility near their college or home and to write a multimodal essay about it. They are offered a series of questions to help them identify the data they will need for the essay and are encouraged to include photographs and links to background information. This assignment gives students practice in doing empirical research on a local site.

For Further Discussion

1. What features do you expect and appreciate in a sports arena? How well does Marlins Park satisfy what you want in a baseball stadium? What stadium would you recommend to friends? Why?

2. What stance does Michael Kimmelman reveal in the title he crafted for his essay? How does the essay support this stance throughout? Is it appropriate for the subject Kimmelman writes about? What would need to be changed in the essay if someone with a different attitude toward Marlins Park were to write about it?

Contributors

Brady Allen teaches composition, fiction writing, honors courses, and literature at Wright State University. He has published short stories in many horror, crime, sci-fi, dark fantasy, and literary journals and anthologies in the United States, England, and Ireland, and some of these stories are collected in his book *Blue Roads and Frontal Lobes*. He has received an Individual Artist Fellowship from the Ohio Arts Council, some of his stories have received honorable mention in *The Year's Best Fantasy and Horror*, and his short story "Slow Mary" has been nominated for a Pushcart Prize.

Michael Boblitt is a former teaching assistant at Wright State University in Dayton, Ohio, where he earned an MA in composition and rhetoric. He enjoys writing fiction.

Adrienne Cassel is Associate Professor of English at Sinclair Community College in Dayton, Ohio. She has designed and taught over a dozen online classes. She teaches academic research writing with an environmental slant and American literature survey courses. Her course "Writing in the Weathered World" won a Curriculum Design Award from the Ohio Association of Two-Year Colleges. A chapter that explains the theory behind the course is published in *Teaching Eco-Criticism and Green Cultural Studies*. Her research interests include eco-composition, eco-poetry, and the ecology of short-grass prairies.

Her poetry has been published in *5 A.M.*, *Flights,* and the *Northwest Review*. She has an MFA from Bennington College and a PhD from the University of Cincinnati.

Jimmy Chesire is a writer, teacher, counselor, and coach. He teaches first-year composition, undergraduate and graduate creative writing, and a course called "Enhancing One's Creativity" at Wright State University, where he is a senior lecturer. He's published a couple short stories, a short memoir piece, a novel, *Home Boy*, and, with the late photographer Inman Irwin, *A Thousand Strikes: T-ball Yellow Springs Style*. He is at work on a second novel.

Carol Cornett recently retired from her position as a lecturer in English and director of the LEAP Intensive English Program at Wright State University. She taught ESL courses in composition, grammar, reading, speaking and listening, and classroom communication for international teaching assistants.

Deborah Crusan is Professor at Wright State University, Dayton, Ohio, where she teaches in the MATESOL program and the TEFL certificate program. She is an active member of TESOL International Association, where she has held the offices of chair (Higher Education Interest Section and Second Language Writing Interest Section) and has also served on the TESOL Nominating

Committee; currently, she serves on the Second Language Writing Interest Section Steering Committee. She is a past member of the Committee on Second Language Writing at the Conference on College Composition and Communication (CCCC) and past president of the Midwest Association of Language Testing (MwALT). Her research interests include assessment for placement of second language writers, the machine scoring of essays, and the politics of assessment. She has published in scholarly journals such as *Assessing Writing*, *TESOL Quarterly*, and *Language Testing*. Her book, *Assessment in the Second Language Writing Classroom*, was published by the University of Michigan Press.

Melissa Faulkner is Assistant Professor of English at Cedarville University in Cedarville, Ohio, where she teaches courses in basic English, composition, and rhetoric, and directs the WAC program. She has authored multiple articles and serves her community by teaching ESL courses to immigrants.

Scott Geisel teaches composition and fiction writing at Wright State University. He is the editor of *Gravity Fiction*, a collection of short stories by college writers. He was Assisting Editor for *Flash Fiction Forward* and *New Sudden Fiction* and a co-founding editor of *MudRock: Stories & Tales*. He was a finalist for the 2008 Eric Hoffer Award for fiction and has a story included in *Best New Writing 2008*.

Paige Huskey is Assistant Professor at Clark State Community College in Springfield,

Ohio, where she teaches writing and literature. She also coordinates the developmental reading and writing program. She holds a BA in literature from the University of Colorado and an MA in literature from Wright State University. In addition to teaching, she writes fiction, poetry, drama, and essays related to literature, teaching, and higher education. Her essays have been published in *The Facts on File Companion to the American Short Story*, *The Facts on File Companion to the American Novel*, and *Special Gifts: Women Writers on the Heartache, the Happiness, and the Hope of Raising a Special Needs Child*, which was an award-winning finalist in the National Best Book Awards 2007.

Carole Clark Papper is Associate Professor in the Department of Writing Studies and Composition at Hofstra University, where she also directs the University Writing Center. Prior to that, she served as the Director of the Ball State University Writing Program (winner of the CCCC Certificate of Excellence). Her scholarly interests include visual literacy, composition theory and pedagogy, and writing center theories and practices. Her favorite courses to teach include the practicum in writing center pedagogy, "From Pictograph to Pixel: The Impact of Writing Technologies on Literacies," and "Navigating the Information Ocean: Research, Writing, and the Web."

Melissa Toomey is a Visiting Assistant Professor of English and Communication at the University of Cincinnati at Blue Ash, where she teaches rhetoric and composition. Her other interests include social movement rhetoric and working class studies.